Martin's Scribbles

Distributed by Radius Book Group
A Division of Diversion Publishing Corp.
443 Park Avenue South, Suite 1004
New York, NY 10016
www.RadiusBookGroup.com

Library of Congress Control Number: 2018957748
First edition: November 2018
Trade Paperback ISBN: 978-1-63576-538-0

Martin's Scribbles

Sort of a Memoir

Martin Holub

Radius Book Group
New York

Contents

Foreword

Why the subtitle "Sort of a Memoir"? Because what follows is not a traditional memoir (i.e., a chronological description of one's life, with recurring themes that lead to a grand summation). Not every event, episode, or adventure, however exciting, that we experience during our lives lends itself to a story, while these scribbles describe only those that do. Consequently, it is not a complete picture of my life; that was not my objective. I only hope that it'll make for an amusing reading.

1969 in London, before leaving for New York.

Arrival in the New World

The year was 1969, when the word on the street in London was "America is a tough place; everybody tries to rip you off." I felt almost cocky, thinking, "Not me. I am not too stupid. I speak English. So I am not going to be ripped off." As it turned out I was ripped off twice within my first few hours on the North American continent.

The first time was in the Customs Hall on Pier 54, where the boat that carried me from Southampton docked. Located on the Hudson River on the west side of Manhattan, the hall was a cavernous space to which passengers were ushered after going through passport control. From the rafters were hanging giant letters of the alphabet. The idea was that you would find your luggage under the first letter of your last name, and sure enough, under the *H*, there was a heap of my baggage—all eleven pieces of it, including a pair of skis, several suitcases, and one large trunk.

After some waiting during which I surveyed the scene, a customs officer came by and reviewed my passport and my customs declaration; he then demanded that, of all my pieces of luggage, I open the large trunk. It so happened that this was the one piece that I had had professionally packed and shipped by a London forwarding company, and as such, its lid was fastened by two steel straps that went around the whole trunk. This is a standard way of securing wood crates and large trunks. There is a special tool to snap and unsnap those straps; with that tool, undoing those straps is a snap, both literally and figuratively, but without it, there is no way to unfasten them with one's bare hands. I explained that to the customs officer. His response—"Not my problem. Call me once you have that trunk open."

What now? I couldn't well leave my luggage unattended and go looking for a hardware store to buy some pliers with which I might remove the straps. However, soon I found that my predicament was not unique. I was approached by two men, one of whom, wielding the coveted tool in his hand, asked me, "Wanna open that trunk?" With a sigh of relief, I said, "Of course, how wonderful. Thank you so much." But before making a move, the man continued, "It'll cost you $20."

I couldn't believe what I heard. In January 1970, twenty dollars was serious money, especially for someone coming from London. To ask that kind of money for doing something that would take only five seconds was beyond my comprehension. My righteous indignation clouded my judgment, and I sent the men away.

Across the hall I noticed a cop leaning against the wall. Being used to London, where bobbies were friends of old ladies and children, I dashed to him and said, "Sir, that man over there is asking $20 for unsnapping a steel strap." The cop, without ceasing to chew his gum, said, "So what do you want me to do about it?" Only half-joking, I replied, "I want you to arrest him. Isn't blackmail illegal in this country?" By turning his head and looking elsewhere while continuing to chew, the cop indicated that further discourse with me was beneath his dignity.

I soon realized the folly of my ways, found the man with the tool, and paid him $20 to open my trunk. With the trunk open, I called the customs officer who, satisfied that it was open, didn't even bother to look inside it. He stamped my form, and I was allowed to leave the Customs Hall. I stowed everything in the storage at the pier, except for two suitcases that I could carry, and went to the street to hail a cab.

Then came the second rip-off. I had a plan of Manhattan and knew the distance between where I was then standing and where I wanted to go. Having consulted my American friends in London, I also knew that the taxi fare should be $3–$4. So when the driver of the first cab I hailed told me that the flat fare from the pier was $12, I sent him away. I did the same to the second and the third drivers. By then I realized that there was a racket, with all the drivers in cahoots. So with suitcases too heavy to carry to the next block, when the fourth cab pulled up, I threw the luggage in the trunk and got in.

What follows has nothing to do with being ripped off, but I want to finish the story of my first few hours in America. The cab I got into at Twelfth Avenue and 54th Street took me twenty-six blocks north and several long blocks east to West 80th Street between Broadway and Amsterdam Avenue, to the apartment of David Roth, an architect my age whom I had met five years earlier in Prague.

David was then in Europe on a Fulbright grant, and when he visited Prague, we spent some two days together. Before we said good-bye, he extended an open-ended invitation to stay with him whenever I found myself in New York. We both understood that this offer was kind of an unspoken joke, because it was made during the Cold War—when it was more likely for me to become a member of the politburo than ever to be able to go to New York. I was living in London when I received David's wedding announcement on which he'd scribbled that he not only had gotten married but also had started his own firm and moved into a six-room apartment. I was duly impressed.

You can imagine my surprise when the taxi drove down his block of West 80th Street.

In 1970 it was a slum. Beer cans strewn around, garbage all over, wobbling men in doorways and on the stoops. When the taxi stopped in front of 205 W. 80th St., I told the driver, "This cannot be the right address. My friend is an architect." He replied, "Well, go in and check it out." I did, and indeed, "David Roth, Architect" was written above one of the mailboxes in the tiny lobby. I soon found out that the six-room apartment was a fourth-floor walk-up railroad flat.

I paid the driver the usurious $12 fare, retrieved my two suitcases, and returned to the lobby. Shortly after I pressed the button on David's mailbox, a greasy-looking, fat woman with a mustache opened the door, looked me over, and addressed me thusly: "What do you want?"

Those were the first words of welcome I heard on the North American continent. I replied, "I am here to see Mr. Roth." The woman looked first at me, then at the two suitcases that nearly filled the lobby, and asked, "With all that?"

By now, David had walked down to the lobby, and it became clear that the fat woman was the superintendent, because David proceeded to discuss with her some housing grievance, like not having enough hot water or some such. Once he was done with that, he turned to me, and we greeted each other. He then carried one of my suitcases up to his apartment on the fourth floor, and from then on, everything was just fine. It was time for cocktails, so we had some drinks, followed by a fine dinner prepared by David's Finnish wife, Marja. Despite the two rip-offs, my first day in the New World ended splendidly.

Peach on the Beach

Barely five months after my arrival in New York City, I experienced a watershed event in my understanding of American democracy. Stanley Gendell, my colleague from Frost Associates, my first New York employer, decided to show me Fire Island. It is a barrier beach strip of land off the south shore of Long Island, accessible only by ferry boats. No cars are allowed. One can take a train from Penn Station to the ferry and be on the island in little over an hour from Manhattan, so it makes for a nice day trip.

One Sunday morning in June 1970, Stanley and I arrived at Fire Island; I no longer remember at what community, perhaps Ocean Beach. We found our way to the beach along a boardwalk that led across the dunes. Next to the boardwalk was a sign with large letters reading, "NO EATING ON THE BEACH."

Life in a totalitarian country, as in communist Czechoslovakia, was full of idiotic orders, restrictions, and rules, so that those who lived in that environment developed an instinct, which became ingrained, to either ignore or circumvent those regulations. Consequently, although I did notice the sign, it struck me as being so preposterous that taking it seriously didn't remotely cross my mind.

Stanley wasn't much of a swimmer, so after taking several long swims by myself, a moment arrived for which I had brought along, in a little plastic box, several juicy peaches. I offered one to Stanley, who declined it, so I proceeded to eat alone. All of a sudden, out of nowhere, a policeman appeared and, in a rather stern voice, informed me that there was no eating on the beach. By this time the peach was eaten, so I wrapped the pit in a napkin and put it in the plastic box. I wanted to show the policeman that I was not littering. He walked away unimpressed.

I was so thick that, even after this episode, I still didn't get it. So after taking another swim, naturally I ate another peach. Before I could put the pit away, the policeman was back, telling me, "You were warned. Now I have to arrest you." He pulled out a pair of handcuffs. This time I knew I was in trouble, mainly from the expression on Stanley's face. It was only due to Stanley's convincing eloquence that I wasn't led away in handcuffs for the crime of eating a peach on the beach.

Stanley told the officer that I had just arrived from Europe and still didn't know what America was all about, that I meant no harm, and that I worked for a prestigious office in the city; he begged him to please not ruin my life by saddling me with an arrest record. I must have looked the part of the naïve innocent Stanley was describing, so the policeman relented and walked away. We left shortly thereafter, had a meal on Main Street on the island, and returned to the city.

I was, however, genuinely perturbed by this incident. Is this America, the land of the free, or the land where you can get arrested for eating on the beach? I had already visited other Long Island beaches, such as Jones Beach and Robert Moses Beach, where people snacked with abandon. So how come that in one little town on Fire Island, one could not eat on the beach?

I spoke about this incident to many people, including some lawyers, and eventually, a picture emerged. In America, any community, large or small, can pass any law, no matter how stupid, and that law will stay on the books until someone challenges it as unconstitutional; if the judge agrees with the challenge, the law is then stricken. But suing a municipality to get rid of an antiquated law is time consuming and expensive and therefore is seldom done. As a result, there still exist many idiotic laws that no one has bothered to challenge.

In a small town in Virginia, for example, if someone steals another person's horse, the owner has the legal right to hang the accused from the nearest tree. In a western Massachusetts town, it is still illegal to taunt someone for not accepting a challenge to a duel. In San Francisco it is against the law to pile horse manure higher than six feet on a street corner. (All these cases were gleaned when I Googled "stupid laws still on the books.") And in a little village on Fire Island, it continues to be illegal to eat a peach on the beach.

An Angel on Wheels

When I was living in Prague, I had heard of a scientist with the same surname as mine, Miroslav Holub. No family relation. He was well known, because in addition to being an immunologist, he was also a writer and a poet. I had not read any of his poems or books, except for one: *Angel on Wheels* (*Anděl na Kolečkách*). It was a nonfiction account of the year he spent in New York in the early 1960s.

Dr. Holub must have struck some Faustian bargain with the communist regime, because in the dark age of the Iron Curtain and the Cold War, when no ordinary person in Czechoslovakia was allowed to travel to the West, he was granted permission to spend a year in the United States. Because of his work in immunology, Rockefeller University had invited him to work in its research labs, and amazingly, the communist government let him go. When he returned home, he wrote a book about his impressions of the United States, specifically New York.

At the time, according to communist propaganda, the United States was a land of Wall Street warmongers, capitalist exploiters, starving masses, and child labor. The state censor would not allow a book to be published that would cast America in a positive light. By focusing on American eccentricities and oddities, however, Miroslav Holub cleverly managed to publish a quite balanced description of the New York scene.

What particularly captured his imagination, and where the title of the book comes from, was an angel on roller skates, an apparition that could be encountered in the early morning hours along Eighth Avenue between 30th and 40th Streets. He described an angel with flowing robes and huge flapping wings who roller-skated in the middle of the avenue. At the time I read the book, I didn't take the chapter about the angel at all seriously: I was convinced that Holub was making it up to make the book more interesting. After all, who could possibly verify it? At the time, the idea of a regular Czech citizen ever being allowed to travel to New York was simply inconceivable.

Fast-forward some ten years. I was then living in New York, working as a design consultant, and one of my clients was a firm in Knoxville, Tennessee. My work for that firm consisted of preparing design proposals for housing and commercial developments, most of which had strict deadlines. It was before the advent of FedEx and other delivery companies, when the only way to dispatch drawings overnight was via the US Post Office Express Mail. The nearest post office that was open twenty-four hours a day was across from Penn Station on 34th Street and Eighth Avenue. There was also a twenty-four-hour blueprinting service on Madison Avenue near Union Square.

On several occasions in those years, to meet a deadline, I would work all night, and by about 4 a.m., I would roll up my drawings and take a cab to the printing service. With the blueprints neatly wrapped in a parcel, I would then take another cab to the twenty-four-hour post office and mail the drawings overnight to my client in Tennessee. If the parcel was mailed before 6 a.m., it would arrive in Knoxville before noon the following day. Once the drawings were mailed, I would saunter to a coffee shop across the street where I'd treat myself to a coffee and donut.

Now, imagine my shock when, on one of those occasions, as I was leaving the coffee shop, I saw the angel. It was about 5:30 a.m., the sun was just rising, and in the light of dawn, the angel was leisurely roller-skating down an almost empty Eighth Avenue. The flowing robe and the flapping wings were just as Miroslav Holub had described them. How I had wronged him to have assumed he had made it all up!

My Mother's Purchase of Art

My mother was released from the communist prison in the late summer of 1951. Although she was never convicted of any crime, simply having been a political prisoner left a black mark, so that no institution was willing to offer her full-time employment. As an art historian, she was eking out a living by taking on freelance assignments for the National Gallery, the Museum of Natural History, the Archives of Nation's Letters, and other government-run institutions. She went from one task to another, with gaps of not working in between. This continued until 1954, when she was appointed an associate professor of art history at the Academy of Applied Art.

In those three years, we were poor as church mice. Toward the end of each month, my mother would summon me to the kitchen table, turn her wallet upside down, and shake it until all the money fell out. Then she would say, "This is what we have to live on until the end of next month." As a thirteen-year-old child with no reference points for comparison, I found nothing unusual about our precarious situation. In fact, it was sort of fun for me. I made a daily budget, figuring out how much we had to spend on public transportation and food to see if there would be any money left for me to go to the movies. I recall no sense of hardship; it was all perfectly normal to me.

It was during those lean years when, out of the blue, we came into big money (relatively speaking). The only permitted artistic style in communist Czechoslovakia then was social realism, which depicted realistically rendered figures of peasants and factory workers performing their tasks. It occurred to my mother that somewhere in storage (with the rest of the stuff that didn't fit into the small apartment the government had moved us to while she was in prison) was a piece of sculpture we owned that might fit the current official vogue. It was an equestrian bronze cast of a peasant wearing a national folk costume done by a mediocre nineteenth-century sculptor—it was basically kitsch. My mother didn't remember how the family ended up owning it. As a work of art, she thought nothing of it. So she offered it to the National Gallery, which, amazingly, bought it for 10,000 crowns.

In terms of purchasing power, 10,000 Czech crowns in 1953 were close to what $10,000 might buy today. At the time, my mother and I were surviving on an equivalent of $200 to $300 per month, so just imagine what an enormous sum of money the 10,000 crowns was for us.

So what did my mother do with this newly found fortune? She bought two contemporary paintings from Libor Fára, an abstract Czech painter, for 7,000 crowns. She put the remaining 3,000 crowns into a savings account to supplement her meager earnings. Again, at the age of thirteen, I found all this perfectly reasonable.

In retrospect, it is amazing what my mother accomplished with the purchase of those two paintings. First, it was an uplifting act in defiance of the drab cultural environment created by the communist regime, in which abstract art was considered bourgeois and decadent and, as such, was not tolerated. Second, those two paintings made an enormous difference in our small living quarters. The tiny space in which we were crammed became somehow more sophisticated. Third, it helped to support and give encouragement to an artist who had no chance to be exhibited or have his work sold.

I don't know what happened over the years to the smaller of the two paintings, but the larger one now hangs in my country house and delights me each time I look at it. In addition to being a fine work of art, it brings back memories of the times and circumstances when my mother bought it, and it fills me with a deep appreciation of her values.

Going to Tehran

At the time of my first trip, in February 1975, there were not yet direct flights between New York City and Tehran, so I decided to go via London and treat myself to a three-day stopover there. It was my first visit of London since I had left it in January 1970.

I disregarded many warnings from friends and booked my flight to Tehran with Iran Air. Before leaving for the airport I called the airline to inquire if my flight was on time and was told, "Absolutely… On time." After arriving at Heathrow, I checked my luggage at the Iran Air counter and repaired to the designated gate. The counter at the gate was manned or, rather, "womanned" by two young, gum-chewing, but otherwise stunningly beautiful Iranian women dressed in smart airline uniforms. I later learned they were designed by Yves Saint Laurent.

Wondering if I had time for a cup of coffee, I asked the ladies when they'd start boarding. With a bored face and without ceasing to chew, one of them announced that the flight was delayed. I asked for how long. She replied, "We don't know yet but minimum three hours." I was incredulous and said, "I called before coming to the airport and was told that the flight was on time." She made a gesture with her hand that could be interpreted as "too bad" or "not our problem." She also failed to disguise her minor amusement over my exasperation. This was my first exposure to what I later found to be a typically Iranian arrogance.

Having found there was a Lufthansa flight leaving for Tehran in less than two hours, I went back to the Iran Air counter in the departure hall and asked if I could have my luggage back. The answer: "Absolutely impossible; once it's gone from here, no way to get it back." Thus I ended up being trapped at the airport for more than five hours. The flight scheduled to depart at 1 p.m. eventually departed a little after 6 p.m.

During those five hours of waiting, I kept going to the gate counter every half hour or so and received numerous replies: waiting for equipment (i.e., the plane), equipment coming from Berlin, landing at Heathrow, ready for boarding in an hour. One or the other of the ladies was always either doing her nails or touching up her makeup. While other airlines in similar circumstances issued vouchers for free meals and drinks, from Iran Air there was never a word of apology—not one "Sorry for the inconvenience"—nothing of the kind.

I was to be met at the Tehran airport by someone from my client's office, but as I later found out, the fellow who came to meet my flight that was to land at 9 p.m. gave up waiting and went home at midnight. When I got off the plane a little before 3 a.m., there was pandemonium. I soon learned that in Iran when a person returns from abroad, it's not just his wife or a friend who comes to meet him, but the entire family, including distant relatives. The families tend to be large, so it's not unusual for one person to be met by a group of twenty people.

Consequently, the airport was a beehive of pushing and shoving people looking for each other and trying to come close to the carousel to get their baggage. It took me an hour to assemble all the pieces of my luggage, including a pair of skis. It was more than one man could carry (my client paid the moving expenses).

Before I could think of what to do next, two burly Iranian men appeared and asked, "Want a taxi?" Again, before I could say yes or no, they grabbed my suitcases and skis and started pushing their way through the crowd. Even with only my carry-on shoulder bag, I had trouble keeping up with them. Once outside, we walked quickly to a car parked at the far end of the lot. The guys threw my things into the trunk, and the skis ended up with me in the back seat sticking out of the window. They mentioned the price, which seemed high, but not unreasonably high, so I went along (as if I had a choice). Then we took off.

It was only when we were on the dark road between the airport and Tehran that it dawned on me that this was no taxi: it was an Iranian version of a New York City gypsy cab. As we hurtled through darkness toward Tehran, it occurred to me that, if they turned on a side road, did me in, and threw me in the river or in a ditch, no one would ever find out what happened to Martin. Fortunately, I escaped this scenario.

However, that something nefarious was in the air became evident as we drove by the Rudaki Hotel, where I had reserved a room. Instead of dropping me off in front of the hotel, the driver passed by the entrance, and drove some one hundred feet farther down the road before stopping. Then both men jumped out, in a flash got all my stuff out of the trunk, dropped it in the middle of the road, grabbed the money I handed to them, got back in the car, and without saying a word sped away.

I walked back to the hotel, woke up the receptionist who woke up a bellhop, who helped me take my things to the room. By the time I was in bed it was after 5 a.m. At 9 a.m. I reported to my client's office. Such was the beginning of what turned out to be my four-year Iranian adventure.

Exchange Trip to Georgia

As life experiences go, this one rates as one of the more memorable ones. During the Cold War, when Czechoslovakia was cut off from the civilized world by the Iron Curtain and its currency was useless beyond its borders, the only way for students to travel abroad was via exchange trips. A given number of students from one Soviet satellite country would be hosted by students from another satellite country, and then the identical number of students from that host country would visit and be hosted by the students from the first country.

A year after graduating from the School of Architecture at the Czech Technical University in Prague, I enrolled in a three-year, postgraduate program for already working architects in the School of Architecture at the Academy of Fine Arts. While a student at the Prague academy, one of my projects received an award: participation in an exchange trip to the Academy of Fine Arts in Tbilisi, Georgia. We students of the academy in Prague went abroad first, in September 1966, with the students from Tbilisi coming to Prague during the next year's spring break.

Georgia was then one of the Soviet republics, and for the Georgian students, traveling to Prague was tantamount to what for us would have been going to Paris. Consequently, we were treated like VIPs. As was normal at the time, our group was chaperoned by an official from the Office of the President of the Prague academy, who was well known to have close ties to the Czech secret police.

Immediately after we landed in Tbilisi, we were ushered to a VIP lounge at the airport, where champagne flowed freely. At the time, every official speech was expected to include toasts to the Communist Party, the workers' achievements, the socialist regime, and so on. Both we and our Georgian hosts had suffered through many years of compulsory Russian-language classes, so even if we were very bad students, Russian was clearly the one language we could communicate in. No matter: it turned out that just as we hated to be under Soviet domination, the Georgians hated being part of the Soviet Union, and consequently, we both hated speaking Russian.

As we were sipping champagne, a handsome, smartly dressed Georgian student came to the microphone to deliver a welcoming speech. The first surprise was that he did not speak Russian as everyone expected, but English (or at least he tried to). The second surprise was that he didn't offer any toast to the party or to the socialist regime, or any such customary pronouncements. Instead, he proposed a toast to the elegant curves of the ankles of the Czech female students. Wow!

Perhaps because my colleagues knew that I spoke a modicum of English, it fell to me to respond to that welcoming speech. After thanking them for their warm reception and for the champagne, in the spirit of my Georgian counterpart, I proposed a toast to the shimmering horizons of the Caucasian mountains, which we could see from the airport. As I spoke, I was watching our chaperone, who was growing visibly nervous because I had not made any toasts to the Communist Party or to the usual socialist ideals.

When the Georgian came back to the microphone, he proposed a toast to the beautiful, sunny weather we were having and expressed his hope that it would last throughout our visit. He further expressed hope that the sun would shine not only outside but also in our hearts, and he finished by proposing a toast to freedom.

Another wow! At the time, freedom was an extremely loaded word because it could have been understood as freedom from Soviet domination. On the other hand, who could object to freedom? Thus our relationship with our Georgian hosts was clinched from the first encounter. We formed an instant bond; we understood each other.

That reception started what turned out to be ten days of euphoric inebriation. I had not experienced anything like that before or since. Our days started with a late champagne breakfast, after which, already in high spirits, we piled into a tour bus and went to see one of the early Christian churches, of which there were many. When we were finished with the day's sightseeing in the early afternoon, we were taken to an apartment or house of the family of one of the Georgian exchange students, where we were treated to a banquet. And what banquets they were!

If I had not experienced it, I would never have thought it possible for a human being to sit down at a table around 4 p.m. and be engaged in continuous rounds of eating, drinking, singing, dancing, and toasting and then more eating, more drinking, toasting, dancing, singing, and so on until well after midnight—that is, for more than eight hours at a time, day after day.

And the toasts! To Georgians, toasting comes naturally; they seem to have an innate need of ritual, of which toasting is just one expression. Taking a sip from a glass of wine without proposing a toast is considered very bad form. They were particularly good at proposing witty toasts full of double entendres. But our toast-proposing skills improved very quickly, and we soon caught up with them. Especially in the late hours, toasting to freedom became de rigueur. And the singing! We were a poor match for the five-voice harmonies of the Georgian spirituals, although we could harmonize Czech folk songs. After a few days of this regime, we had all reached a state of a permanent high, bordering on euphoria.

On one of these rowdy evenings, it fell to me to open yet another bottle of champagne. I was not careful enough, and the cork shot up and got stuck in the cheap, soft plaster of the ceiling. I felt embarrassed about the damage I caused and apologized profusely. But instead of being upset, our hosts procured a stepladder and a pencil, and they asked me to sign my name on the ceiling next to the cork as a memento of the good times we had. Such was the mood of those dinners.

The Czech students were ill equipped to sustain the sheer physical assault of those evenings. The dance of choice was *kozatchek*—that's the dance where squatting men kick up their legs sideways. The Georgians excelled at it, and we tried to keep up with them. However, after we washed many toasts first with champagne, then with wine, then with vodka, and finally with an excellent Georgian cognac, inevitably, one of the Czech students would pass out. Our hosts were neither upset nor surprised by the sight of a stiff body lying in the middle of the dance floor. Out of nowhere a stretcher would appear, the body would be transferred onto it and taken to an adjacent room, and the party would go on. It was all par for the course, nothing to worry about.

Eventually, the ten days were over, and in high spirits we were taken to the Tbilisi railway station where, after tearful farewells and more speeches and more toasts, we boarded a train for a two-day trip back to Prague: the budget of the exchange trip didn't allow for round-trip airfare. It was my first and only experience traveling on the wide-body Russian train, but that would be another story.

Now comes the sad part. When the Georgians appeared in Prague a half a year later, we failed to reciprocate nearly in kind. Most of us had jobs and were busy, but mainly, we were just not interested in spending time with the Georgians. The Tbilisi trip seemed like ancient history. And so having been treated in Tbilisi as royalty, when it came time to return the favor, we gave the Georgians basically a cold shoulder. I am ashamed to this day whenever I think about it.

Strictly Personals

Karen used to like to hear me say that it took me seventeen years to find her. It was a statement of fact. From the time I left my first wife Eva to my first bona fide date with Karen was exactly seventeen years. During that long search for the right woman—in which I left no stone unturned—there were many humorous incidents; this is a story about one of them. Saying that I left no stone unturned is not entirely accurate, because with this one exception, I never answered or posted a personal ad.

The exception occurred sometime in the early 1980s when two of my female friends, independently of each other, cut out and sent me a personal ad from the "Strictly Personals" section of *New York* magazine. Each of the women, who knew me well, added a note, "Martin, here is your woman. You have to answer this."

To paraphrase from memory, the ad read as follows:

> *It is now over four years since my wife and I have amicably separated and later divorced. I have since found another love and have been happily married for over a year. I wish the same happiness for my ex-wife who was not so lucky, which is why I am writing this ad for her. My ex-wife is in her midthirties, a highly educated, extremely attractive, gentle, graceful, and charming woman. However, if you are not comfortable with ambitious, accomplished, and successful women, read no further, because she is all the above. If you are not threatened, answer this ad. You'll be glad you did.*

It was an unusually long personal ad, which must have been exorbitantly expensive to post. I answered it, giving basic information about myself, including my profession and age, and stated that I'd be much interested in meeting the woman described in that ad. I mailed it to the given box number at *New York* magazine and promptly forgot all about it.

About a month later, my phone rang. A woman announced that she was calling about my response to the ad in the magazine. I told her that I was delighted to hear from her and that I was eager to find out more about her—namely, in what field she had accomplished the success her ex-husband mentioned. She told me that she was a writer, currently spending her summer in East Hampton where she was finishing her latest novel. I asked her name and whether she would give me a title of one of her previous books, which I might read. She refused on both counts.

Regarding her name, she said she would not be yet comfortable revealing her identity, and that she'd have to remain nameless until we met. By the same token, giving me a title of her book would be tantamount to giving me her name, so that too would have to wait. Besides, she added, she wouldn't want me, at this early stage, to read any of her books anyway, because they were full of sex, which might wrongly color my opinion of her. My curiosity was stirred!

She lived on the Upper West Side (from my letter she knew that I did as well) and would be returning to the city after Labor Day, at which point she said she'd call me and we could arrange to meet for a drink at some neighborhood bar. During the whole conversation, she did not ask me a single question.

Given it was mid-August when we first spoke, I had to face some three weeks of suspense before laying eyes on this creature. I had, of course, no idea how many men responded to that ad or how many of those responses the secretive writer answered. Labor Day came and went, and my phone rang again. The by now familiar stranger announced that she was back in the city and that, if I were still interested, we could meet for a drink. I responded that I was keenly interested and deferred to her choice of place. She suggested a bar on Amsterdam Avenue, and we agreed on a mutually convenient time. She was clearly in charge.

I arrived at the appointed time in a sparsely populated bar, sat down at the counter, and ordered a glass of red wine. Five minutes later, a pudgy-looking woman wearing knickers entered the bar. My first impression was twofold: first, she looked way older than in her midthirties and, second, she didn't have the figure to pull off knickers: her legs were much too short. Still, she exuded confidence.

I nodded; she smiled and joined me at the bar. I asked her if she had managed to finish the book she was working on in the summer. She said she had and had already delivered the manuscript to the publisher. The second question I asked was when she planned to reveal her identity. My appearance must have put her at ease, because she chuckled and said, "Well, why not right now? My name is Gael Greene." She clearly expected me to know who she was.

While I had heard or seen that name before, I could not quite place it. I certainly had not heard of any writer by that name, and I told her as much. She was evidently disappointed that I didn't know who she was and, with an air of intimating something of great importance, declared, "I am the restaurant critic of *New York* magazine." I explained that I wasn't a regular reader of that magazine, but that, yes, I now remembered her name in that connection and that I might have even read some of her reviews. Then, by way of excusing my ignorance, I explained that I wouldn't put restaurant critics under the heading of writers, which was why it didn't cross my mind that she could have been one. Gael replied that, although she had written several well-received novels, she was still better known as a restaurant critic than as a writer.

I once again asked if she would give me a title of one of her novels so that I might read it. Gael again demurred, saying she'd rather not, because her books might warp my nascent impression of her. We stayed in the bar for more than an hour, each of us drinking three glasses of wine. While I thought that her ex-husband's description of her attractiveness and gracefulness was way overblown and I didn't have the slightest interest in pursuing her romantically, I did find her to be someone whom I'd have liked to count among my acquaintances. Her interests went beyond food and wine. She was well read, au courant on global affairs, and witty, with a dry sense of humor. She was also not a little self-absorbed. From my accent, she must have surmised that I wasn't local, yet she didn't ask me where I was from; in fact, during the whole time in that bar she didn't ask me anything. When the bartender brought us a check, she wanted to pay, but I prevailed and picked up the tab.

When parting, I told Gael that I'd like to keep in touch and asked her if she'd honor me by lunching with me. She said she'd love to and whipped out a pocket calendar to pick a date. I didn't have a calendar on me and told her that I'd have to call her. I still remember how unhappy she looked that she had to give me her phone number. When I called her the next day, it turned out that the earliest open lunch date for both of us was some three weeks later. We agreed to meet at the Museum Café on Columbus Avenue and 77th Street.

When Gael showed up for our lunch date, I was amazed to see that she was wearing the very same unflattering knickers she had donned three weeks earlier for our first meeting. Very few women would wear the same outfit twice. I interpreted that to mean that I didn't rate high on her scale: I was clearly not worth her worrying about her wardrobe. In spite of that, however, we had a pleasant lunch. Gael seemed more relaxed and even more talkative. I remember she told me that the blue shirt I was wearing went well with my blue eyes. It was also during this lunch that she fessed up that there was no ex-husband, that she had written the ad herself. And because she was working for *New York* magazine, the ad had cost her nothing. I complimented her on the clever stratagem.

For the third time, I asked Gael if she would give me a title of one of her books. I said that she should give me credit for being able to distinguish between fiction and reality, so that if she had in her novel a character who was a nymphomaniac, I would not automatically assume that she was one herself. This time she relented and said, "If you really want to read one, get my latest published book. It's called *Blue Skies, No Candy*."

When the check arrived, Gael wanted to contribute, but since I had invited her, I insisted on paying. But I said I'd be glad to let her pay next time, hoping to indicate in this way that, although I was not interested in her romantically, I was interested in staying in touch and having an occasional lunch or dinner together. Also, I felt that since everything had been on my initiative so far (I answered her ad, I paid for drinks at the bar, I invited her to lunch), the ball was now in her court. If she wanted to continue seeing me, the next move would have to be hers.

I have not heard from her since. Gael thus joined a long line of women who, once I didn't pounce, were not interested in being my friend.

After that lunch, I walked to Barnes and Noble on Broadway and bought *Blue Skies, No Candy*. After reading the first twenty of its three hundred pages, I put it down: it was pure trash. I still have the book on a bookshelf in my country place.

How Did I Become an Architect?

Leon Botstein said he knew he wanted to be a conductor ever since he was nine years old. When I was nine years old, I don't think I knew what a conductor was. I was certainly not a precocious child. My parents worried about my lack of ambition and my lack of interest in anything except running around and making mischief. Later on in my teens I developed an interest in skiing and then in going to the balls, drinking wine, and chasing girls. But an inclination toward some profession? Nothing of the sort.

Eventually, the time came when I had to decide to what school to apply. If I were in the United States or in England, I would have enrolled in some liberal arts college and postponed the decision for four years. Unfortunately, in Czechoslovakia (and in other Central European countries), there was no such thing as an undergraduate degree in liberal arts. This had nothing to do with the communist regime; it had been that way since the nineteenth century. We had to decide right after high school what we wanted to do in life and then apply to the appropriate school.

Because my mother was an art historian, the only profession I knew a little something about and could relate to was art history. So I decided to apply to the School of Art History and Classical Archeology at the Philosophical Faculty of Charles University in Prague. However, this was the time of communist centralized planning, and it so happened that the bureaucrats at the Ministry of Culture had determined that there were enough art historians for the time being; therefore they instructed the School of Art History not to accept any new students that year. So that avenue was closed to me even before I submitted my application.

My choices were either to risk being drafted in the army while waiting a year (in the hope that the following year the School of Art History would once again start accepting applications) or to pick another field. It was at this time when two chance—but crucial—encounters decided the course of the rest of my life.

The first one was with Pepa Čihák, my mother's acquaintance and her contemporary: he was an architect, but only by education. He also had a reputation of being a bon vivant who loved good wine and women, so I was intrigued by him. One evening he stopped by our apartment with a few friends to pay my mother a visit. It was on this occasion that he asked me, "Well, young man, what are you going to do when you grow up?" I responded that it was a question that I had recently been pondering very intensively. Pepa's interest was sparked and he asked, "Well, what are you good at?" I responded that my problem was that I wasn't really good at anything. At that, Pepa threw his hands into the air and declared, "It's simple then: problem solved. You should be an architect!"

I had, in fact, already considered architecture. Its confluence of art and technology appealed to me. But I dropped the idea, because everybody I talked to about architecture, including my parents, convinced me that an architect had to know how to draw, had to have a flair for freehand sketching, which was something I decidedly lacked.

The second of the crucial encounters occurred a week or so after my meeting with Pepa Čihák. Walking along a street in Prague, I ran into Marie Benešová, an art historian colleague of my mother's, who was teaching art history at the School of Architecture. As did all grown-ups at the time, she asked me what I was planning to study. I told her I wanted to study art history, but how that plan was thwarted and I had not yet come to a decision what other field to pick. She asked whether I had considered architecture. I answered that I had, but then abandoned the idea because I was not good at drawing.

Marie Benešová was the first person to tell me that the level of drawing an architect needs is a learnable skill. "Martin, you are not expected to draw like Dürer or Michelangelo. We have evening drawing classes at the School, so why don't you come and check it out?" She needn't have said another word: I was in that drawing class that same evening.

It is hard to picture how drearily prudish were those communist years. There were no strip clubs, no *Playboy* or similar magazines to satisfy an adolescent boy's curiosity about female anatomy. So you can imagine my shock when I walked into that drawing class and saw some half-dozen stark-naked women standing on pedestals. I was, however, not destined to draw the naked women. After telling the instructor that I was thinking of studying architecture and needed to pass an entry exam that included drawing, he advised me what kind of pencil, eraser, pencil sharpener, and drawing pad to buy and told me to come back the next day. No question, however, that those naked women were a powerful incentive in my early attendance of those drawing classes.

The next day when I arrived with the required equipment, the instructor directed me to an arrangement of wooden crates on the floor. He then explained the rudiments of perspective—horizon and vanishing points—and told me to have a go at drawing those crates. I wasn't good at it, but trying to get it right absorbed me. The following day I was back, and not only because of the naked women. It was midwinter of 1956 and the entry exams were at the beginning of June, so I had a little more than four months to learn how to draw objects.

Perhaps because it didn't come easily to me, I became obsessed with drawing. After the crates came round objects, such as a group of clay pots. Then, little by little, I drew anything and everything: a chair, a plaster cast we had at home of a torso of Matyáš Braun's *Prodigal Son*, a ceramic jug. I wouldn't stop until the lines on my drawing bore a close resemblance to the object I was drawing. There was certainly not the slightest dash of flair in those drawings, but there was verisimilitude for sure. Much, much later on, my mother told me how all the adults around me at the time were astonished by the change that had come over me. For the first time ever, there was a focus to my life: I had an objective and I was applying myself toward achieving it.

At the beginning of June I took the entry exam. It consisted of three parts. The first was a general interview in which I remember being asked why I wanted to be an architect. That part was easy. Then there was an exam on the history of art and architecture. I was shown pictures of buildings and asked what period they were from, whether Romanesque, Gothic, Renaissance, Baroque, or Rococo. Because of what I had learned from my mother, that was easy for me as well. The final part of the examination was drawing. In the morning we were asked to draw the cubes in the studio, and in the afternoon we went to a nearby park and drew a landscape scene. That part was the hardest, but I squeaked by. At the end of June I was notified that I was accepted at the School of Architecture and Town Planning. I could not wait to start.

In their autobiographies, famous architects often mention how as children they built structures from wooden crates in their backyards or sketched floor plans of houses, but, mainly, they write about how they enjoyed drawing—drawing buildings, landscapes, everything. As a child, I showed absolutely no such proclivities. I was not particularly handy, so I never built anything, plus, as I've mentioned, I wasn't good at drawing. So perhaps, I have spent my life pursuing a profession for which I was ill suited. Be that as it may, once I got into it and tasted it, I had no second thoughts or had ever figured out anything else I'd rather be than an architect.

Bohumír at twenty-one in 1896 as a university student.

My Grandfather Bohumír

My grandfather on my mother's side, the youngest son of a miller, was born in 1875 in the small Moravian village of Sebranice. The custom of the time was that the eldest son would inherit the farm—or, in this case, the mill—and the youngest would receive an education. (I never found out what happens to those in between.) Consequently, after graduating from high school, Bohumír was sent to Brno, where, five years later, he graduated from the Technical University as a chemical engineer. Over the next ten years or so Bohumír worked as a production engineer running chemical factories and dreaming that, one day, he'd have a factory of his own.

His dream came true when he married the daughter of an industrial magnate. Bohumír had invented and patented a new method of making exterior house paints out of locally surface-mined ores; with his wife's dowry he bought the ore mine and started a paint-making factory that he named Teluria. With an eye toward making his own electricity he also purchased a parcel of land through which ran a fast river and built an enclosed shed, purchased ore-grinding machinery, hired five workers, and started churning out barrels of powdered paint. My grandmother proved adept at running the business side of the enterprise, and it grew quickly. In a few years another shed was built, more machines were bought, and there were close to twenty workers working at Teluria.

At that point Bohumír decided that the time had come for him to buy a turbine and start making his own electricity. I don't know how he arrived at the conviction that the best turbines in the world were made in Cleveland, but he resolved to go there and buy one. He bought the turbine before my mother was born, so it must have been a few years before 1913 when Bohumír traveled to Cleveland.

I am, to this day, surprised how little was made of this fact in the family. When I was a child and the subject of the turbine came up, I was simply told, "Your grandfather bought it in Cleveland," as if that were someplace ten miles down the road. Incredibly, that turbine is still generating electricity in Teluria to this day, more than a hundred years later! Other than the turbine itself, the only vestige of Bohumír's trip to Cleveland was a giant Stetson hat that he wore as an old man when he lived in Prague. At the time, it must have been the only Stetson in all of the city. When I asked my mother about the hat, she simply said, "Your grandpa brought it from America when he was there to buy the turbine for Teluria." I am so sorry I don't have any photo of my grandfather wearing his Stetson.

After World War I, Teluria's business continued to grow, and by the mid-1920s the factory was employing more than two hundred workers and exporting paints all over the world. My grandfather was the largest employer in the county. The family had six servants: two maids, a butler, a cook, a

Bohumír at the height of success in 1921.

chauffeur, and a gardener. Abhorring any semblance of ostentation and as if he were embarrassed by his wealth, Bohumír kept trying to hide it. He ordered his mechanic to disguise the Rolls Royce he bought by removing the recognizable *RR* emblem from the hood of the car, saying, "I bought it because it is a most reliable car, not as a status symbol." His coats had fur on the inside, as a lining, because "the fur is to keep you warm, not to show off."

Unfortunately, as the enterprise prospered, the marriage of my grandparents deteriorated. My mother much later concluded that her father suffered from manic depression or what we now call bipolar disorder, a condition that today can be controlled by drugs but was untreatable at the time. Bohumír had a volatile temper, with frequent outbursts alternating with days of melancholy. Feeling unappreciated and unloved both by his wife and by his children, one day in 1935 he attempted suicide. Unfortunately for him, he did not succeed. The bullet missed his heart by two millimeters. A chambermaid of the hotel where Bohumír shot himself found him in the morning in a pool of blood, but he was still alive.

Surviving one's own suicide must be an embarrassing affair, and Bohumír took it hard. He divorced my grandmother, retired from Teluria, handed its reins to his eldest son, and moved into a one-bedroom apartment in Prague. He was sixty-two years old and came to consider the remainder of his life a punishment from God for the sin of trying to kill himself.

What I have written so far about my grandfather is what I learned from my mother and my uncles. The rest of this chapter is from my own memory. I think I was perhaps three or four years old when I first became conscious of my grandfather's existence. He was very fond of me and visited often.

From the vantage point of a four-year-old child, the most striking thing about my grandfather was his appearance. He was taller than anyone around, slender, straight as a ramrod, and with his broad-brimmed hat with a tall crown, there was simply no one like him in all of Prague! When he visited, he would sit with me on the floor and we would play with my toys. He showed me new ways of hitching together various toy cars that I had not thought of before. When I was a bit older, he started taking me for walks. Oh, those were exciting adventures! Even though I didn't yet know how to swim, my grandfather said that if I promised to do exactly what he'd ask me to do, he'd take me boating on the Vltava River. Naturally, I promised and we

Bohumír in 1929 with my grandmother Maryan.

rented a rowboat and paddled all around the river—my very first time on a boat!

I also remember my grandfather taking me to a quarry on the outskirts of Prague, where he not only let me but encouraged me to climb the rock face. I was then perhaps five or six years old. One time I climbed too high, got stuck, and didn't know how to get back down. Standing on a narrow ledge with my nose to the rock face, I didn't know what to do next and was on the verge of crying. My grandfather saw I was in a pickle, and he yelled up to me, "Don't worry a bit; just do what I tell you, and you'll be down in no time. Now, stretch your left hand up until you hit a little root sticking out of the rock. A little to the left—now you have it. Grab hold of it. Now, lower your right hand until you feel the crevice; a little lower—you've got it. Stick your hand in it and grab hold of the edge. Good. Now, lower your left foot, and just keep scraping the rock until you hit a ledge, a little lower—now stand on it." And so it went.

Bohumír in 1934, a year before his suicide attempt.

I was standing with my nose to the rock, so I could not see any of the ledges and crevices my grandfather was guiding me to, but following his calmly delivered instructions, I soon got down. On our way back home, my grandfather suggested that it might be a good idea not to mention this adventure to my mother. Of course, I told my mother everything at once, as I was very proud of my achievement—both that I didn't cry and that, following my grandfather's instructions, I managed to descend.

When I got a little older and was able to negotiate the Prague public transportation, my mother would let me from time to time take a tram by myself to my grandfather's apartment. I'd go on Saturday afternoons and stay with him overnight. Those were great times. While my mother was trying to instill in me some degree of discipline, my grandfather would declare, "In my house we don't live by the clock. We eat when we are hungry, we sleep when we are sleepy, we get up when we wake up. The body tells us what to do, not the clock." This was music to the ears of an eight-year-old boy!

One Saturday visit, which took place shortly after I had returned from summer vacation, stands out in my memory. My mother and I always spent the summer in the country at my grandmother's house next to the Teluria factory in Moravia. At the time, I was completely ignorant of my grandfather's past: his unsuccessful suicide, his divorcing my grandmother, even of the fact that he was the sole founder of the Teluria enterprise and that he ran it until the day he handed over the reins to his eldest son, my uncle Milek, sometime before I was born. Those things were not discussed in my presence. So when my grandfather asked me questions about Teluria—whether a certain shed between the two large halls had been rebuilt or if it was still leaking—I was surprised by his precise knowledge of the factory. On one such occasion, I asked him, "How come, grandpa, you know so much about the Teluria factory?" My grandfather grew incredulous, shouting, "What! They didn't tell you that I built it all?"

In 1945, my grandfather at seventy.

Children don't think figuratively, so I was convinced that what my grandfather was telling me was that he alone—all by himself, brick by brick—built the whole giant complex of buildings. That I found hard to believe. To make sure I understood him properly, I asked, "Grandpa, you really built the whole factory?" My grandfather responded, "Of course I did; there was no one else."

When I returned home on Sunday and asked my mother if my grandfather had built the whole Teluria factory by himself, she quickly grasped that I had taken his answer literally and explained that he hadn't physically built it, but had conceived it and caused it to be built. Therefore, because it would not have existed without him, he was perfectly correct to say that he had built it. I felt better understanding that. Many years later when I recalled this incident, I realized how deeply hurt my grandfather must have been when he saw the disbelief in my face and how he surely considered it yet another proof of his ex-wife's hostility that she hid from their grandson the fact that he, Bohumír, was the founder of Teluria.

During those Saturday visits, my grandfather taught me chess moves, so we played a lot of chess together. While I didn't excel in anything at school, I turned out to be surprisingly good at playing chess, so much so that once in a while I ended up beating my grandfather. I suspected that he sometimes lost on purpose to make me feel good, but he swore that was not the case. My grandfather also taught me how to boil potatoes and scramble eggs. He would let me eat the potatoes by hand. I remember how much I loved eating freshly boiled potatoes with just salt and butter.

My grandfather also liked to tell me stories from his younger years, especially about his time serving in World War I. He was an officer in the Austro-Hungarian army. I no longer remember where he was posted, but his description of how he moved forward during a cannonade has stuck with me. When he found himself in an area bombarded by cannonballs that were making craters all around him, the moment he saw a new crater, he crawled into it on the theory that the cannon shell would never hit the same place twice. Then he waited until he heard another explosion, counting the time between them. Once he heard the next explosion, he quickly climbed out of the crater, ran in the direction he needed to go and, before the next shell was due to hit, he would crawl into another crater, where he would wait for the next explosion—and so it went. I found it hard to imagine a distinguished gentleman like my grandfather engaged in that sort of activity.

The communist take-over of 1948 brought these idyllic visits to an abrupt end. As a prima facie capitalist, my grandfather found himself among the "enemies of the people" who were evicted from their apartments. His eviction was probably a combination of the communists' systematic liquidation of the bourgeois class and of the communist apparatchiks'—who were of humble backgrounds—coveting those bourgeois apartments. In any case, my 74-year-old grandfather had to move and had nowhere to go. As my mother was *only* a daughter of an enemy of the people, we were, for the time being, allowed to stay in our rather large bourgeois apartment and were able to put up my grandfather in the room my mother used to rent to foreign journalists. There were no more foreign journalists in Prague anyway.

A year or so later, my mother found herself in the communist prison. While she was in prison and I was attending a boarding school, my grandfather was once again evicted. This time, however, he was moved to a tiny, two-room flat on the ground floor of a rundown apartment building in a working-class part of Prague. After my mother was released from prison and I returned from boarding school, the three of us tried to live together in that flat, but it was impossible. My grandfather's niece, who had a spare room in her house in a small town in Moravia, came to the rescue and offered to take him in. And so it happened that, of his last two years on this earth, this former industrialist who once employed more than two hundred people spent one year with his niece and the other in an old people's home.

I visited him in both places. Totally resigned to his fate, Bohumír outlived his suicide by eighteen years but never complained. I was fourteen when he died and remember going to Brno for his funeral. I knew he was cremated, but it wasn't until a number of years later that I realized that I didn't know where the urn with my grandfather's ashes was. When I asked my mother, she responded, "The last I heard, it was in the closet of Jožka Sedlmajer, my father's cousin. It was he who picked it up from the crematorium, because he lives in Brno. We need to do something about it, but I just don't know where to put it." Then the exigencies of life took over, and I don't recall that we ever did anything about fetching the urn.

My grandfather in a nursing home in 1953, a year before he died.

Much later, my mother settled the debt she felt she owed her father by writing a book that was translated into English under the title *More than One Life*. Although a work of fiction, it is loosely based on her family, with her father as the main character. She came to believe that he was wronged both by his wife and by his children, and she wrote the book to right that wrong.

Flash Revelations

I have always been fascinated with how some people manage to reveal who they are in one instant—with one sentence or phrase or action—as if stripping naked for all to see.

During Karen's and my six-year courtship—for lack of a better word—the time came for me to meet her father Harold. Karen's parents were divorced, and Harold lived in California with his second wife Mary, who was five years younger than Karen. It was during one of Harold and Mary's rare visits to New York that Karen invited me to dinner at her apartment so that I could meet her father.

As we were sitting in the living room sipping wine and munching hors d'oeuvres, Karen mentioned that McKinsey, the international management consulting firm for which she was one of over four hundred partners, had just elected its new managing director; this election happens once every four years. The managing director is elected by the firm's directors, and because there are more than eighty offices around the world, McKinsey actually hires an outside firm to conduct the election. Describing the process, Karen jokingly said that it was almost tantamount to electing the pope. Harold immediately asked, "What do you mean by that?"

Karen responded that just as the pope is elected by the cardinals, the managing director is elected by the firm's directors. Harold rejoined, "Come on, you don't really believe that the pope is elected by the cardinals, do you?" Karen and I exchanged glances and Karen asked her father, if not the cardinals, who then elects the pope? To which Harold responded, "Oh, no one elects the pope. It's all cooked up in Washington by the CIA, and the cardinals are there just for show." Karen and I exchanged glances once again, and I understood that I was not to argue with her father, not that I had any intention of doing so. Karen said, "Oh, I see," and changed the subject. And so it happened that, within the first fifteen minutes of our acquaintance, I was able to form a very precise idea of my future father-in-law.

One other memorable instance of this phenomenon comes to mind. Sometime in the early 1980s I met Lise, who was an editor for either a publisher or a magazine, I do not recall. She was one of the rare women who wanted to remain friends even after the eros evaporated from our erotic friendship, and friends we did remain for many years. A very attractive woman, she had no shortage of gentleman callers. One of her paramours was someone she referred to as "businessman Bill," because, she said, everything he touched turned to money. She was fond of him, yet I sensed a certain ambivalence. She wanted me to meet him and then tell her what I thought of him, so we arranged a dinner. The plan was that we'd meet at my place, have some wine and nibbles, and then go for dinner to Oenophylia, at the time one of the few fine restaurants on Columbus Avenue.

On the given date, I bought some pâté and cheese at Zabar's and pulled out of my wine rack the best bottle of Bordeaux I had. When they arrived, I could see why Lise liked businessman Bill. He was relaxed, unself-conscious, unpretentious, naturally confident, and self-assured, yet there was something warm and fuzzy about him. After a brief introduction, I opened the bottle of wine to let it breathe. Bill noticed the three wineglasses on the serving table and exclaimed, "Oh, I love wine! Could I taste some?" I responded that, naturally, that was what the wine was for.

While we were still standing, Bill took the bottle and filled one glass with wine to the brim. Then he took the glass, raised it as if he wanted to say "*à la vôtre*," brought it to his lips, and gulp-gulp-gulp-gulp until the glass was drained. Putting the glass on the table and looking at Lise while pointing at me, businessman Bill then proclaimed, "This is the best wine I ever had in my life. Lise, this man knows his wines!" And so before we even sat down, I had a pretty good idea who businessman Bill was.

The next day Lise called me, thanked me profusely for my hospitality, and then said, "You don't need to tell me anything. I saw it for myself."

––––––––––––––––––

When I lived in Tehran, I met an Austrian fellow by the name of Gerhard on the ski slopes of the Alborz mountains; I no longer remember his surname. We met one drizzly afternoon because he and I were the only ones skiing the Poma lift, which was the only one still running: everyone else had either gone home or was drinking coffee at the midmountain lodge. After that rainy day, Gerhard and I met each other often at the slopes and enjoyed skiing together. During our chairlift rides up the mountain we conversed and found out basic information about each other. I learned that he was working for the local office of Ernst & Young, a large American accounting firm, that he had an Italian wife, that they had already been in Tehran three years—but that was all. Our acquaintance did not progress beyond skiing until one weekend, at the end of the ski season, Gerhard invited me to dinner at his house.

It was a large house in an exclusive part of north Tehran, near Darban. Two servants were serving drinks and hors d'oeuvres, and I noticed a cook in the kitchen. As was the norm at the time in Tehran, the company was very cosmopolitan. There were two Ernst & Young colleagues of Gerhard's, one American and one Iranian, both with their wives; a Swedish couple I remembered from the ski slopes; and one unattached Iranian lady. The person who stole the show, at least for me, was Gerhard's wife Angelina. She was lovely in every sense of the word. She was vivacious, exuding joie de vivre from every pore, and moved about with astonishing grace. Yet everything about her seemed genuine, with nothing phony or affected. I was smitten. If she were not married, I would have launched the hottest of pursuits.

When we repaired to the dining table, Gerhard and Angelina sat at opposite ends. Gerhard announced that the main course would be a rack of lamb. Then I noticed that he was surveying the table, as if looking for something. Not finding what he was looking for, he asked Angelina, "Ange, did you get the mint jelly?" With genuine sincerity, Angelina responded, "Oh, honey, I thought you were getting it as the store is right next to your office." Now we all looked at Gerhard, and I saw an amazing change come over him. He straightened up in his chair, leaned forward, composed his features into an extremely stern expression, and, with his head tilted ever so slightly back, spoke loudly, slowly, and ever so distinctly: "Angelina, I am surprised at you. Have you forgotten about my recent promotion? Do you realize how many more responsibilities I now have? And you expect me to worry about mint jelly?"

Unfazed, Angelina responded, "Oh, I am sorry, honey. So because of your promotion, we'll just have to eat lamb without the mint." As if on cue, all the guests chimed in. One said, "Oh, no problem, we don't need the mint." One of the wives added, "I never serve mint with lamb." And on it went. I could see that Gerhard was not entirely happy with this turn of events, but he was smart enough to realize that the only course of action left for him was to go along with the general merriment. So he leaned back in his chair, relaxed his features, and proposed a toast to the fine evening and the fine company. The servants served a very tasty and succulent lamb, and the mint incident was soon forgotten. However, because of that single moment, I was able to find out in a flash what sort of person Gerhard was—something I would not have found out in a lifetime of skiing with him.

———————————

And then there are people's reactions to my place of birth, which quickly reveal a good deal about them. Speaking with an accent, I am often asked where I am from. My stock reply is, "I was born in Prague." The gamut of reactions to this piece of information runs from "Oh!" at the one end of the spectrum, to "Ah, Prague! Franz Kafka, Mozart, *Don Giovanni*, Rilke, ah, how I long to go to Prague!" at the other end. From time to time, out of pure mischief, I ask some of those whose reaction was "Oh!" if they know where Prague is. The responses have included "I've heard of it, but cannot quite place it"; "Is it in Europe or South America?"; "I think it's in France"; "You got me there; I have no idea"; and so on.

I believe I was handed an unfair advantage by being able to sort people out in a flash by their reaction to my place of birth, something I would not have had if I were born in Philadelphia.

First Visit Home

My first visit home since leaving for London in 1967 took place at Christmas of 1983. Some eight years after the Soviet invasion of Czechoslovakia in 1968, once the communist government considered the domestic situation sufficiently normalized, it started allowing some of those émigrés who escaped after the invasion to visit their families back home. But there was a hitch: before applying for a visa, the emigrant had to "rectify" his or her citizenship, which had been marred by escaping (or, as was my case, not returning to) the occupied country.

In practice, this rectifying amounted to paying the government of communist Czechoslovakia for the free education we had received, since most of the people who had escaped had university degrees. At the time, the government calculated the cost of university education to be around $5,000. This was certainly not a grand sum, but the principle of caving in to the communist government bothered many people. Many in the Czech expatriate community condemned those who paid that price to visit their aged parents. I am not sure what I would have done if I had faced that decision.

Those of us who had become US citizens were spared that dilemma. For some reason, the communist government honored a 1927 treaty between the United States and Czechoslovakia, which provided for an automatic loss of the original citizenship should a national of one of the two countries become a citizen of the other country. Therefore, once I became a US citizen, my Czechoslovak citizenship was automatically void, and, consequently, because it didn't exist, it could not be rectified.

I became a US citizen in 1977, which, coincidently, was the year of Charter 77, a Czech manifesto written by dissidents calling for the communist government to honor the human and civil rights provisions of the Helsinki Accords, which, among other countries, had been recently signed by Czechoslovakia. Since, as a signatory of the charter, my mother was not allowed to visit me, I started applying for a visa to visit Czechoslovakia beginning in 1978, and then each year thereafter. On each of those applications, under "reason for the visit" I checked "tourism." And each time, I received a terse notice from the Czechoslovak Embassy in Washington, DC, informing me that my application was denied.

In 1983, I checked "other" and, in the box below, wrote "visit of my mother who is recovering from breast cancer surgery." In due course, I received a notice from the embassy stating that my visa application was being processed and asking me to send in my passport so it could be stamped with an entrance visa. A week later I had in my hand a passport stamped with a visa for a stay of up for two weeks in Czechoslovakia, valid for the next six months.

It was early in December, so I called my mother and told her that I was coming home for Christmas. Naturally, I was excited at the prospect of seeing my mother and other friends I had not seen in nearly seventeen years, but I was also more than a little apprehensive. After all, I was going to a lawless totalitarian country in which I had been sentenced in absentia to four years of hard labor for the crime of not returning after my exit visa had expired. My US citizenship supposedly voided that sentence, but who knows what could happen? Had I disappeared in some labor camp, I didn't think the United States would start World War III for my sake.

Meanwhile, after she signed Charter 77, my mother was subject to the same kind of harassment as was visited on all of its signatories: her driver's license was impounded, her phone was disconnected, and she was frequently interrogated. The preferred time for the police to take her in for interrogation was between 3 and 4 a.m. Worst of all, for several months after issuance of the charter, a policeman was stationed 24 hours a day on the landing outside the front door of her apartment, monitoring her and her visitors' comings and goings. During the first year after the charter was published, my mother was interrogated once or twice a week; gradually, the frequency of these sessions decreased. Eventually, her driver's license was given back to her and her phone was reconnected as well. But the secret police continued to watch her.

So much for the background, and now let me describe my visit. I arrived in Prague on December 21. On our way home from the airport, my mother told me what had happened before I arrived. About a week earlier, two secret police agents had paid her a visit. She knew one of them from her prior interrogations. She found it unusual that this time they were exceedingly polite and even brought her a bouquet of flowers. When they asked to come in, my mother showed them to the living room.

They sat down and the conversation went like this:

"I bet you are glad that we have allowed your son to come for a visit."

"Yes, I am very glad that you did," responded my mother.

"I bet you are looking forward to his visit, yes?"

"Yes, I am very much looking forward to it."

"Well, you know, just because we gave him a visa doesn't mean that we'll let him come in."

"Oh, really? I didn't know that," said my mother.

"Oh, yes, there were those who flew in and we sent them right back where they came from."

"So what do you want from me?" asked my mother.

"Once your son arrives, we'd like to come and have a word with him."

At this point, my mother told me that what made her consent to their request was the thought of my eighty-three-year-old father whom I had not seen in almost seventeen years and whom I might not ever see again if I don't come at this time. Although divorced since 1945, my parents were on friendly terms. The agents knew when I was arriving, so they suggested they would visit the day after Christmas at 10:30 a.m., a quite civilized time. This is what, in the spirit of "guess who's coming to dinner," my mother told me on our drive home from the airport.

Concerned about this turn of events, on the morning of the next day, before going to visit my father, I went to the US Embassy. I told the receptionist that I was worried about my safety and would like to talk to an official to whom I could explain why. It was a slow day at the embassy, and it so happened that the new US ambassador Bill Luers and his wife Wendy had arrived a few days earlier and were just settling in. The receptionist called the ambassador, and, in short order, I was talking to Bill Luers, relating what I had learned from my mother. Mr. Luers was well acquainted with Charter 77 and had high respect for its signatories; he thanked me for the information and asked if I was free to come for dinner the next day. And so on the third night of my visit, I was dining with the US ambassador and his wife at their residence in the Dejvice section of Prague.

Dinner was very informal, just the three of us, but we were served by a Czech butler, which for me precluded any political discussion. There was no question in my mind that the butler was an agent of the secret police, but I wasn't sure if this was also clear to Bill Luers. I soon learned that it was not, when Bill started asking me questions about my mother's involvement with Charter 77.

I responded in the most innocuously vague terms, and when the butler was not in the room, I rolled my eyes and then looked in the direction of the door through which he was coming and going. I then suggested that it would be nice if, after dinner, Bill and I would take a stroll in the garden. In addition to the fact that the butler was working for the secret police, I was also sure that the room was bugged. Bill finally understood my concerns, and we spent the rest of the dinner talking about my four years in Tehran and my take on the Iranian Revolution. After dinner, we put on our coats and walked to the garden.

Once in the garden, I told Bill my concerns about the butler and the bugged dining room. He had eventually understood my suspicions, but at the same time thought that they might be a trifle exaggerated. I told him to not underestimate the efficacy of the Czech secret police. Bill then asked me if I had any idea how he, meaning the US Embassy, could be helpful to the dissident movement. I responded that as far as I knew, the items most coveted by the dissidents were copy machines. Most of the time they were reduced to copying pamphlets on typewriters using carbon paper, because the government saw to it that copiers were simply not available in communist Czechoslovakia. Bill was familiar with the *samizdat* publishing—clandestine and passed hand to hand—so he understood the problem. He then thanked me for the suggestion and, upon my leaving, asked me to see him at the embassy after my meeting with the secret police and report on what had transpired.

By the time I got back to my mother's apartment it was close to midnight, but she wanted to hear about my dinner. When I told her about the Czech butler serving us, our conversation in the garden, and how the ambassador thought that my concerns were exaggerated, my mother rolled her eyes at the naïveté of Western politicians; she then told me that when I next see the ambassador I should tell him to be extra careful about the copiers, because she was certain that the garden was bugged too.

After a pleasant few days with my mother over Christmas, the morning after arrived. At 10:30 sharp, the doorbell rang and the two agents came in. Once again, they brought a bouquet of flowers and were extremely polite. Despite my mother's protests, they took off their shoes and walked in to the living room in their socks. We shook hands and sat down. My mother and I had decided to not offer them anything, so we sat around an empty coffee table.

One of the agents remarked how happy I must be to visit my hometown after such a long time. I nodded, saying nothing. The agent continued, "If there is anything we could do, Mr. Architect, to make your stay here more pleasant, such as giving you tickets to a hockey game, or arranging a tour of a brewery, we'd be only too pleased to do that for you."

The scene looked surreal; I felt like an actor in a Václav Havel play. The break came when my mother excused herself. The moment she left the room, one of the agents turned to me and said, "Mr. Architect, we'd like to talk to you without your mother present. Could we meet in a nearby restaurant at a time of your choosing?"

I thought, having gone this far, why not—so I suggested that we meet at noon the day after next, at U Schnellů, an old restaurant at the corner of the square where my mother lived. The agents rose, profusely thanked my mother for her hospitality (of which there was none), and left.

The plot having thus thickened, in the afternoon I stopped at the US Embassy where I now had direct access to the ambassador, and reported to Bill Luers what had happened. Neither of us knew what to make of it. Bill asked me to keep him posted.

To limit the time of my meeting at U Schnellů, I asked my father to appear there at exactly 12:30 p.m. My father was then eighty-three and looked it. He was half blind with an advanced stage of glaucoma, walked with a white cane, and wore extremely thick eyeglasses and a hat with a wide brim. Altogether, he cut an impressive, respect-commanding figure. There was something almost peremptory in his appearance.

At noon of the appointed day I entered U Schnellů. I saw only one of the two agents sitting in an empty booth and drinking beer; he motioned for me to join him. When I sat down he asked me what I'd like to drink or eat. I responded that it was too early in the day for me to have anything, and I didn't want the state security to spend any money on me. So he came straight to the point: "You see, Mr. Architect, while I now work for the state security, I don't expect to stay in this line of work forever. I would, eventually, like to return to my original profession, which was electrical engineering. I am by profession an electrical engineer, but I've been out of it for so long that I may find it difficult to get back to it. And here is where you might be able to help me."

My face expressed surprise, so he went on: "I know that you are not an electrical engineer, but I also know that you live in America and that America is at the top of the world in electrical engineering."

To my astonishment, he then pulled out a map of Manhattan on which there was an X at West 89th Street where I lived and also at Fifth Avenue and 42nd Street, where the main branch of the New York Public Library was located. The agent continued, "You see, you live over here and a library is over there. Not very far, is it? So I thought you could borrow there a magazine on electrical engineering and send it to me. I would mail it back to you in the required time for you to return it to the library. You could do that for me, couldn't you?"

I responded, "Look, Mr. Officer, although I am not an electrical engineer, I know that it is a vast field that includes low-voltage installations, high-voltage installations, electronics, telecommunications, and many other areas I don't even know about. So if you want me to send you a professional magazine, you need to be a little more specific about what area of electrical engineering you are interested in."

He was clearly surprised by my response. He said, "Oh, any area, it doesn't matter, any magazine would be fine."

It was quite obvious that the guy never had even come close to the electrical engineering field.

Just at that moment, my father walked in. His appearance had the desired effect: our meeting was over. I told the agent that I'd send him some magazine. He managed to tell me that I should send the magazine to my mother, and he'd pick it up from her. We shook hands, and he left. My father and I proceeded to order our lunch. That was the last time that I ever dealt with an agent of the Czechoslovak secret police.

On my way home, I stopped by the US Embassy and reported to Bill this latest installment. He was as much puzzled by it as was I.

My mother shared this whole episode with her fellow Charter signatories, all of whom had vast experience in dealing with the state security apparatus, and they tried to fathom what might have been the objective of this amateurish, bungled enterprise. They concluded that, most likely, the objective was to discredit my mother in the eyes of other dissidents. What a coup it would have been if they could produce to her fellow Charter signatories some evidence of my collaboration and say, "Look, the son of Dr. Holubová is working for us!"

There is an amusing postscript to my encounter with the secret police. About two months after my return to New York, my mother wrote me that the same two agents visited her and asked her if she had received the magazine that I had promised to send them. She said she had not. Of course, she knew that I had never had any intention of sending anything. The agents kept coming, in about two- to three-month intervals, until about a year later, when my mother had had enough and told them, "Look, as an American citizen, my son cannot and will not send you anything. Moreover, he reported all meetings he had with you to the American Embassy."

They were apparently stunned. They left, and my mother never saw them again. The next time I applied for and received a visa for a visit to Czechoslovakia was two years later for my father's funeral. During that week-long stay, nothing untoward happened, and the police left me alone.

The Intelligent Typist

One of my proud achievements in life is that in my sixties I learned to type. Until then, I was fortunate enough to have always had someone type for me. First, the secretary in David Specter's office, where I was renting a drafting table, took care of my typing needs. When I later set up my office in one of the two rooms of my brownstone apartment, it was my friend Harriett who did my typing. She was a paralegal in a midtown law office and kept my stationery in her drawer. At the end of each month I'd dictate over the phone whatever I needed her to type; the next day I'd pick it up, take her to lunch, and that was that. And while I was in Tehran, an American secretary of one of my clients handled all my correspondence.

It must be said that in those years my typing needs were modest, ranging from two to four invoices per month.

When I returned from Tehran, I found I had a new neighbor Jack LoGiudice. Jack was one of the hundreds of prototypical starving actors making a living by waiting on tables; in between auditions, he was only too glad to make an extra buck by typing for me. His living across the hall from me made that arrangement convenient for both of us. However, after a while, as Jack's acting career started to take off, there were times when he wasn't available for a week at a clip, so I started looking for an alternative.

It was at this time in the early 1980s, when I was coming home from a party one evening and was waiting for a bus that I noticed a sheet of paper taped to a lamppost next to the bus stop. I walked closer and saw a notice with the heading "INTELLIGENT TYPIST," handwritten in somewhat shaky block letters. Under this headline was a typewritten paragraph describing the services offered. I remember being surprised by how well written and to the point that paragraph was. At the bottom of the page were tear-off tabs with the phone number, and I took one.

The next day, out of curiosity, I called that number. The phone was answered after the first ring, and someone with a voice that sounded like that of an older man asked, "May I help you?" I said I was calling in response to the Intelligent Typist notice I saw at a bus stop. After thanking me for the call, the gentleman on the other end of the line said that his name was Mr. Bailey and asked me to tell him about my typing needs. Once I finished, he replied that he believed he could be helpful. We agreed that I'd send him a batch of my stationery, and then two days before the end of each month I'd mail him handwritten documents, which he would promptly send back to me typed. Should there be a need for a quicker turnaround, Mr. Bailey would use a messenger service. Throughout our conversation, I was impressed with his measured voice, his speaking in full sentences, his educated accent. I had created a mental image of him as an old-age pensioner, who had time on his hands and wanted to supplement his income.

The system worked like a charm. Over the next several years, the typewritten documents arrived on time, whether by mail or via a messenger, and they never had any mistakes. Throughout this time, Mr. Bailey and I never met, and over the phone, we continued to address each other as Mr. Bailey and

Mr. Holub. Then one day I needed a longish proposal typed overnight. I called Mr. Bailey, explained the situation, and suggested that I'd send him the handwritten proposal by messenger if he could then messenger the typewritten proposal back the following morning. Because he hadn't typed a proposal for me before, I stressed that he needed to pay attention to the layout of pages and font sizes.

Mr. Bailey had a better idea: "Why don't I come over with my typewriter and produce the document at your office? That way you'd be able to proofread it on the spot." I said that would be wonderful. Mr. Bailey added that his schedule was rather full through the rest of the day and wondered if it would be all right if he came to my apartment at midnight. That was perfectly fine by me. This was to be the first time we'd meet in person, and I was curious to meet Mr. Bailey.

At the stroke of midnight my doorbell rang. I heard Mr. Bailey's voice on the intercom, buzzed him in, and went into the hallway to wait for him. I still remember my shock when I saw, climbing the stairs, a short young man in his twenties, of slight build, with a knapsack on his back and greeting me in that familiar voice. He walked in, pulled the latest model of the IBM Selectric typewriter out of his knapsack, found an outlet, plugged it in, situated himself at one of the desks, and in a matter-of-fact manner, set to work.

From the way he handled his typewriter, I could tell that it was his prized possession. I let him work and went on drawing at another drafting board. Mr. Bailey was not a fast typist, but he was steady. I heard even, regular pecking. In about an hour he announced that he was done. I reviewed the proposal: it was impeccable. When I told Mr. Bailey that the proposal was fine, he started putting his typewriter back into his knapsack, clearly preparing to leave. It was now about 1:30 a.m. To continue calling this weird kid, who could have been my son, Mr. Bailey seemed absurd, but I didn't even know his first name. So I asked, "Mr. Bailey, may I offer you a glass of wine?" He said he'd be delighted to have a glass of wine with me.

I only kept good wine, so I opened a bottle of Bordeaux, and we sat down facing each other across the dining table. It became evident that Mr. Bailey knew what he was drinking and that he was appreciating it. The scene—the two of us sipping fine wine at 2:00 a.m. at my office—had more than a touch of the bizarre. The young man sitting in front of me didn't only have the voice and diction of a much older man; his whole demeanor, including his movements, gestures, and bearing, was that of someone of another generation.

I had offered him the wine in the hope that I'd find out more about him, but it didn't quite work out that way. In the end, he learned a lot more about me than I did about him. All he revealed about himself directly was that he lived alone in a studio apartment in the Bronx (at the time the Bronx still had the same area code as Manhattan, so I could not have known from his telephone number that he didn't live in Manhattan), he had a bachelor's degree in English literature from CUNY, and there was some personal problem in his life. When I asked about the nature of the problem, he responded that it was not the time to talk about it but perhaps would be another day.

He did, however, reveal a lot more about himself indirectly by the kind of questions he asked me. It turned out that he knew about the abrogated Munich treaty, the 1948 communist take-over of Czechoslovakia, the Prague Spring, and the subsequent Soviet invasion, because he asked me where I was during those events. He also knew of Charter 77. Having met a number of Americans of his generation, and even older ones, who either never heard of Czechoslovakia or didn't know where it was, I was amazed by Mr. Bailey's grasp of recent European history.

When we were about halfway through the bottle, I said, "Mr. Bailey, from the position of someone much older than you, permit me to suggest that we call each other by our first names. However, while you do know mine, I don't know yours." Mr. Bailey responded that he'd be honored to call me Martin and that his name was Cliff. We shook hands, and I told him that I was happy that we had, at long last, met in person after all these years. He agreed with the sentiment.

Once we finished the bottle, Cliff put on his knapsack and headed for the door. It was now close to 3:00 a.m. I asked him how he was getting home. He said that a Broadway express line would get him to a few blocks from his house. I had to assume that he knew what he was doing.

From then on, instead of using messengers all the time, Cliff started coming over more often. His preferred arrival time continued to be midnight. I think he enjoyed the wine and conversation we always had after his typing was done. After so many years of addressing each other formally, we both seemed to experience difficulties with using first names and kept slipping into Mr. Bailey and Mr. Holub, particularly on the phone. When I saw his youthful countenance, I had no problem calling him Cliff. The subject of his personal problem never came up again.

Once when Cliff was over, he noticed on my desk a stack of invitations to one of my St. Martin's parties. He asked how many guests I expected. When I told him about fifty, he asked if I was employing any barmen. I told him that I never did, that I usually spread food on one table, wine on another, and liquor on yet another, and that folks typically helped themselves. Cliff remarked that a server would make for a classier party and that he would like me to know that he was as good a bartender as a typist.

After that, I felt I had no choice but to hire him. At the party Cliff turned out to be a great hit with my guests, although as a bartender he proved to be a disaster: instead of serving drinks, he kept getting involved in conversations. A few times when introducing him, I unwittingly had slipped into the old habit and introduced him as Mr. Bailey. There was something in his demeanor that made that appellation strangely appropriate, so everyone took to calling him Mr. Bailey. I didn't hire him for the St. Martin's party of the following year, and all my guests were asking, "Where is Mr. Bailey?"

Meanwhile, our professional relationship, including the nocturnal visits, continued most satisfactorily. Then, in 1987, I hired my first full-time employee Larry Brodsky and moved my office out of my apartment into a space I bought on the top floor of a former residential hotel on West 72nd Street. In addition to being a competent architect, Larry was also an excellent typist, so over the next ten years he spent with me, he took care of all the office correspondence. When I broke the news to Mr. Bailey that I would be no longer requiring his services, he took it stoically and graciously wished me good luck. As it was then near the time of yet another St. Martin's party, I sent him an invitation. He called to RSVP affirmatively, thanking me profusely for the invitation—yet failed to show up at the party. I called him the following day; there was no answer, so I left a message asking him to call me back. He did not, and eventually, I let the matter slip from my mind.

It was at least a year, perhaps even two, later when, out of the blue, Mr. Bailey called me. Larry answered the phone, put the caller on hold, and asked me, "Do you know someone by the name of Mr. Bailey? Sounds like an old man and he wants to talk to you." Of course, I picked up the phone, and we had a long conversation. Mr. Bailey was calling to apologize for the no-show at my party. He said that his failure to show up and his subsequent silence had to do with the personal problem he hinted at during our first meeting. He explained that he suffered from bulimia. Although I vaguely knew what that condition was, Mr. Bailey explained that it was an eating disorder whereby sufferers compulsively overeat—so-called binge eating—and then vomit their food, before they start the cycle all over again. He told me he had suffered from this condition for over ten years and had been hospitalized for it a number of times; his last hospitalization had overlapped with the night of the party he had failed to attend.

I was more than amazed; I was dumbfounded. That someone who epitomized calm, measured deportment suggesting rational behavior was suffering from a condition mostly confined to teenage girls, was beyond my understanding. I asked him how he was doing at present. Cliff responded that he was doing fine and hadn't had a bulimia episode in a year. I asked him if he'd like to come and see my new office and have lunch with me. He responded that he'd love to come visit but would not have lunch: he had to eat under controlled conditions that were not compatible with a sociable lunch. So I suggested a lunch-less visit the following week. Cliff accepted, but said that he'd need to confirm it at the beginning of the week. He never did confirm, and that was the last time I heard his unique voice. I've never seen him again. I miss Mr. Bailey.

Apartment Hunting in New York City

I cannot think of a better way of getting to know a city than to look for an apartment in it. I started looking for one in New York City two days after I arrived. I was staying with my friend David Roth, and despite his assurances that I could stay for as long as I needed to, I didn't want to overstay my welcome. As it was, I was well on my way to violating the age-old proverb that says both fish and guests start smelling by the third day.

As it happened, it was a landlord's market at the time in New York, meaning there was a dire shortage of apartments to rent. The guys at my office were advising me to take any apartment I could afford for a year. I could then use that time to get to know the city, learn about the neighborhoods, decide where I'd actually like to live, and then narrow my search in that area until I found an apartment I liked.

But that was precisely what I didn't want to do. There are few things in life that I hate more than moving. I wanted to find an apartment in which I could settle down for the long run. Eventually, I found an apartment in which I stayed for twenty-two years, but that did take a while. My boss, Mr. Frost of Frost Associates, knew what it took to find an apartment in the city, and he was understanding when I needed to run out on short notice and meet a realtor or landlord. I made up the work hours in the evenings or weekends.

Other than working at Frost Associates, looking for an apartment was all I did my first four weeks in New York. Slowly, I learned the tricks of the trade. One source of ads for apartments to rent was the *Village Voice*. It was a weekly available at newsstands on Wednesday afternoons. However, I learned that, at a certain newsstand on Sheridan Square in the West Village, the *Voice* was available on Wednesday mornings after 8 a.m. If I got the paper early, I would get a jump on the competition by calling and making appointments hours ahead of everyone else. Another trick I learned was that if I saw an apartment I liked, I had to write a check for the deposit on the spot. Otherwise, someone else would take it.

I was looking for apartments both in the ads and through real estate brokers. A realtor once called me and said she had a wonderful studio apartment she'd like me to see. I no longer recall what part of town it was in, but I do remember very clearly what I saw when she opened the door. There was a rather large room full of light, but it was in motion: a motion of moving cockroaches. All the walls, the ceiling, and the floor were covered with scurrying roaches. There must have been hundreds of thousands of them.

That constant movement on all six planes made me a little dizzy. The realtor, totally unperturbed, strolled in, crushing the roaches under her feet as she walked. When she noticed that I was hesitating at the threshold, she said, "Don't worry about the roaches; they'll get exterminated. Just look at the apartment." When I told her that I had seen what I wanted to see of the apartment, she shook her head in a manner indicating, "These foreigners, they just don't know about life in New York City."

Another day, a different realtor showed me an apartment on West End Avenue. It was a spacious one-bedroom; the sunken living room even had a dining alcove. It was perfect for me, except it was on the second floor, facing the avenue. Because I had spent my formative years in a ground-floor apartment, I had developed an aversion to living too close to the street. The realtor saw that, although I was interested in the apartment, once I looked out of the window and saw the heads of people walking by on the sidewalk, I became hesitant about renting it. So she suggested that if I gave her a $200 deposit, she'd hold the apartment for me for one more day. I found that reasonable and wrote her a check. It was the first check I wrote on my new checking account in America, and so I still remember that the realtor's name was Bertha Tucker.

Later that day I went by West End Avenue to look at the apartment from the street. From the edge of the wide sidewalk, I could see almost halfway into it. Also, because I like to keep the windows open, I realized that the apartment was bound to be rather noisy. The next day I called Bertha Tucker and told her I would not be taking the apartment. Though she said she'd return the money right away, it took me several months of phone calls before I got the money back—not a pleasant affair.

On yet another day after work, I was going to take a look at an apartment on West 89th Street. Walking down the street, I saw a horse looking out of a third-story window of a building on the north side of the street between Amsterdam and Columbus Avenues. I thought, "How interesting; in America even a horse can get an apartment! Maybe there is hope for me after all." A week later I saw an ad for another one-bedroom apartment on West 89th Street. Remembering that as the street where horses live, I hastened to take a look at the apartment. It was on the third floor of a brownstone between Central Park West and Columbus Avenue.

When I arrived, there were already two female apartment seekers there.

Both the living room and the bedroom were facing south and were flooded with sunlight; at the rear was a kitchen with a breakfast nook, and there was also a decent bathroom. Importantly for me, the apartment was entered via a foyer—a miniscule foyer, no more than 5 feet by 5 feet, but a foyer nonetheless. By then I already knew that most New York apartments had no entry space: you opened the front door and found yourself in the living room. The best features of the apartment, however, were its high ceilings, the bay window with a low parapet, and its view into a mass of green leaves. It so happened that the two buildings directly across the street were completely covered with ivy. The rent was $185/month.

At that point, I must have seen at least two dozen apartments, so that I was able to assess very quickly what was, or was not, acceptable. In this case, two minutes after entering, I knew that this was it. I walked over to the agent showing the apartment and said, "I am taking this apartment. How much deposit do you want?" He replied, "Give me a hundred bucks." I immediately wrote a check and gave it to him. He then addressed the two women who were still walking around, opening closet doors, looking inside the refrigerator, checking the gas stove: "Ladies, you may leave now. The apartment has been taken." Thus began the twenty-two years of my residence on the Upper West Side.

Becoming a Citizen

The process took two and a half years, from January 1975 to July 1977, and could be the subject of a whole separate book. I'll limit myself to only three salient incidents that happened along the way.

I knew that I was eligible to file the petition for naturalization after five years of permanent residence (i.e., possession of a Green Card) in the United States. What I did not know was that once the required period of five years was over, I could not simply file a petition for naturalization; I first had to file an application to file the petition for naturalization. I also did not know that the five years that counted were those immediately prior to filing the petition, not those prior to filing the application to file the petition.

So in theory, one could spend thirty years as a permanent resident in the United States without ever leaving the country, file an application to file the petition for naturalization, leave the United States for six months abroad, and find oneself ineligible to file the petition, because in the five years immediately prior to filing, one has exceeded the number of days one is allowed to spend outside the United States.

More or less, that was what I was in danger of having happen to me. Having spent more than five years (without leaving once) as a permanent resident of the United States in New York, I filed the application to file the petition for naturalization, and the next day I left for Tehran. What followed was a series of missed appointments for interviews at the New York office of the Immigration and Naturalization Service (INS). By the time an INS letter summoning me for an interview would be forwarded to me in Tehran, the date of the appointment would typically be several days in the past.

Naturally, each missed appointment meant lengthening the period before I would be allowed to file the petition for naturalization, thus making it more likely that by the time I would be processed to file the petition, I'd find myself ineligible to do so because I had exceeded the number of days I was allowed to stay abroad prior to filing. Miraculously, the last summons reached Tehran in time to allow me to come back and present myself for the interview within the specified time period.

The purpose of this first of the two interviews was to establish whether my moral character was suitable for being considered for citizenship. My examiner was a congenial chap who took great interest in my personal history, and we pleasantly chatted for over an hour. I returned to Tehran satisfied that, regarding citizenship, things were right on track.

It is against this background that the three incidents I mentioned occurred. First, shortly after returning to Tehran, I received a letter from the director of the New York City office of the INS, Mr. Aiullo. He informed me that, regrettably, during my recent interview, the examiner neglected to ask me an important question. Without providing a notarized answer to that question, my application could not proceed. The question was: "Have you ever committed adultery?"

Now what? Before doing anything else, I decided to find a legal definition of adultery. I had naïvely thought that adultery meant having sex with someone else's spouse. Wrong: as far as the INS was concerned, adultery was sex with anyone but one's legal spouse. In addition to questions such as "Have you ever been a prostitute?" and "Have you ever been a member of the Communist Party?"—those two I liked—my initial application included others about my personal history. So the INS was well acquainted with the fact that, before getting divorced in 1974, my first wife and I had been separated since December 1968. Consequently, stating in 1976 that I had never committed adultery was tantamount to stating that, at the height of my libido, I had not had sex for eight years. So I was confronted with the choice of either admitting adultery or committing perjury.

It was a tough choice, so I decided to seek advice. I had made a social acquaintance of the US consul in Tehran, so I called her and invited her for a drink, during which I explained my predicament. I was struck by how seriously she took my problem—so much so that, before giving me her opinion, she said she would like to seek advice herself. She clearly did not think that it was a trivial matter I was bothering her with.

A few days later, she called me and said that she had consulted an immigration lawyer in Washington, DC. His advice: "Commit perjury." Admitting adultery would open a can of worms that might take years to sort out. So I did as she advised, and no one ever questioned the veracity of my notarized statement that I had never committed adultery.

My petition duly filed, in the next few months there was a need for another personal appearance at the INS office—I no longer remember in what connection—which was the occasion of the second incident. It so happened that I was going to New York for my regular recharging, four-week visit anyway, so I thought that would be a convenient time for the interview. The day after I arrived, I called the INS office in Lower Manhattan and announced my availability. I gave the clerk my petition number and was put on hold. After a while, she picked up the line and said, "Your file has been lost. I am showing its status as 'On Search.'" All this she said in a tone suggesting that a lost file was nothing unusual and happened all the time.

Over the next two weeks, I called at least twice a week, always receiving the same reply—that my file was "On Search." At the end of the third week, hoping to speed things up, I decided to show up at the INS office in person. By then, the receptionist recognized my name. I explained the urgency of my situation, showed her the letter asking me to see an examiner, and told her that I'd be around only one more week before I'd have to leave. Unimpressed, the lady told me that she'd convey the urgency to the appropriate channels.

But I decided to hang around the office and continue to press my case. I had brought a book with me, and so I had read in the waiting room and gone up about every hour to the window to ask whether my file had been found. The fourth or fifth time I did this, the woman exploded and said these exact words: "Mr. Holub, you don't seem to realize that I don't even have to talk to you, because as long as your file is lost, as far as I am concerned, you do not even exist."

I did not quite know how to respond to this outburst, so I decided to leave the cause of my citizenship to fate. I thanked the receptionist for her help and left. However, my having made a nuisance of myself must have had some effect, because the following week I did get a call announcing that my file had been found. I was then able to make a date for my appearance and leave for Tehran satisfied that things were moving along.

The third incident in the process of my becoming a citizen occurred during the final interview. Immigration law requires that a person admitted to citizenship speak English and understand the basic tenets of the US government. The last hurdle before the swearing-in was to establish that I met those two conditions. Sitting in the waiting area outside the examiner's cubicle was a fat woman of about fifty who was called in before me. I was seated right next to the low partition surrounding the cubicle, so I could hear every word they spoke.

"Ah, Mrs. Kapakopulos [or some such Greek name], welcome back. Have you done more studying?"

"Yeah."

"Listen carefully, Mrs. Kapakopulos. This time, I'll give you only three questions. If you answer two of them correctly, I'll give you a pass. Do you understand me?"

"Yeah."

"Very well then. The first question, Mrs. Kapakopulos, is this: What is the capital of New York State? Mind, that I said New York State. What is your answer?"

(after a long pause) "Washington."

"Oh, I am afraid that is an incorrect answer, Mrs. Kapakopulos. Let's try the remaining two questions. The next one is this: Who makes laws in this country?"

(after even a longer pause) "The Republicans."

"Oh, I am sorry, Mrs. Kapakopulos, but that is a wrong answer as well. I am afraid you'll have to do still more studying. Do you still have the little booklet I gave you last year?"

"Yeah."

"You really must try to read it, Mrs. Kapakopulos. Answers to all the questions that I ever asked you are in that booklet. Come back once you've read it, OK?"

"Yeah."

I am sure that, eventually, Mrs. Kapakopulos passed and was granted citizenship. After all the challenges on the way to my becoming a citizen, this last interview was a walk in the park for me. When I was called in after Mrs. Kapakopulos, I thanked the examiner for the entertainment provided by the INS for free. He seemed to appreciate my joke. It was only a few years since Richard Nixon had resigned; I don't remember how the interview began, but we spent most of it talking about Watergate. The examiner must have surmised that my understanding of how our government functions was satisfactory, because he did not even ask me any questions. I was sworn in on my next visit home.

Naftee Man

When I lived in Tehran, most apartments and houses were heated by oil-fired stoves. The stove brand of choice was the US-made Magic Chef, and it was quite efficient. One centrally located stove comfortably heated my entire two-thousand-square-foot apartment, including the bedroom if I left the door open. The distribution of the heating oil, called *naftee* in Farsi, was, however, rather primitive.

Each neighborhood had its *naftee* man, who pulled a cart with a large barrel of oil through the streets in the early mornings and in the evenings, while shouting "*naftee, naftee, naftee.*" If folks needed oil, they would open the window and call down to the *naftee* man to ask him to fill up their stoves. He would then fill up one or two cans with oil, come into the house or apartment, and fill up the oil tank, which was an integral part of the stove. I had an extra can that I always had him fill up as well. On the ladder of occupations, the *naftee* man was somewhere near to the bottom rung. Most were illiterate.

One day when I called the *naftee* man to fill up my stove, there was a stack of neatly folded shirts on my dining table. I had picked up my shirts from the laundry the night before and had not yet put them away in the closet. When the *naftee* man entered the room, he immediately spotted the shirts and was dumbfounded, probably never having seen so many shirts in one place before. He looked at me, then at the shirts, and said, "Those shirts, all yours?"

I confirmed that those were all my shirts. He came closer to the table and counted them: "One, two, three…seventeen! You have seventeen shirts!" He looked both incredulous and bewildered. Then he brightened up, flashed a smile, and continued, "Look, you, seventeen shirts, me, only one. So if I take one of yours, you'll still have sixteen shirts and I only two. So Mister, one shirt for me, yes?"

As he started reaching for the shirt at the top of the stack, I said, "No, you cannot have one of my shirts. I'll give you a nice tip for bringing me the *naftee*, but no shirt." He still didn't give up and tried once again, reminding me that, even if he took a shirt, I would still have sixteen left. However, once he saw that I was firm in my refusal to give him a shirt, the *naftee* man quickly finished his job, thanked me profusely for the *baksheesh*, and left.

Fast-forward some twenty-five years. I was married to Karen, my mother was visiting, and we had invited a bunch of friends to dinner. Two of our guests had also spent time in Tehran, so when we started reminiscing, I shared the story of the *naftee* man who wanted my shirt. When my mother learned that I had not given him the shirt, she was upset that I could have been so heartless.

In my defense, I explained, "But mama, isn't that the very nub of communism? If I gave him the shirt, the next time he might say, 'Look, you have twelve pair of pants and I only one. So if you give me one, you'll still have…' and so on. And then why should he not ask my landlord, 'Look, you own ten apartment buildings while I own none, so why not give me one?'"

My mother concluded that I was so traumatized by communism that I had lost my perspective, failing to see the difference between a shirt and an apartment building.

Two Percent

From the time I started studying architecture and through the following fifty-plus years, I never had second thoughts about becoming an architect, nor had it ever occurred to me that there is anything else I'd rather do. So what follows is neither sour grapes nor is it written with a chip on my shoulder; these are simply my observations.

Architecture is a profession that looks wonderful from the outside, but not so much from within it. From the outside, what could be more exciting, rewarding, fulfilling, and satisfying than working at the intersection of art and technology, designing spaces for people to live and work in, creating forms and shapes that define our time in history? From within, however, the picture is a little more sober. Suffice it to say that, according to a survey of the profession in the *Wall Street Journal*, whose findings are confirmed by my own observations, only about 2 percent of all architects get to do their own work; that is, get to develop their own designs. One might then ask what the remaining 98 percent of architects do. Fortunately, there are many highly skilled occupations both within and outside the context of an architectural office.

Within architectural offices, many of those in the 98 percent work for those in the 2 percent. Each *starchitect*, such as Renzo Piano, Frank Gehry, Richard Meier, Jean Nouvell, and Norman Foster, to name a few, employs a large number of architects to help translate their designs into structures. The last I heard, Frank Gehry employed 160 architects, Norman Foster more than 600, and Richard Meier close to 200 architects. (The thought that 160 architects get up each morning, go to work, and have to find satisfaction and fulfillment in helping Frank Gehry be Frank Gehry sends cold shivers down my spine.) But even when we come down from the stratospheric heights of starchitects, all the way down to little boutique offices such as Martin Holub Architects, each of those small firms employs one, two, perhaps four or five architects whose job is to help the principal of the office realize his or her designs. Depending on the workload, I used to employ between one to three architects who had to find satisfaction in helping me turn my designs into construction documents—in other words, helping me be Martin Holub Architect.

Among the noncreative occupations within an architectural office are project managers, administrators, project architects (sometimes called job captains) who supervise teams of production architects preparing working drawings, as well as site architects specializing in construction support services; lately, every large office has an IT manager who supervises the digital production of construction documents, as well as three-dimensional visualizations of the project designs.

Outside the context of an architectural office architects serve as facilities managers, manufacturer representatives, building department examiners, shop drawings preparers in contractor's offices, specifications writers, building department expeditors, zoning consultants, building inspectors, renderers, cost estimators, waterproofing consultants, facade consultants, and much more besides.

Every large corporation and every university have facilities departments typically staffed by frustrated architects. These professionals take care of the buildings in the office park or on the campus, deciding which ones need new windows or a new roof, a new elevator, or the like. When a new building needs to be built, they conduct the search for an architect. The New York chapter of the AIA has a special committee on corporate architects, a category that includes facilities managers. When we, for example, specified Sussman windows for the Dominican chapel we were designing, an architect working for the Sussman Corporation prepared the shop drawings. Typically, we put our specs on the drawings, but when a New York State agency required that specifications for our design of the community center on Roosevelt Island be placed in a separate book, we hired Construction Specifications, Inc.—a firm of specification writers headed by Steve Pine, FAIA, and employing many architects. Writing specifications for other architects is all they do.

In the era of manual drafting, I used to personally draw all our perspective renderings. However, photorealistic visualizations are now prepared on the computer, and we hire Petrino Visuals to make them for us. Petrino Visuals is a small firm headed by Joe Petrino, an architect, who employs three architects who specialize in preparing 3D renderings for other architects. That's all they do. You get the idea. There are many jobs for architects outside of the context of an architectural office.

For example, sometime in the 1980s a woman walking along a sidewalk on the Upper West Side was killed by a brick that fell off a building onto her head. As a result, New York City enacted Local Law 11, which mandates that the facade of every building over a certain height must be inspected every five years by a licensed architect or engineer, who certifies that the facade is safe. If the facade needs repairs, the architect prepares documentation for and then supervises the execution of the repairs. In the wake of that law a number of architectural offices sprung up that specialize in Local Law 11 inspections. It is a steady work, as the inspections are mandated every five years, recession or no recession.

And then there is the fact that every large cooperative apartment building in Manhattan has an on-call architect. These architects provide services in connection with the building's maintenance, be it installing new windows, fixing the roof, replacing the boiler, or repairing the facade. In addition, when apartment owners want to renovate their own residences, co-op architects review those architectural plans to make sure that they do not propose work that might be harmful to the building's integrity.

Yet even if an architect manages to be in those 2 percent who develop their own designs, it doesn't automatically mean that he or she is doing exciting work; it simply means that the architect is doing his or her own work, which is often far from exciting.

A little-known fact outside the profession is that the process of preparing the construction documents for any project involves a lot of tiresome drudgery. There is no fun and glory in assembling door and window schedules, in making phone calls to confirm that the products specified are still available (i.e., have not been discontinued), in picking the door hinges, or in detailing the cabinets in the laundry room. Yet as long as it is our baby, meaning our design, just as we wipe the bottoms of our babies with love (or so I imagine), we do all of it and more with alacrity, propelled by the desire to see our designs built. However, the thought of doing that kind of work for somebody else's design is another thing that sends shivers down my spine. And the sobering truth is that this is precisely what a vast majority of architects do for their entire professional lives: they work developing somebody else's designs. I am eternally grateful for the fact that I never had to do that.

Some time ago I was at a dinner party attended by geezers of my vintage and their wives, when the hostess had the wisdom to ask each of us what single achievement made us most proud. We were all certainly of an age when a question like that could be asked, so we took turns around the table answering it. A PhD biologist had discovered a method of birth control for ticks and mosquitoes with the potential of severely limiting the spread of malaria. Another guest's most proud moment occurred when he was a student in a school of engineering and came up with a different solution to a mathematical problem that even the professor didn't know about. A violinist who played with the New York Philharmonic said that her most proud moment was when she was selected for a solo part in a Mahler symphony. Another woman shared that her most proud moment was the birth of her first son.

When my turn came, I just couldn't think of a single achievement I felt most proud of, so I took a pass. As usually happens, it wasn't until a few days later that the answer came to me. I am not sure if achievement is the right word for it, but I confess that I am mighty pleased with the fact that, with the help of luck and circumstance, I managed throughout my professional career, even in my employment years, to stay in those 2 percent of architects who do their own work. Never ever did I have to work developing a design that was not mine, which gives me a good feeling. That would have been my answer, had I the presence of mind to think of it.

Outside the town hall.

First Wedding

My first wife, Eva, was my classmate in the School of Architecture in Prague, meaning we met when we were both seventeen. We became friends in the first year, but did not become lovers until the sixth year of our studies. When her mother found out that we were actually lovers, she found the situation unacceptable. In her book, we only had two choices: either stop seeing each other or get married. We definitely didn't want to stop seeing each other, nor did either of us want to get married: we both felt twenty-four was much too young an age to get married. So the status quo dragged on. Each time Eva came home from a date, there were tears and cries, with her mother urging her to leave me or to make me marry her.

Eva was quite close to her mother, and the conflict was hard on her. She faced a choice of either breaking up with her mother or with me. Neither seemed feasible to her so eventually, she suggested to me that, to end this impasse, we should get married. I felt cornered. I was in love but, still, getting married at twenty-four seemed ridiculous to me. After all, my father didn't get married until he was thirty-seven.

I discussed the situation with my mother, who was very fond of Eva, and she urged me to go ahead and marry her. So I gave in, but in the most immature and juvenile manner, of which I am not proud to this day. I told Eva, "So you want to get married? OK then, let's get married. But let me tell you, all I am going to do is to show up. You'll arrange the rest." She accepted the bargain. To drive in the point that this marriage thing was no big deal, just something we were doing to appease her mother, I suggested to Eva that she keep her name. I could see that she was hurt. In hindsight, this was clearly not an auspicious start of a marriage.

There was, however, one more wrinkle: Eva's mother wanted us to have a church wedding. I need to explain two things about getting married in church during the communist era. First, according to the official ideology, religion was the opium of the masses. Consequently, the state did not recognize religious marriage. For the marriage to be legal, one had to get married by civil authorities; that is, at city hall. A religious wedding therefore had to be in addition to the civil one. Although not forbidden, marriage in church was much frowned on by the authorities and left a black mark on the dossier of whoever chose it. For me, all this provided an incentive to get married in a church: I saw it as an act of defiance.

The second thing that needs to be explained and that has to do with me personally is that in my late teens and early twenties I was in a particularly anti-Catholic mode. I have since mellowed, but at the time it seemed to me that Catholicism was the other side of the coin of communism. The dogma, the hierarchy, the rule by fiat, the fact that no questioning was permitted, the infallibility of the pope—all of this seemed to me tantamount to the directive of the Communist Party. Therefore, it would have seemed duplicitous of me to go through the motions of the religious ceremony while feeling about the church the way I did. So I resolved to speak to the priest who was going to marry us to tell him my opinion of the Roman Catholic Church and then to leave it up to him whether he still wanted to marry us.

I got the priest's contact information from Eva's mother, called him to make an appointment, and went to see him. After patiently listening to my diatribe against the Catholic Church, the priest thanked me for my frankness and said, "Sure, I'll be happy to marry you."

Newlyweds with my mother.

So after the ceremony at the town hall was over, the whole wedding party repaired to a nearby church for the religious wedding. Before we exchanged our vows for the second time, the priest in his talk came to this passage: "There may come a time when the husband and wife will disagree upon an issue before them. Should such an instance occur, the Church advises that you discuss the matter thoroughly and advisedly. However, if you still find yourselves unable to reach an agreement, then it shall be the husband's position that shall prevail." That was the Roman Catholic credo in 1963. I wonder if it still applies.

I gave Eva a glowing smile of extreme gratification. My willingness to please her mother not only by marrying Eva but also by marrying her in church was richly rewarded. Eva gave me a look in return that suggested she understood the irony.

As a short postscript, about two years into the marriage—when I was still in love and things between us were going well—one evening in a romantic mood, I suggested to Eva that it would be nice if she now changed her surname to mine. She flatly refused and dismissed the subject with "Too late now, daddy-o."

A Close Call

Sometime in the late 1970s or early 1980s I was in Boston and, at a party of a friend, met Nancy Williams, a very prim and proper young lady; she was originally from Birmingham, Alabama, but by the time I met her was a consummately New Englander. We hit it off and I visited her in Boston several times before she paid me her first visit in New York.

Instead of going to a restaurant, Nancy decided to cook us dinner in my apartment, so we went to my local supermarket to shop for the ingredients. While we were in the produce area, in came a large man wearing a narrow brim hat pulled down his forehead to his eyebrows, chomping on a lit cigar. The guy, who must have weighed four hundred pounds, was a casting director's dream for a character of an uneducated hick.

Nancy had the wisdom to inform this man that there was no smoking in the food store. Well, that got him going. He unleashed a barrage of expletives, which I no longer remember, except that the words "fuck" and "fucking" figured prominently in his speech. As Nancy and I were obviously together, I felt it incumbent upon myself to do something to protect the lady's honor. So I said, in a consciously low, measured voice, "The least you can do is be polite."

That really fired the man up. He came up to me, uncomfortably close, and sneered, "Listen, you pip-squeak, I have to take this shit from her, but I don't have to take it from you. Why don't you and I go outside and talk about it? Eh? Let's go outside and talk about it. Eh?"

I stepped back and responded that I had gone there to shop, not to discuss. Perhaps because he didn't know what to say next, he walked away with a dismissive snort and a gesture indicating that further communication with me was useless. Nancy and I proceeded with our shopping, but I had a strong suspicion that the guy was not done with me. My hunch turned out to have been correct.

When we came to the checkout line, I saw the guy waiting for me on the other side of the counters, seething: there was no escape. When we had finished checking out, he came up to me and said in a loud, threatening voice, obviously meant to be heard by others, "Well, now you've done your shopping, so we can have a little discussion outside, yes?"

People around us took notice that there was going to be some sort of confrontation and started gathering for the spectacle. I'd been shopping in that supermarket for more than ten years, so the cashiers and other employees knew me by face, and I saw them standing around, waiting for the theater. No one called for help; no one tried to intervene. All I saw were expectant faces waiting for the next move.

With a grocery bag in each of my hands, I made for the door with a frightened Nancy following close behind. My adversary barred my way with his huge bulk, saying, "Don't even think about getting away; we are going to have a little talk, aren't we?" Trying to play to the crowd, I replied in a louder voice than was necessary, "What do you want from me? Look, anyone who takes one look at you and me can see that you could make mincemeat out of me in very short order. Now, what would that prove? Would it make smoking in food stores acceptable?"

The guy was taken aback and, seeing that all eyes were now trained on him, I could see that he got nervous. As he had in the produce department, he snorted dismissively, waved his hand indicating disgust, and walked out of the store. Nancy and I walked home without incident, and she cooked a fine veal Milanese dinner. That dish is also known as "Veal from the Garden": breaded veal cutlets topped by chopped arugula, tomatoes, and onions. Washing it down with a Chianti Classico was a pleasure.

Ginsberg

In the West, the year 1965 was the time of the Beatles. In Czechoslovakia, it was the dark age of the Cold War and of communist rule, and in Prague many young men adopted the Beatles' style of long hair. Because this fashion clearly came from the West, the communist authorities frowned on long hair and called the young men who sported it hooligans. Consequently, wearing shoulder-length hair became a subtle sign of protest against the regime. Eventually, however, as the fashion exploded and every young man who wanted to be hip let his hair grow long, it lost its initial meaning of protest and became simply fashion.

How did we know about Beatniks and the Beatles? Living in Czechoslovakia, we had a complex about being cut off from the civilized world by being on the wrong side of the Iron Curtain, and to remedy that complex, we tried hard to follow and keep up with the goings-on in the West. We managed this by listening to Voice of America and Radio Free Europe and by reading the occasional issue of *Time* or *Life* magazine, *Paris Match*, or *Der Spiegel* that a foreign visitor left behind or that a lucky Czech citizen who was allowed to go behind the Iron Curtain brought home. Those magazines were then carefully circulated and thoroughly read, both to learn what was going on in the free world and to practice our English and other foreign languages.

On one particular night in the spring of 1965, a bunch of us were sitting and drinking in Viola, a wine bar in downtown Prague. It was late, way after midnight, the time of night when all that needed to be said was said, and we all knew it. Yet instead of calling it a night, we ordered another bottle of wine. And it was then that the door opened, and a man with flowing, shoulder-length hair and a beard to match walked in.

Trying to be funny, in perhaps a louder voice than I intended, I said to my buddies the Czech equivalent of "Why is it that every asshole these days has to look like Allen Ginsberg?" The man who'd walked in stopped in his tracks, came over to our table, and said, "Excuse me, I heard someone say my name. I am Allen Ginsberg."

At first, we didn't believe him. Meeting Allen Ginsberg in the wee hours of the night at a bar in Prague was at the time a totally absurd proposition. One of my buddies who spoke the best English of all of us got up to greet the man, saying, "Oh, so you are Allen Ginsberg? How nice to meet you. I am Jack Kerouac." And he offered the stranger his hand. The man, grasping that he was being mocked and not being believed, responded, "Look, like it or not, I am Allen Ginsberg. I don't care if you believe me or not, but if you want proof, here is my passport." We looked, and, sure enough, the man in front of us was Allen Ginsberg.

We apologized for not believing him, explained the long odds of meeting someone like him in a Prague bar, ordered yet another bottle of wine, invited him to join us, and proceeded to practice our English on him. Allen Ginsberg seemed delighted that he was known in Prague and graciously suffered our interrogation. First of all, we wanted to know what brought him to Prague. He explained that things had gotten a little hot for him in the United States (he didn't elaborate and we didn't press) and that he'd decided to take a year off and travel around the world, heading east. After sailing across the Atlantic from New York to Southampton and spending a few weeks in London, he had wended his way through France and Germany.

Prague was his first stop behind the Iron Curtain. From Prague, Allen intended to travel by train and bus through Hungary, Romania, and Bulgaria into Istanbul, and then on through Turkey into Syria, Iraq, Iran, Afghanistan, and onward, moving east until he ended up in Tokyo. I must confess that, due to the vast amount of wine we consumed that evening, that's about all I remember of our conversation with him. I do remember, however, that we stayed at the Viola bar until it closed at 4 a.m., after which we stood in the street in front of it and kept on talking, God knows about what. I didn't get home until a little before 6 a.m., and I had to be at work at eight o'clock, but when you are twenty-six, you can do that sort of thing.

More than ten years later, when I found myself in Tehran, I met Bob Landsman, another New York architect seeking his fortune in Iran. Over dinner one night, I shared with him the story of how I met Allen Ginsberg in Prague. Bob asked me when that happened. When I told him that it was in 1965, Bob continued, "Well, now we know that after Prague, Allen Ginsberg made it at least as far as India, because in the fall of 1965 I bumped into him in the American Express office in Calcutta." It so happened that in 1965 Bob had also taken a year off to travel around the world, except that he was moving westward, starting in Japan.

Now let's fast-forward thirty years since that night when I met Allen Ginsburg; it is 1995, and I'm in New York. In some newspaper or magazine, I saw an announcement that Allen Ginsberg would be talking in a high school auditorium in Lower Manhattan. Driven by perverse nostalgia, I decided to go. The five-hundred-seat auditorium was half full. His talk was blabber. I would not have stayed if I didn't want to talk to him afterward.

I was not the only one wanting to talk to Allen, so I patiently waited my turn. When we finally stood facing each other, I asked him if he remembered a night in a bar in Prague thirty years ago. Allen Ginsberg looked at me with a totally unanimated, uninterested, unengaged face and said that he had no recollection of such a night. I then asked him if he remembered ever having been in Prague. After a moment's reflection, he replied, "I guess I do." I wished him good night and left.

Early Sex Stories

Three-year-old Martin.

The first recorded manifestation of my lifelong interest in female breasts occurred at the age of three. I know this incident more from my mother's telling, although I do have my own vague memory of it. At my grandmother's house in the country, which was adjacent to the factory, there was a large garden—and in the middle of it was a gazebo surrounded by hazelnut bushes. A long, winding path led from the house to the gazebo. One summer day my mother was sunbathing with her top off, lying on a deck chair in a clearing between the bushes near the gazebo. She heard her three-year-old toddler son coming along the path and so put her broad-brimmed straw hat over her chest. When I reached her, I demanded that she remove the hat so that I could see her breasts. She first refused, but apparently, I made such a nuisance of myself, shrieking my repeated requests that she remove the hat that, to shut me up, she relented. As is well known, when women lie on their backs, their breasts sort of disappear. According to my mother, when I saw what was there to be seen, my face fell in disappointment and I waddled away. Some might argue that this story doesn't belong in a chapter on sex stories, but I think it does.

There was a custom when children of my and earlier generations were born that their parents started writing what were known as baby books. In these diaries parents recorded major, and many not so major, events in the early lives of their offspring. I found my baby books, covering my development from birth to five years old, when I was liquidating my mother's Prague apartment after she died in 2001. I also found my mother's baby books written by my grandmother, dating from 1913 to 1917. Although written a generation apart, these books were so similar as to be nearly interchangeable. Both were written in the first person, addressing the child:

Today you were very pleased with yourself because it was the first time you managed to turn over all by yourself....When I came to your room this morning, you were for the first time standing, holding on to the railing of your crib....Today you took your first three steps before you fell down. You found it funny, clapped your hands and tried again. That meant crawling back to the coffee table, pulling yourself up to the standing position, then turning around, in the process of which you fell down a few times before you managed to stand with your back toward the table. Then, very gingerly, you took one, two, three, four wobbly steps before you fell down. That effort exhausted you so much that you stayed lying on the carpet and immediately fell asleep.

And so on and so on. My baby book entries were mostly written by my father, with an occasional note by my mother. I must admit that even though they were all about me, I found the books a very boring read and skipped through them quickly. It wasn't until I opened the book dated 1943, written when I was four and a half years old, that I found a real gem.

It was in July of that year, when my mother and I were spending the summer at my grandmother's house in Moravia and my father had traveled from Prague to join us for a week, that he wrote this entry:

In the afternoon, while your mother was in town visiting Aunt Boženka, your Uncle Radko and I were sitting and talking in the garden gazebo while you were playing with the fire truck you got for Christmas. It was hot and when Amálka [my grandmother's cook] brought us the afternoon tea and some freshly baked cookies, she was wearing a loose blouse with a lower cut than usual. To put the cups and saucers from her tray on the low table next to which you were standing, she squatted, so that her head was level with yours. While standing next to her, you were unabashedly peering into Amálka's cleavage. When she left I told you that it was a very bad form to so obviously stare down ladies' blouses. You looked at me genuinely sur-prised and, with a totally unself-conscious sincerity, you said, "But dad, I am very interested in breasts." Then, to my amazement, you asked, "Do you think Amálka's breasts are bigger than mama's?" I told you that it was completely irrelevant and that you shouldn't worry about things that don't matter one way or another. I could see that you were not entirely satisfied with that answer, but you went back to playing with the fire truck.

Unlike the first incident, I have no recollection of this one, but it must have occurred because my father would certainly not have invented it.

––––––––––––––––––––

Because I was born in December, I started attending grade school when I was five. To get to the all-boys' school in which my parents enrolled me required taking public transportation, which in this case meant a tram. During my first year, either our maid Amálka or my mother would accompany me to the school and later would pick me up. During my second year, since getting to school on time was critical, I was still accompanied by my mother or Amálka; however, I was deemed competent enough to get home by myself, whether by taking a tram or by walking. This story happened on one of my walks home from school, either during my second or third year of grade school. I was six or seven years old at the time.

The walk home required crossing the Jirásek Bridge, which is the last bridge built across the Vltava River in the center of Prague. At that time of year, there were many people leaning over the railing of the bridge feeding the gulls. As I was walking along, I noticed a man in baggy pants. There was something peculiar about him. Although he was leaning over the railing, he was not feeding the gulls. Instead, while supporting himself on his left elbow, his right hand was inside the pocket of his pants. But it wasn't just resting there: it was moving vigorously back and forth. I felt something nefarious was going on.

Knowing nothing of masturbation and fascinated by this spectacle, I stopped and watched. After a while, with a combination of the brazenness and innocence of a child, I asked, "Mister, what are you

Walking across Jirásek Bridge with my mother.

doing?" The man turned his head, looked me up and down, and, while continuing to move his hand, calmly answered, "I am playing with it. And why shouldn't I? After all, it's mine, isn't it?"

I remained still, pondering this answer, while the man continued to watch me. Then he asked, "Do you want to see it?" I indicated with a nod that, yes, I would. The man told me to follow him and started walking toward the riverbank. I knew he was heading to the public toilets that were built into the first pier of the bridge on the embankment. He entered the men's room and I followed. We were alone. The man unbuttoned his fly, and out came the first erect penis I ever saw.

I was astounded by its size. I had no idea that even a grown man's penis could be that big. The man observed my fascination and said, "You can touch it if you want to." I wanted to, and I did. It was warm and as hard as a rock. The man continued, "You can play with it if you want to." I did not know what he meant by that, and it was probably at this point that, for the first time, I began to feel that I was where I should not be and was doing what I should not be doing. So I said to the man, "Mister, I have to be going now; my mother is waiting for me." He said, "OK, good-bye. Feel good." I left and, amazingly, that was all that took place between us.

I could not wait to get home to tell my mother about this latest adventure of mine. Before Amálka served us lunch, I spilled it all out—from the first moment of noticing the man on the bridge to leaving the men's room. I noticed that my mother was listening intently. When I was done, she told me, "Martin, the man you met was a pervert. It is not his fault. Perversion is a disease. This particular pervert happened to be a kind man, but not all are. There have been cases when they actually harmed the boys they were with. So the next time you see a grown man acting unnaturally, better avoid him."

As always, what my mother said made sense to me, so I nodded and said I would avoid such men. It wasn't until many years later, when I was a grown man myself and my mother and I were reminiscing about that incident, that she told me how petrified she felt as I was innocently relating my adventure on the bridge and how hard she tried to appear calm all the while her heart was racing.

———————————

My next clear memory that has something remotely to do with sex is of an experience I had in third grade in an all-boys grade school in Prague. I was seven when it happened. Among my classmates was Josef Mocek, who was a year older than the rest of us since he had had to repeat a grade. That made him sort of a class elder: he knew things the rest of us did not.

One day after school Mocek came up to me and said, "Holub, do you want to see cunts?" I had only a dim idea what he was talking about, but I was curious, so I answered, "Cunts? Well, sure; yes, I want to see the cunts." "OK," said Mocek, "follow me."

We boarded a tram and rode to the Yellow Baths, which was a bathing establishment on the Vltava at the southern edge of Prague. There was a large deck floating on the river from which people could jump in the water and swim, as well as changing rooms and showers on the shore. And this story is concerned with the women's showers.

The showers—a grid of pipes with chain-activated shower heads on top—were located in a large enclosure open to the sky. About fifty women could shower there at a time. Near the only entrance was a small hillock with a tree and a few bushes on it. Mocek figured out that there was a spot near the tree from which we could get a good view inside each time the door opened. And because there was a lively traffic of women coming in and out of the shower area, the door opened quite often. Nobody paid attention to two small boys crouching near the bushes and looking inside the showers. Mocek crowed, "See the cunts?" Hard as I looked, all I could see were black triangles between women's legs. So I said to Mocek, "Where are the cunts? I see no cunts."

Mocek was furious, "You idiot; don't you see the black triangles?" I said, "Sure, I see the triangles, but those are not cunts, those are just hairs." Mocek shouted at me, "No, you stupid; those are the cunts." I did not believe him and went home disappointed.

Then in the summer of 1949, between fourth and fifth grade, I attended a YMCA summer camp. A boy my age whose name I no longer remember came up to me and said, "Holub, do you want to fuck?" I didn't quite know what he meant by that, but trying to be cool about it, I said, "Sure." The boy said, "OK, then let's go to the bushes." When we came to a little clearing, he dropped his shorts, gripped his little pecker with both hands, and commanded me to do the same. When I did, he came closer to me and rubbed his pecker against mine. I asked, "Are we fucking?" He replied, "Sure, we are fucking." After a while we got bored, pulled up our shorts, and walked back to the camp.

After my fourth-grade year, the communists abolished the all-boys' school as bourgeois, so for the fifth grade, I attended for the first time a co-ed public school, where I fell hopelessly in love with my classmate Milada Andělová.

At the time, I had absolutely no idea how children were made, nor was I much interested in finding out. Yet this ignorance did not prevent me from fantasizing what a bliss it would be if Milada and I were lying naked and snuggled in a bed, rubbing our bodies together. Despite knowing nothing about sexual intercourse, this fantasy was very real, and I was tormented by its unattainability.

The boarding school of George of Poděbrad owned a ski lodge in the mountains of north Bohemia. Strictly speaking, "owned" was not the correct word because, after the communist putsch

In 1950, when my mother was in prison.

of 1948, no one in Czechoslovakia owned anything. Yet the school held the title to the lodge it used to own and could still use it. In the 1950–51 school year, while my mother was in the communist prison, I was a boarder at that school, and during the midterm break in February 1951, I found myself at that ski lodge.

The school had boarders from sixth to twelfth grades. At the time of that midterm break I was in seventh grade and was one of the youngest kids staying in the lodge. It was a Spartan establishment with one huge co-ed dorm full of bunk beds. Of some thirty kids on that ski vacation, there were perhaps a half dozen high school girls who were fifteen, sixteen, and even seventeen years old. To twelve-year-old me, they appeared like grown women. We slept in sweat suits under woolen blankets without any sheets. Deprived of my mother with whom I used to cuddle, I was perhaps starved for a female touch. Sensing that those grown girls liked me, during the milling about before the lights were turned off, I boldly jumped into bed with one of them and snuggled up.

The first time I did it, I half-expected to be thrown out, but instead, I found myself warmly embraced. So I snuggled closer and, in so doing, started fondling her breasts. To my surprise she let me, so I kept on fondling. Caressing breasts for the first time in my life made me feel a little dizzy. I was in seventh heaven, and when I left her bed to go sleep in mine, I was already thinking about the next time.

The following night, I did the same, albeit with a different girl, who also let me fondle her breasts. And so on, night after night—a different girl, same experience. I was a harmless child, and, who knows, perhaps those girls had some motherly feelings of their own. I remember nothing of the skiing during that vacation, but sixty-five years later I still remember the breast fondling.

When my mother was released from prison in 1951 and we moved to the proletarian neighborhood of Žižkov, it was the first time I came into contact with working-class kids. As I mentioned, the communists abolished the all-boys' school I attended through the end of fourth grade; for fifth grade I went to a regular public school in our neighborhood, and then I attended another public school the following year. For the seventh and half of the eighth grade, while my mother was in prison, I was in the boarding school in Poděbrady, so that the Žižkov school I went to in the second half of the eighth grade was the fifth school I had attended. Consequently, I was well used to changing schools and getting acquainted with new classmates.

Typically, when making new acquaintances, kids asked each other questions such as "What does your father do?" and "What does your mother do?" I was used to answers like my father is a dentist, a lawyer, an engineer, a journalist, and so on, and my mother is a teacher, a nurse, a librarian, an accountant, and such.

In Žižkov, however, when I asked a kid what his father did, I was always met with an astonished expression and the same reply: "What do you mean? He works in the factory, like everybody else." Then when I asked what his mother did, I was met with even more bewilderment: "What do you mean?" When I explained that I was asking what his mother's profession was, the kid would give me an uncomprehending stare and would reply, "She is at home, like all mothers." I quickly learned that my background was very different from theirs.

With my mother. I am thirteen.

In hindsight, it seems to me that these working-class kids grew up faster. At twelve, I was still a child, while most of my male classmates already had deep voices and were physically more developed and the girls had already started sprouting breasts. It was in this environment that I was standing in a group of my new classmates when one of them, out of the blue, asked me, "Holub, are you jerking off?"

Caught by surprise, I lied: "Of course, I am jerking off." The kid said, "I don't believe you." I insisted that I was absolutely jerking off. Then another boy jumped in, saying, "OK, if you are jerking off, then tell us what it looks like and smells like that comes out of you." I was caught: I didn't know what semen looked like. So I made up a description: "It is a thick, yellowish liquid that smells like rotten hay." They all burst out laughing, knowing that I had no idea what I was talking about, and I felt humiliated. It did not take long, however, before I was able to answer that question correctly.

I started these early sex recollections with breasts, and I am going to finish with breasts. The breasts in question were those of Mrs. Blažena Bassová. At the time, I was thirteen and taking private English lessons from her; she was then in her mid-sixties. She was a friend of my mother's friend who, before World War II had spent a few years in England and was now supplementing her meager pension by giving English lessons.

Mrs. Bassová was a short woman whose salient feature was her enormous bust, which absolutely fascinated a thirteen-year-old boy in the throes of puberty. We would usually sit catty-corner at her dining table, giving me the full view of her magnificent profile. Because of her short stature, the bottom of her bust was just at the level of the tabletop, so that when she leaned over to reach for something, her bust seemed to move an incredible distance across the table. As yet unaware of the function of a sturdy undergarment, I marveled at that imposing cantilever. I yearned to touch and feel those breasts, but of course, that was out of the question. As is evident, whatever English she taught me, those breasts remain the single strongest memory of my lessons with Mrs. Bassová.

And there is a humorous postscript to this story. Some forty-five years later, I was visiting my mother in Prague. One afternoon she hosted a tea for a group of longtime friends, among whom was the well-known photographer Dagmar Hochová, who was my age. Once we established that she was a niece of Mrs. Bassová, she asked me if her aunt had given me a solid enough foundation of English that I was then able to build on when I moved to London. After giving Dagmar the account of my lessons with her aunt—the chief feature of which was my fascination with her bust—I noticed that she was not at all amused. The second thing I noticed on taking a closer look at her was that, under a loose top, she had a bosom the size of her aunt's. It was clearly a family trait.

St. Martin's Parties

Perhaps one reason the tradition of giving children the names of saints has persisted in most of Europe for centuries is that it gives each child another yearly celebration, in addition to his or her birthday. On the given saint's day, sometimes called the saint's feast day, the child who has that saint's name has a party and gets presents. Each day of the year has at least one saint assigned to it; some days are assigned more than one saint, and some saints have more than one day. For example, there are four St. Johns: St. John the Baptist, St. John the Apostle, St. John the Evangelist, and St. John Chrysostom, also known as Gold Mouth. I don't know which of those was my father's saint, but I do remember that his feast day was May 16.

This tradition is so firmly entrenched that the communists did not dare interfere with it, even though they believed that religion was the opium of the masses and did their best to do away with it. Consequently, even during the communist era, calendars printed in Czechoslovakia still listed a saint per day. In fact, the feast day celebrations were perfectly secular, and few people thought about the actual saint who was being honored on the given day. For children, their saint's day was an occasion to receive presents, and for adults it was a time to throw a party or go out for a fine dinner. On feast days of saints with common names, such as St. Joseph's Day (March 19) or St. Wenceslas's (September 28), Prague looked like New York City on St. Patrick's Day.

And so I have celebrated St. Martin's Days on November 11 ever since I can remember. My first St. Martin's party on the North American continent was in 1970, when I invited perhaps half of the design department of Kahn & Jacobs, where I was then working. For most of my colleagues, the concept of celebrating one's name day was a novelty, and they were delighted that they would now have one more reason to throw a party. That was fine for those with names like Paul, Thomas, Stephen, or Charles, who could easily look up the feast days of their saints, but tough luck for those with names like Craig, Hunter, Shahita, or Gary.

After the success of the first St. Martin's party, I had one every year. In those early years, the refreshments were simple: I just bought plenty of fine cheeses, pâtés, and cold cuts at Zabar's. The wine of choice in those days was Gallo Hearty Burgundy. I also carried on the tradition during my four years in Tehran. There were enough Europeans in the ex-pat community who were familiar with name day celebrations so unlike in the United States, no explanations were required, and my huge apartment easily accommodated sixty-some people. Those were pre-email times, so I would just call folks to invite them.

After my return from Tehran, I started designing and printing invitations. Typically, I would take a segment of an architectural drawing I was working on and turn it into a graphic, with letterpress printing on the invitation, walk it over to the offset print shop around the corner, and print the required minimum of a hundred copies.

Yes, St.Martin's Party Again:

Sun 11 Nov 6 PM 41 W 89

RSVP 724 7113

Hope you can come to

St. Martin's Party
Tue 11 Nov 8 PM
41 W 89 NYC

RSVP 724 7113

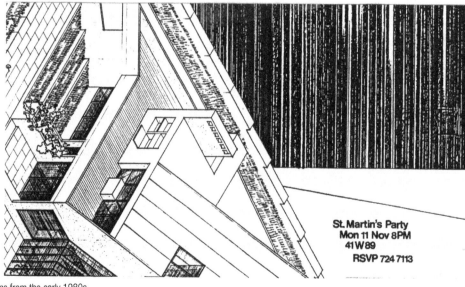

St. Martin's Party
Mon 11 Nov 8PM
41 W 89
RSVP 724 7113

Invitations from the early 1980s.

After a while, two problems surfaced. The first was that I knew more single women than single men, so I started asking my male acquaintances to bring along their male friends. The second problem was that, while the list of invitees kept growing, the size of my apartment did not. Although it looked bigger than it was because of my design and its high ceilings, it was still only a 550-square-foot, two-room apartment. In hindsight, I am astonished by how many people I was able to pack into that small space. If I didn't have a list of attendees of all my St. Martin's parties, I would never believe that there were often fifty to sixty people in attendance.

Those tight quarters were perhaps one reason folks liked those parties. I've been told that they had a feeling of coziness not always present at other gatherings. If you stand with your face six inches from somebody else's face, it's hard not to start a conversation. Add to it that I spent the evening introducing people who didn't know each other, and it's easy to see why by the end of the night everybody had become acquainted with each other, which, again, is not the norm at parties of that size.

Another feature not always found at other parties was the many toasts and jokes. Sometime between 10 and 11 p.m., I always stepped on a bench next to the fireplace and proposed a toast to St. Martin, noting particularly his capacity as a patron of wine. Then I would open the floor for other toasts, of which there were always many. Finally, I'd tell a mildly risqué joke and invite the multitudes to tell more jokes, and they happily obliged. In hindsight, I think that all of this contributed to the warm feeling my St. Martin's parties were known for.

Then, sometime in the mid- to late 1980s a third problem arose: the St. Martin's party clearly got to be oversubscribed. How could I solve that problem? Before the next party, I took the list of invitees and deleted everyone I had not heard from since the last party. That, however, did not quite work. The day before, or even on the morning of November 11, my phone would start ringing and people would ask, "Martin, isn't it about the time of the party? I didn't get an invitation!" I didn't have the nerve to tell them, "My dear so and so you didn't get an invitation, because you were not invited." Instead, I'd lie and say, "Oh, it must have gotten lost in the mail, so just come on over." It was also about this time when Karen started appearing in my life and the St. Martin's parties became, little by little, fancier. I started hiring help, and the refreshments became more sumptuous.

A major change came in 1991, when I moved in with Karen, and we started having the St. Martin's parties at our freshly remodeled Upper East Side apartment, which was more than twice the size of my bachelor digs. We'd hire two servers, and Karen saw to it that the food was a feast. There were still toasts and jokes, yet something was missing. For one thing, because there was more space in which to spread out, the coziness created by the tight quarters was gone. For another, there was somehow a lower turnover of guests, so that the same crowd kept showing up year after year. All in all, I had an impression that the parties were growing stale—no more the rambunctious merriment of years past.

The death knell of our St. Martin's parties rang during the 1996 edition, when I accidentally overheard one guest telling another, "These parties have lost the element of rowdiness." That was all I needed to hear. When I shared that with Karen, we decided that the next party would be the last one, and the invitations for the following St. Martin's party did include a note to that effect. During that final party,

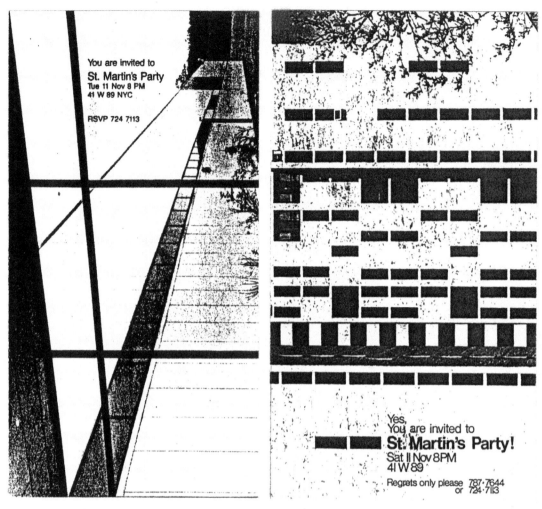

You are invited to
St. Martin's Party
Tue 11 Nov 8 PM
41 W 89 NYC

RSVP 724 7113

Yes,
You are invited to
St. Martin's Party!
Sat II Nov 8PM
41 W 89

Regrets only please 787·7644
or 724·7113

**St. Martin's Party
as usual...
Wed 11 Nov 8PM
41 W 89
RSVP 724 7113**

Invitations from the late 1980s.

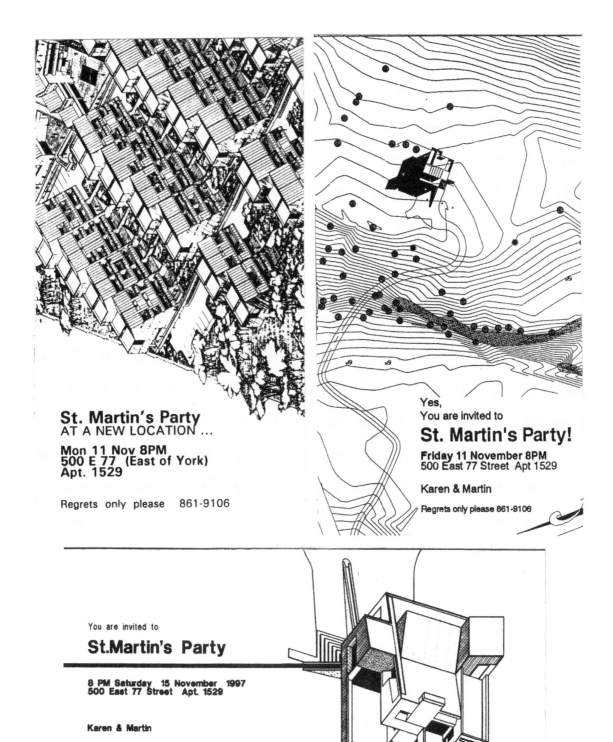

St. Martin's Party
AT A NEW LOCATION ...

Mon 11 Nov 8PM
500 E 77 (East of York)
Apt. 1529

Regrets only please   861-9106

Yes,
You are invited to

St. Martin's Party!

Friday 11 November 8PM
500 East 77 Street Apt 1529

Karen & Martin

Regrets only please 861-9106

You are invited to

St.Martin's Party

8 PM Saturday 15 November 1997
500 East 77 Street   Apt. 1529

Karen & Martin

Regrets only please   861-9106

Invitations from the 1990s.

folks inquired what made us discontinue the tradition. I responded truthfully, saying that we felt the parties had grown stale. There were only mild protestations.

The following year I turned sixty, and instead of a St. Martin's party, we decided to have a ball. We hired an orchestra that played at the waltz balls we went to, rented an old, cavernous stable in West Village that was turned into an event space, and put on a gala—black or white tie for the men, ball gowns for the women, the works! From then on, every five years we did something mildly loony. For my sixty-fifth birthday, we hosted a dinner in Death Valley, California. Only sixteen people showed up. Five years after that, we hosted a dinner in Prague, which drew thirty-six attendees, Prague clearly proving to be a stronger draw than Death Valley. For my 75th, my third-wife-to-be Sandra and I hosted dinner in the Ruby Tuesday Lodge at the foothills of the Smoky Mountains in Tennessee. I forget the exact number of guests, but it was somewhere close to thirty.

I have often wondered why it is that some people throw parties and others don't. Does it spring from an emotional need to mark watershed anniversaries, like milestone birthdays? Not for me: I see a milestone birthday as simply an excuse for a party. People who like giving parties can find many excuses to do so. In my early years in New York, in addition to my St. Martin's parties on November 11, I used to have parties on January 23, the anniversary of my arrival in the New World. But I also know people who dislike parties because they are not conducive to having serious conversations. While still living in Prague, I remember my mother telling me, "Parties are not vehicles for profound conversations. They are vehicles for finding someone with whom you might want to have a profound conversation." Though I've kept that in mind ever since, I also think that the answer to the question of why some folks do and some don't like giving parties lies in the same sphere as the answer to the question of why some folks like broccoli and others prefer cauliflower.

My First and Last Job in America

My first employer in New York was the firm of Frost Associates. Ignorant as I was about the United States while living in London, when I decided to come to America, there was one thing I did get right (I don't know how) and it was this: if America, then New York or San Francisco (I would now add Chicago). Accordingly, I started applying for jobs in those two cities.

Today there are a number of types of work visas for foreigners. In 1969, however, there was only one legal way to work in America and that was to immigrate. The immigration officer at the US Embassy in London told me that the fastest way to obtain immigration status (i.e., getting a Green Card) was to have my immigration application sponsored by a prospective employer. Consequently, in each of the job applications I was sending to architectural firms in San Francisco and New York, I mentioned that, should a job be offered, I would also expect the firm to sponsor my immigration application.

I am sure that this contingency reduced the number of responses I got, but eventually, a letter arrived from Mr. Frederick Frost of Frost Associates in New York. He wrote that my application was being considered, asked for more samples of my designs, and requested a letter of reference from my British employer. In short order, after submitting the requested material, I received another letter from Mr. Frost offering me employment and stating that the firm would be happy to sponsor my immigration application.

What followed were more forms to fill out, more references to submit, and then an interview at the US Embassy. Finally, a letter arrived from the New York office of the US Immigration and Naturalization Service, confirming that I could apply for an Immigration visa at the US Embassy. The whole process took a little over four months which, as I came to know later, was at the speed of lightning compared to how long it takes to obtain a Green Card these days.

I wrote Mr. Frost thanking him for his sponsorship, purchased passage on the boat from Southampton to New York, gave a month's notice at my London employer, informed my landlady, and started packing. It was early January 1970 when another letter arrived from Mr. Frost:

Dear Martin,

Since we offered you a job last year, things have changed for the worse at our office. Many commissions we counted on receiving are being held up so that we actually had to let a few people go. In short, it would be better for both of us if you do not arrive at this time and wait until we get more work.

However, if you have already made arrangements for the trip, we shall certainly honor our offer, but we cannot guarantee you employment for any length of time.

Sincerely yours,

Fred Frost

Although I still have that letter, I didn't have to look it up, because after close to fifty years, I still know it by heart. What now? I quickly resolved to stay the course, even though I didn't know what to make of the sentence "We cannot guarantee you employment for any length of time." Would I have a job for a month? A week? A day?

I decided the die was cast and so wrote Mr. Frost, thanking him for his letter, expressing optimism about the future of his firm, and announcing the day of my arrival, January 22, 1970. Fortunately, by the time I reported for work at Frost Associates, they had received a commission for a private school in Manhattan, and I was asked to develop a conceptual design for it. It took me a little over two months to design the school and have it approved by the client, after which Mr. Frost called me to his office, "Martin, we have absolutely nothing else for you to design. We have people to prepare the construction documents and, besides, you don't yet know the American way of working drawings (he was correct). So I am very sorry but we have to let you go." Thus ended my first job in America.

So that was why, less than three months after my arrival in New York, I found myself on the street looking for a job—my second and what turned out to be my last one. If I were looking for just any job as a staff architect with a firm, finding employment would have been easier, but I was looking for a position of a designer. Someone suggested that I call I. M. Pei's office. At the time, I had no idea that I. M. Pei was well on his way to becoming one of the most respected architects in the United States. For me his was just another firm to call. I still remember that I made that call from a phone booth on 57th Street, across the street from Carnegie Hall. A receptionist answered, and when I told her that I was calling about potential employment, she said I needed to speak with Mr. Easton Leonard and that she would connect me with him. It is amazing to me that I still remember the name of a guy whom I never met, with whom I had one five-minute telephone conversation some forty-eight years ago.

Mr. Leonard came to the phone, asked how many years of experience I had, and then asked what kind of job I was looking for. I responded that since all my ten years of experience were solidly in design, I thought I could be most useful in the capacity of a project designer. Mr. Leonard's response was as follows: "Young man, we already have a designer here. His name is I. M. Pei, and all of us in the firm are honored that we can help him realize his visions. Think about it and, if you'd like to work within this context, call me back and we'll schedule an interview."

Although his response was perfectly logical, I found it to be a sobering statement, and I didn't call back. I needed to be developing my own designs. Why? At the time, I steadfastly believed that the only way to be an architect was to design and that, if I were not designing, I would only be a hired hack working for a living.

I shared my conversation with Mr. Leonard of I. M. Pei with Stanley Gendell, a former colleague from Frost Associates, and he suggested that I call Kahn & Jacobs. He reasoned that it was a large firm with no design personality, and because I had a strong design portfolio, chances were—if they also happened to need someone—that I might get into its design department. So I called Kahn & Jacobs and was interviewed by the director of design. Julian Van der Lancken was an amiable man in his midsixties, on the cusp of retirement, no longer needing to prove anything. I could sense that he liked me, but more importantly, he liked my portfolio and hired me on the spot. I'd be the most junior of five senior project designers, but I would be developing my own projects. I was in seventh heaven.

Kahn & Jacobs was both an old and an old-fashioned New York firm, founded in the 1930s by Ely Jacques Kahn, a French architect. At the time I was hired, it had more than 150 employees and its main line of work was high-rise office buildings. It had a design department, a production department, a plan desk, a model shop, its own building department expeditor, and a chief draftsman. I was given a cubicle in the design department and was assigned to prepare one design study after another.

About eight months into my employment, there started to be signs that the firm was hitting a slow period. Each week several people from the production department were let go. Van der Lancken told me that no one was building high-rise office buildings at the time and that the firm was desperately trying to diversify. It was probably in pursuit of diversification that Mr. Jacobs (Mr. Kahn was no longer around) sought and was given a commission from the New York Board of Education to design a public school in the Bronx.

The contract called for the submission of three schematic designs. Mr. Jacobs asked the director of design to pick three designers, each of whom would develop one design. I was one of the three and so entered into an unofficial intraoffice competition. We three knew that the client would select only one of the designs to be developed and eventually built. Meanwhile, the situation of the firm continued to deteriorate, with more and more people being let go each week. I paid no mind to it, being fully absorbed by developing my design for the school. Eventually, the deadline came, and the three schematic designs were sent to the Board of Education.

Two weeks later we were notified that my design was chosen. I was jubilant, not only because my design was going to be built, but also because my job was now secure for at least a year, which is how long the design development and the subsequent supervision of the working drawings preparation would take. I threw myself into the design development and was meeting regularly with the client's representative, an architect from the Board of Education. In the design department, I became like a hero.

This probably all went straight to my head, because about a month or so into the design development process, I decided to ask for a raise. I thought, "I've been with the firm for well over a year now, my work has been uniformly well received, my design was selected by a client for realization, so why not?" I called Van der Lancken's extension and asked if I could stop in to see him. He told me to come right over. I walked in to his office, sat down, and said, in so many words, that I believed I merited a raise. Van (that's what we called him in the office) put his elbows on the table, propped his forehead against his hands, and for a long time said nothing. Eventually he straightened up and said, "Ah, Martin, Martin, you have no idea what's been going on behind the scenes. The sad truth is that I actually have to let you go. If you hadn't called me, I would have called you tomorrow. You'll have two more weeks to bring the design of the school to a state where someone else can take over; then you'll get a month's severance and will be gone."

Then Van explained that Kahn & Jacobs Architects was in the process of merging with Hellmuth, Obata & Kassabaum (HOK), a much larger firm from St. Louis, Missouri. One condition of the merger was that HOK was bringing its designers to New York and Kahn & Jacobs's design department would be gradually dissolved, including Van himself. I was the last designer hired, so I was the first to go, never mind my school design. To this day, I am the only architect I know who was fired while asking for a raise.

I started feverishly working on the design of the school, trying to tie up all the loose ends. My colleagues could not believe how hard I worked. They kept telling me, "Martin, you've been fired, why are you knocking yourself out? Don't be ridiculous." Still, the school in the Bronx was my baby, and I was trying to do all I could to ensure that it would get built as I had designed it.

So much for my second and last job in America. I never found another employment. Instead, I started working as a freelance design consultant for other architectural and engineering firms, which very slowly paved the way to private practice.

Some thirty years later, when Karen and I were driving along the elevated section of Bruckner Boulevard on the way to our house in the Hudson Valley, I happened to look to the left, and there was PS 151 in the Bronx—my last project at Kahn & Jacobs—right below the highway. I recognized it instantly: the layout, the massing, and the volumes were exactly as I had designed them. But even in that blink of an eye, I could also see that the finishes were not mine. It then took about another five years before we found time on our way up to the country to make a little detour and drive by the school to take a closer look.

It was a bittersweet experience. The satisfying part was to see that the school worked as I had intended: the gym and the cafeteria on the south end of the site, closest to the highway to buffer the noise; the kindergarten on the opposite end with the elementary school, middle school, and high school all surrounding the inner courtyard, interconnected yet separate. It was a school day, and the little kids were playing in the yard just as I had imagined they would.

But it was sad to see that the skin of the building was not what I had designed. Bricks were substituted for the precast concrete panels; stock aluminum windows with thick frames were substituted for the thin members of steel-framed windows. There's more to a building than a well-functioning plan, which is the reason you won't find this school among the completed buildings in my portfolio.

Banishment

In communist Czechoslovakia, every able-bodied citizen had to work. If someone was found not working, he or she was labeled a parasite, which was a punishable offense. However, while work was an obligation, it was also a right, meaning everyone was entitled to employment. In the centrally planned economy, the government placed every university graduate in a job. One didn't have to accept it, but if one failed to find a job on one's own, one was guaranteed that job placement.

In June 1962, at the end of the sixth year of the program at the School of Architecture, when those of us who had made it that far had already passed all the exams and defended our thesis projects and when the date of the graduation ceremony was already set, we were called to assemble in one of the auditoriums to be handed our job placements. Out of about thirty students, there were among us five known members of the Communist Party, none of whom were originally from Prague. Naturally, the coveted placements were at the institutions in Prague; less desirable ones were in the provinces.

The dean of the School of Architecture, Professor Janu, distributed the placements, calling the students' names one by one and announcing the name and location of the institution in which each was placed. My placement was in the national contracting firm Konstruktiva's branch office located in the town of Litvínov in northwestern Bohemia. I had no intention of working for a building contractor or of moving to Litvínov, and I was confident that I'd find a job in Prague, so I didn't take that placement at all seriously.

When he was finished handing out the placements, the dean asked if there were any questions. Although I spent the six years at the School of Architecture worrying that I might be dismissed—either because I would fail reinforced concrete calculations or some such exam, or because the personnel officer would discover my class origin—I now felt secure, considering myself safely out of the university's clutches. So I raised my hand and said that I did have a question. I asked the dean to help me understand if it were just a coincidence, or if it happened by design, that all the members of the Communist Party who were originally not from Prague received placements in Prague, while most of us who were from Prague received placements in the provinces.

The room fell deadly quiet. The dean's face got red. He opened his mouth, and then he closed it. Then he opened it again and closed it again. Someone chuckled. The dean finally said, "This is neither the time nor the place to discuss this sort of thing." Everybody in the room, including the dean, knew that it was not an adequate answer, but he said nothing more. Then he asked if there were any more questions. There were no other questions, and we were dismissed.

I didn't think much about this incident. It hadn't occurred to me that I had caused the dean to make a fool of himself in front of a large audience and that there might be consequences. A few days later, a large group of us students was celebrating the forthcoming graduation, and we got mixed up in a pub brawl involving East German tourists. Because it was an international incident, the police were called in to investigate. No charges were filed and no blame assigned. But imagine the glee that Dean Janu must have felt when he found on his desk a list of students who were involved in a disturbance that had been investigated by the police, and my name was on it! He immediately decided that I was the main instigator of the disturbance and that I should be punished by having my diploma suspended. Consequently, instead at graduation, I was given not my diploma, but the following document on the letterhead of the School of Architecture of the Czech Technical University:

To Whom It May Concern:

This is to confirm that Martin Holub fulfilled all requirements of the study of architecture at the Czech Technical University and may use the academic title of ing. arch. However, for disciplinary reasons, the Dean's Office has temporarily suspended Martin Holub's diploma, pending his demonstration of positive attitude toward the working class and our socialist regime.

Signed Deputy Dean

This changed the game. The first consequence was that I couldn't well ignore my job placement in the northwest corner of Bohemia, because I could not demonstrate a positive attitude toward the socialist regime if I refused the employment that the regime had secured for me. So I packed a suitcase and took a bus to Litvínov, where I reported to the office of the national enterprise Konstruktiva.

It was a blighted region of the country, known for strip mining and oil refineries. The largest refinery there was still known at the time as Stalin's Works. Konstruktiva was involved in several construction projects inside this vast complex of buildings. When I walked in with my suitcase to Konstruktiva's office, the receptionist asked me why I had come. Judging from her looks that she wasn't a hardline communist, I indulged in a bit of irreverence and told her that I had come to prove my positive attitude toward the socialist regime. With a mock serious face, she responded that I had come to the right place. We immediately formed a bond.

This is a perfect example of how the communist regime worked. Except for a small number of committed communists, the so-called true believers, the rest of us knew that it was a farce, yet we all played along. I soon learned that Konstruktiva was a national firm and that Litvínov was only one of its many offices. The company was headquartered in Prague, where it had its own architectural office. It soon became my objective to be transferred to the Prague office once having, of course, proven my positive attitude. But how does one prove one's positive attitude toward the socialist regime? By producing a letter from someone of authority stating that one had demonstrated such an attitude.

I was assigned to one of Konstruktiva's building projects inside Stalin's Works. My job was to supervise the excavation of trenches for the concrete footings and foundation walls for a huge new warehouse. I reported to the superintendent, Mr. Buble. It was from him that I heard for the first time the adage "Well, they pretend to pay us, so we pretend to work." His second credo was "What you've once eaten, nobody can take away from you"—and he certainly took it to heart. He must have weighed close to four hundred pounds and yet was surprisingly nimble. Although he and I hit it off immediately, unfortunately he was not high enough on the ladder of authority to write the letter confirming my positive attitude. That would have to come from Mr. Buble's boss, the project manager Mr. Hampel, whom I had yet to meet.

Mr. Buble explained that the manager supervised a number of projects, only one of which was ours, and that he came around to check on things no more than once a week. Furthermore, it was then July, and he was on vacation; he would not return until sometime in August. I was very eager to meet this man on whom my fate depended.

When he finally came in mid-August to inspect our work, I breathed a deep sigh of relief. Mr. Hampel was a man in his late fifties or perhaps early sixties: he was the type who had seen it all, had nothing more to prove, and was coasting along toward retirement. From his refined looks it was also obvious to me that working on construction sites inside an oil refinery would not have been his first choice. Mr. Hampel was extremely curious how I ended up in Stalin's Works. He said there were not many architects working for Konstruktiva at that location. When I told him why, he was mightily amused. Although he did not say so directly, he indicated that, in due course, obtaining the desired letter would not be too difficult for me.

I cannot say that my life in banishment was a great hardship. Courtesy of my employer Konstruktiva, I lived in a tiny one-room apartment with all requisite life necessities and for a very reasonable rent. From there I could walk to a station from which the tram would take me to the front entrance of Stalin's Works. In the evenings, I could also walk to a restaurant in the nearby high-rise apartment building Koldům, where I met a number of other banished professionals—teachers, doctors, and chemical engineers—all of whom could not find work in Prague (whether because of their bourgeois class origins or other reasons that displeased communist authorities) and had to come to the provinces. We formed a "Brotherhood of Banished Citizens," swapped stories, drank wine, sang songs, and had a lot of fun together. I used to ride a motor scooter at the time, so when the weather was warm, I'd ride on the weekends to Prague. Later on, I found a nearby ski resort Bouřňák, which was accessible by train, and spent the winter weekends skiing. So on the whole, my banishment was bearable.

Still, when spring came, I started feeling increasingly restless. I wanted to show the world what wonderful buildings I could design, and instead, I was wasting my time in the provinces. By coincidence, a friend of my soon-to-be-wife Eva was Alena Šrámková, the wife of the architect who was the director of Konstruktiva's architectural atelier in Prague. Through her, an interview was arranged for me with her husband, Mr. Šrámek. At the time, I had no other designs to show except for my schoolwork, so I brought with me photographs of my thesis project. I asked Mr. Šrámek if there would be a place for me in his atelier once I disentangled myself from Litvínov. He leafed through my thesis project and said yes. Hallelujah!

It was now early April 1963, and back in Litvínov, I waited for Mr. Hampel's next visit to our construction site. When he came, I told him about my interview at Konstruktiva's architectural office in Prague and timidly asked if he thought it might be time for him to write that letter. Mr. Hampel asked me how long I had been working at Konstruktiva. When I told him that it had been only nine months, he suggested that we wait until the end of April, when he could reasonably write that I had worked there almost a year.

I could see his point. Some zealot in the Office of the Dean might think that nine months was not long enough to demonstrate one's positive attitude toward the working class and the socialist regime. So we agreed that Mr. Hampel would write the letter at the end of April. It was only three weeks away, but I was so impatient at the time that it seemed an eternity. At the end of April, Mr. Hampel called me to his office in Konstruktiva's building in Litvínov. The receptionist who'd greeted me on my arrival ten months earlier quipped, again with mock seriousness, "It's so nice to see, Mr. Holub, how your relationship to the working class has improved." Mr. Hampel let me read the letter his secretary had just typed before he mailed it to the Dean's Office: it was a masterpiece. I thanked him profusely. With a letter like that, I could have run for the politburo!

Things really started moving then. Within a week, I received a notice from the Dean's Office informing me that I would be presented my diploma at the graduation ceremony of the class below mine at the end of June. In mid-May, I started working in Konstruktiva's architectural office in Prague. It was an intrafirm transfer, so that I didn't have to give notice in Litvínov; I had only to say good-bye to Mr. Buble and Mr. Hampel. And on July 6 of that year I got married.

In retrospect, those ten months in banishment were an excellent experience, both professionally and personally. But of course, at the time, I couldn't appreciate that. All I saw was a delay in getting ahead.

Stroke of Luck

The first order of business in the years after the communist revolution of 1948 was the liquidation of the bourgeois class. Consistent with that long-term objective was preventing the children of the wealthier members of the bourgeoisie, the so-called enemies of the people, from obtaining a higher education. Because my grandfather was a textbook example of an enemy of the people and my mother's ideological dossier was stained by having spent time in the communist prison (never mind that after eighteen months of pretrial custody all charges against her were dropped), some people familiar with that era of Czech history have wondered how it was possible that I was allowed to attend the School of Architecture of the Czech Technical University.

My mother and I firmly believed that the answer to that question is a simple one: the year I graduated from high school was 1956. For the communist empire, it was a pivotal year because of two events. The first one was the meeting of the 20th Congress of the Communist Party of the Soviet Union. It was at this congress—only three years after Stalin's death—that Khrushchev accused him of having indulged in a "cult of personality" and, at the same time, revealed the existence of the numerous prison camps in which multitudes of innocent people were imprisoned by Stalin.

It is hard today to imagine the shockwaves those revelations sent throughout the communist empire, because it's impossible to conceive of the level of worship of Stalin required by the communist regime, which lasted even after his death up until that 20th Party Congress in 1956. When a pupil referred to the leader of the Soviet Union as Stalin, a zealous teacher would immediately correct him that the proper appellation was "Great Stalin." There was a statue of Stalin in the town square of every provincial town in Czechoslovakia (as was also the case in all other Soviet satellite countries), and in Prague a ten-story Stalin stood on a pedestal high above the Vltava River, visible from most points in the city. There was a framed photograph of Stalin on the wall at every government office, in every classroom from grade school up to the Charles University auditoriums, in every store—simply every-where. And on Stalin's seventieth birthday in December 1948, all day long there flew over Prague a formation of more than a hundred airplanes forming the letters *J V S* (Joseph Vissarionovich Stalin) and the numeral 70. At night the planes were lit, making for an eerie spectacle. I was ten years old at the time and remember it vividly.

Given this level of officially demanded adulation, you can perhaps appreciate the shock Stalin's denunciation caused in communist cadres. And that shock was soon to be compounded by the second pivotal event of 1956: the Hungarian uprising. Since apart from a few true believers, the vast majority of communists in Czechoslovakia were spineless opportunists, the revolution next door suddenly made them shake in their boots. They thought that if Stalin could be denounced and if the people of Hungary had the guts to rise against the communist regime—both events that were hitherto unimaginable—then anything could happen. For a fleeting moment, the thought that the communist regime in Czechoslovakia might collapse was not out of the question. And just in case it did happen, the opportunists in charge were hedging their bets; they did not want to be branded as the perpetrators of the liquidation of the bourgeois class, so they became less orthodox in executing their ideological agenda.

And it so happened that, in my enormous luck, I was applying to the School of Architecture during that improbable and fleeting moment. That timing is probably the single stroke of luck that had the greatest influence on the course of the rest of my life. There was a high probability that, had I applied one year earlier or one year later, I would not have been accepted. My boarding school roommate Václav Havel, who was two years older and had graduated from high school in 1954, was barred from attending the university because his father was an enemy of the people. That brief moment of uncertainty ended in November 1956, when the Soviet army brutally crushed the Hungarian uprising and communists all over Eastern Europe breathed a palpable sigh of relief. But by that time, I was already an eager student of architecture.

How I Danced with a Feminist

One of the means I used during my seventeen-year search of looking for the right woman for me was attending various professional or business networking meetings. In the early 1980s I attended Jerry Rubin's Business Networking Salon in the Palladium nightclub on 14th Street. Yes, the very same Jerry Rubin of the Chicago Seven—who, along with Abbie Hoffman was one of the counterculture icons of the 1960s—eventually ran business networking salons.

To be admitted one had to be either an independent professional or run his or her own business, but I don't think this rule was strictly enforced. Rubin's salon struck me more as a dating scene than a professional meeting. Whatever it was, one of the people I met there was Phyllis Chesler, a plump woman with an engaging smile. She told me she was a writer. After a short conversation, it was clear that she was smart, quick-witted and had a dry sense of humor. We exchanged cards and went our separate ways.

Today I would probably Google her, but we met long before the age of the internet, so I stopped in Barnes & Noble and asked the woman at the information counter if the store had any books by Phyllis Chesler. She looked her up and announced, "Oh yes, she's written a number of books. You'll find her in nonfiction, under 'Feminist.'" The word "feminist" gave me pause, but I didn't let that deter me. Although I had zero sexual or romantic interest in Phyllis, I called her the following week and asked her if she'd honor me by dining with me. She responded that she'd be delighted. I asked her if she'd prefer to go out or let me cook her something simple in my apartment. Because she ate out all the time, she thought that dining in would be a treat. And so it happened that, two weeks later, Phyllis Chesler rang my doorbell and came to dinner.

The conversation flowed freely, as did the wine, and about halfway through the linguini al pesto, apropos of something I have since forgotten, Phyllis propounded the following theory: the entire fashion industry was dominated by misogynistic gay designers who intentionally designed clothes in which only ultrathin models looked good, but in which the rest of regular-figured womankind looked ridiculous. They did it on purpose because they hated women, and they had single-mindedly decided that only being tall and slender was beautiful, while short and plump was not. And as if to prove her point, she went on, "Why is it that I cannot even buy a bra that would fit me in Manhattan but have to schlep to Brooklyn to a plus-size store?" Only then did I notice what an enormous bust Phyllis had.

Stunned by that outflow, and perhaps with my tongue loosened by the amount of wine I consumed, to my surprise I found myself saying, "My dear Phyllis, it is not the gay fashion designers who decided that tall and slender is beautiful, while short, fat, and squatty is not. That perception has been around ever since the beginning of the history of Western art, starting with Mesopotamian, followed by Egyptian, Greek, and Roman art and going on to Romanesque, Gothic, Renaissance, and Baroque art up until the present day." Amazingly, Phyllis took it calmly. She didn't slap me, nor did she walk out. We simply changed the subject and talked about something else. The evening ended pleasantly, with my walking Phyllis to Central Park West where she caught a cab.

Phyllis and I saw each other one more time. Perhaps three weeks or a month later, Bob Landsman called me, said that he had two extra tickets to a performance at BAM in Brooklyn, and asked if a lady friend and I would like to join him and his date for the performance and dinner afterward. As it happened, none of my female acquaintances were available, and then I thought of Phyllis Chesler. I called her and she was happy to join us. After the performance, which I no longer can recall, we had a fine meal at Peter Luger Steakhouse, and Bob drove us all home, as we all lived on the Upper West Side.

Having once cooked for her and then taken her to a performance and dinner, I was convinced that if Phyllis wanted to maintain contact—which might or might not develop into a friendship—the ball was definitely in her court. I have not heard from her since. Phyllis thus joined a long line of women who, when I didn't pursue them romantically, had no interest in maintaining a friendship.

I had yet another memorable and, in some regards, more successful encounter with a self-avowed feminist. During several consecutive summers in the early 1980s, I was part of a group of acquaintances who rented a summer house in the Hamptons. That particular summer, the house we rented was in Westhampton, and one of my housemates was a woman who could turn just about any issue between heaven and earth into a matter of the oppression of women. Not enough women in the US Army? Oppression of women. Not enough female senators? Oppression of women. High cost of a good haircut? Oppression of women.

One night after dinner we all went to a country music dance hall on Montauk Highway. At one point, the woman—whose name I no longer remember but whom we all took to calling "The Feminist"—and I were the only ones left at the table while everyone else was dancing. I had no choice but to ask her to dance. When we reached the floor, I held her and attempted to dance to the tune that was playing. After two or three turns, she suddenly stepped aside and asked, "Why is it that it is always the men who have to lead?" I responded, "You may have a point, so why don't you lead?" And I went limp.

A short and slight woman, she tried valiantly to lead me while I tried my best to follow, but it just didn't work. Eventually we stopped trying, and I give The Feminist credit for admitting that men lead on the dance floor not as part of the male conspiracy to oppress women, but because their bigger bulk gives them inertia, which makes it easier for women to follow. We spent the rest of the evening dancing, with The Feminist happily following.

My Take on Iran

At the end of 1974, when my plans for going to Tehran were already in place, *Harper's Magazine* published a scathing article about Savak, the secret police of the Shah's regime. It noted that the regime tolerated no opposition whatsoever and described Savak's efficacy in subduing any dissent. That the Shah's regime was authoritarian was well known. Some of my left-leaning acquaintances actually held it against me that I was going to work in Iran, because to them working there was tantamount to endorsing the brutal regime. While I did not share that view, the *Harper's* article did stir my antioppression and prodemocracy sentiments so that I arrived in Tehran strongly prejudiced against the Shah's regime.

It didn't take long, however, before I started revising that prejudice. Growing up in communist Czechoslovakia, I knew a thing or two about what it was like to live under a totalitarian regime, and what I was observing around me in Tehran did not jibe with that picture. In stark contrast with communist countries from which people were escaping at great peril, Iran's borders were completely open. My Iranian acquaintances confirmed that anyone who wanted to leave could do so. I was also surprised to see the *New York Times*, *Paris Match*, *Der Spiegel*, and a whole spectrum of Western newspapers and magazines readily available at Tehran newsstands—something unthinkable behind the Iron Curtain.

I also found copies of Karl Marx's *Das Kapital* in bookstores, with translations in many languages.

Another feature of Iran that didn't correspond with my experience of totalitarian regimes was the free flow of money. While the Czechoslovak crown was completely useless outside the country, the Iranian rial was readily convertible to all major currencies, with no restrictions on the amount, which was certainly not the case in the Soviet Bloc countries. Also, while in communist Czechoslovakia one did not talk back to the police, I was surprised to see many instances of ordinary citizens engaging in lively arguments with the police.

What made me reconsider my belief in universal democracy was an official Iranian government statistic, according to which 71 percent of the country's population was illiterate. It hit me that you cannot have a participatory democracy when over two-thirds of the people are unable to participate in it. Clearly, a country like that needs an authoritarian ruler. Now, the benefits of autocracy obviously depend on the type of ruler, and as authoritarian rulers go, I was coming to see that the Shah was not a bad one. He was secularizing the country, getting women out of *chadors* and into the workforce, and building schools, hospitals, and universities. Instead of military service, literate young men had the option of joining a Literacy Corps and teaching illiterate villagers how to read and write. It was hard to disagree with programs like that. And last but not least, the Shah was a staunch ally of the West.

Then there also was in Iran something that struck me as disarmingly honest. Unlike communist Czechoslovakia that pretended to be a democratic country while it was everything but, there was no such pretense in Iran. The Shah's rules were quite clear: Iran was a monarchy, and he was the king.

You didn't have to agree with him, but you had to keep your disagreements to yourself: dissent was not tolerated. If you didn't like the policies of his government, you were free to leave. If you stayed and went on living peacefully, you'd do well and have a good life. If you made trouble, you'd be put in prison. It was simple as that.

And so having arrived in Tehran on an especially anti-Shah note, within the first six months I came to believe that—given the circumstances of that underdeveloped, two-thirds illiterate country and considering its geopolitical situation—the Shah's government was probably the best that could be hoped for.

During my almost four years in Tehran, I attended many dinners at the houses of my Iranian clients and their friends, all of whom were educated in the West. Many of them were vehemently anti-Shah. The refrain at those dinners was "We have to get rid of the Shah." Sometimes I timidly asked, "Suppose you do get rid of the Shah; then what? Is there an organized opposition ready to step in?" The answer was invariably, "Well, there isn't, but we'll figure that out later. First, we must get rid of the Shah." We all know what happened once they did get rid of the Shah, but little is known about how it came about.

There was at the time an Islamic cleric by the name of Ruhollah Khomeini. He has been exiled by the Shah's government because he was stirring unrest among the religious, uneducated merchant class known as *bazaaris*, demanding a greater role of Islamic religion in politics. Khomeini was then living in France and smuggling into Iran cassettes with his fiery speeches calling for the overthrow of the Shah. In the spirit of "the enemy of my enemy is my friend," the Soviets cleverly sought to undermine the Shah's government—which with its pro-Western stance was a thorn in their side—by supporting Khomeini's smuggling operation.

Soon, instead of a few hundred cassettes floating here and there, thousands were coming into Iran across the Caspian Sea. Anti-Shah rhetoric was something totally unknown during the twenty years of the Shah's regime and, therefore, was tremendously intoxicating to Iranian denizens, even to those who didn't want to get rid of the Shah. I remember how excited my clients were whenever they got hold of a Khomeini tape. They would invite their friends over and together would listen to it behind closed doors.

In his speeches, Khomeini shrewdly downplayed his religious fervor and his vision of an Islamic state; in that way he managed to co-opt the intellectual left and the students, who shared one and only one common goal with the *bazaaris*: to depose the Shah. It was this most unlikely coalition of two segments of the population that had absolutely nothing in common, except for sharing the objective of removing the Shah from power, albeit for completely different reasons, that ultimately brought down the regime. To my knowledge, the role of the Soviet Union in fomenting that coalition has been little acknowledged.

The End of an Era

That was the word on the decks of the ship *Bremen*, on which I sailed to America. It's hard to believe, but in 1969, which is when I bought myself a ticket for this transatlantic passage, crossing the Atlantic by boat was cheaper than flying. It was much cheaper if you had a lot of luggage, which I did. Five years later, when I traveled back to Europe for the first time, it was already cheaper to fly.

I consider myself fortunate to have caught this ending of the era when crossing the Atlantic by ship was the norm, for it was a magnificent experience on many levels. First, there were the passengers. People who sail to America on a boat in January are decidedly not leisure travelers, but folks who have a purpose, who go there for a reason. That made for an interesting collection of fellow passengers. A couple I met onboard (he was a professor of astronomy at Yale, returning from a year's sabbatical in France) became my clients some four years later. Some older sea salts claimed that it was their fortieth or fiftieth crossing, and they looked the part.

In addition to the company, the beauty of the sea passage itself made the journey remarkable. When we set out from Southampton, the weather was so mild that we were sunning in the reclining chairs on the decks. Then, a few days later, we found ourselves in a snowstorm, at the end of which I was traipsing on the decks in a foot of snow. Wooden decks covered with snow rendered the ship uniformly white. From the upper deck, the sight of a completely white ship floating on a black sea was phantasmagoric.

Another memorable feature of the trip was the nonstop social frolicking. It so happened that, according to all seasoned ocean crossers, the sea was exceptionally rough during that voyage. As a result, the majority of passengers were in their cabins vomiting, and only a small group of us whose stomachs were not affected by the rocking of the boat were taking our meals in the dining room. That made for a particularly convivial group of partiers who loved drinking and dancing, both of which were aplenty. In the afternoons there were tea dances in the lounge, and during dinners wine flowed freely; then there was after-dinner dancing in the ballroom, and when that ended around midnight, the hardcore partiers repaired to the bar, where a combo played into the wee hours.

To be served breakfast, one had to show up in the dining room within a certain time period: between 7 and 9 a.m. Because of my late-night partying, I did not make it to a single breakfast. To get a sorely needed cup of coffee in the morning, I had to wait until the bar opened at 11 a.m. and then beg the bartender to make me some coffee.

When I'd first learned that the boat trip would take a week, I could not imagine how I would pass all that time. I decided I would catch up with my correspondence and read some novels. Needless to say, I had not written a single letter nor read a single page of a novel by the time we arrived in America. Those days had just flown by in an alcoholic haze. And that was despite being on the boat for even longer than a week.

The original schedule had us going from Southampton to Halifax, and then on to New York. On about day five of the trip, the captain's bulletin announced that, because of the rough seas, the boat was proceeding more slowly than expected. As a result, even if we skipped Halifax and went directly to New York, which is what the captain decided to do, we'd arrive one day later than planned. The few passengers going to Halifax would be given train passage from New York. Consequently, I went to the boat's telegraph office and sent a cable to Frost Associates announcing that because of the late arrival of my boat, I'd be reporting for work one day later than expected. It made me feel very worldly and grown up to send that telegram from the middle of the ocean.

My Mother

Everybody has a mother, and each person's relationship with his or her mother is unique. Having observed many such relationships, I have concluded that the relationship of my mother and me was truly extraordinary. Of course, first I thought it was normal, not knowing anything else. But the older I got, the more I became convinced that the relationship my mother and I had was not typical. With the exception of my obstreperous teenage years, my mother was my best friend in the truest sense of the word. And as I grew older, I believe I became her best friend as well. How did that happen?

I can only speculate, but I think the close proximity in which we lived between the time I was twelve and twenty-two years old—the most impressionable time in a person's life—had something to do with it. While my mother was in prison, a communist apparatchik claimed our bourgeois apartment, and we were moved to a two-room, ground-floor, cold-water flat in Žižkov, a working-class part of town. We went from about a 1,500-square-foot, three-bedroom, two-bathroom apartment with a maid's room to a flat of no more than four hundred square feet.

And we managed to adapt to this much smaller space thanks to my mother's ingenuity. Without any training as an architect or interior designer, using common sense and imagination alone, she divided the space into several tiny but distinct areas using armoires and bookcases as room dividers. We ended up with a tiny kitchenette, a dining area, a sitting area with a coffee table, and a corner with a writing desk; she even found space for an upright piano. It was crowded, but bearably so. The sleeping arrangements were also ingenious. My mother slept on a bed with two mattresses on top of each other that, with the help of a nice cover and many pillows, served as a sofa during the day. At night, when the coffee table was moved aside, there was just enough floor space for the top mattress on which I slept. Thus we slept within a few feet from each other all those eleven years we lived in that flat.

It was, of course, impossible to accommodate all the furniture from our former apartment into a space a quarter of its size, so friends helped, taking a piece or two each for safekeeping. Still, there remained an upholstered rococo armchair that no one had space for and that absolutely could not fit in our new small flat. The solution? We put it in the bathtub.

The bathroom in our new flat was a tiny room with a bathtub, a coal-fired hot-water boiler, and nothing else; the toilet was in a separate stall, and there was no shower or bathroom sink. For our daily ablutions, we had to boil water on the gas stove and pour it into the kitchen sink. When we wanted to take a bath, it was my job to go to the basement and bring up a bucket of coal. Then I had to make a fire in the boiler, and a half hour later, there was enough hot water in the boiler for two full baths. Having to remove the armchair out of the bathtub seemed like a small addition to this production. No wonder we went through this process once or twice a week at the most.

Visiting my mother in Marienbad in 1960. She is forty-seven, I am twenty-one.

I described our living arrangements to explain what I meant when I said that my mother and I had lived in close proximity. I wonder to this day how I managed to do all the drafting required during the six years of architecture school, when the only place in that flat for the drawing board was on top of the dining table. Most nights, after the dinner dishes were taken off the table, the drafting board went on top of it and I started drafting. At the time, it was the only thing I knew, so I didn't consider it a hardship.

Things got better in 1962, when we managed to move to a much larger apartment in Malá Strana, a quite desirable part of town. How this happened bears explaining. To further its goal of liquidating the bourgeois class and, at the same time, deal with an acute housing shortage, the communist government decided what was a reasonable apartment size for a single person, a married couple, a family of three, four, and so on. Those who lived in apartments whose size exceeded the stated limits had a choice of either leaving town, moving to a smaller apartment (an impossibility because apartments of any size were hard to find), or paying an exorbitant surcharge for each square meter in excess of the allotted area.

We knew two families who were living in a nineteenth-century apartment house that had originally one apartment per floor. Sometime after World War I, those giant apartments were split into two per floor, but the sizes of those smaller apartments were still way over the prescribed number of square meters. Consequently, our friends were paying huge surcharges for those extra meters and were looking for a way to decrease the size of their apartments without moving. They knew of our dire housing situation and proposed that we create a third apartment on that floor by taking two rooms from each of the two adjacent apartments and building a new bathroom and kitchen.

At the time, my mother was an associate professor of art history at the Academy of Applied Arts, and I was in the fifth year of the School or Architecture and earning good money as a freelance graphic designer. We could afford the small cost of building the new kitchen and bathroom and enthusiastically accepted our friends' proposal. It was an incredible stroke of luck and also my first opportunity to design something, however modest, that would actually be built.

That is how we came to leave our cold-water flat in Žižkov and move to an apartment three times its size in Malá Strana. My mother and I continued to live together, although in much larger quarters. I was twenty-three and for the first time in my life had my own, rather sizable, room. I lived in that room alone for only a year, however, because the following year my new wife moved in with me. From our perspective today, it seems bizarre that newlyweds would live with one of their parents, but in communist Czechoslovakia that situation wasn't at all unusual. For a young couple to get an apartment of their own was just not possible. There was a waiting period of ten to fifteen years for an apartment in one of the state-constructed, concrete-paneled housing projects in the suburbs of Prague. So I continued to live with my mother until I left for London in August 1967.

My mother and I then didn't see each other until a year later in July 1968, when she came to visit me in London. During the Prague Spring, she was able to get an exit visa without a problem. That was the first time in our lives we were apart for a year. The next time we saw each other was another year later in August 1969, when she came again to London. Then in December of that year, we met in Paris. Unbelievably, more than a year after the invasion, it was still possible for my mother to take a class of students from the Academy of Applied Arts on a field trip to Paris. At the time, we already knew that I was leaving for America and that we might not get to see each other for some time.

My mother in 1967, when I left for London.

We had no idea, however, how long it would be before the communist regime would allow her to visit me. It wasn't until 1974 that my mother was, at long last, given an exit visa for a visit to the United States. A year earlier, fully five years after the invasion, the communist authorities in Czechoslovakia were still not confident enough in their "normalization" efforts; they decided to require every working citizen to sign a declaration that he or she approved of the Soviet invasion of the country in August 1968. Of course, it was called not an invasion but rather "brotherly help from the friendly armies of the Warsaw Pact." And so from the factory floors to the Academy of Science and from university classrooms to the ministries, department store employees, research scientists, everyone was required to sign this declaration.

My mother was the only faculty member at the Academy of Applied Arts who refused to sign it. As a result, and combined with the fact that her son was an illegal emigrant—that is, a convicted felon—she was told she could no longer teach and had to retire. She was sixty at the time and didn't want to retire, but she didn't protest too much because she knew that retirement would put her in the category of people who could easily get exit visas. The government's calculation was simple: when a retired person didn't return from a trip to the West, the regime saved the cost of his or her pension. And sure enough, when my mother submitted yet another application for an exit visa (together with the required notarized confirmation that I would pay all expenses relating to her trip), this time she received an exit permit for six months in the United States. Hallelujah!

At the time my mother was planning her first visit to America, I was spending a lot of time in Tennessee. One of my clients for my design consulting services was located in Knoxville, where I had also been appointed a visiting professor of design at the School of Architecture at the University of Tennessee. Eventually, in those years I was spending ninety to a hundred days a year in Knoxville. My stays there never lasted longer than three or four days at a time, but I made a lot of those trips.

It so happened that one of those trips was scheduled to begin the day after my mother's arrival in New York. Somehow, I didn't think that presented much of a problem. After five years of not seeing each

On her first visit to New York in 1974.

other, we were so thrilled knowing that we'd be together for half a year that the fact that I had to leave for a three-day business trip the day after she arrived seemed but a small wrinkle. My mother was fluent in English, and I had complete confidence in her ability to orient herself in the new city, so I thought she'd be fine. The day after her arrival, before I took the taxi to the airport, I showed my mother where the nearest supermarket and subway station were and how to lock and open the door of my apartment. Each evening I called her and made sure that she was all right. Looking back, I now think that my decision to leave her alone for three days was a little reckless, even though she was indeed fine.

Over the next half a year, my mother took a bunch of trips to visit friends in San Francisco, Chicago, and Washington, DC, while I continued making trips to Tennessee. So we weren't together all the time, but we spoke daily. While we were both in New York, we played house in my apartment. My mother determined that the cutlery I possessed (it was a camping set, which had its own stand on which forks, knives, and spoons were hanging on hooks and which I thought was cute) might be fine for a student, but was totally unsuitable for a grown man of thirty-five. So we went out and bought a fine new set at Fortunoff, which I use at my country house to this day.

I cannot think of any subject I could not discuss with my mother. We talked about politics (both local and international, as well as the situation in Czechoslovakia), religion, books we'd read, films and plays we'd seen, women I had met, clients I had served, people we knew—everything. When she left at the end of the six months, the apartment felt especially empty. But by the time my mother was leaving, we already knew that I'd be going to Tehran at the beginning of the following year, and we agreed that she'd come to visit me there later that year. We had correctly assumed that because the communist regime gave my mother an exit visa to go to the United States, it would certainly let her go to Iran. One of the ironies of the Cold War was that communist Czechoslovakia was doing a brisk business with the ultraright regime of the Shah. A consequence of that relationship was that in 1975 there were direct flights between Prague and Tehran on both Czechoslovak Airlines and Air Iran.

I'd have been happy to buy my mother a ticket on one of those direct flights to Tehran, but she refused, thinking it cost too much money. Instead, as a retired person who had lots of free time, she elected to travel as follows: she flew on the Soviet airline Aeroflot from Prague to Moscow, which was then very inexpensive, and then from Moscow to Baku, where she boarded an overnight boat to Bandar-e-Pahlavi, an Iranian port on the southern coast of the Caspian Sea.

And so on one fine day in October 1975, I rented a car and with my friend Elina drove from Tehran across the Alborz Mountains to pick up my mother from the boat arriving at Bandar-e-Pahlavi. Even when we factored in the car rental and the night in a hotel for the three of us, the cost of my mother's travel was less than one-third of the plane ticket from Prague to Tehran. Such was the wide gap between the costs of travel inside and outside of the Soviet Empire.

1976 in Tehran.

The drive from Bandar-e-Pahlavi to Tehran lasts about five hours, most of which is spent crossing the Alborz Mountains, which separate the wet Caspian coast north of the mountains from the desert climate to the south. That transformation—from the lush greenery to the bone-dry desert—after passing through a tunnel on top of a mountain pass was quite dramatic. You leave luxuriant vegetation on the north side of the tunnel, and when you emerge on the south side, you see nothing but sand and stones. Add to it the beauty of the snow-capped mountains—jagged, rugged, rocky peaks—and you have one majestic scene. Although Elina and I had passed through it on our way north, it took my mother to wake us up to the beauty of the journey. Or perhaps, it was more dramatic going from lush to dry than the other way around. In any case, my mother was ecstatic. I still remember her shrieking with delight, "Go slower, go slower, let me look! Oh, look over there! That rock looks like Giacometti's man, and over here is a Hans Arp, and beyond is Henry Moore!"

On that visit, my mother stayed with me until mid-January, and in those three months we once again played house, this time in my grand Tehran apartment. Ah, what an apartment it was! Although it had only one bedroom, its overall area must have been well over two thousand square feet. It had an enormous living/dining room with a rather large nook for a built-in bar; the kitchen was big enough to accommodate a breakfast table; the bedroom had a king-size bed and its own bathroom; and there was a large foyer from which all spaces were accessed, including a spacious powder room. During a St. Martin's party, the apartment swallowed sixty people quite comfortably. I gave my mother the bedroom, and I slept on a sofa bed in the living room.

I worked long hours, but we had weekends to explore Tehran and take some trips. One memorable trip was to Persepolis. We were both familiar with the place, because at the School of Architecture I had to draw the capitals of its columns, which consisted of bulls' heads, while my mother lectured about it in her art history classes at the Academy of Applied Arts. If someone had told me at the time when I was struggling with those bulls' heads that in seventeen years I would find myself in Persepolis looking at those columns, I'd have said, "Go on dreaming."

We also visited Isfahan. We both agreed that this much-celebrated place was vastly overrated. The huge square is a kind of Potemkin's village. Most of the facades of the upper stories of the houses defining the square had nothing behind them, except the diagonal struts supporting those gables. But the scale of the square is impressive: it was indeed designed for the man on the horse.

During those wonderful three months, little did we know that it would be another five years before we'd see each other again. My mother's return trip to Prague was no less exotic than her journey from Prague to Tehran. She began it on a train from Tehran to Yerevan, the capital of Armenia, which at the time was one of the Soviet republics. It was a twenty-four-hour train ride. After a night in a hotel in Yerevan, on the third day, she flew on Aeroflot from Yerevan to Moscow, and on that same day from Moscow to Prague. All that rigmarole to spare her son from buying an expensive plane ticket from Tehran to Prague.

Once again, my apartment—this time in Tehran—felt very empty after my mother left. Though I consoled myself with the thought that she'd come again the following year, that visit was not to happen. The following year was 1977, the year of Charter 77, a dissident manifesto criticizing the Czechoslovak government for failing to observe international norms of human rights, specifically the human rights section of the Helsinki Accords, which, among other countries, was signed by Czechoslovakia. My mother was one of some two hundred of its first signatories, and she and her fellow signers were subjected to the worst persecution and harassment of the "normalization" era. Other than the frequent, middle-of-the-night interrogations, the harassment included confiscation of her driver's license, disconnection of her telephone line, and a policeman sitting twenty-four hours a day on the landing outside her apartment, monitoring all comings and goings.

In the spring of 1977, when the communist regime in Czechoslovakia was in the throes of hysterically denouncing the Charter 77 signatories, my mother applied for another exit visa for a trip to Iran. To her surprise, it was granted, and we were both elated. This time my mother allowed me to buy her a plane ticket for a direct flight from Prague to Tehran on Czechoslovak Airlines. On the day of her departure, she went to the airport and boarded the plane. A few minutes before takeoff, however, two secret police agents came on the plane, asked for Dr. Holubová, told my mother that she could not leave the country, and escorted her off. The plane was then held up for another half hour, because that was how long it took to retrieve my mother's already checked luggage.

And so it happened that in the afternoon of the day I was going to pick up my mother at the Tehran airport, the phone rang at my office. To my surprise, it was my mother calling, who in a calm voice told me she was not coming and then explained what had happened. The consensus among my mother's friends was that the communist authorities had deliberately orchestrated this incident to instill fear, not only in my mother, but also in all charter signatories, and to drive home the point that they were all powerful and in full control—that they could do anything, anytime, anywhere.

Thus started the period of some four years during which my mother applied every year for an exit visa while I, at the same time, as a freshly minted US citizen applied for an entry visa to Czechoslovakia. All that effort was to no avail: for four years in a row, all our applications were denied. For reasons we never learned, this spell was broken in 1981 when, without warning, my mother's annual application for an exit visa was granted and her passport was stamped with a permit for a six-month stay in the United States. The last time we had seen each other was five years earlier, in January 1976. This would be my mother's second visit to America, seven years after her first one. Having lived through two five-year periods of forced separation, we didn't know what to expect next. Would she be allowed to come again the following year? Or would it take another five years? Although we didn't dwell on it, under the surface that question was always there.

After my return from Tehran in January 1979, I had substantially remodeled my brownstone apartment, which I'd kept during my four years in Iran. I added lots of new built-in cabinets and shelving on which were displayed art objects both old and new. This was the first time my mother saw this new arrangement. Tired as she was when I brought her home from the airport, she immediately recognized two brass coffeepots we had bought together in Tehran, which I had displayed on two different shelves. My mother suggested that they might look better if they were next to each other: "Could you try that, Martin?" I did as she suggested, and lo and behold, they did look much better together. Then she just could not help herself and went on, asking, "Could you move that Boulle box next to that Calder mobile? They would go well together." And they did. And so on and so on, until perhaps 9 p.m., which was 3 a.m. her time. When it came to arrangements of paintings on the wall or objects on the shelf, my mother's eye was unerring. I learned a lot from her in this respect.

The next morning Mary Greenebaum, the woman in my life at the time, called me and asked how my mother was, after my not seeing her for so many years. I told Mary that she was in great form and that, despite being dead tired, we had spent her first evening in New York rearranging objects on my shelves. Mary was incredulous: "What, she comes and starts telling you how to rearrange your apartment? What nerve! That's unbelievable! It's not her apartment; what business does she have telling you how you should display your objects on your shelves in your apartment?"

I responded that my mother happened to have a very good eye and that I was glad to see that she hadn't lost her touch—not to mention that I was grateful to her, since all her suggestions had improved the overall arrangement. And so it happened that Mary managed to get negatively prejudiced against my mother even before she met her. Needless to say, she was not in my life for much longer.

The rest of my mother's stay went by much as had her first one seven years earlier. This time she visited friends in Los Angeles, Montreal, Chicago, and Washington, DC; each trip lasted about a week. By then she also had a bunch of friends of her generation among the Czech émigrés in New York City. I was no longer going to Tennessee, but I did go out west for a week of skiing. Overall, it was a lovely time, and once again when she left, I faced an empty apartment and that uncertainty of when we would get to see each other next.

As it turned out, we got to see each other at least once a year for the next nineteen years, until the end of my mother's days in 2001. The Cold War climate gradually warmed, a process that started with perestroika and ended with the demise of the Soviet Empire. This warming was probably the reason my mother was given an exit visa in 1982 and then every year until the annus mirabilis of 1989, when the communist regime in Czechoslovakia collapsed and we could visit each other at will. Those yearly visits were no longer six months long, but closer to six weeks. Yet we still took lots of trips. One year, we visited my mother's cousin in Fort Lauderdale and then spent several days driving all the way to Key West and back. Another year we spent a week on St. Croix in the Virgin Islands, and the following year we enjoyed a week on Sanibel Island off the west coast of Florida.

Folks from landlocked countries like Czechoslovakia tend to develop a romantic relationship with the sea: not having it causes us to yearn for it. So the day after we arrived in Fort Lauderdale, my mother, her cousin Věra Hořák, and I headed for the beach. It was the week of Thanksgiving, and swimming that late in the year feels luxurious for northerners. We couldn't wait to jump in the ocean. To our dismay, when we arrived at the beach, we saw that the lifeguard's high chair was empty and that there was a black flag flying from the mast attached to it.

I explained to my mother that the black flag meant that the ocean was deemed too rough for swimming. Indeed, there were only a few people on the beach. We were then standing on higher ground from where we had an unobstructed view of the ocean. My mother remarked that the waves were rough only where they broke near the shore and that the water beyond was quite calm. She said, "Look, if I could hold on to you and if you'd help me get through those waves, we could get to swim in those calm waters beyond." Věra offered to stay on the beach, and my mother and I did exactly as she had suggested. She held me around my neck, we dove under the waves, came up on the other side, and then spent a half an hour swimming in a rather calm sea.

We did much the same on our way back to the shore, except this time we didn't dive under the waves but let them push us onto the beach. While we were wading through the shallow water by the beach, we noticed a large group of people, perhaps twenty in all, looking at us. Their stares suggested a mixture of awe, fear, and astonishment, as if we were some exotic animals. Věra stood a little distance away, so we walked toward her. She told us that when the folks on the beach saw us diving under the waves, they got agitated and wanted to call the police. Věra had to tell them that we were both strong swimmers and that we knew what we were doing. Still, they continued to watch us incredulously; perhaps, they had never seen a woman of my mother's age swim the way she did and for as long as she did. My mother was then in her early seventies, and I was in my late forties. Czechoslovakia was a country where a ten-year-old would not advance from fifth to sixth grade unless he or she could swim across the pool and back, so we didn't think what we did was anything out of the ordinary.

After the Iron Curtain ceased to exist, I visited my mother in Prague every year, and she came to New York every year as well, so in those last ten years of her life, we saw each other twice a year. And there was the wonderful period when she was a Bunting fellow at Harvard University and lived in Cambridge, Massachusetts, from September 1991 until the end of June 1992. In those ten months, I called her daily and visited her in Cambridge at least one weekend a month.

1988 in Long Island.

After a while, my post–Iron Curtain visits to my mother acquired a routine. My friend and business partner St'opa Hrubý would pick me up at the Prague airport after I had arrived at about 8 a.m. on a direct flight from New York. He would then drive me to Malostranské Square, where my mother lived. When I got out of the car, I'd look up at the fourth-floor bay window of the building where my mother lived and would see her waving to me. St'opa would then help me carry my suitcase upstairs, say a quick hello to my mother, and disappear. I'd drop my suitcase in my room and go to the living room, where my mother would be waiting. I would sit down in an armchair, and she would sit in my lap.

No words were spoken. The room was so full of love, you could cut it with a knife. Eventually, my mother would venture, "Would you like some tea?" And so we'd have some tea and only then would start to talk. And talk we would for the rest of the day.

My mother had a streak of playfulness, one manifestation of which was her fondness for fashion. During the Cold War years, there were no Western fashion magazines available in Czechoslovakia, and it gave my mother enormous pleasure when I managed to send her, via someone traveling to Prague, an issue of *Vogue* or *Harper's* or *Elle*. Her former students once told me that my mother had the reputation of being the best-dressed woman at the Academy of Applied Arts where she taught. That was quite some distinction, considering that art schools typically attract a fashion-conscious crowd. In my view, she was an exemplar of the difference between being fashionable and being elegant. While seldom fashionable, she was always strikingly elegant. As a child, I was always half proud and half embarrassed by my mother's appearance, because she did not look anything like the mothers of the other kids I knew.

Interestingly, however, her keen eye did not help my mother catch on quickly to the cultural differences concerning fashion. For example, when she arrived in London in 1968 for her first visit, we were invited for Sunday lunch by an English couple of her generation; I had already been to their house a number of times. When she saw me putting on a sweater, my mother was incredulous: "You don't mean to go to Sunday lunch in a sweater, do you?" I replied, "Yes, mama, it's OK; trust me, I've been there before." She thought her son had taken leave of his senses, and she did not relax until we arrived and she saw the lady of the house wearing casual slacks and her husband a sweater much like mine. Slowly, slowly, it did sink in that the cultural mores relative to fashion in London were different from those in Prague.

Yet my mother still did not learn. Six years later, one morning on her first visit to New York, I was going out to run some errands in the neighborhood. I was wearing a pair of jeans that had a minor tear over one knee. When my mother saw that I was going to walk out in those jeans, once again she could not believe it: "You are not going to walk out in those trousers, are you? Didn't you notice that they have a hole in one of the pant legs?" I said, "Yes, mama, I know about the hole. It's OK; I am not going to church; I am going to the cleaners. Do yourself a favor: go to Broadway and pay attention to what people wear; you'll see that anything goes." My mother's response: "Just because anything goes does not mean that you should be going around looking like a vagabond." (In my mother's defense, I have to say that this was before Bloomingdale's and Bergdorf Goodman were selling pre-torn and prefaded, high-priced jeans.)

Despite these differences, my mother and I were each other's fashion consultants. She sought my opinion as I did hers. Most of the time I had no comment, because to my eyes my mother was always dressed just right. The few times I did have a suggestion, she listened. For example, when I said, "Mama, I think for where we are going you are overdressed," she would respond, "Really? Should I put on the black pants instead of this skirt?" She had a good sense of my wardrobe and from time to time would say something like "I think you should buy some black corduroy pants; you only have a couple of those fancy gabardine ones and there are occasions when the cords would look better." Or "Martin, you definitely need to buy a new tuxedo; this one is just too worn out.

There's nothing worse than a worn-out suit, and a worn-out tuxedo is even worse than a worn-out suit." Ah, those were the times.

On one of my last trips to visit her in Prague, once we started talking, the first thing my mother said was "I have to show you the new hat I bought." She left the room and reappeared wearing a splendid hat. It was a work of art, and it suited her perfectly. It was a great pleasure for me to see what joy the purchase of a hat could bring her at the age of eighty-eight.

Now I need to mention something I am ashamed of to this day. As I mentioned earlier, during 1950 and 1951, my mother spent close to one and a half years in pretrial custody in a communist prison. At the time she was released after the trial in the late summer of 1951, I was spending my summer vacation at my father's country place in the mountains in northeast Bohemia. The first thing my mother did when she walked out of the prison was to call my father and ask him to send me to Letovice, a small town in Moravia where she was going to spend some time in the country at her aunt's house. And now comes the shocking part.

I was twelve at the time and was having fun running around with kids my age. When my father told me that my mother was out of prison and expected me to go to Letovice, I did not want to go. Incredible! I had not seen my mother for one and a half years, and when I was able to see her, I was reluctant to go: playing with my buddies seemed more important. My father had to convince me that I had to go, that my mother was waiting for me. Of course, once I stepped off the train in Letovice and saw my mother standing on the platform waiting for me, my eyes welled up. I ran to her, we embraced, and I was so very happy to have her back that I immediately forgot about my reluctance to come.

It wasn't until years later that, as a young adult, I remembered the time when I didn't want to go see my mother who had just been released from prison. When I shared my reluctance with my mother, she reassured me that I didn't need to feel any shame about it: "You were a puerile child of twelve. It's quite normal for children of that age." Still, to this day, whenever I think about it, a feeling of shame rushes over me.

I left Prague in August 1967. Since then, unless she was visiting me, my mother and I were in epistolary contact, exchanging letters weekly and sometimes more often. We had to assume that those letters would be read by communist censors. To make sure we'd know if any letters disappeared, we numbered them, which is how I know that, except for those years when she spent six months in the United States, my mother and I exchanged upward of fifty letters per year. This letter writing gradually stopped in the late 1980s, when international calling became easier and less expensive. After the Velvet Revolution of 1989 I was calling her once a week on Wednesdays and eventually, twice a week, on Wednesdays and Sundays.

So there were at least twenty years of fifty letters a year, which makes for more than a thousand letters my mother wrote me. They are now in a suitcase in the basement of my country house, with each year of letters in a rubber-banded bundle. The National Literary Archive in Prague has a dossier on my mother, and the archivist tells me that they would very much like to have those letters. When I was liquidating my mother's apartment in Prague after she died, I found a similar suitcase with the thousand-plus letters I had written her, similarly tied in annual bundles. I am not sure why, but I brought those letters with me to America and put them in the same suitcase with my mother's letters to me.

While she was at the Bunting Institute at Harvard, my mother started writing her memoir. After she returned to Prague, it took her another five years to complete it. The nonfiction book, whose title would be translated in English as "Off the Road, on the Road," was published in 1997 in Prague. To my mother's surprise, it turned out to be a great success. It went through several printings and had a number of laudatory reviews from prominent critics. Excerpts were read on Prague radio, and my mother appeared on TV several times to talk about it. So unexpectedly, at the age of eighty-six, she had her proverbial fifteen minutes of fame. It was bittersweet, however, because by the time she gained the stature and renown that guaranteed that anything she would commit to paper would get published immediately, she had run out of strength. She no longer had the energy required for the concentration needed to write.

A Bunting fellow, at her apartment in Cambridge, Massachusetts, in 1992.

I mentioned earlier that there was no subject my mother and I couldn't, or wouldn't, discuss, and that included her death. After she had several ministrokes, we both knew what to expect, so I raised the question of where she'd like to have her ashes interred. There is a family grave in Moravia, in a town near the village where she was born, so I had always assumed that that would be where she'd like her urn to go, but I was mistaken. My mother pointed out to me that neither her mother nor father were buried there; more importantly, she thought that having her urn there would burden me with having to travel to Moravia each time I would visit Prague. So we started to look at cemeteries in Prague, but no place spoke to us. We kept on looking at more cemeteries (there are many in Prague) without finding any that appealed to us.

Then, one day, when my mother was visiting me in the United States and we were driving to our country place, we passed a Quaker cemetery on the side of the road about five minutes from my house. It was situated in a lovely meadow, with tombstones gently strewn about and a view of the distant hills. I slowed down, pointed out the meadow, and asked my mother, "How about over there?" We got out of the car and walked around. There were graves dating to the early 1820s and 1830s. My mother liked the spot and was happy to think I'd be driving by each time I went to or from our house.

And so it happened that my mother was later buried there. I called the Quakers and purchased a lot at the cemetery. Then, when my mother was a few months shy of her eighty-ninth birthday, she suffered her last stroke. After the service in a Prague church, I took the urn with her ashes with me to New York. I designed the tombstone, had it made by a local tombstone maker, and, with only my wife Karen and a few close friends around, interred the urn under it. Nine years later, I added the tombstone of my wife. The next one will be mine. On the advice of the tombstone maker, I have already designed it and sent him a print.

My mother at eighty-seven, a year before she died.

In the spring of the following year, there was a memorial service for my mother in the Dominican Chapel I designed in Sparkill, New York, about a half-hour drive from Manhattan. The chapel is attached to the existing Dominican Convent and was completed the year my mother died. It was under construction a little over two years, during which time I was making regular supervisory visits. During what turned out to be her last visit, I took my mother along to see it in June 2001, when the chapel was nearly finished. The Sisters were charmed by her and invited us for lunch. My mother loved the chapel, and so did the Dominican Sisters, which is how it happened that when she died later that year, they offered to hold a memorial service for her.

During that last visit, which at the time we didn't know would be her last visit, my mother spent the weekends at our house in the country, as she had done ever since Karen and I had built it. On the weekend before returning to Prague, my mother and I wanted to stay in the country one more day, while Karen needed to be at work on Monday morning. So on that Sunday night I drove Karen to Poughkeepsie where she took the train to the city, and I returned to the house. After dinner, my mother and I repaired to our respective bedrooms. The house is designed so that the guest bedrooms are on the first floor and the master bedroom on the top floor, with the living room, dining room, kitchen, and study in between. When lying in bed with the lights out, I heard my mother climbing the stairs to my room. The master bedroom is an open loft, so there are no doors. My mother got in the bed on Karen's side, we snuggled, and we slept happily until the morning—as if she had a premonition that it would be the last visit.

Even when people love each other the way my mother and I did, misunderstandings can occur. In early June 2001, to mark her eighty-eighth birthday, her friends and admirers organized a festive evening in her honor in the literary wine bar Viola in Prague (yes, the same one in which I had met Allen Ginsburg thirty-six years earlier). It was less than two weeks before her planned trip to New York. Because I knew that I would see her shortly, it did not even occur to me to fly to Prague for the sake of one evening. When she arrived in New York a short time later and was showing me photos taken that evening and I saw that there was assembled the literary crème de la crème of Prague, I could not help exclaiming, "Oh, how I wish I had been there!" To my shock, my mother replied, "I was wondering why you did not come." If only she had given me the slightest hint that it would have pleased her if I had come to her party, I would have done so! But she didn't, and I'll regret that I didn't go for the rest of my days.

My mother's memorial service was held in this Dominican chapel.

My mother has now been dead for more than seventeen years, and I can say, without exaggeration, that there hasn't been a single day since she died when I haven't thought, "Oh, I wonder what she would think about this or that?" or "What a pity that I cannot talk to her about this or that." I suspect it'll go on like this until the end of my days.

Rusty Goat

When the country house Karen and I had built in the Hudson Valley was completed, I thought that it could help me generate more residential commissions in Dutchess County. To that end, in a rare spurt of marketing activity, I had the house professionally photographed, picked the best shot, and had a postcard made. I then hired a mailing list broker and ordered lists of Dutchess County real estate brokers, insurance agents, doctors, and lawyers. I also ordered a list of Manhattan subscribers to *Hudson Valley Magazine*. These lists contained more than twelve thousand addresses. So I printed the requisite number of postcards, hired a mailing outfit, and had them bulk mailed.

I learned that in the mail-order business, a 3 percent response is considered a hugely successful campaign, with a rate of 1 percent to 2 percent being more typical. I received some thirty phone calls, which is less than one-quarter of 1 percent. Moreover, none of those thirty calls were about design services. They were all questions regarding some feature of the house shown on the postcard, such as the type of garage doors, wood siding, stucco, roof, or windows used.

I was ready to write off the whole campaign as a total flop when another phone call came: "We have a thirty-acre compound near Staatsburg and would like to build a six-car garage, a new pool house, and a major house addition. We've already interviewed other architects, but we like the house on your postcard and would like to talk to you. When can you come see us?" We made a date for the next Saturday. I had to pinch myself to make sure I wasn't dreaming, but then I reminded myself that I didn't have the job yet: I was just going to be interviewed.

The following Saturday, driving to the given address, I was in for a few surprises, the least of which was an especially amateurish sculpture of a goat—made of rusting metal scraps—on the side of the entrance to the driveway. The next surprise was the size of the house at the end of the long driveway: it was enormous. Other than its size, the house was most unremarkable, being the kind of builder's special most probably not designed by an architect. On the lawn next to the house, I saw two fire trucks. Then the door was answered by a maid wearing a little white apron, definitely not the norm in Dutchess County. Walking through the entry hall I saw a cook through the open door to the kitchen.

But the biggest surprise of all came from my potential clients themselves. I expected a middle-aged couple, but instead Mr. and Mrs. Hahn (I changed the name) appeared to be in their mid-thirties. It was a hot summer day, and both Todd and Mary Hahn wore shorts and T-shirts, so that I could see that the legs and arms of both were covered with tattoos. The most striking feature about them, however, was how they talked. During our short introductory conversation, it quickly became apparent that both of them were congenitally unable to utter a sentence without some form of the word "fuck" in it.

It turned out that Todd was a trader at the American Stock Exchange. In Manhattan, they had an apartment in Battery Park City. While Mary stayed mostly in the country, Todd commuted back and forth via helicopter. There was a helicopter pad, which I was shown later, on the Rusty Goat compound. They had no children. When I asked Mary how she spent her time, she responded, "Oh, I've always been very fucking good at doing nothing." The most amazing thing was that this tattooed couple, who spoke like truck drivers and looked the part, liked my contemporary, minimalist architecture. While Todd was perusing my brochure, he kept exclaiming, "Wow, this is fucking beautiful! What a great fucking view! Fucking fantastic terrace!" and so on…

When he was going over the list of projects I'd completed, Todd came to the name of Sheila Nussbaum, a client for whom I had designed two retail art galleries in New Jersey—the first one in Millburn and then, five years later, another one in Princeton. Todd asked me if it was the Sheila Nussbaum from Millburn whose husband's name was Howard. She clearly was someone for whom Todd had a great deal of respect. When I confirmed that it was indeed her, Todd responded, "This is fucking amazing! Her son Rick was my best fucking buddy in high school." Then he turned to his wife and said, "If Sheila Nussbaum asked Martin to design her gallery, and then five years later came back and asked him to design another one, that's fucking all I need to know. I am ready to sign him up." Mary nodded, indicating her agreement.

However, I still did not believe that they would really like what I would design for them. So I suggested that before they hire me, it would be a good idea if they saw our house and experienced its spaces to have a better appreciation of what I might do for them. After all, it was only twenty minutes away. They heartily agreed, and Todd asked if we could go straightaway. I called Karen and told her that I was bringing over my potential clients to see the house.

When we got out of our cars, Todd announced, "Yours must be the longest and steepest fucking driveway in the whole fucking county!" Then when Karen saw the tattoos and heard their language, she thought I had lost my marbles bringing those folks over. But their commentary on our house captured its spirit, and they were bubbling with enthusiasm. Mary declared, "This is just a fucking beautiful space! It is sparse, but still fucking warm and cozy." Todd liked the fucking beautiful black matting on the terraces and noticed how it connected with the black rubber tiles in the dining room, making the space seem bigger. The visual acuity of this couple was startling. Where did it come from? However, it was not the time to ponder this question. Before they left, Todd and Mary pronounced themselves thrilled with the house and said they couldn't wait for me to start designing their projects. When I said I'd mail them an agreement, Todd's response was "Just fucking FedEx it."

I did as Todd requested, and within forty-eight hours I had in hand a signed agreement and a check for the initial payment. Todd and Mary told me that the most urgent of the three projects was the garage. It was to house the two fire trucks, two Hummers, two Porsches, and an assortment of Harley-Davidson motorcycles and snowmobiles. When I asked if they had a budget for the garage, "No fucking budget" was the answer. Because of the distinct sizes of the three types of vehicles, the garage practically designed itself. Todd was obviously proud of his automobiles, so I conceived of the garage as a display case for the vehicles, making its doors of glass. The conceptual drawings were ready within a week, and I presented them to Todd and Mary the following weekend. Their verdict: "Fucking perfect! Exactly what we fucking want."

The six-car garage.

We completed the design development and construction documents in record time and then arranged to fast-track the construction, meaning that the contractor started pouring the foundation while we were still drawing the details. While the garage was under construction, we started developing the pool house. The same scenario was repeated: Todd and Mary gave us a specific list of spaces they wanted in their pool house, we presented them with a conceptual design that they approved in its entirety, and we started working on the design development and then on construction documents. Once again, the foundations were poured while we were still finishing the drawings. And in the same way, we moved onto developing the design for the house addition.

Without question, Todd and Mary were the best clients we ever had. They were uniformly enthusiastic about our designs and always approved them on our first submission; once they approved them, they never changed their minds, never had any afterthoughts, and always paid on time like clockwork. It all seemed too good to be true, and as it turned out, it was.

Eighteen months after we were hired, the phone call came in December 2000. By this time the garage had been built, the working drawings for the pool house were completed and its footings and foundation walls poured, and the design development phase of the house addition was close to completion. Larry answered the phone and handed it to me. I picked up and Mary went right to the point: "Martin, we have to fucking stop the whole fucking thing. Todd had a financial setback, we are out of fucking money, and on top of that, we are getting fucking divorced. Send me an invoice for what we owe you and stop work effective immediately, OK? Good-bye." She hung up, leaving me no chance to say anything. I was stunned.

At the time I received this call, I was in the process of developing a computerized bird's-eye rendering of the whole compound showing the existing house, the addition, the pool house, and the garage, which I intended to give Todd and Mary for Christmas. I had about a half day's work left to finish it, so after I hung up with Mary, I continued working on it. The next day I had it framed, and the following Saturday I took it to the Rusty Goat compound. I could see that the construction work on the pool house had stopped. Nothing had been done since my last visit. Todd was not in evidence, but Mary was home. She was surprised to see me, saying, "Didn't I tell you it's all fucking over?" I remember that it made me think of an Edward Albee play.

I told Mary that I had made that rendering as a Christmas present for them before I knew that it was all over and had not charged for the time it took me to prepare it. Because it was of no use to me, I wanted her to have it as a token of my appreciation for what great clients they were. I could see that she wasn't interested in anything I had said. She glanced at the rendering, said something like "fucking impressive," and put the picture away. She then shared with me that Todd had run away with a Bulgari heiress. She added, "It'll cost him fucking dear, I'll fucking see to that." That was the last time I saw Mary Hahn.

About a year later, I found out through a real estate agent we knew that the Rusty Goat property was on the market for $2 million but that it was not selling because the 4,500-square-foot garage was a liability. No one knew what to do with a building that huge. Maybe another year later, I learned from the same agent that Rusty Goat had finally sold for $800,000, which was less than half of the replacement value of the existing house and the garage alone, never mind the thirty acres of land. Hearing this news reminded me of the rendering, and I thought that it would be nice to have it, so I called Mary Hahn's cell phone. To my surprise, she answered.

I asked her how she was doing, but she clearly was not interested in chitchat. So I asked her if she still had the picture I gave her the last time we saw each other. She said she had left it in the house. I found the name of the new owner of Rusty Goat on the Parcel Access website and called him. He said he had no recollection of ever seeing the picture I described but suggested I call his mother, who now lived in the house. When I asked her about the picture, she replied, "Oh yeah, I seen the picture; it's in the pantry." I asked if I could come get it. It was the first time I saw the garage in more than four years. Without any cars inside, it looked bizarrely monumental.

The Rusty Goat rendering now hangs in the TV room of our country house.

How Communism Helped My Career

Under communist rule, there was no such thing in Czechoslovakia as a private architectural office. Consequently, there were no starchitects with recognizable signature styles, such as Frank Gehry, Richard Meier, or Zaha Hadid, who get so many commissions that they need to employ other architects who help them be Frank Gehry, Richard Meier, or Zaha Hadid. All Czech architects worked in state-owned offices and were designing projects assigned to them by that office. No architect had to look for clients or work for another architect.

There was another important difference between being an architect in a centralized socialist economy and being one in a capitalist economy. In the latter economy, young architects fully expect that for a number of years after graduation they will be working for other architects, drawing bathroom details and preparing door schedules of projects they did not design. In contrast, young Czech architects during the communist regime were expected to start designing immediately after graduation, and many of us, including me, did just that (although I was delayed by ten months of my banishment).

And so it happened that, in the four-plus years between the end of my banishment and my departure for London, while working at the architectural office of the building contractor Konstruktiva, I had developed a portfolio of building designs that, as I found later, no twenty-eight-year-old architect working in the West could possibly hope to assemble. True, only one of those buildings was actually built—the rest were studies or proposals and some competition entries—but that was not unusual in Czechoslovakia at the time. Much was designed, and very little was actually built. To design buildings that would actually get built was the main reason I yearned to work in the West.

Interestingly, although no cultural or news magazine from the West was allowed to enter communist Czechoslovakia, scientific, technical, and architectural magazines were permitted to come to the Technical Library of Charles University. When we were students, we used to spend many hours in that library perusing *Architectural Record*, *Domus*, *Architectural Review*, *Progressive Architecture*, *Architecture Aujourd'hui*, and many other architectural magazines from Western Europe and the United States. In those magazines, we saw a dramatically different level of architecture from what we saw going up around us. Our separation from the outside world bred a certain naïveté. For example, I was truly convinced that the only thing that kept me from designing the kind of buildings I saw in those magazines was my being on the wrong side of the Iron Curtain. I was in for a rude awakening.

I spent my first year in London working for the Department of Architecture of the Greater London Council, designing plans for a variety of housing units, which were then used by project architects for housing developments in the City of London. Although I was living in London, which was exciting, my work situation was worse than what I had in Prague. There I was designing buildings that were not being built, but in London I was only designing floor plans to be used sometime in the future for a project I wouldn't even be involved in. So after a year, I was eager to find a job with a private firm.

That was my first time ever interviewing for a job. (My job at the London Council was offered to me, via mail, on the basis of an application form and submitted samples of my work.) I noticed early on that the people who interviewed me were surprised by the size of my portfolio. Some even seemed suspicious. I remember one architect at a large firm who, when interviewing me and leafing through my portfolio, came to a project of an office building and asked, "What role did you play on this project?" When I responded that I was the project designer, he looked skeptical. He probably expected me to say that I had detailed the windows or designed the bathrooms. So I pointed out the title block in the lower right of each drawing, where he could see my name. I could see that he was still not convinced; he asked, "So you were really responsible for the overall design?" I said I was, just as with all the other buildings in my portfolio. He appeared stunned, and mumbled, "Very impressive, very impressive." I no longer remember how the interview ended, except that I was not offered a job. Eventually, however, a medium-sized firm offered me a design position, which I happily accepted.

Clearly, having this kind of portfolio assured that either I was not offered a job at all or, when I was, it would be as a designer, not a draftsman or a detailer. Architects get ahead by assembling portfolios. The best ones are made up of completed buildings, but nobody expects a twenty-eight-year-old architect to have such a portfolio, so portfolios of building designs are the second best. And it was only by working in communist Czechoslovakia that I was able to assemble the kind of portfolio I had when I arrived in London. Two years later, it stood me in good stead in New York as well. This is what I mean when I say that the communist regime helped my career.

Another unexpectedly fortuitous result of my time in Czechoslovakia was that, because of the many hours I had spent in the Technical Library perusing Western architectural magazines, when I arrived in London, I found myself better informed about contemporary British architecture than my English colleagues. This earned me a reputation of being a learned guy, which, although it was completely false, didn't hurt.

First Honeymoon

I have already described the circumstances of my first wedding, so this story is about our subsequent honeymoon. I am writing this to give witness to the times because from today's vantage point, the whole experience appears so totally absurd that if I had not lived it, I would find it hard to believe.

The year was 1963, and Eva and I were both twenty-four years old. Though she had once been to Moscow, I had not yet been abroad. Neither of us had ever been to the seashore. So we decided to use our honeymoon to take a trip to the sea. Of the two seas available to us, the Black Sea and the Baltic, we opted for the Baltic because it was closer. To get there meant traveling either to East Germany or Poland. Because two years earlier while we were still students, I was prevented by the Interior Ministry from going on an exchange trip to East Germany, we decided to try for Poland. However, at the time, even going to another Soviet Bloc country wasn't that simple: an ordinary citizen couldn't just apply for a visa to Poland and go. No, to go abroad, even to a brotherly socialist country, one had to be a part of an organized group. The group most readily available to us was the Czechoslovak Youth Institute, since every person our age was automatically a member.

So we went to the travel bureau of the Czechoslovak Youth Institute and inquired about trips to the Baltic Sea in Poland. There were several, and we picked one whose timing worked for us. Again, it was not as simple as saying that we'd like to go on this trip. Since we were planning to go abroad, to be included in the group, we needed to bring two letters of recommendation—one from our employer and the other from the communist cell of our domicile. The letters were expected to state that we were upstanding citizens with positive attitudes toward the socialist regime and the working class and, as such, deserved to be included in the given trip abroad. We easily obtained the required letters. Both the givers and receivers of those letters knew it was a charade, but we all went through the required motions. There was no other choice: if we wanted to see the sea, this is what we had to do.

The trip itself was for ten days; its destination was Swinouscie (German Swinemunde), a small seaside resort town where we were to spend six days, followed by two nights in Warsaw on our way back. Travel was to be by train. On the given morning, we were met at the Prague main railroad station by our guide, an employee of the Czechoslovak Youth Institute who was in charge of the group. We all knew that he was more than a guide; he was our group leader, and in addition to guiding the trip, he was to be a guardian of its ideological purity. As it happened, he was a rather pleasant chap in his early thirties, clearly the oldest member of the group. I no longer remember his name, so let's call him Franta.

The first time Eva and I met the rest of the group was at the railroad station. There were ten of us, of which we were one of two married couples. Three of the remaining six singles were young women, and three were young men. Except for our leader Franta, everybody had a university education. We turned out to be a congenial group, so the eleven-hour train ride passed quickly. We sang Czech folk songs, drank wine, swapped stories and jokes, slept some, and before we knew it, we had arrived at

Swinouscie. We were met by Franta's Polish counterpart, an employee of the Polish Youth Institute who was an attractive woman named Wanda. It was then late evening, so without much ceremony we were taken to the college dorm where the Czechoslovak Youth institute had arranged for us to stay. It was summer, the time of vacations, so the dorms were empty, and the arrangements all made good sense.

There were two large rooms with bunk beds in the dormitory building, one for women and one for men, plus two rooms with four beds each, one of which rooms was already occupied. Franta wisely decided that the married couples should take the remaining room with four beds, while he went with the single men to the men's dorm, and Wanda repaired with the single women to the women's dorm.

With the other couple, we rearranged the four beds into two larger beds, and then for a measure of privacy, we put one of the two armoires in between them. There was, of course, absolutely no acoustical privacy. What amazes me when I write this is how, at the time, we didn't find any of this absurd; on the contrary, it all seemed perfectly normal to us. We knew when we signed up for the trip that there was no such thing as a private room on the Youth Institute trips.

On the second or third day of our stay at the seashore, I was approached by the husband of the couple with whom we shared the room. With a wink, he asked me if Eva and I could go to the movies that evening and added that they would be happy to do the same for us the following night. Naturally, I agreed, and I told him that they could count on having the room to themselves that evening. However, I knew that Eva could not enjoy our intimacies under those circumstances. Consequently, we are the only couple I've known to this day who spent their honeymoon without sex.

Now, a word about the comparative merits of Poland and Czechoslovakia at the time, which are best summed up by a joke that was then going around. A Polish dog goes to Czechoslovakia while a Czech dog decides to go to Poland. It so happens that they meet at the border. The Czech dog asks the Polish dog why he is going to the Czech lands. The Polish dog says that he wants to buy some nylon stockings and some pork chops. Then he asks the Czech dog why he is going to Poland. The Czech dog replies, "Oh, just to bark some in a freer land." The Czechs had more money to spend while the Polish regime was less oppressive. How did this manifest itself? Polish movie houses were showing American Westerns, and there was a modicum of Western goods available in Polish stores, things such as Colgate toothpaste, Knorr soups, or hugely overpriced Levi's jeans.

And so it happened that the first Western Eva and I ever watched was in the Swinouscie movie theater, though I no longer remember what it was.

The Czechoslovak Youth Institute arranged a few boat trips for us on the Baltic, and the rest of the time we were left alone on the beach.

I still remember my first sight of the sea. Eva and I just could not wait, so we ran to the beach before breakfast that first morning, but what a disappointment! I expected this dramatic element I knew from photographs and movies, with roaring waves breaking on the rocks or on the beach. Instead, on that particular day the Baltic was as calm as a lake, with only a minor ripple here and there. Fortunately, the waves, and quite big ones, came a day later.

Once our days at the seashore were over, we were again on a train, this time bound for Warsaw. The sleeping arrangements at a Warsaw college dorm were much the same as those at the seaside, except that our four-bed room was much smaller, so there was no space for an armoire between us. Warsaw was Wanda's hometown, and she was eager to show us its nightlife. Consequently, we spent both nights there dancing until the wee hours and then slept during most of the train ride back to Prague. When folks at our offices asked us how our honeymoon was, both Eva and I responded, "Oh, wonderful, simply wonderful!" The funny thing is that we truly meant it.

Sotheby's

When I returned from Tehran in January 1979, I had no clients waiting for me, so I was casting around for design consulting assignments. Someone suggested that I call Oliver Lundquist of Lundquist & Stonehill, a medium-size architectural firm. I called and explained my situation, and we made a date for an interview.

Mr. Lundquist appeared to be in his mid- to late sixties and had the looks of a prototypical New England Brahmin, complete with the tweed jacket, the bow tie, and the tousled gray mane. He appeared to have reached the stage of life when he no longer had to prove anything, looked comfortable in his skin, exuded rectitude, and inspired trust and respect. He took time to leaf through my portfolio, was intrigued by the number of projects I had designed in Iran, and then, with charming frankness, told me that over the years what had kept Lundquist & Stonehill afloat was its work for the auction house Sotheby's.

At the time, Sotheby's occupied a block-long building on the west side of Madison Avenue between 76th and 77th Streets. It was a large edifice from the 1930s full of showrooms, galleries, offices, and auction halls, and it had a continuous need for some alteration or improvement, such as installing a new elevator, moving partitions, adding new stairs between two floors, installing new flooring or new lighting, and so on. Lundquist & Stonehill was Sotheby's default architectural firm and was doing all that required work. However, it had never been asked to design anything conceptual until then. Sotheby's had recently asked the firm to produce a design feasibility study to help them decide whether to buy a Kodak warehouse on York Avenue and 72nd Street and convert it into a much larger auction house than the one on Madison Avenue.

Oliver Lundquist asked me if I'd be interested in preparing that feasibility study for them, as I appeared to have the requisite qualification and experience. I was, of course, thrilled, thinking that by a stroke of luck, I had managed to walk into the right place at the right time. I received the plans of the Kodak warehouse together with the program of spaces required by Sotheby's and set to work. With my structural engineer Hans Gesell, we determined what segments of the warehouse floors could be removed to make two-story-high spaces for an auditorium and lecture halls, galleries, and a loading dock. Our conclusion was that the warehouse indeed could be converted into an auction house. Within two months, we had prepared a presentation showing exactly how. It included plans of all the floors showing diagrammatic layouts of the required spaces, plus a few additional sections.

When I presented our submission to Oliver Lundquist, he was overjoyed, saying that it was precisely what was wanted. He reiterated that at this point there was no way of knowing if this study would lead to anything, that its sole purpose was to help Sotheby's decide whether to buy that warehouse. I said that I was hoping that, if Sotheby's did decide to buy it and to go ahead with the project, Lundquist & Stonehill would then ask me to turn this study into a set of design development drawings. Oliver's reply was "You can bet on it." We shook hands, and that was that.

Shortly thereafter, I received my first corporate commission to design archives for a major fabric house in Manhattan, then I received another assignment, and soon I forgot all about Sotheby's and the Kodak warehouse.

Perhaps two years later, I was at a party in a downtown loft where I met a man who told me that he worked for Sotheby's. When I asked him if he'd heard anything about the Kodak warehouse, he told me, "Of course I have. I was the one who transacted its purchase." I asked if Sotheby's was going forward with the project of turning it into its new auction house. He said their architects were busy working on it. And who were their architects? "Lundquist & Stonehill."

The next morning, I called Mr. Lundquist and told him that I heard that the firm was working on the Sotheby's project. I still remember his response: "Oh, we are going great guns on it! And, Martin, your plans worked out perfectly. We didn't have to change a thing; all we had to do was to follow your lay-outs." While he was talking, what went through my head was that without a written agreement, I didn't have a leg to stand on. I was asked to prepare a feasibility study, I got paid for it, and, beyond that, Lundquist & Stonehill had no further obligation to me. Consequently, spilling bile, thereby creating bad feelings, would be of no use. So I responded the only way I could, saying, "Glad to hear that, Oliver. Good luck."

How I Did Not Become a Fashion Model

Even in communist Czechoslovakia, where ready-to-wear clothes were so uniformly dreadful that no even slightly fashion-conscious person wore them, there were fashion magazines. Fashion magazines had a need for fashion models, which gave rise to modeling agencies, which were much like those in the West, except, of course, on this side of the Iron Curtain, they were all state owned. And so it happened that one of the modeling agencies in need of male models dispatched an agent to the School of Architecture to look for them.

I remember an older (he was probably forty), well-dressed man who came and sat in on a class on the history of architecture and then mingled with us students during the break between the lectures. When the break was over and before we piled into another auditorium for the next lecture, the man approached first Honza Bočan and then me and took us away from the horde of students. At the time, having a business card was not the norm in Czechoslovakia, so I clearly remember it when he handed us his card, said that he was working for such and such a modeling agency, and asked us if we'd be interested in earning some money as models. Honza, clearly a faster draw than I was, asked how much.

During my summer vacations between my university years, I was earning what I considered to be decent money on archeological digs, spraying hops, as a truck driver's helper, and shoveling coal in a coal mine. However, the hourly rate that the guy from the modeling agency casually quoted was something like the highest rate I ever earned multiplied by ten. The man clearly enjoyed watching our shock as we absorbed the information he had just imparted, and then he suggested that we call the agency and make an appointment at our convenience. Honza and I did as we were told and a few days later showed up at the agency. There we saw more staff members at the agency, were photographed, and eventually signed a contract for on-call assignments at the given hourly rate. As we left, our heads were reeling. What a hoot! I could not wait to get home to break the news.

When I got home, I found my mother and my stepfather having tea with our family friend, the philosopher Jan Patočka. Elated, I announced, "My dear friends, hold your hats; we'll be going downhill to a new era." I showed them the contract and briefly explained what had happened. They passed the contract to one another in silence and all looking very serious and concerned. I was puzzled by their reaction. Then Jan Patočka spoke: "Martin, you need to reconsider this. In a little over a year you'll graduate and enter the profession. You'll want to be taken seriously and be respected as an architect, and this could jeopardize that goal. Just consider: can you imagine a young Corbusier having been a fashion model? Or Walter Gropious, or Mies van der Rohe? To have been, even briefly, a fashion model is just not compatible with an image of a serious professional."

If my mother or my stepfather had spoken those words, I would have probably argued with them, but because they came from Patočka, whose opinions were highly respected by everyone I knew, I did consider them seriously and came to agree with what he said. The next day I called the modeling agency and told them that I had a change of heart and, instead of modeling, would be concentrating on my studies. Honza Bočan, however, went ahead with the modeling. Pictures of him modeling now a hat, now a sweater, and then a coat appeared in a number of fashion magazines, and while still at the university, he did suffer his share of derision. Fellow students would taunt, "Here comes the pretty boy! Make space for the model. Where are the cameras?" But as time wore on, his modeling career was forgotten and did not seem to harm his professional reputation in any way.

How times change! Not even Patočka could have predicted that forty years later, respected professionals would be eager to be photographed in Levi's jeans and have their pictures plastered on New York City bus stops; the thought that it might harm their reputations wouldn't even enter their minds. And something else occurred to me many years later: how bizarre that, in the centrally planned economy of communist Czechoslovakia in which no market forces existed, the powers that be considered it appropriate to pay fashion models several times what coal miners earned!

Woodstock College

It must have been in late 1971, or early 1972, when I read in the *New York Times* an article about Jesuits from the Woodstock Theological Seminary at Columbia University who served a noon mass at St. Paul's Chapel on the Columbia campus. The services were described as highly unusual. For one thing, they were in open defiance of the Vatican in that women were allowed to offer the Eucharist. For another, gays were welcome. Furthermore, because most of the celebrants had PhDs in theology, the homilies tended to have a scholarly quality. All of that sounded quite interesting to me.

Never having been a churchgoer and having weathered a rabid anti-Catholic phase, I decided to go check it out. The Columbia campus was within a comfortable walking distance from my West Side apartment, and the starting time of the service was convenient, so the following Sunday I walked up to Columbia University, found St. Paul's Chapel, and sat down in a pew. Looking around, I quickly saw that this was a congregation of educated people. The few times I had attended a mass, I was always put off by the sanctimonious atmosphere, punctuated by too many "Lord is great," "Jesus loves you," and similar phrases that I found meaningless, not to mention all the genuflecting and bowing each time someone passed the altar. There was nothing of the kind during this service. I still remember that the Gospel reading was about the prodigal son and that in the subsequent homily, the celebrant parsed and dissected that story in a meaningful way.

There is a moment during each mass when people petition God, and after each petition, the whole congregation responds, "Lord hear our prayers." Among many of the petitions offered, such as "May my father recover from his surgery" or "May my daughter be safe while she is in Africa," a woman in a clear voice gave this one: "May the papacy cease." The congregation replied, "Lord, hear our prayers." There were no chuckles, no raised eyebrows; no one seemed startled or perplexed. The service went on.

After the mass, everyone was invited for coffee and cookies in a community room in the basement, so I joined them. I noticed several smart (in both senses of the word) young women, and because those were my looking-for-the-right-one years, that alone was a powerful incentive to return. Then I caught sight of a man with a white mustache and a goatee, who bore a strong resemblance to Thomas Masaryk. He looked approachable, so I went up to him and asked if anyone else had ever told him that he looked like Thomas Garrigue Masaryk. To my shock, he didn't know who I was talking about. (This was before I had met Americans with advanced degrees who had never heard of Bismarck or Franz Kafka and weren't sure if Maria Theresa was a movie star or a figure skater.) When I told him that Thomas Masaryk was a close friend of Woodrow Wilson and the first president of Czechoslovakia, he was mighty flattered.

As we continued to talk, I learned that he was an artist and that he made a living working for a company that provided lighting fixtures and stained-glass windows for new and renovated churches. His name was Willy Malarcher, and this was the beginning of a friendship that lasted more than twenty-five years. It was also the beginning of my more or less regular attendance—which lasted about twenty years—of the noontime services of the Woodstock congregation. Unless I was out of town or had a deadline to meet and had to work, each Sunday I'd walk up to the Columbia campus and attend the Woodstock noon mass.

After a number of Sundays at St. Paul's Chapel, I started recognizing some fellow attendees. In particular, one older fellow's behavior caught my attention. He always wore the same worn and crumpled suit and always sat in the same seat in the front row, but what I noticed was that this senior citizen behaved like a pupil eager to please his teacher. He was the embodiment of supererogation: smoothing the cloth on the altar that did not need smoothing, slightly moving the candlestick that didn't need moving, wiping the seat of the presider's chair that didn't need wiping.

There was something pathetic in seeing an old, gray-haired gentleman behave like an eager beaver. "Strange," I wondered. "Whom is he trying to please?" At the coffee and cookies gatherings after the mass, I noticed that he would corner people, who then would have difficulties getting away from him. When I asked Willy about this man, he said, "Oh, yes, that's Leo. He used to be a Jesuit, who then dropped out to get married. He then got divorced, and now he'd love to be taken back into the order, which, of course, is not going to happen. In the meantime, he manages to make a nuisance of himself." Knowing this, Leo's peculiar behavior, although not less repulsive, at least made some sense to me.

Even though I tried to avoid him, always standing at the opposite end of the room, there came a day when Leo managed to corner me in the community room after the mass. Without any prompt from me, he explained that, of all the Sunday services in Manhattan, for an intelligent person this was without question the best one around. I did not disagree, but that didn't stop Leo from continuing. He kept on belaboring the point, repeating himself, as if he were wound up and couldn't stop. During his whole soliloquy, he didn't ask me a single question. Eventually, to get away, I told Leo that someone was waiting for me. After that encounter, I was always extra careful to be on the other side of the room from where Leo stood.

In 1974 when my mother was allowed her first visit to America, she was interested in coming with me to the Woodstock mass, about which I had written her in my letters. She, too, noticed the improbable antics of the senior eager beaver in the first row. I told her Leo's story, and because he was at least her contemporary, if not older, she was touched by it. After the service, in the community room Leo noticed a new person and made a beeline for us. We exchanged a few sentences, and Leo, noticing my mother's accent, asked her where she was from. She responded that she was from Czechoslovakia. To my utter consternation Leo replied in Czech, "How interesting, so am I! I was born in Prague, came here before the war, and never returned." So I had been avoiding my compatriot! When he had talked to me a few years earlier, I did not detect any accent and always assumed that he was American born.

Listening to Leo talk in Czech, I was struck by how his personality changed when he spoke in his native tongue. He no longer appeared as an anxious, eager-to-please, nonstop-talking, overbearing senior citizen, but, on the contrary, as a rather relaxed geezer with a self-deprecating sense of humor.

He even asked us questions. During her stay, my mother came with me a few more times to St. Paul's Chapel. Each time, after the service, she got into a long conversation with Leo. Sometimes I was standing by; other times I was talking to someone else. Before she returned to Prague, my mother told me that Leo shared with her that he had an older brother in Prague with whom he had not been in touch for more than forty years. She asked him why not. Leo said that because he had never accomplished anything, he never had anything positive to say, and so he had not written; in that way, enough time had elapsed that eventually he thought it was too late to write. But now he asked my mother to find his brother and, if he were still alive, to tell him that he, Leo, was also still alive. This was how we learned that Leo's surname was Mladen. Leo said that his brother's name was Albert and that he lived in Prague.

A month or two after she returned to Prague, my mother reported that she had found Leo's brother. It was not difficult: there was only one Albert Mladen in the phone book. When she called the number, a woman answered the phone. My mother identified herself and asked if she was speaking to Mrs. Mladen. When the answer was yes, my mother explained that she had recently returned from New York, where she happened to have met Leo, who asked her if she could find his brother Albert and tell him that he was still alive. Mrs. Mladen became very emotional. She said that her husband was in his nineties and was extremely frail and that since they had not heard from Leo for more than forty years, they had long assumed that he was dead. She was worried that the news that Leo was alive might be so moving for her husband that it could jeopardize his health. She said she'd have to break the news to him gently, at the right time.

A week later, Albert Mladen himself called my mother and asked her if she would honor him by accepting his and his wife's invitation to tea, because he'd so much like to hear her account of meeting his brother. My mother, of course, accepted. She later wrote me that Albert, although frail, was still a handsome man: he was a rare example of an old-style gentleman, a disappearing species in communist Czechoslovakia. As she told him beforehand that she didn't have Leo's address, at the end of their meeting Albert Mladen gave my mother an envelope, hand-addressed to Leo, and asked her if she could ask me to hand it to Leo. Albert was ten years Leo's senior, and my mother wrote that, although he had not heard from him for so long, he still exhibited a fatherly solicitousness toward his younger brother.

And so a few weeks later, enclosed in my mother's letter was the envelope with Albert's letter to Leo, which had been left unopened by the communist censors. When I handed it to Leo the next time I attended the Woodstock liturgy, he was, at first, speechless. Then in a disbelieving tone, he said, "You mean your mother found Albert's name in the phone book, went to visit him, and he gave her this letter and asked her to mail it to you?" When I said yes, we went over the story once again. We were speaking Czech, so he ought to have been in his relaxed geezer mode, but instead, he was stiff, as if frozen. He showed no emotion, took the envelope, put it in his pocket, and said good-bye.

Shortly thereafter I left for Tehran, so the next time I saw Leo wasn't until some six months later when I returned for my first trip back to New York. On my first Sunday back, I walked up to St. Paul's, and after the mass I asked Leo if he and his brother had gotten together. He responded that it was hopeless: "He is too frail to travel and I have no money." Over the next four years I saw Leo sporadically, during my visits back from Tehran. The subject of his brother never came up again.

After my return from Tehran, for the next decade or so I kept going to the Woodstock mass every Sunday I was in town, unless something else was happening or I had to work. I continued to find the sermons interesting and even thought provoking. Often they were delivered by clergy of other religions. I remember listening to a rabbi, a Baptist preacher, a Hindu priest, and a female Episcopal priest.

One Sunday in the early 1980s, the homilist was Father Daniel Berrigan, the renowned peace activist. This was shortly after he had served a short jail sentence for damaging warheads in a nuclear missile facility in Pennsylvania. He and six nuns had managed to trespass onto a General Electric factory, where they expressed their pacifist feelings by denting with hammers the noses of several missiles, whereupon they were arrested, which was, of course, what they wanted.

In circles such as at Woodstock College and the whole Columbia campus, Father Berrigan was a hero. What vexed me during his homily was that he clearly assumed that everyone in the congregation shared his pacifist feelings and approved of his activism. In fact, his self-righteous certainty irked me so much that after he finished delivering his sermon, I raised my hand. Father Berrigan saw me and asked if I had a question.

I said I didn't have a question but wanted to make a statement. Father Berrigan motioned to me to speak. I said that only because he appeared so certain that everyone here shared his views, I felt compelled to tell him that I, for one, totally disapproved of what he had done in Pennsylvania.

Father Berrigan graciously thanked me for expressing my opinion. Even this short exchange would be unthinkable during a mass in any other church I can think of, but at the Woodstock congregation it felt quite natural. I mention it to illustrate the atmosphere at those services.

In 1991, I moved in with Karen, who lived on the extreme east edge of the Upper East Side, way over on York Avenue and 77th Street. Suddenly, my trip to the Columbia campus became not just less convenient but downright inconvenient. It was too far to walk, and there was no simple way of getting there by public transportation. My choices were to take either two buses or a cross-town bus all the way to Broadway and then the subway uptown. Either way, instead of a twenty-minute walk, it would be at least a forty-five-minute commute. So I stopped going. Years later, when reflecting on my twenty years of churchgoing, I had to admit that it had nothing to do with God and everything to do with my social needs, the convenient location, and a measure of intellectual curiosity.

War Memories

When people find out my age, I sometimes get asked if I have any memories of World War II. Well, I do, but not the kind you might expect. One is of air raids. Because German munition factories and warehouses were located at Prague's outskirts, during the last year of the war, the city was subject to frequent Allied air raids. Since it was long before the advent of smart bombs, it sometimes happened that the bombs missed their intended targets and, instead, hit a Baroque church or a Gothic city hall. But on the whole, Prague largely escaped serious damage from the bombing.

I was attending an all-boys grade school at the time, and we pupils loved the daytime air raids. It so happened that across the street there was an all-girls grade school and the basements of both schools were connected. Since during air raids everybody had to go to the basement, this was one opportunity for the boys to chase the girls, pinch them, pull their braids, and do whatever six-year-old boys do to six-year-old girls. Nighttime raids were less loved but were regarded only as an annoyance. To be woken up in the middle of the night, have to get dressed while half asleep, and then have to rush to the basement of our apartment building with all the adults was, of course, no fun, but it was no major suffering either.

I remember very clearly one air raid in particular. It happened on a weekend afternoon when I wasn't in school. I was walking with my grandfather across the Jirásek Bridge, and when the sirens announcing the air raid went off, we were smack in the middle. It is a long bridge, and there was no chance that we'd make it to either end in the required time. According to the Civil Defense instructions, when one could not get into a shelter within the allotted time—I no longer remember how long that was—one was to lie down wherever one was. My grandfather told me to lie down and he did the same, stretching out on the sidewalk. We were not the only people who found themselves in the middle of the bridge, so folks were lying down around us. I remember finding it quite humorous that all those grown-ups were lying flat on the sidewalk in their fine clothes.

Then we heard the planes and explosions, most of which sounded distant except for one, which seemed to be quite close. The raid was over in a couple of minutes. When we heard the sirens sounding the end of the raid we got up and looked around. There was a sort of collective gasp as we looked toward the end of the bridge, and there, on the embankment—at the corner of the street that continued the line of the bridge—what used to be a six-story apartment building was now a smoldering pile of rubble. So that was the explosion that had seemed so close! (Incidentally, that parcel of land remained empty over the next fifty or so years, until in the mid-1990s a ludicrous-looking building designed by Frank Gehry was built on it.)

To this day I remember another strong image that we saw when we neared that pile of rubble. In those days in Prague, one could still occasionally see a wagon, typically with beer barrels on it, being pulled by a team of oxen. There, at the end of the bridge, we saw such a wagon, with both oxen lying motionless on the ground, presumably dead. From the snout of one of the oxen flowed a prodigious amount of dark-red blood. My grandfather explained to me that it was probably the strong blast of air from the bomb and the subsequent explosion that had killed the oxen.

Another war memory I have is of Uncle Viktor. Viktor Kaufman wasn't my real uncle but was my father's colleague from law school and an old friend. He was a frequent visitor, often dining with my parents. One day, when I was perhaps five years old, Uncle Viktor had dinner with my parents and did not leave. There was a large walk-in closet in our apartment, where my parents set up a cot on which Uncle Viktor slept from then on. When my parents had other visitors, Uncle Viktor would stay in the closet. I was told not to mention to absolutely anyone that he lived with us. And so it went for perhaps more than a year.

For a child of five, everything is normal, so I didn't much wonder why Uncle Viktor was living in our closet. Then, sometime toward the end of the war, suddenly, Uncle Viktor was gone. I asked my parents where he went and was told that he went west to join the Americans. Again, I accepted that at face value and did not question it. Soon after, I started going to school, and I forgot all about Uncle Viktor.

It wasn't until I was a teenager when my father told me the whole story of Viktor Kaufman. The day he came to dinner and then did not leave was one of the days when the Gestapo was rounding up Jews for transport to Auschwitz and other camps. Viktor got word about it through a friend, so he left his apartment in the morning and walked the streets the whole day until he came to dinner at our place. During dinner, he told my parents what was happening and asked my father if he knew of some place in the country where he could hide. My father thought that going to the country would be dangerous and offered to put him up for the night.

The next day my father went to Viktor's apartment. In the corridor, he met Viktor's neighbor whom he knew by sight from his many previous visits. The neighbor told him that the day before the Gestapo indeed had come, and furious that Viktor wasn't home, they broke down the door, ransacked the apartment, and left. When my father reported this news to Viktor, they concluded that since he was now a wanted man, it would be too dangerous for him to go outside; he needed to stay put where he was. And so he stayed, never leaving the apartment for more than a year.

Then, sometime early in 1945, he cracked up. He had been following the progress of the war on our short-wave radio and knew that General Patton's army was already in Germany, while the Red Army was in eastern Poland and was rapidly advancing toward Berlin. Clearly the war would be over in a few months, but Viktor just could not wait any longer. He got it in his head that he'd be able to make it through the Western Front to the Americans' line where he could join the US Army. Despite protestations from my parents, one night he left, and we never heard from him again.

My other memories of the war are from its end, from what came to be known as the Prague Uprising. The time was early May 1945, May 5 to be exact. General Patton was in Pilsen, the Red Army was in Berlin, and the war was clearly over. After six years under German occupation, the folks in Prague could not wait for the Germans to leave and started taking down the German-language shop signs and displaying Czechoslovak flags.

I was sitting with my paternal grandfather Josef in our living room when my mother came home, all smiles, waving Czechoslovak flags. I remember my grandfather getting all excited and shouting, "Have you lost your mind? Don't you know those flags are forbidden? You are going to get us all arrested!" My mother responded, "It's all over, the war is over, these flags are everywhere!" However, she didn't yet know that the German soldiers, instead of leaving, had started shooting at the folks who were taking down the signs and putting up the flags. This is how the Prague Uprising started. Czech citizens had started building barricades, mostly from cobblestones, to prevent German tanks and armored vehicles from moving around. Intense shooting was suddenly heard all around the city.

Word went out that Prague was in trouble, and Czechs were needlessly dying. Patton's army could have reached Prague in less than two hours, but FDR had agreed in Yalta that Prague would be liberated by the Soviets, so Patton was prevented from sending help. My father heard on BBC radio that a Red Army tank battalion had been dispatched from Berlin to liberate Prague but that it would take two days for the tanks to get to us. Meanwhile, the fighting in the streets continued.

A rumor reached us that a German tank had broken through a barricade and fired its gun into an apartment building, causing its collapse. We had not left our apartment in three days. Then, on the fourth day, the sounds of shooting intensified, and we heard some artillery shells as well. The streets then quieted and we heard shouts: "The Russians are here, the Russians are here!" We heard no more shooting, looked out the windows, and saw no Germans in evidence so we—meaning my parents and I, together with everybody else—poured out of every building and walked over to the main street, which was already lined with people. For a six-year-old kid it wasn't too difficult to sneak through the crowd, and I soon found myself standing in the first row. Sure enough, in a short while, we first heard and then saw what we took to be Soviet tanks slowly rolling down the street.

But then, somebody shouted, "This is not the Red Army; this is General Vlasov's Army." We looked, and sure enough, those tanks did not have the hammer-and-sickle emblems of the Red Army. Now, let me explain about the army of General Andrey Vlasov. It was a testament to the anti-Bolshevik feelings within the Red Army when, convinced that the Russian people would be better off under Hitler than they were under Stalin, in 1943 Vlasov was able to persuade a whole division of the Red Army to defect and join the German army in fighting the Soviets. By the end of the war, with the German army decimated, Vlasov saw that he had bet on the wrong horse and tried to surrender to the Allies. In the process, he managed to liberate Prague from the last vestiges of the German resistance. Shortly thereafter, the whole of Vlasov's Army was captured by the Soviets near Pilsen; Vlasov himself was sent to Moscow where he was hanged for treason, and his army was shipped to Siberia and never heard of again. After the communist take-over of Czechoslovakia in 1948, the fact that Prague was liberated by the renegade General Vlasov and not by the Red Army disappeared from all history books.

However, in the euphoria over the end of the war, the distinction between the Red Army and Vlasov's Army was lost, and the Russians of whatever army were welcomed enthusiastically. They were our liberators! Some of the tanks pulled up on the side of the road, and soldiers jumped out, shook hands, and embraced the local populace. I was hoisted on top of a tank, and there is a black-and-white photograph of me with a grinning, broad-faced Russian soldier. Later in the day, there was dancing in the streets, singing, and general merriment. When the actual Red Army tanks finally arrived from

Berlin the following day, although there was no need for them to fight the Germans because that had already been taken care of by Vlasov's Army, in the spirit of the end-of-the-war rejoicing, they were welcomed too. The news about their raping and pillaging in the countryside came out later.

Things were, however, still a long way from being back to normal. Sitting at the breakfast table the day after the tanks arrived, we suddenly heard a distant shot, followed by a crack in the window. I saw a neat round hole through both panes of the glass and another hole in the parquet floor by the window. Then we heard shouts from the street: "Sniper! Everybody step back from the windows!" It turned out that a lone German sniper had holed up in a spire of the nearby church, from where he was shooting people in the streets as well as inside apartments. It took the rest of the day to take him down, during which time we couldn't go outside or come close to the windows. Anytime I forgot about this injunction and strolled near a window, my mother went ballistic, shouting, "How many times do I have to tell you? Get away from that window!"

Perhaps a week after the liberation, one morning I looked out of the window of our third-floor apartment and was astonished by what I saw. The whole street, both the roadway and the sidewalks, was solidly covered with German prisoners of war lying exhausted on the ground, in silence, with only occasional moans: "*Wasser, bitte, wasser, bitte.*" I called my mother. She looked out and concluded that they had probably marched a day and night without food or rest, until they could go no farther and collapsed. She started filling one of our larger pots with water. Now my father entered the picture and asked what she was doing. My mother responded that she was taking some water down to the prisoners. My father was incredulous, saying, "What, have you forgotten all the atrocities the Germans committed over the last six years? Have you forgotten the concentration camps? Have you forgotten what they did to the Jews? And now you are going to give them water?"

I remember this incident because I'd never before heard my parents argue. If they ever did, it was never in my presence. (Little did I know that at that time they had probably already filed for divorce, because a little over three months later, by the start of the next school year, they were divorced and my father had moved out.) My mother responded, "I have not forgotten anything, but I doubt that those guys lying outside barely alive had to do with any of it. So I am going to give them some water." With several tumblers in one hand and a large pot of water in the other, she left the apartment. I remember looking out the window and watching her offer the water to the Germans. Soon I saw women coming out of other apartment buildings along the street doing the same. A similar argument probably took place in other households, with the women prevailing.

Simon Alexander

The last of the three jobs I held in London was for a large firm by the name of R. Seifert & Partners. It had more than two hundred employees, working in some dozen studios scattered all over London and operating more or less autonomously. I was the only designer in the studio that was headed by a South African architect, Simon Alexander. My work consisted of producing conceptual designs for developers, mostly of hotels, office buildings, and shopping malls.

Simon was one of the partners of R. Seifert & Partners, and as such, his role was 100 percent administrative and managerial. Most of the time, he didn't even have a drawing board in his office. However, he did possess an architect's ego, which, from time to time, compelled him to show to himself and to the world not only that he was a capable administrator and manager but that he could also design. At such times, he asked for a drawing board to be set up in his office, rolled up his sleeves, and, over the next few days, labored over a design of a hotel or some other commercial edifice.

The problem for me would arise when Simon finally arrived at some design. Because I was the only person around who ever designed anything and appeared to have earned his respect as a designer, he'd call me to his office, where he'd show me his design and ask for my opinion. Because his designs were uniformly dreadful, this put me in an awkward situation. Not only was Simon a very nice person, but he was also at least twenty years my senior and, most important of all, he was my boss!

I could not bring myself to say the designs were wonderful, so I often muttered something about "interesting," because I just couldn't think of anything else to say. Simon was not stupid, however, so he knew straightaway what I thought and, with a dejected look, would throw his pencil on the board and say, "OK, Martin. Why don't you just take it over and fix it."

As this scenario was repeated every two months or so I sought advice from my architect friends how to handle it. In short order, I had compiled a list of innocuous, meaningless phrases to use on similar occasions without insulting or hurting the person seeking one's opinion. You could always say, "There is a nice scale to it" or "It has pleasing proportions." Or you could try these phrases: "It has a nice feel about it" or "Wow, this is special!" The best one is "You've done it again!"

I'll never know if Simon saw through me when I uttered these phrases to him. But in at least half of the cases, after I told him that his design had a nice feel about it or some such nonsense, instead of asking me to take it over and fix it, he'd pass it on to a project architect and instruct him to develop it. In the years since, these bromides have stood me in good stead on many an occasion.

Skiing in Jackson Hole in 1972.

Yevtushenko in Jackson Hole

I had always thought that Yevgeny Yevtushenko was a phony and that he must have struck some Faustian bargain with the Soviet politburo. How else would it have been possible that, as a certified dissident, he was allowed to travel to the West? While other dissidents, like Andrei Sakharov, were banished to Siberia, Yevtushenko traveled all over Western Europe as well as to the United States. Yes, in the early 1960s his poem "Babi Yar"—in which he acknowledged Soviet silence about the Nazi massacre of more than thirty thousand Jews near Kiev during World War II—launched him into the ranks of dissidents, yet I didn't trust him. My suspicions were proven correct during my first ski trip to the American West.

The year was 1972, and in March Gerry Jonas and I went skiing in Jackson Hole in Wyoming. These days, Jackson Hole is a fancy ski resort with a Four Seasons and other luxury hotels, but at the time it was a spartan ski village. Gerry and I stayed in a small hotel room with a bunk bed. One night after dinner in one of the few restaurants around, when we ordered one more glass of wine, we became aware of some commotion at the other side of the room. Waiters (mostly college kids) were running back and forth, taking bottles of champagne and buckets of ice to a table at which sat two men. After taking a closer look, it seemed to me that one of them looked like Yevtushenko. I also recalled that, a week or so earlier, I had read in the *New York Times* that Yevtushenko was visiting the United States.

I shared my thoughts with Gerry. His response: "Nonsense, what would Yevtushenko be doing in Jackson Hole?" Indeed, meeting a Soviet dissident in an American ski resort was a bizarre idea. However, the casual and relaxed atmosphere of the ski village restaurant, plus the wine we had consumed so far, made me lose whatever inhibitions I might have had, so I got up, walked over, and addressed the gentleman who looked like Yevtushenko in Russian. (During my schooling in Czecho-slovakia, I had gone through eleven years of compulsory Russian.) I asked him if he happened to be Yevgeny Yevtushenko.

He got up and, in a very histrionic manner, threw his arms around me. He was genuinely thrilled to be recognized in this far-flung outpost: it had made his day. He commanded me to join them and promptly poured me a glass of champagne.

When I told him I was there with a friend, Yevtushenko asked me to bring him over. We switched to English when Gerry joined us. Yevtushenko's English was halting, but he was able to communicate in it. The fellow with him was an American, someone from the State Department assigned to be Yev-tushenko's escort on his travels through the United States. The champagne flowed copiously, and the histrionics continued.

When Yevtushenko found out that I was a Czech, he fell to his knees in front of me, the palms of his hands pressed together as in prayer, and he pleaded for my forgiveness for the terrible things the Soviets did to Czechoslovakia in 1968. It was not yet four years since the invasion, and the memory of it was still raw.

I told him that I'd never forgive Brezhnev, but that I did not hold him, Yevtushenko, personally responsible for it, so that he didn't need to apologize. He seemed satisfied with this response. I also thanked him for writing "Babi Yar," and he seemed pleased that I knew about it. As time dragged on, Yevtushenko became less and less coherent as the prodigious amount of champagne he had drunk caused his English to fail him. It was only after the bar had closed that he agreed to go to bed. His companion had long since excused himself.

On the whole, I was satisfied that the impression I had of Yevtushenko prior to meeting him was correct: he was a phony buffoon.

My Lecture in Prague

In hindsight, other than that my mother had been receiving exit visas for her visits to the United States every year since the early 1980s, another sign that change was in the air was the fact that I got a visa for a two-week visit to Czechoslovakia in September 1989. The Cold War was still on, and the Iron Curtain was very much in place. Although I had applied for visas many times, until then I had only been granted them twice: the first time on humanitarian grounds while my mother was recovering from breast cancer surgery in 1983, and the second time two years later for my father's funeral. Karen had never been to Prague and wanted to go, so although I didn't have high hopes, I applied for the visa once again. Under the reason for the visit, I checked "tourism." To my great surprise, the visa was granted. Hallelujah, let's go! I called my mother to tell her we were coming, and she was thrilled.

The plan was for Karen to spend a week in Prague with me and then leave for Vienna, where I would join her three days later. That would give me a chance to see some friends who didn't speak English; visiting them with Karen along would not have made much sense. Also, my mother and I wanted to make a day trip to the country and climb Blue Mountain near the village where she was born.

Two days before our departure my mother called me and said that a bunch of her young architect friends, feeling isolated on the wrong side of the Iron Curtain, had asked her if I could meet with them and talk about current American architecture. In her words, it would be "just an informal discussion around a table. Bring some slides; they have a projector." Pressed for time as I was, I went to the slide library at the School of Architecture on the Columbia University campus and randomly picked about fifty slides of projects I knew about, including some of mine. I packed the slides in my suitcase and promptly forgot about the whole thing.

The first week in Prague passed quickly. Given my experience during my first visit home six years earlier, I was understandably a little nervous, but this time there was no evidence of the security apparatus, so I quickly relaxed. I remember that Karen left for Vienna on a Friday and that I was to join her on Tuesday of the following week. My get-together with the young architects was to take place on Saturday afternoon. My mother told me that they were to call and tell us where to meet. I expected we'd meet at someone's apartment.

Saturday morning someone called and told my mother that we were to come to the Technical Museum. The meeting was set for 3:00 p.m., so after lunch I took the slides and we went to the museum. When we approached it, my jaw dropped. On each side of the entrance door there was a printed poster that read,

Czech-American Architect Martin Holub

Will talk about

CONTEMPORARY AMERICAN ARCHITECTURE

Today at 3:00 p.m.

I turned to my mother and she was as surprised as I was. I was dumbfounded for two reasons. First, who could think such a thing was possible at all at a time when, according to the official ideology, America was an enemy—a country of capitalist exploiters, Wall Street warmongers, and starving masses—and when emigrants like myself were considered traitors. The Technical Museum was a public institution and that a traitor would be allowed to talk there about America was something incredible. The second reason I was flummoxed was, of course, that I was totally unprepared.

We arrived about twenty minutes early so that I'd have time to put the slides in the carousel. We were directed to the main auditorium, which seated three hundred people and which was already half full: people were that starved for news from the West! When the time came for me to come to the podium, the auditorium was full, with a few people standing. I saw in the audience Marian Bělohradský, an old professor of mine from the Academy of Fine Arts, and even after twenty-two years away, I still recognized many other faces. I also noticed a man about my age sitting in the front row, looking at me in a most unfriendly manner.

I thought that the only way out of this pickle was to tell the truth, so I said that there must have been some misunderstanding; some wires must have crossed, because I didn't have any lecture prepared about American contemporary architecture. I explained that I thought I'd be sitting with a small group of my mother's friends around a kitchen table showing slides and talking about them instead of facing an audience of three hundred people. I later realized that in the climate of the time and the place, it was actually perfectly believable that a small meeting could snowball into a three-hundred-person gathering in an auditorium. Folks seemed to understand my predicament, and I felt friendly vibes. Someone called out, "It's OK, Mr. Architect; let's get on with the slides." So I did.

The slides I selected were the most uncontroversial collection of American architecture completed in the 1970s and 1980s. Because postmodernism still reigned supreme, for good measure, next to the fine examples of contemporary buildings, I had thrown in a few postmodern ones, such as Michael Graves's Municipal Building in Portland, Oregon, and Charles Moore's Piazza d'Italia in New Orleans. I stressed that I was showing those postmodern buildings not because I liked them, but as examples of what was being built in America at the time. Predictably, the Czechs had little use for the postmodern stuff, so we were all in agreement.

Throughout my talk, I was aware of the hostile stare coming at me from the man in the first row. Finally, he exploded. I remember it was when I was showing pictures of the Sea Ranch in northern California that he shouted at me mockingly, "Mr. American Architect, do you take us all for idiots? Why are you showing us buildings we are all familiar with?" The room fell quiet. Not knowing what else to say, I addressed the audience: "Is there anyone else who thinks I take you all for idiots?" The whole auditorium roared, "No!" One man shouted, "It is a unique opinion of someone who is an idiot himself." The audience burst out laughing. The man in the front row got up and, with a lugubriously defiant expression, left.

Once folks calmed down, I continued with the slides. Later, I learned that the man was one Milan Knížák, a well-known self-promoter, rabble-rouser, agitator, and provocateur, someone who'd use any occasion to hype himself. After the Velvet Revolution, he became first the director of the Academy of Fine Arts and then of the National Gallery.

There was another incident worth mentioning that took place during the lecture. During the Q&A session after the slides, someone asked me whether there was any building that had been built in Prague since I left that I liked. I responded that I quite liked the new television tower. At that point, another man shot up and said, "Mr. Architect, you are perhaps not aware that what once was a television broadcasting tower has become a jamming tower, jamming the Voice of America and Radio Free Europe, and as such it has become a symbol of the hated regime."

I could not believe what I was hearing. That the man was not afraid to say those words in an auditorium with three hundred people, whom he could not possibly have all known, was something incredible. I would not have been at all surprised if the state security apparatus had sent an agent over to monitor the event. However, this was not the time to ponder this. I responded to the man that I was indeed unaware that the television tower was doubling as a jamming station, but that it didn't change my opinion of its architecture. I later learned that the man was Zdeněk Lukeš, a respected architectural historian and curator. When there were no more questions, the show was over. I sent my mother home and went to have dinner with my old friend Sťopa.

The next morning my mother and I lighted out for Moravia, to a place where she was born and where I spent a big part of my childhood. The factory my grandfather started, which was since nationalized, was still there. We parked my mother's car at the foot of Blue Mountain and started climbing. The weather could not have been better; it was like Indian summer. Blue Mountain is more of a hill than a mountain, so it took us less than an hour to get to the top, where there is a beautiful view. Our hearts beat faster there. We had a little snack at the top and started on our way down. Soon we were at the car and on our way back to Prague. It was a wonderful day.

But now comes the rub. Before we got to the main highway—I was driving—a policeman hailed us down. This was not an unusual occurrence in totalitarian Czechoslovakia; it was just a routine checkpoint. However, my heart sank, because at that moment I realized that my passport was in my suitcase at my mother's apartment and that the only form of identification I had on me was my US driver's license. A scenario of what was going to happen next flashed through my head: I pictured myself spending the night in the Moravian jail while my mother drove to Prague to fetch my passport and then drove back with it on Monday morning. Then I saw myself calling Karen in Vienna to tell her that I would be arriving a day late. And that was the best-case scenario.

But what happened next was yet another sign that the times were a-changin'. I pulled over, rolled down the window, and waited. The policeman came by and asked me for my identification and driver's license. In Czechoslovakia every citizen was, and I believe to this day is, obliged to carry at all times an identification card. I told the policeman that I didn't have an identification card and that I was an American citizen visiting my mother. He asked me for a driver's license, and I gave him my New York State one. He studied it carefully, confirmed that the picture looked like me, and handed it back to me. He did not even ask me for a passport. He looked at my mother and said, "I don't need your identification card because I can see that you are his mother." Then he waved us off. We drove on in silence, both being stunned. After a while, my mother spoke, "I can't believe this. Pinch me. Did it really happen?"

Two days later I was sitting on a train to Vienna, mulling over the events of the last ten days. First, that I got the visa at all was unusual. Then that an emigrant, a traitor, was allowed to talk about American architecture at a public institution was even more astounding. Furthermore, that Zdeněk Lukeš was not afraid to call the television tower a symbol of the hated regime in a crowded auditorium was simply incredible. And lastly, that in the country where everyone is required to carry an identification card at all times, a policeman didn't even ask a visiting emigrant for a passport was something beyond even my imagination. Taken together, all these events seemed to indicate that some change was in the air. It turned out that my hunch was correct, because less than two months later, the Velvet Revolution was under way.

Mrs. Weiner

Strictly speaking, she was not a Mrs., because she never married, but my mother considered addressing an elderly lady as Miss anachronistic, so we called her Mrs. Weiner. Her story was a moving one. When Mrs. Weiner was still a child, sometime before the turn of the twentieth century, her mother became infatuated with an American businessman visiting Prague and eloped with him to Chicago, taking her seven-year-old daughter along and leaving her broken-hearted husband behind.

Even at that tender age, the daughter understood that what had happened was not quite right and, when they reached Chicago, she wrote a letter to her father. Over the next forty-plus years, the daughter and the father continued to write letters to each other. The daughter had not married, the father had not remarried, and at the end of World War II, they found themselves living alone, one in Chicago and the other in Prague. The daughter was then in her midfifties, the father in his late seventies. In 1945, Czechoslovakia was a free country, and no one anticipated that in less than three years it would be separated from the free world by the Iron Curtain. So the father wrote his daughter a letter suggesting that she come back to Prague to live with him, where they could be alone together. The daughter liked the idea and arrived in Prague before Christmas.

Her father died two years after her return to Prague, but she didn't have the presence of mind to return to Chicago, so after the communist take-over of 1948 she found herself trapped and living alone in Prague. (This was the story my mother told me. Thinking about it today, I find it unlikely that the communist government would have kept an American citizen in Czechoslovakia against her will. So perhaps Mrs. Weiner stayed on willingly, thinking, like most people at the time, that the communist nonsense would blow over and things would soon return to normal.) However, because she was a Czech American, the communist authorities considered her highly suspect of engaging in subversive activities and subjected her to frequent interrogations. To make ends meet, she started giving English lessons. I don't know how my mother made her acquaintance, but sometime in the late 1940s she hired Mrs. Weiner as one of my many English tutors. I never knew her first name; for me she was always Mrs. Weiner.

Because I had zero interest in learning English, I did zero studying, and consequently, my progress was close to zero. That did not sit right with Mrs. Weiner, who didn't enjoy teaching a child with no interest in learning. One time, before leaving, she told my mother, "Martin is a very smart child; he just thinks too slowly." When Mrs. Weiner was out the door, my mother hit the ceiling; she asked me, "Do you realize what she meant when she told me that you think slowly? It is a polite way of saying that you are dumb. Is that how you wish to be perceived? If yes, then continue to not study."

I no longer remember if that perfectly sensible admonition changed my behavior, because shortly thereafter, my mother was taken to prison and my English lessons with Mrs. Weiner ceased. However, in retrospect, I think that Mrs. Weiner was correct in her assessment of my abilities, because in general I do think slowly. Quick repartee is definitely not my forte. Whenever I find myself in a confrontational situation requiring an exchange of words, most of the time it is not until the next day and, in some cases, until the next week when I realize with crystal clarity what I should have said. But I am digressing: this is a story about Mrs. Weiner.

The next time she appeared in my life was some seven or eight years later. I was fifteen or sixteen years old and in love with American pop music. The affection that Czech youth had for rock and roll and the blues was enhanced by the fact that, though that music was not forbidden outright, it was frowned on by the communist establishment as something decadent and bourgeois coming at us from the hostile West. Consequently, whenever rock 'n' roll and blues music was played by Czech bands at balls or tea dances, it had to be preceded by an explanation that it was the music of oppressed black people in America.

But what helped more than anything else to heighten the popularity of rock 'n' roll music in Prague in the mid-1950s was an American radio station called Radio Luxembourg. It had nothing to do with Luxembourg, was broadcast from London, and was chiefly aimed at American troops stationed in West Germany. Unlike Radio Free Europe or Voice of America, Radio Luxembourg was not jammed. It played current American pop music nonstop, and it was through this station that we learned about Elvis Presley, Buddy Holly, Fats Domino, the Everly Brothers, Bill Haley, and many other rock musicians. I was thrilled that I could make out some, if not all, of their lyrics—and this is where Mrs. Weiner comes in. But first let me insert a few words about her physique.

Perhaps the reason Mrs. Weiner never married was her size: she was enormous. She was not tall, just exceedingly fat. The sight of her gentle and kind face, with an intelligent expression, on top of that mountain of flesh was quite extraordinary. But because of her warm and bubbly personality, one quickly forgot about her size.

When my mother was released from the communist prison, she took a year to complete her dissertation and obtain her doctorate. Then there followed some three years of hardship, when no one dared to offer her a full-time job, until she landed a position as an art history professor at the Academy of Applied Arts. At that point some people she knew before her imprisonment started drifting back into her life, and among them was Mrs. Weiner—this time not as my English tutor, but as a friend from better times.

When my mother remarried, Mrs. Weiner was from time to time our dinner guest. It was around this time, perhaps in 1955 or 1956, when I got hold of an LP titled *Rock around the Clock* by Bill Haley and the Comets. It was a prized possession, but was not exactly my possession. I had it on loan from my classmate Honza Bílek, whose father was a member of the Communist Party and, as such, was allowed to go on a business trip to West Germany, where he purchased the record for his son. The album was a collection of songs with a seductive, bouncy, rock 'n' roll rhythm that just made you want to dance. I still remember the lyrics of some of the songs: "Down around the corner / In a little school / Children learn a lesson / 'bout the golden rule."

The trouble was there were many lyrics that I didn't understand, and that was when I thought of Mrs. Weiner. I asked my mother if the next time Mrs. Weiner came to dinner, we could play her the record and ask her to write down the lyrics. My mother was thrilled that for the first time in my life, I exhibited an interest in learning English, but at the same time, she was apprehensive that this kind of youthful music would be too much for an old lady in her seventies. Well, she needn't have worried.

The moment I put the record on, Mrs. Weiner started twitching to the rhythm, and then the twitches became jerks, until she couldn't contain herself, got up, and started dancing. The sight of that enormous body shaking to the rhythm of rock 'n' roll could have easily been embarrassingly comical, but Mrs. Weiner managed to remain graceful. Then something came over me. I got up, joined Mrs. Weiner, and the two of us jitter-bugged in the middle of the living room. My mother and the other grown-ups around the table were delighted with this performance. I then played the record again, and Mrs. Weiner was only too happy to write down the lyrics for all the songs on that record. I still have that sheet of paper with the lyrics.

That is the last memory I have of Mrs. Weiner. I no longer remember how, or why, we lost touch with her.

Coincidences

In the fall of 1977, when I was in New York on one of my recharging trips from Tehran, Alicia Legg invited me to dinner. Alicia was a curator at the Museum of Modern Art (MoMA) and a friend of my mother. The reason she invited me was that one of her younger colleagues, Jennifer Licht, also a MoMA curator, had recently returned from a business trip to Tehran and she wanted us to compare notes about the place. Jennifer was English, and once she was done describing the vibrant international art scene in Tehran at the time, she proceeded to regale the dinner guests with another story. She mentioned that on her way back from Teheran, she had made a stopover in London, her hometown. While in London, she was taken by her English friend, an architect whose name I no longer remember, to dinner at the freshly renovated apartment of a Czech couple, both of whom were also architects. My ears pricked up. Jennifer had no idea that I was Czech, and she went on describing that apartment.

It was a very small two-bedroom unit in a recently completed residential development near Marble Arch. Instead of filling a tiny living room with the standard sofa-armchair-coffee table furniture, which would have left little room to move about, the architects did away with furniture altogether; instead, they installed an aluminum rail in the shape of an oval, which was raised about ten inches off the floor. Inside the oval was plush carpeting installed over a thick underlayment, which made for a pleasantly soft floor. Over the carpet were strewn many cushions in the same color as the carpet. Clipped to the aluminum rail were a number of objects: a small TV set, a number of trays serving as side tables for drinks and hors d'oeuvres, and a few lighting fixtures. Guests were invited to take off their shoes and make themselves comfortable inside the oval by propping cushions against the aluminum rail and leaning against them. Jennifer thought that it was quite an ingenious solution for a very tiny space.

At one side of the living room was a small dining alcove just big enough for a table for four or perhaps five diners. The dining table was made of a perforated sheet of aluminum that, when not being used, was folded against the wall. Another memorable feature of the apartment was the entry to the kitchen, which was on the other side of the living room from the dining alcove. It was neither a door nor an opening but a porthole, a concession to the architectural fashion of the time. The porthole entry consisted of an oval opening that began some eight inches above the floor, meaning one couldn't just walk in but had to step over it to enter.

Jennifer then went on describing the dinner party itself. After they were done lounging inside the oval while drinking wine and eating appetizers, the guests were asked to come to the table. Jennifer's friend, who was a little older and more rotund than the other guests, had to be helped to his feet. While at the table, to the embarrassment of the hostess, small objects such as salt-and-pepper shakers and small coffee spoons kept falling through the holes in the perforated aluminum sheet. When they finished the first course, Jennifer's friend tried to be helpful by taking some dirty plates back to the kitchen. However, on his way to the kitchen, he had to pass a narrow passage between the wall and the aluminum rail, tripped over the rail, and fell headfirst into the oval carpeted area. Because of the soft carpet and the many cushions, he didn't get hurt and nothing got broken, but it took a while—helping him get up and picking up the dishes scattered all over the carpet—before they could sit down again and start the main course.

Jennifer was the star of the last act. When the dinner was finished, this time it was she who was taking some dishes back to the kitchen. She managed to negotiate the narrow strait between the wall and the rail; however, presumably due to the amount of wine consumed, she forgot that she had to step over the bottom edge of the porthole entry into the kitchen and tripped over it—sprawling herself and the dishes all over the kitchen floor. Unfortunately, that floor was not as soft as the one inside the oval; it was tiled. Consequently, a number of dishes got broken, and Jennifer badly bruised one of her knees.

Once they were on the street, Jennifer and her friend could not stop laughing over how they managed to turn what was to be an innocuous dinner party into a slapstick comedy. She felt like they were in the Jacques Tati movie *Playtime*. It was only when she got to this moment of telling her story that I said, "Jennifer, you have perfectly described the apartment of my ex-wife Eva and her current partner Jan Kaplický."

The room fell quiet. Jennifer's face went crimson red; she dropped her chin, opened her mouth, then closed it, and started repeating, "Oh, I am so sorry, I am so sorry, I am so sorry," until I had to interrupt her, saying, "Jennifer, you have no reason to be sorry. I left Eva nine years ago and I am glad that she found someone she seems to be happy with." The conversation around the dinner table resumed, and people started guessing the statistical odds of her story being about my ex-wife. Given that there are some eight million people in London and another eight million in New York, the odds would seem to be something like one in 32 million.

Talking of startling coincidences, here is another one. In the spring of 1968, I took a week's vacation from my job in London and went to ski in Switzerland with my mother's cousin Jean Heidler and his wife Paola. At the time, they lived in Geneva, and that winter they were renting a chalet in Verbier, where I joined them. One day when I got separated from Jean and Paola and was skiing by myself down an easy slope leading to the bottom of another lift, someone hit me from behind and we both fell down. While falling, I heard the person who had run into me utter the words *"Do prdele!"* a typical Czech curse that only a native could utter.

When we were both lying on the ground, I turned around and saw that the person who hit me was a man of my father's age, who kept repeating, *"Veuillez m'excuser, monsieur, je suis désolé, veuillez m'excuser."* Being certain that he was my countryman, I addressed him in Czech. In deference to his age, rather than berating him, I indulged in mild sarcasm: "It is a good idea, my dear sir, to ski in control of one's speed." He was obviously delighted to hear me speak Czech, smiled broadly, and replied in Czech, "I am so glad I ran into a countryman. The last time, I hit the Shah of Iran and his bodyguards were not amused. By the way, my name is Pavel Tigrid." I could not believe my ears and stupidly asked, "Are you *the* Pavel Tigrid?" He responded, "Well, I don't know anyone else by that name, so I must be him."

During the Cold War, in Czech émigré circles, Pavel Tigrid was a highly respected publisher of a Czech literary review, *Svedectvi* (*The Witness*), which was published in Paris. It was a bimonthly magazine in which Tigrid published Czech writers who were banned in communist Czechoslovakia. As were most Czech emigrants, I was a subscriber, which I promptly told Mr. Tigrid while we were getting up. He then asked me how I came to be skiing in Switzerland.

Most Czech emigrants at the time had left Czechoslovakia after the communist take-over in 1948 and, consequently, were Mr. Tigrid's age, give or take up to ten years in either direction. Because I was in my late twenties, he was naturally curious and perhaps even suspicious about what I was doing on the west side of the Iron Curtain. Once I told Mr. Tigrid my story and he was satisfied that I wasn't a communist spy, I took the liberty of inviting his wife and him for après-ski drinks at Jean and Paola's chalet. I was sure that they had heard of him and would be interested in meeting him. I was correct on both counts. When I met Jean and Paola for lunch and told them what had happened, they were heartily amused and looked forward to meeting Pavel Tigrid.

It turns out that the story of this particular coincidence had two episodes, of which Pavel Tigrid's running into me while skiing was only the first. The second one unfolded when Pavel and his wife Ivanka entered the chalet. When Jean and Ivanka took a look at each other, they first froze, and then they both shrieked, "Goodness, is that you?" Then they explained that they had been friends in Prague and had not seen each other in more than twenty years. With the Prague Spring under way in Czechoslovakia and the students' demonstrations going on in Paris, there was plenty to talk about, so the Tigrids ended up staying for supper. When they were gone and I was alone with Jean, he confided that he and Ivanka had been more than friends back in Prague.

A footnote: twenty-four years later Pavel Tigrid became the Minister of Culture in Václav Havel's administration of the free Czech Republic.

When I was working in the design department of Kahn & Jacobs Architects in New York, one of my colleagues was a Polish architect named Steven Hildebrand. We were not close friends, but sitting in the same room for over a year, we became well acquainted. After the demise of Kahn & Jacobs in 1971, I heard via the grapevine that Steven had trouble finding another job and that he had moved to France.

Fast-forward seven years to 1978. I had stopped in Paris on my way from Tehran to New York (or from New York to Tehran, I no longer remember) to visit my *petite-amie* Marie-Jose. One day we were walking down Boulevard Saint-Michel when, out of the blue, I saw Steven Hildebrand coming toward us. Naturally, we were both surprised to see each other. Steven said he thought I was in Tehran. I introduced him to Marie-Jose, explained my situation, and asked him what he'd been doing since our Kahn & Jacobs days. He said he had gotten married and was living in Strasbourg, where he was working for a local architectural firm. He was in Paris just for a day, having come that morning on the

TGV and was returning the same evening. We wished each other good luck, shook hands, and continued on our respective ways. After we parted Marie-Jose remarked that, considering that one guy was in Paris on a day trip from Strasbourg while the other one was there stopping over for a few days on his way to (or from) Tehran, the odds of our running into each other must have been infinitesimally low. And she did not even know what happened next.

Fast-forward sixteen more years to 1994. Karen and I were on our first trip together to Paris. On our last day there, we went to see the recently completed American Center by Frank Gehry in Rue de Bercy. While walking around the building we ran into, yes, Steven Hildebrand. I think we were again both equally surprised. After introducing him to Karen, I asked if he was still living in Strasbourg. Yes, he was, and he was again in Paris on a day trip, returning to Strasbourg later that afternoon. The main purpose of this trip was to see Gehry's building. We talked a bit about mutual acquaintances from our Kahn & Jacobs days of almost a quarter century ago, then wished each other good luck, and continued to walk around the building in opposite directions.

Even if we account for the fact that once we were both in Paris on the same day, the chances that we would run into each other at the site of a new building designed by a noted American architect were higher than meeting elsewhere, I find that coincidence extraordinary. But consider the chances alone of the two of us being in Paris on the same day. And that it had happened twice I find beyond extraordinary. Since then, each time I am in Paris I expect to run into Steven Hildebrand, but so far, to my great disappointment, the third meeting has yet to happen.

————————————

When I lived in London, I was good friends with Mark Ransom, who was the head of the glass department at Heals, one of the premier department stores specializing in contemporary furniture, lighting, home furnishings, and accessories. One fall Mark organized at Heals an exhibition of contemporary Finnish glass. Glass design luminaries such as Tapio Wirkkala, Timo Sarpaneva, and Oiva Toikka all participated and attended the opening to which Mark finagled an invitation for me as well. At the time I was already a proud owner of a set of eight Tapio Wirkkala glass tumblers, something I didn't fail to mention when I was introduced to him. I still have two of those tumblers some fifty years later.

It also happened that my best friend during my first years in New York, David Roth, who was also an architect, was married to a Finnish woman by the name of Marja Mustanoja. When they later had a son, they asked me to be his godfather.

Some years later when I was living in Tehran and was to have dinner with Desai, an Indian architect, he called me about an hour before we were to meet and asked if he could bring along a Finnish ceramist; as he put it, she was "a very vivacious young woman." I said I would, of course, be delighted to meet her.

When I arrived at the appointed restaurant, Desai and the young woman were already there. When he introduced her as Elina Sorainen from Finland, just to be funny and to show off my knowledge of Finnish design culture, I responded, "Ah, Tapio Wirkkala, Timo Sarpaneva, Oiva Toikka." And then, just for the hell of it, I threw in the name "Marja Mustanoja."

Elina laughed while I was reciting the names of the designers we both knew, but when I said, "Marja Mustanoja," her face grew stiff, and she said, "What, Marja Mustanoja? She was my high school classmate!" Just to make sure that it was the same Marja Mustanoja, Elina asked if Marja was married to an American architect. I confirmed that she was indeed and added that the American architect was a good friend of mine and that I was the godfather of their son. Would you venture to figure out the odds of something like this happening?

Dora Mazálek, a daughter of my mother's first cousin, has been living with her husband Bogi in Toronto since 1968. They have one daughter Ali, who turned out to be a computer genius. She graduated from the Media Lab at MIT and now holds two IT professorships, one at the University of Toronto and one at Georgia Tech. Her professional brilliance, however, did not extend to her personal life. Seven years ago, she married a man who quickly sired twins and, thereupon, disappeared. At the time of his disappearance Ali was living in Atlanta. To help her take care of the twins, her parents took turns staying with her there.

Dora informed me of these developments sometime in 2011, which was when Sandra appeared in my life and I was visiting her frequently in Knoxville. At the time, Dora and I had not seen each other for more than ten years, and, as Knoxville is only a three-hour drive from Atlanta, I suggested to her that when we were next both in the South, we might meet somewhere halfway between Atlanta and Knoxville, say, in Chattanooga. Over the next three years we kept trying to pull this off, but it just never worked out. On the few occasions when we were both in the South at the same time, either one or the other of us was too busy to take a day off and drive to Chattanooga. Eventually, we stopped trying.

In July 2015 Sandra and I were driving from Knoxville to spend two days in Snowbird Lodge in North Carolina. The lodge is near the town of Robbinsville in the westernmost corner of the state, jutting between Georgia and Tennessee. It is one of the most remote and desolate areas I know of in the eastern United States: there are miles and miles of wooded mountains and nothing else. The road to the lodge was not paved until 1995. Before then, there was a dirt trail that only jeeps could navigate. When we were about halfway between Knoxville and Snowbird Lodge, I received on my iPhone an email from Dora: "Martin, are you by any chance in Knoxville? Ali and I have rented a cabin on a lake in North Carolina, not far from Tennessee, and we'll be here with the twins over the next two weeks. If you happen to be in Knoxville, would you consider coming over for a day of swimming in the lake?"

Sandra was driving, so I responded, asking where exactly in North Carolina was the cabin. It was on a lake near the town of Hayesville. I then looked up Hayesville on Google Maps and, to my astonishment, found that it was less than twenty miles from Robbinsville. So I wrote to Dora that we were on our way to a lodge that was only a half hour from their cabin and suggested we meet for lunch someplace halfway between. We picked a Mexican dive in a little town the name of which I no longer remember. We had a pleasant lunch the following day, and Sandra thus met another of my very few and far-flung relatives.

During lunch, we reflected on the likelihood of such a meeting taking place: that a mother living in Toronto and a daughter living in Atlanta decided to go on vacation and picked a lake—of the thousands in between on which they could have rented a cabin—that was a stone's throw from the lodge in which Sandra and I had chosen to spend a few days. Furthermore, that Sandra and I, who live in New York and come down South only sporadically, chose to do so at the same time Dora and Ali chose to vacation there. Also, that from the huge number of lodges in the Smoky Mountains, we picked the one near Hayesville. Ali the math whiz entered some data into her laptop computer, such as the number of two-week vacation slots in the summer, the number of lakes between Toronto and Atlanta on which one could rent a cabin (we guessed one thousand), the number of days Sandra and I were likely to spend in Knoxville in the summer, and, of those days, how many two-day slots there were for us to pick for our short sojourn in the mountains. After a while, she came up with a likelihood of less than 0.00001 percent that our paths would coincide, meaning there was less than a one in a million chance of all those factors converging and something like that happening.

Sometime in the early 1970s, while my mother was still teaching at the Academy of Applied Arts in Prague, a group of American arts educators visited the school; this was a highly unusual occurrence during the Cold War, but from time to time visits like that happened. Because she was the only one on the faculty who spoke English, my mother was in charge of showing the group around the academy. When she wrote me about it, describing what a breath of fresh air the Americans provided, my mother mentioned that she particularly liked a fellow with a Slavic name, Rudy Osolnik, who was the chairman of the Department of Woodwork and Ceramics at Berea College in Kentucky.

The two of them hit it off, so that my mother invited Mr. Osolnik and his wife to tea at her apartment the following day. At the time I was already making many trips to Tennessee and my mother knew that Kentucky was an adjacent state, so she sent me Mr. Osolnik's card and suggested that the next time I was in Knoxville I should drive to Kentucky to visit him. She told him about me, showed him some of my projects, and Mr. Osolnik said that he'd love to meet me. However, whenever I was in Tennessee, my hands were full designing or teaching so that, although Berea is only a two-hour drive from Knoxville, I never found time to go there, and soon I forgot all about Rudy Osolnik.

Two and a half years later, in 1974, my mother was forcibly retired and, as a retiree, found herself in a category of people who were allowed by the communist regime to travel to the West. (The reason was simple: if they did not return, the regime would save on their pensions.) When she was staying with me on her first visit to the United States, I took my mother along on one of my trips down to Knoxville. At the time, one of my clients in Tennessee was Buck Ewing, the chairman of the Arts Department at the University of Tennessee. I was designing a guesthouse on his property. When he learned that my mother was in town, he invited us to his house for dinner. Knowing that my mother was an art historian, Mr. Ewing added, "We have a houseguest whom I am sure she'd enjoy meeting."

You've probably already guessed that the houseguest turned out to be Rudy Osolnik. Now, think about the chances of that encounter happening: Rudy coming from Kentucky on the day my mother was on her once-in-a-lifetime visit to Knoxville and the two of them meeting at Buck Ewing's house. Needless to say, it was a memorable dinner.

The third time Rudy Osolnik's name appeared on my radar screen was some forty years later. One summer night Sandra and I were staying in a little inn on Fontana Lake in North Carolina. Sitting on the terrace overlooking the lake, we were sipping wine before dinner when we were joined by an elderly couple who too had brought their wine. When we learned that the man was a retired professor of English literature at Berea College, I asked him if by any chance he knew Rudy Osolnik. He told us, "Ah, Rudy! Of course we knew him. A great guy and a good friend of ours. Died about ten years ago."

Stateless in Tehran

Although I was a permanent resident of the United States (in possession of the coveted Green Card), once my Czechoslovak passport expired in 1971, I became stateless. That is the official designation for people without citizenship (i.e., without a passport). To enable its stateless permanent residents to travel abroad, the US government issues them a travel document called a Reentry Permit to the United States. It is a little booklet that is narrower and taller than a regular passport because it is meant not to look like one. To drive home the point, it says on the first page, "This Is Not a Passport. It Is a Permission to Reenter the United States." The second page contains all the information about the bearer that a regular passport would have, and the following pages are left blank for visa stamps. Because not many stateless people travel internationally, not every Passport Control agent is familiar with this document. I found myself often holding up the Passport Control line at the airports while the agent looked for his superior, who would tell him that it was all right to stamp the reentry permit with an entry stamp. It was with this document that I entered Iran in 1975.

During my first few months in Tehran, I became acquainted with a Finnish ceramic artist named Elina Sorainen, whom I mentioned in my earlier chapter on coincidences. She was a lively party girl who had already lived in Tehran several years, was fluent in Farsi, and generally was a star of the expatriate community. The Czechoslovak equivalent of July 4 is October 28, marking the birth of Czechoslovakia from the ashes of the Austro-Hungarian Empire at the end of World War I in 1918. The communist regime continued to honor that day, and somehow Elina finagled an invitation to the embassy of the Czechoslovak Socialist Republic in Tehran for a reception to celebrate the October 28 anniversary.

The fact that at the time Czechoslovakia was a totalitarian communist country was lost on Elina, and knowing that I was a Czech, she asked me to go with her to the reception. I explained to her that I was stateless and, as such, without the protection of the US Embassy; that I had been sentenced in absentia in Czechoslovakia to four years of hard labor for the crime of not returning when my exit visa expired; and that, consequently, I absolutely could not set foot in the Czechoslovak Embassy. Elina was intrigued by all that, but she hatched a solution: "Why don't you come with me incognito? I'll introduce you as a Finnish architect who is visiting me from Finland. How about that?"

Now I was intrigued in turn but still resistant to the idea, believing it to be too dangerous. But Elina was charming and persistent, so eventually I relented and agreed to the subterfuge of going with her to the reception as a Finnish architect. And so we went. I was introduced to the Czechoslovak ambassador as Martin Wirkala.

One of the ironies of communist Czechoslovakia at the time was that it was doing a brisk business with the ultraconservative regime of the Shah of Iran, particularly in the areas of arts and sugar refineries. Consequently, there were in Tehran a number of Czech artists working on the Shah's museum, as well as engineers working on the refineries. These were folks who had been sent to Iran by their employers—that is, by the Czechoslovak government—and it was only natural that they would show up at the reception. Thanks to these people, the atmosphere at the reception was quite congenial.

Attractive Czech waitresses were butlering tasty hors d'oeuvres, champagne flowed amply, and I was hearing Czech spoken all around me. And so it happened that, when a waitress was offering me yet another caviar toast, the word "*děkuji*," which is Czech for "thank you," slipped from my mouth. Perplexed, the waitress asked me how I came to speak Czech. I had the presence of mind to lay another lie on top of the first one, and I told her that a long time ago, my father was a diplomat posted at the Finnish Embassy in Prague, so as a child I spent two years going to a Czech school. That sounded plausible enough, and I was not questioned further.

About an hour into the party, I noticed that the ambassador and the senior diplomats had disappeared, leaving behind some of the junior staff along with the Czech artists and engineers, plus a number of assorted hangers-on from the Tehran expatriate community, such as Elina and myself. The last time I had seen Elina, she was surrounded by a clutch of Czech graphic designers on the far end of the room. Throughout the evening, I had observed a sullen Czech man who didn't mingle, always standing by himself and watching the crowd. I had a feeling that he was watching me.

Sometime after the ambassador left, the engineers and artists burst into singing Czech folk songs, all of which I knew from my childhood. After close to two hours of drinking champagne, I felt pleasantly relaxed and joined the singing. No one questioned my provenance anymore; that I was supposed to be a Finnish architect was totally forgotten. All of a sudden, a man who looked familiar came up to me and said in Czech, "Goodness, Martin, what are you doing here? I thought you were in America." I recognized Mr. Souček, my former boss from the Konstruktiva office in Prague.

I explained that I was indeed living in New York, but that I was working temporarily in Tehran. Mr. Souček was the one who had approved my unpaid leave for my first year in London and then again for the second year, when I asked for an extension after the Russian invasion. So although he was a member of the Communist Party, he was a good sort. He was now posted in Iran to supervise the construction of one of the sugar refineries designed by Konstruktiva.

Eventually, someone sat down at the piano, and a smaller group formed around it, including Elina and the graphic artists with whom she was by now extremely chummy. With my cover completely blown, I joined in, and we continued singing and drinking. The atmosphere was very congenial, the singing making everyone feel a little homesick. Out of the blue, the sullen man who I thought was watching me appeared and addressed the group, pointing out that the reception was scheduled from 7 until 9 p.m. I looked at my watch and was shocked to see that it was close to 11 p.m. It took me some time to disentangle Elina from her new friends, but soon we said our good-byes and were on our way out.

It wasn't until the next morning when I fully realized how reckless I had been the previous night. My behavior was a textbook example of how alcohol can dim one's judgment. When I told my mother about it later, I thought she would have a heart attack. "Did you realize, you dimwit," she asked, "that the embassy you were in was a Czechoslovakian territory? That as a stateless person without the protection of any country, you could have easily been detained and then shipped back to Prague?" She could not believe what stupid behavior her son was capable of. In hindsight, it was perhaps the dumbest thing I've ever done and another instance of my guardian angel watching over me.

First Time Out

Isolation breeds naïveté, so at the time I was living in communist Czechoslovakia, I was truly convinced that the only thing that kept me from designing buildings of the caliber I saw in the Western architectural magazines was my being on the wrong side of the Iron Curtain. This firmed up my resolve to do everything possible to get to practice architecture in the West. To that end, after graduating from the School of Architecture in 1962, I kept applying for any employment or stipend in the West I could find. Through a German architect I met in Prague, I was offered a job with an architectural firm in Munich. Next I applied for and was granted a stipend for a year of postgraduate study at Brown University in Rhode Island. Then I answered an ad in *Architecture Aujourd'hui* and was offered a job with a firm in Paris. Similarly, I was offered a job in Rotterdam and in Stockholm. But all to no avail, because I was never allowed to leave the country.

When a citizen of communist Czechoslovakia wanted to go abroad, he or she needed an exit visa, which would be granted or denied by the Ministry of Interior. Because Czechoslovak currency was useless beyond its borders, an application for an exit visa had to be accompanied by an invitation from an individual or an institution, confirming that he/she/it would cover all expenses in connection with the applicant's stay abroad. In each of the above instances, I applied for the exit visa with a copy of a letter offering me employment or a stipend, and each time I received from the Interior Ministry a notice informing me that my application was denied, because my "trip was not deemed to be in the best interest of the Czechoslovak Socialist Republic." The same language was used in all of the denial notices.

I appealed all the denials and, in due course, received denials of all the appeals. Each of the denials of the appeals contained this sentence: "The decision is final; no further appeal is possible." It became a sport for me: filing an application, receiving the denial, appealing the denial, receiving a denial of the appeal.

Meanwhile, as the political climate was becoming milder, more and more of my friends and colleagues were managing to finagle invitations from the West and to receive exit visas for trips beyond the Iron Curtain. Even my wife Eva was able to go to Paris for a UIA (Union Internationale des Architectes) convention. I knew the reason for all those denials of my exit visa applications: there were just too many strikes against me.

I was the wrong class origin. My grandfather on my mother's side was a wealthy industrialist, so my family was in the category of "enemy of the people." In addition, many of our relatives (my grandmother, my uncle, and three of my mother's cousins) had escaped and were living in the West. And although she was not convicted of any crime, to have a mother who had spent time in the communist prison left another bad mark on my dossier. Finally, my opinions of the communist regime were well known. Consequently, all those denials were not altogether surprising. Still, I felt increasingly frustrated, like a wild animal in a cage.

In the fall of 1966 a group of German students arrived in Prague. They were the first part of an exchange trip between the Academy of Fine Arts in Prague and the Kunstakademie in Düsseldorf. I managed to get included in the group of Czech students from the academy who were to go to Düsseldorf the following year. For an exchange trip, people did not apply for exit visas individually, but the academy applied for the whole group. I thought that, with my name hidden among some fifteen other names, there was a chance that the Interior Ministry might overlook it and I'd get to go.

Because I was the only one from our group who spoke a modicum of German, I became an unofficial contact person between our students and the Germans during the week of their stay in Prague. We hit it off. They loved Czech beer, so after seeing the numerous cultural sites, each day we ended up in one of Prague's many pubs or bars. The Germans had a great time and were genuinely looking forward to returning our hospitality when we'd go to Düsseldorf a few months later.

It turned out, however, that I had miscalculated the chances of my being able to go to Germany. A few weeks after the German students departed, I was notified by the presidium of the Czech Academy that it had received from the Interior Ministry the exit visa for the group but that my name was crossed out from the list. I could not go. As always, with no hope but as a matter of principle, I filed an appeal.

Meanwhile, the group of our students minus me went to Düsseldorf and had already returned. They reported that the first question the welcoming Germans asked on their arrival was "Where is Martin?" When the Czech group told the Germans that I wasn't allowed to come, there was stunned silence. Each of the Germans had a relative, a friend, or an acquaintance living in East Germany, so they understood what life under communism was like.

A few months after filing the appeal, I found an envelope from the Ministry of Interior in my mailbox. I thought I knew what to expect, so you can imagine my shock when I opened it and read that my appeal was processed favorably, and I was hereby notified that if I took this letter along with my passport to the Ministry, they would stamp it with an exit visa for a one-week trip to West Germany. I could not believe it. Maybe it was a mistake? My friends allowed for the possibility of a mistake and advised me to move fast before it was discovered.

The first thing I did was to call Professor Hoehme at the Kunstakademie in Düsseldorf. He had accompanied the group of students that visited Prague, and after one drunken evening, he and I came to be on a first-name basis. I told him what had happened and asked if I could come straightaway to Germany. He said, "Absolutely, come as soon as you can." A half hour later Hoehme called back, said that he had spoken to the president of the Kunstakademie, and instead of the agreed-upon one week, they decided to fund my stay for two weeks. And even better, I'd be staying at his house instead of in the student dorm!

So I grabbed the letter and my passport and rushed to the visa section of the Interior Ministry, wondering along the way how to extend my exit visa from one to two weeks. The clerk at the counter turned out to be a pleasant-looking older woman. I told her my story; she was sympathetic to my plight and wrote "15 days" on my visa stamp. I then ran to the visa section of the West German

Embassy. After showing them the letter from the Interior Ministry and telling them that this was to be my first trip out after five years of trying, my passport was stamped with an entry visa on the spot. Thus in a little over four hours since I had opened the letter, I was ready to go. To say that I was elated would only partially describe my state of mind: I had to pinch myself to make sure that I was not dreaming.

But before I left I had to make a few practical decisions. Because I now had two weeks to roam about West Germany instead of one, I decided to drive instead of taking a train, which would give me more flexibility of movement. To drive from Prague to Düsseldorf takes about seven hours, two of which are within Czechoslovakia. To use the time allotted to me in the West most efficiently, I decided to start driving that same night, stay overnight in a motel near the border, get up early the next day, cross the border, and be on my way to Düsseldorf.

There was one last knotty issue to tackle. During the communist era, it was illegal for Czech citizens to own Western currency. While the German students were in Prague, one night one of them had run out of Czech crowns and had asked me if I could let him have some crowns in exchange for German marks. Although it was illegal to do so I had happily obliged. That is how I came into the illegal possession of sixty German marks. Naturally, I wanted to take those marks with me on my trip. The question was where to hide them.

Given my history, it was reasonable to expect that I would be searched at the border crossing by the Czech border guards. My wife, mother, and I mulled over all the possible places to hide the sixty marks, until we settled on the following. I would roll up those three bank notes into a tight roll and insert it inside a buttered bun with some salami. I would then put that snack inside a clear plastic bag, which I would leave on the passenger seat in plain sight while going through the border crossing. We thought it would look so innocuously natural that no guard would think of looking inside the bun.

I executed the plan exactly. Don't forget that still hovering over my head was the possibility that the exit visa was given by mistake, which might soon be discovered, in which case all border crossing posts between Czechoslovakia and West Germany would be alerted not to let me through. To minimize that possibility, I left that same evening and checked into a motel in Rozvadov, the nearest small town to the border crossing. The next morning I got up at 6 a.m., and a little before 7 a.m., with my heart beating fast, I pulled up to the gate at the border.

Four guards surrounded my car. They looked glum and bored, but not unfriendly. They asked me to open the trunk, the only words spoken. They looked inside rather perfunctorily and, amazingly, that was all. I handed over my passport, which they stamped with the date, the hour, and the minute of my crossing—and I was waved on! The bun with the sixty marks inside it attracted no attention. Some two hundred feet down the road was the West German border gate. What a difference! The guards were in good humor; one of them looked in my passport to make sure that I had an entry visa and then said, "Welcome to Germany." I was on my way.

So finally, at long, long last, I was in the West. I drove through the first village with its neat, clean, freshly whitewashed houses that looked markedly different from the drab village houses in the Czech lands at the time, and then it sank in: I was really in the West. For the first and only time in my life, I started hyperventilating. I only learned later that is what involuntary, rapid breathing is called. I pulled up by the side of the road, got out of the car, and for the next half hour or so I walked in the meadow by the side of the road until my breathing steadied. Then I drove on. That's what communism did to a grown man. I was twenty-eight at the time.

I drove through Nuremberg, stopped for lunch in Mainz, and by midafternoon arrived at the Kunstakademie in Düsseldorf, where I received a hero's welcome. Professor Hoehme told me that later that night there would be a reception in my honor at the president's house. I was clearly being treated as a victim of communism. Describing the following two weeks of driving around West Germany with Kunstakademie students as my guides would be another story. On the night before my exit visa expired, I crossed the border back to Czechoslovakia.

After this first venture to the free world, the second and the last one followed four months later. Without anyone knowing it at the time, the makings of the Prague Spring, which was to occur the following year, were clearly under way. What better proof of it could there be than the following: Shortly after returning from West Germany, I learned via the grapevine about an architectural firm in London that was known to hire architects from abroad. I applied for a job, was offered one, then applied for an exit visa for a year's stay in England, and—to my utter astonishment—was granted it. What was I to make of it? Only a half a year earlier, I was not allowed to go for a one-week trip to West Germany, and now I could go for one whole year to England? But instead of pondering the reasons behind this amazing development, I packed up, left for England, and arrived in London on August 21, 1967.

At the time, I was convinced that a year later I'd be back in Prague. Or, when I let my imagination run wild, I thought that if things in London went swimmingly well, I might apply for an extension of the exit visa for another year. Two years in London were the ultimate bliss that I could imagine at the time. Although there were signs of mellowing, of which my one-year exit visa was one, at the time, no one anticipated the full swing of Prague Spring several months later, nor its brutal squashing by Soviet invasion exactly a year to the day after my arrival in London. Once I saw Soviet tanks rolling down the streets of Prague, it didn't take much imagination then not to return.

Once in London, I applied for an extension of my exit visa, which was granted, and ditto a year later. And I applied again yet another year later when I was already in the United States and knew full well that I would not be returning anytime soon to the Czechoslovak Socialist Republic, where "normalization" was in full progress. Still, for the sake of my parents, I applied at the Czechoslovak Embassy in Washington, DC, for another extension. In response to my application, I received a letter from the embassy, which is translated as follows:

Esteemed Mr. Holub:

In response to your application, we wish to inform you not only that any further extension of your exit visa is out of the question but that your last extension given in London was invalidated by the Interior Ministry's directive no. xxxx, which presently renders you staying abroad without the consent of the Czechoslovak Authorities. We appeal to you to return to the Czechoslovak Socialist Republic with the swiftest dispatch you are capable of. Upon your return, you are to report to the Interior Ministry within three days of your arrival.

Sincerely yours,

Signed Director of Visa Section

I still have that letter. It was the last contact I had with the Czechoslovak authorities. Some three years later, my mother was notified that her son was sentenced in absentia to four years of hard labor for the crime of not returning after his exit permission expired.

Advocate

Everyone needs an advocate from time to time, but it seems to me that architects need them more than most. There was a time in the late 1960s when Vincent Scully, a professor of the history of architecture at Yale and a well-known author and lecturer on architectural history, never ended a lecture, no matter on what subject, without remarking that the best living architect in America was Robert Venturi. Robert Venturi then had under his belt a house he designed for his mother and a book he wrote called *Complexity and Contradiction in Architecture*. And that was all. To make a living, he had to teach. However, if someone of Vincent Scully's caliber continued to promote you consistently over a sustained period of time, people would eventually take notice. We'll never know if Robert Venturi would have achieved the renown he eventually had without Vincent Scully's advocacy.

The closest I ever came to having an advocate was in the person of Jonathan Barnett. Jonathan was one of the principal architects at the Urban Design Group, which was set up in the New York City Department of Planning during John Lindsay's administration and was tasked with revising the zoning book of New York City. Uncharacteristically for a city agency, it happened to be staffed by a group of extraordinarily gifted and dedicated individuals. One of their legacies that continues to this day is incentive zoning, whereby in exchange for providing some useful public amenity, such as a park or a playground, a developer gets to build a few more floors of his apartment or office building. Thus the developer gets to make more profit by selling more apartments or office space, and the public gets an amenity it would otherwise not get: a win-win situation all around.

In 1971 when I was let go from Kahn & Jacobs and was looking around for another design job, someone suggested that I call the Urban Design Group. I did, arranged for an interview, and when I showed up, the person who interviewed me was Jonathan Barnett. I was then thirty-two years old, and Jonathan was perhaps ten years older. When he leafed through my portfolio, I sensed that he liked what he saw, but at the same time he surmised that preparing zoning laws would probably not be my cup of tea. As he told me later, he thought mine was a portfolio of someone who wanted to design buildings that would be built. So he asked me if I was familiar with what the Urban Design Group did. I said that all I knew was that they were working on revising zoning laws. He said that was mostly what they did, but that from time to time there might be some design study to be prepared; however, the purpose of such studies would be to demonstrate the effect of the zoning they were proposing and not to build something. While he was talking, what was going through my mind was this thought: "I might as well have stayed in Prague, where I was designing one study after another for buildings that were not getting built."

Jonathan must have been reading my mind because, after some discussion of projects in my portfolio, he said, "Look, I think you'd be much happier with a firm where you could be working on projects to be built, but if you don't find such a job, you can always come back here and we'll take you in." I thought that was an extraordinarily magnanimous offer, and I was profoundly grateful for it. As things developed, I did not return; although I did not find another full-time position, several design consulting assignments came my way, and I forever left the employment track. Three years later I left for Tehran but kept in touch with Jonathan Barnett. We were both members of the Architectural League and often met at its functions. The subsequent city administration dissolved the Urban Design Group, and eventually, Jonathan found himself working for a large developer; I think it was Arlen Realty. Among other things, that company developed the Museum Tower on top of the Museum of Modern Art.

While in Tehran, I met Jack Robertson, an internationally known American architect and planner, who was at the time working for the Shah, designing a master plan for a new district of Tehran. This came about when Mehdi Karabekian, a young Iranian architect who used to work at my office in Tehran and then for Jack Robertson's firm, decided that Mr. Robertson and I should meet. I was fond of Mehdi, so even though I had no idea what good could come out of my meeting Mr. Robertson, to please Mehdi I said yes. An opportunity presented itself at the Iran-American Society, where Mr. Robertson was scheduled to deliver a lecture about his project and Mehdi was helping him arrange his slides. Before I could take my seat for the lecture, Mehdi came rushing to me and led me to the back of the room where Jack Robertson was fiddling with the slide projector. He said to him, "Mr. Robertson, this is Martin Holub, whom I told you about."

Everyone is a little nervous before delivering a lecture, including even Jack Robertson, which perhaps caused him to let his guard down and not be as polite as he usually was. With several pointed questions, he determined that I was neither a potential employee, nor a potential client, nor even a connection to a client. Having thus concluded that I was of no use to him, he said, "Nice to meet you," and turned back to the slide projector. Clearly, the audience was over. I replied that the pleasure was mine and went to sit down. Mehdi observed the scene in bewilderment.

After Khomeini's 1979 revolution, approximately 100,000 Americans working in Iran all had to leave in an unseemly haste, and that included Jack Robertson and me. Once again, I found myself in New York looking for work. Among other contacts, I called Jonathan Barnett to ask if he had any leads for me. He was still working for Arlen Realty, and to my great surprise, he said, "Well, Martin, as it happens, I might have an idea for you. Have you heard of Jack Robertson?" I told Jonathan that I had not only heard of him but actually met him. His response: "Well, he is now working for Arlen on a variety of projects and I think it would behoove you to meet him. I'd be happy to arrange a meeting." I told Jonathan that I didn't see what good could come out of meeting Jack Robertson a second time, but he was insistent. Robertson had a number of projects he was involved in, and Jonathan thought it was possible that he might send a smaller one my way. So I thanked Jonathan and told him that I'd be glad to meet Jack Robertson once more.

What followed was a replay with only minor variations of my meeting with Mr. Robertson some three years earlier in Tehran. When I showed up at Arlen's offices on the Avenue of the Americas, I was ushered into a small conference room. In short order, Jonathan walked in with Jack Robertson in tow. After a quick introduction, I asked Mr. Robertson if he remembered our meeting in Tehran. He looked at me blankly, his face showing not the slightest sign of recognition. After a while he collected himself and said that he did recall our meeting, when it was obvious that he did not. Jonathan mentioned that during the four years I had spent in Iran, I had designed a number of projects there and asked Jack if he was interested in seeing my Iranian portfolio. What could he say? Mr. Robertson began looking at my portfolio, but it was clear to me that Jonathan was more interested in my work than he was. When he finished, he said, "Nice work. Thank you for coming over." Then he got up, we shook hands, and Mr. Robertson left the room. Jonathan and I looked at each other; he shrugged his shoulders and said, "You just never know, Martin, what may come of it." Then we went out and had a fine lunch at Trattoria Dell'Arte.

The next and last piece of advocacy that Jonathan Barnett performed on my behalf was introducing me to John Portman. After leaving Arlen Realty, Jonathan wrote a book titled *The Architect as Developer*. It was about John Portman, the Atlanta architect known for designing flamboyant hotels with tall interior atria. Portman was also one of the first architects to develop his own projects. During the writing of the book Jonathan spent a lot of time in Atlanta, and the two men got well acquainted. At the same time, Jonathan got to observe Portman's organization, both its architectural and its development arms, up close.

Sometime after the book was published and well received, Jonathan conceived the idea that John Portman and I would benefit from meeting each other. He said that he had already mentioned me to him and that Portman expected me to call him. When I called Portman's office in Atlanta and said that I was phoning at the suggestion of Jonathan Barnett, I was instantly connected with Mr. Portman. He knew exactly who I was, said that Jonathan sang my praises, told me that he'd be in New York the following week, and asked whether I would be available for breakfast next Wednesday at 8 a.m. in the Edwardian Room of the Plaza Hotel. All that in one sentence! When I replied that I'd be happy to have breakfast with him, Portman quickly added, "And bring your portfolio. See you there." And then he hung up. The whole conversation took less than two minutes.

That was the only power breakfast of my life. When I showed up at the Edwardian Room five minutes before eight, the receptionist told me that Mr. Portman was expecting me and led me to a small booth. The most impressive feature of John Portman's appearance was his hairdo. It turned from the back to the front of his head, not in a straight line but with sideways sweeps, and yet it stayed miraculously in place. I remember that Mr. Portman ordered soft-boiled eggs. During breakfast, we talked about my work in Iran. Mr. Portman leafed through my portfolio, studying it far more closely than Jack Robertson had some three years earlier. He asked questions. What material was that? Where was the second means of egress? How do you get from the garage to the lobby? Why didn't you use the same concrete finish as you did over here? And he listened to my explanations. When he was about halfway through, he closed the portfolio and said, "I want you to come to Atlanta." Then he took a small blank card from his pocket, wrote a name and a phone number on it, and told me to call when I was ready to arrange my trip. Mr. Portman got up, and we shook hands. That was the last time I saw him. The whole audience took less than a half hour.

My trip to Atlanta was the first time I flew business class. I arrived the night before my appointment and checked into the Portman-designed Peachtree Hyatt Hotel on Peachtree Street. The next morning, I walked along Peachtree Street to the high-rise office building where John Portman Enterprises took up several floors. The receptionist led me to the managing director of the architectural office, whose name I no longer remember—let's call him Mr. Jones. He was an amiable chap without any pretense that he was anything but an administrator. He showed me around the architectural studios full of white-shirted architects. In the South, at the time, the architect's uniform was still a white shirt and tie. There were more than sixty architects in that office.

After the tour of the studios, Mr. Jones took me back to his office and said, "I am going to start you at $50,000." I was shocked: in 1982 that was a very nice offer for an architect. Yet I hadn't come to Atlanta to get a job. I told Mr. Jones that I was looking for a project, not for employment. Now it was Mr. Jones's turn to be shocked. Not trying to disguise his amazement, he asked me, "Does John know this?" I said that during our short meeting it had not come up, but that I had assumed that Mr. Portman knew from Jonathan Barnett that I worked on a per-project basis as a design consultant for other offices.

At the mention of Jonathan's name, Mr. Jones perked up, and then he continued, "I am sorry for the misunderstanding about your role here. I don't even have to talk to John about this. I run his architectural office, and I can tell you we've never had a design consultant here. If you want a job, you can start tomorrow, but no consulting." I told Mr. Jones that even if I wanted a job, I could not start tomorrow as I had several projects on the drawing boards that I'd have to finish first. Mr. Jones said that they would be happy to wait for me to wipe my slate clean before starting my employment with John Portman Architect.

At that moment a thought flashed through my mind: What if I did take that job for a couple of years? I'd keep my apartment with an office in New York, I'd rent a pied-à-terre in Atlanta, and chances are I'd get to design larger projects than I could generate by myself. With those projects under my belt, I might then be able to get similar projects on my own. So I said to Mr. Jones, "May I ask a question? Suppose I take this job. Then suppose I design a project that gets published. Could I expect a byline, something like, 'Designed by Martin Holub of John Portman Architect'?" The response was swift: "NO WAY. We all here work for John Portman and are proud of it. If you could not work within that context, there is no place for you in this company." I told Mr. Jones that, unfortunately, he was right: there was no place for me there. We parted amicably, and I took a cab to the airport.

The next morning, I called Jonathan Barnett and reported on what occurred in Atlanta. Jonathan responded, "Oh, you should have insisted on speaking to John before you left. He might have been more broad-minded." Might have been, but we'll never know.

Scared in Times Square

In the spring of 1971, I was preparing for the architecture license exams. Yes, although I had already had nine years of experience since graduation and many designs under my belt, in America I couldn't even call myself an architect unless I had a license to practice. So I had to take the license exams. They consisted of a total of seven exams, one of which was structural design. An enterprising structural engineer, Mr. Hoffberg, was giving classes in structural calculations aimed, specifically, at helping architects prepare for the structural part of the exam. Generations of New York architects had taken Hoffberg classes, and I was one of them. The classes were held once a week on Wednesdays from 6:00 to 7:30 p.m. in the Hotel Iroquois on West 44th Street. It so happened that on this particular Wednesday, during my lunch break, I had bought a pair of shoes, so that when I was walking after class along 44th Street toward the subway station in Times Square, in addition to my briefcase, I was carrying a shoebox under my arm.

Before I crossed Sixth Avenue near Times Square, a slight, short, black man who looked like Sammy Davis Jr. asked me if I could spare a quarter, something not at all unusual in New York City. As always in such situations, I responded that I could not. What was unusual, however, was that the guy did not move away but started walking beside me, repeating, "C'mon, man, you can spare a quarter, cain't you?"

Still, I didn't feel at all threatened because, first, the guy was of slight build, much shorter than me, and walked with a bit of a limp; second, the sidewalk was full of people. By now, we had crossed Sixth Avenue, and the guy was continuing to limp by my side, muttering something about the quarter. Then, all of a sudden, he snatched the shoebox from under my arm and, his limp notwithstanding, started running away. I easily caught up with him and grabbed the box back. To my amazement, the guy started shrieking, "Gimme that box! It's my box; he took my box!"

I then began walking as fast as I could toward Times Square, with the guy on my heels and shrieking, "Gimme that box!" No one paid much attention. But I started to panic and did something stupid. When we reached Times Square, I saw two black vendors standing behind a table full of tourist tchotchkes. I turned to them and said, "Can you guys help me? This man here is bothering me." One of the peddlers gave me a cold, unconcerned look and told me, "Give him that box; it's his box." I walked away and, in a full-blown panic, shouted at the top of my lungs, "Can anybody please help me?"

It was Times Square in the rush of pretheater, sidewalks overflowing with throngs of people. A few of them turned their heads, looked at me, and kept on walking. The little black man kept on shrieking, "Gimme that box!" I was looking around hoping to catch sight of a policeman, but no cop was in evidence. Suddenly I saw a taxi with its light on, so I promptly flagged it down. The cab pulled up and I got in. However, my pursuer was also quick, and just before I could close the door, he grabbed hold of it, preventing me from closing it. Cleverly, he stood on the other side of the door, holding it fully open, so that the only way for me to push him away was to get out of the cab, which was something I didn't want to do.

Now we come to the theater-of-the-absurd part of this story. While I was sitting in the cab, the guy, supremely confident and composed and still holding the door open, kept repeating, "Come out of det car and gimme me det box. You ain't going nowhere befo you gimme det box." To make things more interesting, the cab driver shouted, "Shu de doo o git out; I ain't drivin' with da open doo." Caught in the middle, I pleaded with the driver, "Can you just please get me out of here? Don't you see that this man is bothering me?" The driver responded, "Shu de doo," while the black guy kept demanding that I get out of the cab and give him my shoebox.

But I stayed in the cab, playing for time, hoping to see a cop. Meanwhile, masses of people were moving in both directions along the sidewalk. No one paid any mind to the little drama by the curbside. The whole thing probably didn't take more than a couple of minutes, but it seemed like an eternity. Suddenly and inexplicably, the Sammy Davis Jr. look-alike let go of the door and disappeared into the crowd. Perhaps he saw a cop moving in our direction or someone else he did not want to meet: who knows? Finally, I was able to close the door of the cab and we drove off. This incident—along with the one I described in "A Close Call"—is one of only two instances during my forty-eight years in New York City when I felt in physical danger.

Karen

I met Karen in the summer of 1979 in Westhampton. She had rented a cottage on the beach, with her friend Becky, and I was staying in a group summer house with a bunch of friends and acquaintances. New York City single folks flock to the Hamptons in the summer not only for the splendid beach but also for the garden parties. So that its residents can be invited to these parties, each group house throws one party per summer. This creates a scene where there is at least one party to go to each weekend. Most of the group houses are on properties with big lawns, so the parties are typically outdoors; hence the famous Hamptons garden parties.

On the Saturday in July when it was our house's turn to throw a party, it was raining, which rendered a lawn party not feasible. We had no choice but to move the party indoors, but fortunately the house was plenty big. Crashing a group house party is easy, because if someone appears at the door whom you don't know, you automatically assume that it is a friend of one of your housemates, which was precisely what I thought when two attractive young women, one blond and one brunette, entered our living room. And so as I was standing nearby, instead of asking whom they knew, I asked them what they would like to drink. Once I had served them drinks, we started conversing. After introductions, it turned out that the brunette was Karen and the blond was Becky. I remember being impressed with how Karen spoke in measured, full sentences.

It wasn't until about a half hour into our conversation, after our basic personal coordinates were established, that I ventured to ask the question of whom they knew in the house. Karen answered, "Nobody. We were driving around looking for a party, saw a critical mass of cars outside your house, and decided to crash."

I was charmed by her honesty. And that's how we met—by Karen crashing my group house party. However, the sparks were decidedly not flying at the time. Even worse, we took a dim view of each other's existence. As we confessed to one another many, many years later, I was at that time naïve enough to truly believe that only someone who was not smart enough to become a scientist, doctor, lawyer, journalist, engineer, architect, and so forth would work for a giant corporation such as the management consulting firm Karen was employed by; Karen was naïve enough to truly believe that a freelance architect could only be someone who was not smart enough to work for a corporation or an investment bank. I am exaggerating only slightly: neither of us was that naïve, but nevertheless we held a strong hint of those views.

And so over the next seven years, we remained distant acquaintances. When we ran into one another on the beach, we'd sit down and talk; when we met at a Westhampton discothèque, we'd dance. We also exchanged Christmas cards. Once when my Tehran buddies Tom and Charlie were visiting me and we were planning to go out to dinner, they asked for female company. I hit my phone book and started calling all the women to see if any might be available on short notice to join us. When I came to the *K*'s, I called Karen, and she was free and happy to join us. We had a pleasant evening. Another time Karen invited me to a party for Becky's birthday. But that was the total extent of our social intercourse over those seven years. Neither of us felt motivated to call the other and make our contact more frequent.

Then in the fall of 1985 I printed the second edition of my office brochure and, of course, sent it to everyone in my Rolodex. That included Karen, and astonishingly, she was the only one who called me and thanked me for sending it to her. At that time, we probably had not seen each other for over two years, so we had a long chat. The shocking news was that Becky had died of a brain tumor earlier that year. I was once again reminded of Karen's precise way of talking, with no superfluous words.

At the end of our conversation, I asked her if she'd like to have dinner with me. She said she'd be happy to, so we both opened our calendars trying to come up with a date when we both had a free evening. It was mid-November, and the earliest night we could find was two months later, on January 23, 1986. It's amazing what dates one remembers! When that day neared, I called and asked Karen if she'd like to go to a restaurant or would she rather have dinner at my apartment. She was eating out all the time and said that having dinner in someone's house was always a treat. We agreed she'd come over at 8 p.m.

I was busy at the time, both professionally and socially, and my search for the right woman was in high gear. So this dinner with Karen was no big deal; it was just one of many such meals. When the day came, I bought some fine cheeses and pâtés at Zabar's and prepared to cook linguine al pesto and make a tomato and onion salad. I still remember that for dessert I served Pepperidge Farm Milano cookies. And, of course, it was all washed down with a fine Côtes du Rhone. We had a nice evening full of lively conversation, ranging from the meaning of life to the books we'd read, movies we'd seen, and trips we'd taken. There was absolutely no flirtation, no footsies, nothing of the kind. Karen was dressed like a suburban matron; her fashion sense at the time was not very sophisticated, but I didn't mind, because I didn't think of her as a potential romantic interest. Close to midnight Karen announced that it was a school night and that she had to go home. I walked her to Central Park West where she hailed a cab.

In those days, my MO relative to women was to take the first step, such as inviting the woman I wanted to get to know to dinner and then, having expended the time and money, I would lean back and wait to see what would happen next. I have not kept records, but I'd venture to guess that more than half of the women I treated to dinner did call back and said something to the effect of "Thank you for dinner; I had a good time." And perhaps half of those who did call and thank me would add, "The next time is on me," or something along those lines. That left a vast number of women who never called me back. The frightening thought is that if Karen had not called me after our dinner, we'd have missed all those wonderful years we were to spend together. But then again, if she had not called, she would not have been Karen, who turned out to be as far from a "princess" as a woman can get.

So the day after our dinner, Karen did call and told me how much she enjoyed our evening and that the next time was on her. I was glad that she wanted to have a next time, and once again we both hit our calendars to find a mutually convenient date. This time, instead of two months ahead, we found a date in late February, some four weeks later. I remember our second dinner was in an Italian restaurant on the Upper East Side that no longer exists. And so started a series of dinners, always in restaurants (except for the first one), and as the dates grew ever so slightly closer together, we were growing ever so slightly closer as well. One dinner during that period stands out in my memory. It must have been dinner number six or seven, because it was already warm enough to sit outside.

In my long search for the right woman, I had grown allergic to women who considered it their birthright that the man always pays. I was happy to note that Karen didn't belong to that category. Without saying anything, we alternated in paying the bills, as we did in picking the restaurants. During this particular dinner, it was my turn to pay. Imagine my horror when the check arrived, and I pulled out my wallet and saw that my credit card was not in it! I then remembered that in the afternoon, I was buying something over the phone and must have neglected to put my card back in the wallet after giving the merchant the card number. Profoundly embarrassed, I told Karen what had happened. To this day I remember how impressed I was with the sincere grace and ease with which Karen handled the situation. She matter-of-factly took the check and pulled out a card from her wallet, saying, "Martin, don't even think about this; it is a nonissue."

Throughout all those dinners, nothing physical happened between us. A peck on the cheek when meeting and saying good-bye was all. We didn't become intimate until late July, more than six months after our first dinner. We were dining in La Petite Marmite, a French restaurant on East 49th Street. I dined there so often that I had an account there. After dinner, we were in a very pleasant mood as we walked up First Avenue and held hands for the first time, and I felt moved to say, "If you asked me to come home with you, I'd be happy to oblige." Karen swiftly responded, "Consider yourself asked," and hailed a cab.

This was the first time I ever set foot in Karen's apartment. If someone had told me then that I would be living there in five years' time, I would have thought they were out of their mind. The apartment looked terrible: it was an architect's nightmare. The color scheme was green and yellow. The wallpaper pattern matched the sofa upholstery. There was shag carpeting in the bedroom: horror! Karen's saving grace was that she knew it was bad. She explained that she and her ex-husband had hired a decorator when they first moved to the apartment fourteen years earlier, and nothing had been done to it since. She'd been meaning to have it redone but just hadn't gotten around to it.

Nothing much changed after that night; the frequency of our dinners did not accelerate much, and both of our calendars continued to be full. The only difference was that, after each dinner, we would spend the night at Karen's or my apartment. I did not suspend my search for the right woman and continued to see the Polish artist Ewa, whom I had started seeing a year earlier. And I had no idea whom Karen was seeing in between our dinners. Sometime in late August, we took a weekend trip to a beach resort on Shelter Island. It was the first time we were together for more than just one night.

Summer of 1986 at Westhampton Beach.

149

Over time and very gradually, our dinners continued to occur closer together, and by about Christmas of 1986, we saw each other nearly every week. Then Karen made a request. At the time, I did not yet know how rare it was for Karen to ask for something. She said that she didn't like being alone on Saturday nights. For someone who works for himself, Saturday night is no different from any other night, so I was only too glad to accommodate Karen's request to see each other on Saturdays. From then on, we would only call each other when one of us could not make a certain Saturday, such as when Karen was to be away on business or I would be skiing out West. After perhaps four or five months of seeing each other regularly every Saturday night, from time to time we started slipping in one midweek night.

It was around this time when Angela Ule, a wife of a friend, who knew of my perpetual search for the right woman, called me and said there was a woman whom I might enjoy meeting. I called the woman and after a half-hour chat we determined that we'd like to meet. I asked where she lived and was shocked to find that she lived in the same large apartment building on the Upper East Side in which Karen lived. Fearing that I might run into Karen in the lobby but always curious to see how people lived, I offered to pick her up. After a disastrous dinner in Le Refuge, a French restaurant in the neighborhood, I walked her back to her building, and we said good-bye in the lobby. The dinner was disastrous not because of the food, which was fine, but because very soon after meeting her it became clear to me that I had zero interest in her, which meant another wasted evening. Such were the rules of the game; you just never knew.

But the real point of this story is that, after dropping the woman off in the lobby of her apartment building, I walked down the street, and on the corner of York Avenue, I saw a phone booth. I walked in and called Karen. When she picked up, I confessed all that happened: that I was calling her from a phone booth down the block after a disastrous blind date with a woman who lived in her same building. While most women would have sent me packing, Karen's response was this: "Well, since you are here, why don't you come over?" That was precisely what I had hoped for. I mention this episode because I think it captures Karen's straightforwardness and total lack of pretense.

During my seventeen years of searching for the right woman, there came times when I noticed that the woman was taking our relationship more seriously than I was. At such times, I felt it incumbent to have a talk with her and tell her how I felt. The talk went something like this: "Dear so-and-so I am very fond of you, I very much like the time we spend together, and I certainly hope we'll remain friends forever. However, I don't think I have in me whatever it takes to make you 'my woman.'" I was perfectly sincere when I spoke those words. Quite understandably, most women with whom I had this talk walked away. Happily, not all did.

I am embarrassed to admit it now, but I thought that with Karen the time for the talk had come sometime in the fall of 1987, when we had arrived at seeing each other twice a week. To my amazement, after delivering my usual spiel, Karen looked me in the eyes and said, "Martin, you are hard to leave." That was all. We never returned to the subject again. To my delight, Karen stayed in my life.

During 1988 we continued to see each other at least twice a week and took more trips together—to Hawaii, Bar Harbor, and Montauk. In hindsight, the watershed moment for me was my fiftieth birthday in December 1988. Karen decided to host a dinner party for a group of fourteen friends of mine, all of whom she had met, since by then she had already attended three St. Martin's parties. Because she was embarrassed about the appearance of her apartment, she had it catered in my place. It was an elegant affair, and it was during this dinner when it finally hit me: "This woman truly loves me." Afterward, I suspended my search, phased out the Polish artist, and was happy with Karen being my one and only squeeze. (A word about the "search" at that time: when someone called me and suggested I meet so-and-so I invited so-and-so to dinner, and that was that. I was no longer proactively searching.)

December 1988, my fiftieth birthday party in my apartment.

And it was in January 1989, when we were having dinner in Acquavit to celebrate the third anniversary of our first date, that I felt moved to say to Karen, "If we go on meeting like this, by about 1992 we might be ready to get married." I was not being funny; I was absolutely sincere when I said those words, and as she told me much later, Karen understood that because she felt similarly. She nodded and said that 1992 might be a good year to evaluate things. So from then on, when folks would ask me what was going on with Karen and me, since we'd been seeing each other for quite a while, I'd reply, "Well, if things go on the way they have been, we might get married in 1992."

Interestingly, the one person who, for reasons I don't comprehend to this day, found this to be the most ridiculous and embarrassing thing she'd ever heard was my mother. Whenever she heard me, during her yearly visits, say to someone over the phone that I might be getting married in 1992, she would hit the ceiling. "For crying out loud, Martin, don't ever say that! Saying in 1989 that you might be getting married in 1992 is absurd and stupid," she would tell me. Still, that's how Karen and I felt. So we kept moving on. There was no coup de foudre; we just slowly kept growing on each other.

In 1990 Karen asked me if I'd take on the renovation of her apartment. In hindsight, it is remarkable to me, but the truth is that, even at that late date, it didn't occur to me that I'd be one day living in that apartment. I was simply designing an apartment for Karen, one room at a time. Yet just a little over

In Prague, on the eve of the Velvet Revolution, September 1989.

a year later, in June 1991, I moved in with Karen. The impetus for this decision was that a McKinsey colleague of Karen needed to move with her husband out of their apartment during its renovation, so I rented them my apartment for what was to be a half year. It was only after we started living together that it became obvious that I wasn't going to move back, and from then on, I was designing the apartment for both of us. It was clear that, should we ever live together, it would be in Karen's apartment, which with its two bedrooms, two bathrooms, separate dining room, and balcony was more than twice the size of my bachelor pad. Sometime toward the end of 1991 we picked May 16 of the following year as the date for our wedding. It would then be 1992, and it felt right to get married.

Having picked the date, the next thing to decide on was the venue. Karen was the most irreligious Jew I've ever met; she never set foot inside a synagogue (her parents were both confirmed atheists). I was a lukewarm Christian, or so I thought at the time. Karen's only request was that she didn't want Jesus to have anything to do with our wedding. And we both wanted something other than a standard-issue city hall wedding. We checked out the Unitarian Church on Lexington Avenue, but didn't like the pastor. One day while walking along First Avenue at 44th Street, I noticed a sign for the United Nations Interdenominational Chapel. It was a contemporary space on the ground floor of a high-rise office building. Immediately, I thought to myself, "This is it!" In the evening, I told Karen about it, and she agreed wholeheartedly. The next day we called, found that the chapel was available on May 16 in the afternoon, and booked it.

Having decided the date and the venue, we needed to figure out who would marry us. After some reflection, we both thought of our friend Willy Malarcher. He was an artist making a living as a liturgical design consultant (in which capacity he recommended me for several church jobs). He was also a deacon and, as such, had the authority to officiate at weddings. We invited Willy and his wife for dinner and asked him if he'd be willing to marry us in the UN Interdenominational Chapel. He quickly responded that he'd be honored to do so. Karen gave him a sheet of paper on which she had typed what she considered to be important about marriage and married life. Her dominant theme was that marriage was not simply about the exaltation of love but was far more about the quotidian grind. For Karen, a fitting symbol of the daily slog was oatmeal. The last thing to take care of was the invitations. The first line read, "The Wedding, at last…"

On May 16, we were surprised when Willy showed up at the UN Chapel with a box of Quaker Oats oatmeal, which he put on the altar, but we let it be. And so we were married on a box of oatmeal. After the wedding, we repaired with fifty-some friends and acquaintances in a chartered bus to our reno-vated apartment for a catered reception. The toast I proposed went something like this:

People marry for a reason. The most common reason is start-ing a family, and it makes indeed perfect sense to be married if you plan on having children. Then some folks marry for real estate reasons, such as keeping a rent-controlled apartment, while others marry for insurance reasons, such as being added on to your spouse's health plan. None of the above applies to us, so one might ask why are two old farts like us (Karen was forty-seven; I was fifty-three) getting married? There is one reason and one reason alone: to declare to each other and to the world that we mean this, that we take this relationship seriously. In other words, the only reason is love.

Wedding reception in our renovated apartment, May 1992.

Little did I know at the time that twenty-three years later I'd be proposing much the same toast at my third wedding, but that's another story.

Things didn't change much after the wedding. Having seen increasingly more of each other for more than six years, and having lived together for the past year, the marriage made little, if any, difference in our lives. As time passed, we kept incrementally realizing what a good fit we were and our love grew. Of course, we didn't realize it at the time. The only wrinkle for me was that Karen never fully warmed up to my mother, which troubled me greatly. She liked and respected her but never became a true friend. I understood that, given the troubled relationship Karen had with her own mother, seeing how my mother and I were just two chips off the same block must have been hard for her. But even that improved over time. My mother died in 2001, and during the last two years or so of her life, Karen became an exemplary daughter-in-law.

We were both workaholics, which had been a problem in some of my earlier relationships, when women I was dating would complain that I never wanted to do anything or that I kept working all the time. There was no problem of the sort with Karen. We both liked working late, so when we weren't doing anything social or cultural, we typically met at home at 9 o'clock in the evening. There were times when I wanted to finish something, so at 8:30 I'd call Karen at her office and ask, "Sweetie, could we make it 9:30 tonight?" To which Karen would swiftly respond, "That's fine. I could use the time as well. Let's make it 9:45."

Yet Karen was never far from tears, whether from joy or sorrow, real or perceived. It sometimes happened that we had a misunderstanding as to when I was expected to come home. If it so happened that I arrived a half an hour or forty minutes later than she expected, I'd find her in tears: "Where have you been? Why didn't you call?" Those were tears of joy, because she was happy to see that I wasn't dead, lying in a gutter of a heart attack or stroke as she had been imagining. But once she snapped out of it, being ever so honest with herself as she was with everyone else, she'd flash a smile and say, "Do you know what's so pathetic? That I am not crying over you, that you might have suffered some harm. No, I am crying over myself, because the rest of my life is predicated upon you being in it, and should that not be the case, I don't want to live it."

When she retired from McKinsey in 2004, everyone including Karen was worried what a workaholic like her would do with all that free time. It turned out there was nothing to worry about. Karen threw herself with abandon into all the things she didn't have time for while she was working. She enrolled at NYU in classes on international politics, worked on improving her French, kept up with all the museum exhibits, joined a book group and read voraciously, arranged our trips, organized all the drawers in our apartment, and simply had a ball. Then one day everything changed.

In 2005 Karen decided to switch from her family doctor, whom she had been seeing since she was a teenager and who was then in his mideighties. During their initial appointment, her new doctor, Dr. Cantor, asked her if she had ever smoked. She had but had stopped twenty-four years earlier. Dr. Cantor suggested that she have a CT scan of her lungs, "just to have a baseline." Karen did as she was told. Then one sunny morning late in November—I still remember it was a Thursday

At Karen's retirement party at the Rainbow Room, June 2004.

Outside of Bohemian Hall in 2007.

morning—while we were having breakfast and the mood was warm and congenial, the phone rang. Karen picked up and I could hear the voice on the other end: "Karen, this is Dr. Cantor. I am afraid I have some bad news. The CT scan of your lungs showed a tumor in the upper right lobe that is consistent with the signs of lung cancer. We have to move fast. I have already made an appointment for you with the pulmonologist in our group."

Our universe collapsed! But we didn't know that at that time; we were sure we were going to lick it. The surgery to remove the tumor was scheduled. Because the tumor was caught early, it would be fine, or so we were told and fully believed. The surgeon removed the whole lobe, and Karen was pronounced cancer free: the PET scan showed no cancer anywhere in Karen's body. We had to cancel our ski trip scheduled for January, but by March Karen was already well enough to go skiing in Vail. And indeed, she was cancer free for the next two and a half years, or so we thought. We resumed our normal lives. In June 2006, we traveled to Europe to celebrate both my fiftieth high school reunion in Prague and the wedding of my godson in Bamberg. We took our usual two ski trips to the West per year, both in 2007 and in 2008.

In June 2008 Karen started having pain in her upper neck. When the pain didn't go away in two weeks or so she went to see Dr. Cantor. Given Karen's history, Dr. Cantor prescribed a CT scan of her head. The scan showed a tumor on the brain. Karen did her research and found that, indeed, if lung cancer spreads, it most often goes to the brain first. Once again, things started to move fast. This time the "good news" was that the tumor was operable. The brain surgeon removed the tumor, and once again, Karen was pronounced cancer free. And once again, we fully believed it. When Karen recovered from the brain surgery, we resumed our normal life. In September 2008 we took a trip to Charleston, South Carolina, and then in November to Prague, where we hosted "The Dinner in Prague" to mark my seventieth birthday.

After her brain surgery, Karen was to have a control brain scan every three months, so we lived from scan to scan. However, when the first two scans turned out clear, we stopped fretting and went on with our lives. We took another two ski trips in 2009. The January one was to Sun Valley, since Karen's doctors advised her to avoid elevations above eight thousand feet and Sun Valley is a low-elevation resort. That was our last ski trip on which Karen still skied. The next one was to Aspen, but Karen no longer went skiing. She said that she didn't want to risk injury and that coping with cancer was enough. It turned out to be our last ski trip. Perhaps this is a good place to insert a paragraph about Karen's skiing.

Skiing in Alta in 1994.

It's a miracle that Karen ever skied at all. I cannot think of a person more unlikely to take up skiing than her. To begin with, she was not well coordinated at all. She was afraid of heights and suffered from vertigo. Nor did she like speed. She never did any sport whatsoever, not even ice skating, because she'd convinced herself that she had weak ankles. (Orthopedists tell me there is no such thing.) Yet Karen recognized that skiing was an important part of my life and that if she wanted to spend winter vacations with me, she had to come along. She didn't want to become one of the nonskiing wives, so at the age of forty-five she started taking skiing lessons. She learned slowly but steadily, and after some five years of lessons, she became a very gracious intermediate skier.

In Prague, after the brain surgery of 2008, eighteen months before she died.

Over the twenty-four years we were together, Karen and I took thirty-nine ski trips together to eighteen resorts between Taos, New Mexico, and Whistler, British Columbia. Karen came to love our ski vacations, yet the actual act of skiing remained her least favorite part of them. She loved the chair rides, the scenery, the après-ski, the whole atmosphere of a ski resort—if only it could all come without having to ski. Being a closet travel agent, she also loved the planning, choosing hotels, and making reservations. Much, much later, when I no longer had her, it dawned on me what an enormous act of love it was that Karen had skied at all.

But back to 2009. In May, Karen's control scan showed another metastasized tumor on her brain, which had not been there three months earlier. Her oncologist recommended radiosurgery, the so-called Gamma Knife. It is a procedure whereby a multitude of rays converge on the tumor and destroy it. Karen did her research and found that the survival statistics of those whose lung cancer metastasized into the brain were grim indeed and that the prognosis of those who had a second metastasized tumor was even worse. However, her doctors insisted that she was not a statistic and that her chances were good. So we went through with the radiosurgery. The only good thing about it was that the recovery was pretty quick. Karen rested the day after the procedure but went about her normal life the next day.

The August control scan showed yet another tumor. Again, she was not a statistic, so she underwent the same procedure again. In October, we traveled to Munich to attend a friend's birthday celebration, and then we spent a week touring Provence. Throughout, Karen felt fine, and we almost forgot about the Damocles sword hanging over our heads. When we returned home, Karen booked our January ski trip to Whistler.

At the end of November, she started having headaches, and her radio surgeon put her on steroids. At the beginning of December, Karen started having trouble seeing from her left eye. She saw her ophthalmologist who found nothing untoward and sent her to see a retina specialist who didn't find anything wrong with her eye either. The next eye doctor Karen saw was a glaucoma specialist who also didn't detect anything. Meanwhile, her eyesight continued to deteriorate. Finally, I no longer remember at whose suggestion, Karen saw an oncological ophthalmologist, Dr. Dinkin, at New York Presbyterian Hospital. When his eye examinations failed to reveal any reason Karen was losing her sight, he prescribed an MRI of her eye sockets. We were to see him again the following day.

That was the day before Christmas Eve, and on our way home from the MRI we stopped at Sables on Second Avenue and bought caviar, our once-a-year indulgence for Christmas Eve dinner in the country. By now, Karen was practically blind in her left eye, and the vision in her right eye was worsening. Our ski trip to Whistler looked increasingly less likely to occur, but we were still hoping for a nice Christmas at our country place.

On the morning of Christmas Eve, we went to see Dr. Dinkin. He let us read the MRI report and showed us the images on the screen. The report described and the images showed cancer cells attached to the optic nerves. There were more of them on the left nerve, which corresponded with the state of Karen's impaired vision. At long last, the mystery of her loss of eyesight was solved. Why none of the respected specialists whom Karen saw since she started losing her vision thought to check for cancer is another mystery. It pointed out the main problem with the treatment she received during her last days, which was that Karen didn't have a doctor coordinating her care. She had a plethora of specialists, but not one doctor to oversee the whole picture.

Dr. Dinkin suggested a massive intravenous infusion of steroids in Karen's bloodstream in the hope of flushing out the cancer cells and improving her eyesight. So instead of driving to the country, Karen was admitted to the hospital. We paid extra for a private room. I came over in the evening and brought the caviar and vodka. While she was hooked up to the IV, Karen enjoyed our little Christmas festivity. The three days of the steroid infusion didn't produce the desired result—that is, Karen's eyesight did not improve—and the attending physician decided to perform a spinal tap.

The lab test showed that the cancer had spread into Karen's spinal fluid. In retrospect, that was the death knell, although no one said it at the time. Strangely, the medical response to this finding was whole-brain radiation. Karen was warned that there might be some residual brain impairment but was promised that there was a good chance that her eyesight would improve. She was discharged from the hospital, and each day over the next ten days we walked down to 72nd Street to the Radiation Department of New York Presbyterian Hospital, where Karen received her radiation treatments.

Meanwhile, we were making arrangements to make our apartment suitable for a blind person, which is what Karen now was, although she still had minimal vision in her right eye. We bought digital clocks with extralarge numbers and also a white telephone with large numbers. Apple had just come out with a new iPhone that had voice recognition software, so we bought it as well. When we were at the Apple store they told us the phone cost $425 but that if we waited until March, we'd be able to buy it for less than half that cost. We bought the phone that day, and Karen was then able to command the phone to call whomever she wanted to speak to. That was one device that really helped.

Although during the ten days of her radiation therapy Karen was still able to walk the five blocks to 72nd Street and back, shortly thereafter she started losing the strength in her legs. She no longer felt secure walking unsupported, so we bought her a walker, with which she was able to navigate around the apartment. In hindsight, I think this was a significant development. Yet when I reported it to her doctors, none of them was impressed by it.

When the radiation treatments failed to improve Karen's vision, her brain surgeon together with her radiation surgeon and the oncologist proposed a last-ditch attempt to restore her sight. They suggested installing a shunt in Karen's skull through which chemotherapy would be infused into her spinal fluid. A shunt is a hole in the skull leading to the interstitial space surrounding the brain, which contains the same fluid that is in the spine. The doctors did stress that the procedure would not extend Karen's life, but that there was a good chance that it would restore her sight. My thinking was that her last days would be happier if she could see, and Karen agreed, so we went for it. In retrospect it was a mistake, but once again, there was no doctor who could connect all the dots and say, "Hold your horses; this doesn't make sense."

As with the two previous surgeries, we had to report to the hospital at 5:30 a.m.

I still remember that the date was January 19. When we left our apartment at 5:00 a.m. and were walking down the corridor toward the elevator, Karen using a walker and I supporting her, a premonition flashed through my head: "She is not coming back." It turned out to be correct. I'll now mention another consequence of Karen having no doctor. After the surgery, with the shunt in her head, she was lying in the recovery room, waiting for the oncologist to administer the chemo. Only then did we learn that Karen's oncologist, Dr. Ruggiero, did not do this procedure. Evidently, pouring chemo through the shunt is a specialized procedure that not every oncologist is skilled to perform. The brain surgeon installed the shunt but gave no thought to what happened next. It was only in the recovery room that the attending physician began looking for an oncologist skilled in this procedure. It took twenty-four hours before he found one, during which time Karen was kept in the recovery room with all the attending beeps and commotion, instead of the quiet of her private room (for which we'd paid a handsome extra sum).

While Karen was in the hospital, she couldn't stand the hospital food, so I brought her breakfast from the deli, and then for lunch and dinner, I would bring her favorite dishes from nearby restaurants. She couldn't see, so I had to feed her. But she ate everything with gusto and didn't lose her appetite until a few days before she died.

While she was in the hospital, Karen and I had no time to talk. I was either foraging for food, feeding her, talking to her doctors, arranging for an overnight private nurse, or setting her up for the night with her radio and earphones. If I managed to get to my office at all, it was for a maximum of two hours per day, and while there I spent my time emailing with Karen's doctors. It felt like I was running on a treadmill. It was probably a good thing that I was so busy, because otherwise I'd have cried all the time. As it was, I cried only when I was by myself, which was not often.

When after three doses of chemo Karen's sight did not improve, the doctors concluded it was not working and that there was nothing more medicine could do for her. They recommended that she be moved to a hospice. Karen and I agreed, and I started looking for the best one. I soon discovered there was uniform agreement that the best hospice was Calvary Hospital in the Bronx. After hearing many positive testimonials, I came to agree—but reluctantly, because it was in a remote area of the Bronx and was difficult to get to; there was no chance that I could see Karen three to four times a day as I had while she was in a hospital eight blocks from our apartment. Karen agreed that the quality of the care and the reputation of the place were more important than the number of my visits. In hindsight, I am not sure we made the right decision.

During our drive to the hospice in the ambulance, I was with Karen and one paramedic in the back. Karen, although by now completely blind, was alertly following our trip, commenting, "Now we are driving north on York Avenue, now we are getting on FDR Drive, now we are crossing the Willis Avenue Bridge." After that point she lost the route, because we were entering the terra incognita of the Bronx. When the paramedic saw how profusely my tears were flowing, he handed me a box of Kleenex.

After the three hectic weeks in the hospital, I was looking forward to the peace and quiet of Karen's private room at Calvary; in fact, all the rooms were private, and we didn't have to pay extra for it. I installed her in a rather nice one, but unfortunately, she couldn't see just how nice it was. Supper was brought in, and I fed Karen. It was the first time she didn't eat with relish and left more than half of the meal on the plate. I attributed this lack of appetite, perhaps incorrectly, to the hospital fare. After supper Karen fell asleep, and I left. I remember it was a Thursday night.

On Friday morning, I ordered a plate of Karen's favorite linguine al pesto from Petaluma restaurant, took a bottle of Zinfandel from our wine bin, walked down to 73rd Street to pick up the dish, and then took a taxi to the Bronx. I arrived at Calvary Hospital just in time for lunch. I warmed up the linguine in the hospital kitchenette's microwave and started feeding Karen. Although it was her favorite dish, she ate less than a quarter of it and drank barely one sip of the wine. So it was not the hospital fare that caused her not to eat much the previous night: something else was at play.

I stayed with Karen for the better part of the afternoon. We talked about current goings-on, who called, who left a message; I told her our friend Waltraud had set up a schedule on a special website where folks who wished to visit Karen could sign up for a particular time slot, to avoid five people showing up at the same time. It didn't feel like a propitious time for serious conversation, for telling each other what a wonderful time we'd had over the twenty-four years together, for saying good-bye. Not having that serious talk then was another mistake on my part, because, as it turned out, that Friday afternoon was the last chance we could have had that conversation.

When I showed up on Saturday, the attending nurse told me that Karen was very agitated. I walked into her room and saw Karen tossing around, flailing her arms violently, and muttering something incomprehensible. I held her and spoke to her, but she took no notice. The nurse then walked in and gave Karen an injection of some tranquilizer; I suspect it was morphine. I guess the nurse wanted me to see how Karen was so agitated before she administered the tranquilizer. Karen quieted down very quickly. I stayed with her another hour or so held her hand, and spoke to her, but she showed no sign of knowing that I was there. She breathed peacefully, and her heartbeat was regular.

On Sunday when I arrived, the nurse informed me that Karen continued to be unresponsive. It was an apt description. Again, I stayed a couple of hours with her, held her hand, and watched her breathe. She did not appear to register my presence. The same occurred on Monday, which was the last time I saw Karen alive, if that is the right expression. On Tuesday, I just called the nurse in the morning, afternoon, and evening. Each time she told me that Karen continued to be unresponsive. It was the same on Wednesday morning, afternoon, and early evening.

That evening, February 17, my close friend Peter Kussi and I attended a function at the Bohemian Hall, after which we had dinner at the Atlantic Grill on Third Avenue. When I got home a little after 11 p.m., the voice mail light on my phone was flashing, so I listened to the messages. The last one was from Calvary Hospital, asking me to call the given number. I still remember the subsequent conversation, word for word.

"My name is Martin Holub, and I had a message to call."

"What room number is dis about?"

"My wife is in the room number 442."

"Hol' on."

After a long wait, "Well, we keep 'em in d' room for an hour and den we put 'em in d' mortuary, so are you comin' over or what?"

"Are you telling me that my wife died?"

"Oh yeah, she died."

"I am not coming over; put her in the mortuary."

"OK, good night."

"Good night."

On Thursday morning, I called Krtil Funeral Home and asked them to pick up Karen's body from Calvary Hospital. I remembered that when my mother had died nine years earlier in a Prague hospital, there was no room available where I could sit with her, and I had missed that. The Jewish custom of sitting shiva made a lot of sense to me, so I asked the Krtil Home if it had a room where I could sit with Karen's body before they took it to the crematorium. The answer: "Yes, viewing room for $500 extra." I said, "All right, I'll take it."

My biggest regret was that Karen and I did not have a chance to say good-bye to each other. I thought we'd have plenty of time while she was in hospice, but it didn't work out that way. I later learned that zonking out terminally ill patients with strong doses of morphine is not an uncommon practice in hospices.

A long time before she was diagnosed with lung cancer, Karen and I discussed the fact that we were unlikely to die together (we always assumed that I'd go first), and we both agreed that we didn't want funerals after our respective demises. Karen said, "I don't want a funeral—have a party." And so we did. A little over two months after she died and after a very unceremonious internment of her ashes (next to my mother's) at the Quaker cemetery near our country place, I put on a catered party at our hilltop house: 116 people from all over the country came to celebrate Karen's life.

I was touched by how many people told me what a legendary couple we were. I had no idea how much it showed; we certainly did not put our love on display. In fact, we never even said to each other the words "I love you." We never talked about it, because I guess we both felt that stating aloud something that was so obvious would somehow cheapen it. (As I write this, I realize that, perhaps for the same reason, neither my mother nor I had ever said those words to each other.) Ah, how right Khalil Gibran was when he said, "And ever has it been that love knows not how deep it is until the hour of separation." Just as with my mother, not a day has passed since Karen died without my thinking of her.

All matchmakers work on the premise that, to be romantically attracted, people need to share a lot of common interests. I don't speak from personal experience, having never availed myself of a matchmaker's services, but I know people who have used them. The first thing you do after you've paid the fee is to fill in a long questionnaire that asks you to state in great detail all your proclivities, likes, and dislikes, so that you can be matched with someone of a similar turn or mind. Thus if you state that you like operas, trips to Europe, skiing in the Rockies, fine wines and good restaurants, the matchmaker will produce someone who also likes operas and so on.

Karen and I proved this strategy to be, if not complete nonsense, at least not universally effective. When we first met, we had precious few interests in common. Karen told me many years later that, before she met me, she'd never been to an art gallery or an art museum, she did not ski, and she didn't know much about wine. So did we even have any interests in common? Well, we both liked the beach, although for different reasons (Karen didn't like swimming in the ocean), we both had subscriptions to the New York Philharmonic, and we both were avid readers, but that was about it. But having interests in common proved to be unimportant.

What was important was that we shared the same values. We both valued honesty, clarity, directness, openness, integrity, and talking to the point. We abhorred pretentiousness, affectation, dissembling, prevaricating, and half-truths. Consequently, we had the same take on people: when I thought someone was an asshole, I could be sure that Karen was of the same opinion, and vice versa. Although we had very different lines of work, we both loved what we were doing and enjoyed working hard. We had the same sensitivity to color, light, space, shape, and form. And when we went to an art exhibit, we always ended up playing the following game: if you absolutely had to take home one painting or one piece of sculpture, which one would it be? Even though Karen knew next to nothing of art history, more often than not, we picked the same piece of artwork.

This was quite remarkable given our different backgrounds. With my mother an art historian, plus the thorough grounding in art history that I got in the School of Architecture, plus a lifetime of looking at pictures, I carry a lot of baggage when looking at art, while Karen carried none—and yet we'd pick the same picture. Karen's sensitivity to light, space, form, and color is shown best is our country house, which is spacious and airy and has a lot of light. Karen had a proclivity to depression, but whenever she was in that house, it was as if she blossomed; while there, she always had a smile on her lips. I attributed this to Karen's extraordinary, inborn sensitivity—something far more important than whether she liked to ski.

Olives in Varna

One of the many absurdities of life on the wrong side of the Iron Curtain was that, by the age of twenty-five, I had yet to taste an olive. I knew about olives from literature. From reading Hemingway, I knew that people drank martinis with an olive, but I had no idea what olives tasted like because they were simply not available in communist Czechoslovakia; there were not even canned ones. Neither were avocados available, but that is another story; this one is about olives.

The year was 1964, and in July I was flying with my mother-in-law to Bulgaria to join my wife Eva, who was already there with her father and her two younger siblings. She was at the time teaching at a special institution for students from the Third World called the University of 17th November, and as such, she had two months of summer vacation. Since going to Bulgaria required two days and one night of travel on the train and I had only two weeks of vacation, I got to fly.

In addition to never having tasted an olive, another consequence of life in a communist country was that, at the age of twenty-five, this was my first ever airplane ride. One of the stupidest fashions ever must have been dressing up for a plane ride, but so it was in the sixties. Consequently, I was wearing a white shirt with a bow tie, tailored pants, and a sports jacket. (This is a good place to explain that, at the time, having clothes tailor made was by no means a luxury but the norm. The ready-to-wear clothes were so uniformly dreadful, with baggy pants and ill-fitting jackets, that anyone who had even the slightest sense of fashion had their clothes made.) My mother-in-law wore an elegant summer dress.

Our final destination was Nesebar, a fishing village on the Black Sea, halfway between Varna and Burgass. To get there one took a two-hour flight from Prague to Varna, where one then boarded a southbound boat for a three-hour voyage to Nesebar. We had about three hours to kill between arriving in Varna and boarding the boat, so having checked the luggage at the harbor, we walked around and looked at the boats. Eventually we spied a seafood eatery called Automat (having gone through eleven years of compulsory Russian, I could read Cyrillic); it was a sort of fast-food seafood place, where people ate standing at high tables. When we entered, all heads turned in our direction because we were, by a long shot, the best-dressed people in the whole joint. The seafood on display looked scrumptious, but what caught my attention was one whole display case full of olives.

I had no idea that olives could come in so many shapes, colors, and sizes. Before World War II, you could get any type of food in Prague that was available in Paris or London, so I assumed that my mother-in-law knew what olives were from the time before the war. I asked her whether those were olives in the display case, and she indeed confirmed that they were.

I proceeded to order a sampling of olives from each kind on display, ending up with a heaping plate of olives. I ordered nothing else. When I carried the plate with the olives to our high table, I once again saw all heads turned in my direction. People just didn't know what to make of this guy in a white shirt and bow tie who came into this seafood place and ordered nothing except for one large plate of olives.

I could see that my mother-in-law was somewhat alarmed, pointing to the olives and asking, "You mean to eat all of them?" It was clearly foolish of me to order that many olives without knowing what an olive tastes like, but eat them all I did. I liked the taste of the first one so slowly, one by one, sampling the tastes of all kinds—some pitted, some not—I kept on eating the olives until they were all gone. This was before my *H. Pylori* ulcer days when my stomach was still in good shape, and there were no untoward gastrointestinal consequences of my foolhardy act. But throughout the end of our stay in Nesebar, my mother-in-law never failed to regale anyone who came to visit with the story of how Martin ate a whole plate of olives in Varna.

Legal Victory

When I was commuting to Tennessee to do design work for my client Barber McMurry and to teach, I also picked up several jobs for local clients there. One of them was a house for (let's call her) Christine Dash, who was referred to me by my friend Jasan. Christine was one of Jasan's many paramours, and he had the good sense not to enter into a business relationship with her, so he recommended a New York architect to her. And she liked having a New York architect.

Christine was an attractive divorcee who had divorced well. There was nothing wrong with the house she lived in, except it wasn't contemporary. She had a dash of sophistication rare in Tennessee and wanted a contemporary house, which is why she needed an architect. She had purchased a two-acre lot in a high-end subdivision in West Knoxville and gave me a very detailed brief of her plans. Clearly, she had given a lot of thought to the design of the house. I remember that one of the two guest bedrooms was to be next to the master bedroom and the other in the remotest possible part of the house. Among other features, she also wanted within the house an outdoor space shielded from view where she could sunbathe naked.

I didn't find it difficult to comply with all her wishes, and at my first presentation of the schematic design, I showed Christine the layout, which she approved enthusiastically. We swiftly moved into the design development phase, and after I presented the drawings to her, she professed to be thrilled with them. She asked for a 3D model, which is not a standard part of the service, but I hired a student who built a fine cardboard model, and Christine was delighted. She signed off on the design development set of drawings, and we moved into the construction documents phase. As is usual, I billed Christine monthly, and, up to this point, she had paid my invoices promptly. The following month I didn't spend much time on Christine's job, so I decided to delay billing until the end of the next month. Then, just before the end of that month, Christine called me in New York and announced that she was suspending the project. She said that she had lost a lot of money in the stock market and her stockbroker had advised her that she couldn't afford to build a new house just then.

This was the summer of 1974, when there indeed was a recession—the Dow Jones had dropped significantly, and many people did lose money—so I took Christine's announcement at face value. I told her that I understood and that I stood ready to resume the project should her situation change. The next day I sent her an invoice for the time spent since my last billing. It was for around $2,500, which brought my total billing well below the not-to-exceed limit stipulated by our agreement. When no payment arrived by the end of the following month, I resent the invoice. Another month passed with no payment, so I resent the invoice once again. I also called Christine several times, each time leaving a message on her answering machine. All to no avail: she never called back.

One of my acquaintances in Knoxville was a lawyer who had a fitting name, James Justice. He was a friend of Jasan, and the three of us often dined together. When I was in Tennessee in December 1974—on my last trip before leaving for Tehran—I called James and told him about my uncollected

The Rokeby Apartments in Nashville, Tennessee.

fee. He asked me to come over to his office and bring along my agreement with Christine, as well as all my invoices. When he examined the documents, James said that the law was on my side and that he'd file a suit to obtain a judgment at the Knox County Courthouse, adding, "It'll cost you a filling fee of $12." As I was leaving for Tehran in a few weeks and not sure when I'd be back, James asked me to write him once I knew when I would be returning and he would schedule the court hearing for the time I'd be in the country.

It turned out I was back in the country for my recharging trip half a year later, in June 1975. I needed to go to Nashville in connection with the Rokeby Apartments project, which was then under construction. The next morning, I caught a flight to Knoxville, saw James Justice, and together we went to the courthouse. James told me that Christine Dash had been duly served, and he was sure that she would show up. She did not, and so I received the judgment automatically. The judge added some damages to the amount of the unpaid invoice, so that I walked out with a judgment in excess of $3,000. However, it is one thing to obtain a judgment and quite another to collect the money. When I asked James, "What next?" he told me that I'd have to hire a collection lawyer to collect the money for me. He added that the collection lawyer's fee was typically done on a contingency basis, meaning I'd pay only if he or she managed to collect. James thought that, in this particular case, the collection would be a breeze.

Well, breeze or not, during the next four years of moving between Tehran and New York, as well as during the following nine years in New York, I just didn't give the matter much thought. It wasn't until 1988, when I was moving my office from my apartment to the space I bought on 72nd Street and Columbus Avenue, that I came across the file folder for Christine Dash, in which I found the judgment from 1975. I called David Soeiro, the lawyer who had assisted me with the purchase of my office space. He told me first, that judgments never expire and, second, that they actually accrue interest. He also gave me the name and phone number of a lawyer who specialized in collecting judgments. I called the lawyer, who asked me to fax him a copy of the judgment. He then called me back to say that he needed to do some research and would get back to me within a week.

Before the week was over, the lawyer called and told me a number of pieces of information. He found out that Christine Dash had moved to Jacksonville, Florida, where she lived in a five-thousand-square-foot house in a high-end subdivision and that she owned three cars. Further, he had located a Jacksonville lawyer who was willing to do the collection, and the two lawyers would work together and split the 40 percent commission. Lastly, the lawyer told me that my judgment with the accrued interest was now worth over $5,000 and that, given Ms. Dash's circumstances, the chances of collecting the whole amount were pretty good. In conclusion, he said that if those terms were all right with me, he'd fax me his agreement, which I should sign and fax right back. I did as he said.

Perhaps two weeks later, Christine Dash called me. It was the first time I'd heard her voice in fourteen years, since the summer of 1974 when she called me to tell me that she was stopping the house project. This time she affected a weepy pleading tone, saying, "Martin, why are you ruining my life? I am coming out of a very difficult period, putting the pieces of my life back together, and now you appear out of nowhere, determined to destroy me all over again. Why are you doing this? Please stop ruining me." For emphasis, she punctuated her talk with histrionic sobs that sounded insincere even over the phone.

I told Christine that it was a little too late to pay the invoice I'd sent her fourteen years ago or to respond to the many messages I had left on her answering machine back then that she had ignored. I also told her that I had not come out of nowhere, that I was in the same place all along, and had she wanted to get in touch with me, she knew exactly where to find me. In conclusion, I told her that if she wanted to blame someone for this situation, all she needed to do was to look in the mirror. I tried to speak in as calm and measured a voice as I was capable of, because I wanted to convey my resolve that I was not going to be tricked into taking pity on her. It seemed I succeeded because she never called back.

In another two weeks, I received from the lawyer a check for over $3,000. It was a sum very close to the original judgment, and the interest covered the lawyers' fees. I felt extremely satisfied, but not because I got the money—I would have been fine without it—but for the principle of it. Justice was done; the person at fault was punished. That doesn't happen often, but when it does, it feels good.

Studio 54

I've always found it puzzling that a guy like myself, someone who likes dancing, drinking, and partying, never took to the New York disco scene of the 1980s. On the few occasions when, through some circumstance, I found myself in one of the discos, I could not wait to get out of there. For one thing, the decibel level of the music rendered any meaningful conversation impossible. For another, a disco was not an environment conducive to asking a woman you didn't know to dance. People tended to stick with the partners they came with. On top of that, there was the humiliating procedure of getting in, whereby some low-life standing at the fire hydrant next to the velvet-roped entrance decided, purely based on appearance, who might and who might not be allowed to enter. Altogether, for me, the disco was not an attractive scene.

One of the best-known discos at the time was Studio 54 on West 54th Street. It had a reputation as a place where the rich and famous, movers and shakers, congregated, and thus it was really difficult to get in. One late night sometime in the early 1980s, my friend Jeff Vandeberg and I were returning from a dinner party in midtown, wending our way to the subway station on 57th Street and Eighth Avenue. It was way past midnight, so we were surprised when we saw a large crowd of people spilling from the sidewalk onto the street. We looked up at the street sign and saw that we were on West 54th Street. Then we realized that we were outside of Studio 54, and the crowd we saw was made up of people trying to get in.

Jeff and I decided to stick around and observe the scene. Yes, there was the proverbial bouncer standing on a fire hydrant (or was it a chair next to a fire hydrant?), pointing at individual people or couples. He would say, "The blond lady in the red coat, yes, you, and your escort, you may go in." The couple advanced, two attendants parted the velvet rope, and they happily sauntered in. Next, "You with the dotted bow tie, yes, you." A rotund older gentleman advanced through the parted velvet rope. We were surprised that someone of his stature would subject himself to this positively undignified procedure. When we heard, "You with the hat, yes, you with the fedora, and your buddy," we realized that he was pointing at me (I was wearing a rather jaunty hat that night). We looked at each other and thought, "What the hell, why not?" and walked through the parted velvet rope.

Once inside, we found a cavernous space pulsating with music and people, although it was now close to 2 a.m. The music was so loud that, to communicate, Jeff and I had to talk into one another's ears. Even though we had more than enough to drink that night already, we decided to tie one more on. Sitting at the bar while facing the dance floor, we watched the scene. Despite the loud and throbbing music, the atmosphere was far from joyous. We didn't see anyone laughing or even smiling. Perhaps because of the late hour, the prevalent expression on people's faces was a lugubrious stupor. Then we noticed that not everyone on the dance floor was dancing. Some people were just hanging out looking around; others were walking about.

Jeff and I decided to move to the dance floor, where we promptly lost each other. Once on the floor, I noticed that the dance area was divided by a wall into two sections of different sizes: what we had been looking at was the larger of the two, and there was a whole other area behind the dividing wall, accessible by passages at both ends of the wall. I walked to one of those openings to take a peek into the other space and noticed a sign, "Private Party," on the wall next to the passage. Despite the sign, I saw people moving freely between the two spaces, so I walked through the opening to the space behind the wall. It was smaller, with a lower ceiling, and so more intimate, and it was packed with more people than the space on the other side. The music was less loud there, making some conversation possible; you could hear others' voices. Fewer people danced in this back space; most were just standing around, looking about.

I turned around and found myself standing next to Andy Warhol. We were facing each other, our faces about eighteen inches apart. Although I was in his direct line of sight and his eyes were open, it was clear to me that he did not see me: he was in another world. So I didn't even attempt to address him; instead, I continued to observe him. It was a spooky sight: he was wearing thick pancake makeup all over his face, and his eyes were not moving, but were fixed as if in a torpor. The only sign that Andy Warhol was actually alive was that he was standing upright, quite straight, not wobbling.

After what seemed like a long time but was perhaps not more than several minutes, Andy Warhol suddenly turned around and, with a slow but steady gait, walked toward one of the passages to the front room. Though no one else paid any mind to him, I followed. The front room was by now much emptier. When we walked in, I noticed that two men sitting at a nearby table got up and walked toward Andy Warhol. One of them was holding his coat. They helped him put it on, and the three of them walked toward the front lobby. I was glad to see that Andy Warhol was not entirely alone. I later learned that he was a regular fixture at Studio 54, which was perhaps why no one paid any attention to him.

The music stopped at about 4 a.m. and it would have then been possible to converse, except everyone was leaving. I found Jeff at the bar and asked him if he'd noticed Andy Warhol. He hadn't. We walked out, and I took a taxi home.

Ideological Dossier

On graduating from the six-year program of the School of Architecture at the Czech Technical University, we were to receive not only a diploma certifying our academic achievement but also certification of our ideological fitness to face the world. This personal, ideological dossier—a type of an ideological report card—was prepared for each graduating student by a committee consisting of the four Communist Party members of the graduating class, plus two or three sympathizers (i.e., friends of those party members). The committee was chaired by Assistant Professor Slíva, who also chaired the faculty's Communist Party cell.

The thirty students in the graduating class were split evenly between men and women. One of my classmates was Alena Hejdová, a very plain and homely young woman. On top of that, she was also hopelessly untalented in architectural design. Consequently, throughout my six years of university attendance, I paid Alena zero attention, as if she were air. She simply didn't exist for me.

At some point after we had taken our final exams, we were told that the committee preparing the ideological reports had completed its work. We were asked to assemble in an auditorium where, in the name of openness and transparency, the individual reports would be publicly read. At the given time, we filed into the auditorium. Chairman Slíva and the committee members sat on the podium, facing the assembled class. I was sitting next to my future wife Eva. A committee member started reading the individual reports, one by one. They were all variations on the same theme. Comrade so and so through his/her extracurricular activities, his/her summer jobs, as well his/her conduct in their respective domiciles, had demonstrated a positive attitude toward the working class and the socialist regime. He/she participated in the activities of the university chapter of the Czechoslovak Youth Institute, sang in the university Glee Club, and in the design studio was always eager to help his/her colleagues, and so forth. After each report was concluded, Chairman Slíva asked if there were any comments. There never were any.

After more than half of the reports were read, it was time for mine. It was a devastating report, which included statements such as "Comrade Holub always avoids any participation in the activities of the Czechoslovak Youth Institute. His mocking attitude toward our socialist regime is well known. He often initiated disturbances at public gatherings, showed disrespect to his superiors." There was silence when the reading concluded. Chairman Slíva asked if there were any comments. More silence. It was known at the time that Eva and I were a couple, so if she had said anything, it would have carried no weight. The silence was deafening. Suddenly, a hand went up. All heads turned in that direction. It was Alena Hejdová, who stood up and said, "I think that report is too harsh. Martin couldn't get a job with that kind of report, and I don't think he deserves that." There was a murmur of agreement in the room.

Chairman Slíva took the floor and said, "OK, if you all agree that the report is too harsh, it can be modified. Do you all agree that it's harsh?" A unanimous "Yeah" issued from the room. The chairman continued, "All right, any suggestions as to what to add or what to delete?" My friend Petr Krejčí stood up and said that other reports included mentions of that person's summer jobs and that he knew that I had done manual labor every summer, including spraying hops with herbicide, which we had done together. Somebody else stood up and said that if I had done physical labor every summer, then my attitude toward the working class could not have been all that bad, so why not mention that? Chairman Slíva kept nodding, and one of the committee members kept revising my profile, so that when it was finally reread, it ended up being almost as bland as the rest of the reports. And none of this would have happened without Alena Hejdová, someone whom I had completely ignored throughout the six years we spent in the university.

Once the meeting was over, I rushed to her and thanked her. However, it wasn't until many years later, when I was reliving this episode in my memory, that I came to realize that my thanks was nowhere near adequate relative to what she had done for me. Of all my classmates, she was the one whom I had paid least attention to during the six years of university, the one whose existence I barely registered. And yet she was the one who stood up and, at some personal risk, spoke in my defense—and all I did was to say thank you. On reflection, I wanted her to know how much I appreciated what she had done and that I had never forgotten it, but of course, there was no way of letting her know that while I was living in New York during the Cold War. Then, unexpectedly, more than thirty years later, an opportunity presented itself where I could let Alena know about my feelings, but unfortunately, again I blew it.

It was in the early 1990s, shortly after the Velvet Revolution. I was visiting the Prague office of ARA/Praha-New York, a Czech American architectural firm I had recently founded with my friend and partner Stʼopa Hrubý. One day when leaving the office and rushing to a meeting, I ran into Alena in the foyer. It was the first time we had seen each other since we left the university. I said, "Goodness, Alena, how nice to see you, what are you doing here?" She explained that my partner Stʼopa had hired her to do some work. She too appeared to be in a hurry, and it seemed to me that this was neither the right time nor place to let Alena know how often I had thought of her in the last thirty years. So instead, I asked her if she'd be around and whether I'd have another opportunity to see her. She replied, "Oh yes, I'll be around," and we each ran our separate ways. As it turned out, that was the last time I saw Alena Hejdová. Unless another opportunity miraculously presents itself, she'll go to her grave without the slightest notion of how grateful I was and still am to her.

Construction photo taken in 1978 of the apartment building Arash still lives in.

Iranian Architect

In the summer of 2014, I received the following email:

Dear Mr. Holub,

I am a young Iranian architect and I was born and still live in the building you have designed in the Gheytarieh neighborhood in Tehran. Ever since my childhood, I have felt fortunate to be living in a special, unique, beautiful building. I have researched all the projects you had done in Iran, and I'd like to write an article about your work for an Iranian architectural magazine. Do I have your permission?

Respectfully yours,

Arash Tabidzadeh

This email made me feel old, but also strangely satisfied! It was a nice ego massage, to be sure. I responded to Arash that he did indeed have my permission, and I asked him in which of the two apartment buildings designed by me in Gheytarieh he was living. I also expressed my doubts that any editor would want to publish an article about an American architect who had worked in Iran under the Shah's regime. He replied that he was well aware that I had designed two apartment buildings in the Gheytarieh neighborhood and that he lived in the one completed first, known as Gheytarieh I.

I then asked Arash a favor: would he take some photos of both buildings and email them to me? My request clearly pained Arash. He responded, "Mr. Holub, I'd be happy to take pictures for you but, please, understand that we live here under very difficult circumstances. Your buildings have not been maintained since they were completed. Please keep that in mind." Once I got the photos, I understood what Arash was talking about. The buildings were finished in a light-beige stucco, which was now covered with streaks of dirt. However, other than being dirty, the stucco had held up well; there was no peeling or cracks. The large windowpanes were all intact as well, so I wasn't altogether unhappy with what I saw after more than thirty-five years.

When I thanked Arash for sending me the photos, I mentioned that a thorough power washing would make his building look like new. He responded that he knew that, but that the financial

One of the photos Arash sent me. I suppose...

170

situation of his family, as well as that of the other condo owners, was such that spending money on cleaning the building was totally out of the question. I did not ask about the article, and after his first email, Arash never again mentioned it. Apparently, my hunch proved to have been correct, and I never heard from Arash again.

Too Late

As in all schools of architecture around the world, architectural design was the main course in the curriculum of the School of Architecture of the Czech Technical University. All the other classes, such as on the history of architecture, materials such as steel and concrete, building construction management, and so on, were in support of design, which was taught in design studios led by renowned professors. Each semester the professor would assign a project that we would then work on, in frequent consultations with the professor and his assistants, during the next five months. At the end of the semester, the completed designs were pinned to the walls of the studio for grading by a consortium of professors. After the grades were assigned, the drawings were kept up for a few weeks and then taken down. Now I am coming to the point of this story.

In the long and wide corridors there were pinup boards between the windows and the doors on which drawings were pinned. After the design drawings were taken down from the walls of the studios, the professors would selected a few that they pinned to the boards in the corridors, where they stayed during the whole next semester. Clearly, those were the drawings that the professors deemed to be worthy examples of studio work: they were teaching tools that showed the younger students what designs and presentations were considered exemplary. Throughout my six years at the school, I always very much wished that some of my drawings would be selected for display in the corridor, but that never happened. Even though I had always received the highest possible grades for my designs, no professor ever picked any of my drawings to display. That was quite disappointing for me.

Fast-forward some three or four years when I was working as a designer in the architectural office of the contracting firm Konstruktiva. It so happened that a colleague of mine, Věra Hylišová, needed to go to the School of Architecture either to pick up something or see someone, I no longer remember. When she returned to the office, she was all excited, exclaiming, "Martin, your drawings are all over the School! In all the corridors, there is a Martin Holub drawing anywhere you look." By that time, however, I no longer cared whether my work was displayed or not. I didn't even bother to go to see which of my drawings had been selected for display. It was too late.

Here is another story about how sometimes when you strongly wish for something, it may eventually come about, but at the wrong time or too late. Next to designing buildings, what I most like doing is skiing. However, as an architect, I never was able to ski for more than two weeks a year. So throughout my twenties and thirties I harbored a dream of taking one entire winter off, renting a place at some fine resort, and being a ski bum for a whole season.

It was, of course, a totally unrealistic fantasy. During my employment years, it would have been preposterous to expect that any employer would ever consider giving me a four-month leave of absence or that finding another job would have been easy had I taken so much time off. And once

I started working on my own, closing the office for the ski season was something completely out of the question. So the dream remained a dream.

And then, unexpectedly, when I was in my early forties, I was suddenly presented with a possibility of realizing my dream—if not fully, then to an extent hitherto unimaginable: I was given gratis a two-bedroom apartment, for one whole month, in a condominium building a short walk from the chairlift in Park City, Utah.

True, it was not for the whole season, but to be able to ski one entire month was something I had never done before, and in contrast to taking off the whole season, it was realistic: I could afford it and I could arrange my schedule to get away for that long.

This all came about because some good friends of mine, Chuck and Suzanne Rowan, a couple I had met in Tehran, asked me if I would develop a design proposal for a ski lodge to be added to the Edelweiss Condominiums, which they were managing in Park City. I agreed enthusiastically because I always wanted to design a ski lodge. But because Chuck and Suzanne were doing it on spec, all they could pay me were my expenses. They were planning to show my finished proposal to the condominium board and, convinced that the benefits of adding a Martin-designed lodge to the existing nondescript building were self-evident, they were quite optimistic that the board would approve it. When it did, I not only would collect my fee for the proposal but also would be given a commission for the lodge.

Well, as it happened, the board didn't go along with the idea: they thought the condo was making enough money for its owners as it was and that no new lodge was needed. However, prodded by Chuck and Suzanne, the board agreed to let me have an apartment for a month as a consolation prize.

And what an apartment it was! It was a two-bedroom, two-bathroom corner unit on the top floor with one large window looking toward the mountains and another down the valley. All my visitors would have their own bedroom and bathroom. Chuck and I picked a time slot from mid-February to mid-March, and I was all charged up to go. However, as the time was drawing closer, I began to feel that taking a month off wasn't perhaps the best thing to be doing at that time in my career. But another feeling—that I couldn't not accept that most generous offer of my friends—prevailed, and soon I was on my way to Park City.

My first visitor was Jim Cotton from California, another member of the XX Club (when we were in Tehran, we were ex-pats and after we returned, we became ex-expats; hence, members of the double-X club). Jim knew Chuck and Suzanne from Tehran, and the four of us had some good times together, spent both skiing and dining. I only invited good skiers, and the next visitor was Beverly Taylor, an old friend from New York. And so it went, one guest after another, each staying three to four days. Sometimes there was an overlap with two guests at a time, which we handled by using a convertible sofa in the living room. All the guests knew each other from my St. Martin's parties. There was plenty of fresh powder and the skiing was great.

Then something unexpected happened. Toward the end of the second week, I began to feel that I had had enough of skiing. I was surprised, because I had never felt that way before. Whenever I had skied for two weeks at a time before, I had never felt I'd had enough, and I had always felt sorry when it was over. And now, having a once-in-a-lifetime chance to ski for a whole month, I felt like going home after two weeks. How could this be?

In any event, I couldn't go home, because I had one more guest coming. Tom Rooney, another member of the XX Club who was then living in North Dakota, was coming for three days of skiing the next day. He too knew Chuck and Suzanne, and they were looking forward to his visit. After three more days of skiing with Tom, I decided I was going home: I just couldn't wait to get back to work and to my city life. The problem was how to tell Chuck and Suzanne. I could have made up some excuse, such as a crisis with a project under construction, but they were too good friends to lie to.

However, once I told them the truth, I was sorry I had. I should've made up some excuse, because my leaving while I could have skied for another two weeks was for them something totally incomprehensible. That a sane person in full command of his or her faculties would rather work than ski was simply beyond their ken. Once I realized that, I didn't even try to explain it. Instead, on my last night at Edelweiss, I invited Chuck and Suzanne to dinner at the best restaurant in Park City. They tried hard to behave as if nothing had happened, but I felt that my leaving early definitely cast a pall on our relationship. Fortunately, it was only temporary, and when I returned the following year, the incident of my early departure was forgotten.

So what's the moral of the story? I guess that it takes some time to know when we have outgrown something, to acknowledge that, and accept it. Accepting the offer to ski for a month was like trying to wear a twenty-year-old tuxedo that no longer fit.

Teaching

"Those who can, do; those who can't, teach." I've heard this adage attributed both to George Bernard Shaw and to Mark Twain. Whoever wrote it, nowhere is it truer than in my beloved profession of architecture. There are, of course, stellar exceptions to that rule (Louis Kahn comes to mind), including many practitioners just starting out who teach part-time to supplement their income and stop immediately once they no longer need to do so. But having taught at three vastly different institutions at different times, spanning fifteen years and two continents, I can state unequivocally that most of my colleagues who taught full time could not hold down a job or make it on their own.

I think that to be a good teacher, one needs to have a teacher's mentality, meaning one needs to derive satisfaction from explaining something one is very familiar with to someone who is not. By that definition, I clearly do not have teacher's mentality, and not only as far as architecture is concerned. I happen to be a good skier, so I often get asked if I could ski with someone and give some pointers. I dread those situations.

So why did I teach at all? Although I never sought teaching positions, I didn't have the nerve to decline them when they were offered to me. My reasons were mercenary. I was well aware that the general public (i.e., potential clients) did not know the truth about those who teach architecture. Most people still believe that, if you are a university professor, you must be good in your field. Consequently, having taught at such and such a university adds value to your résumé. In addition, I never taught full time, but always as a visiting or an adjunct professor of design. I know that many architects will give you all kinds of lofty reasons for why they teach, ranging from wanting to give back what they received when they themselves were in school to learning from their interactions with the students. Well, not me.

My first teaching position was at the Architectural Association in London in 1969. It was (and still is) a well-regarded school of architecture where luminaries such as Rem Koolhaas, Zaha Hadid, Peter Cook, Daniel Libeskind, and others all later taught. At the time, the AA, as it is called, put an overriding emphasis on the development of students' creativity, pushing all the practical aspects of the art of architecture to the back burner. Emblematic of this approach was the fact that the master of one of the fifth-year classes (called "forms") was not an architect, but a sculptor who was making a living by teaching full-time at the AA. His name was Trevor Long (amazing to me that I still remember his name almost fifty years later), and he was the reason I was offered the part-time teaching job at the AA.

I met Trevor at a party, and we talked about architecture. He told me that he was teaching at the AA and expressed interest in seeing my designs; the following evening I went to see him at the AA on Bedford Square with my portfolio and that was all it took. Trevor told me that if I wanted the job of being a design critic to his class during the last semester of their fifth form, meaning for their thesis projects, I should go to the dean's office and see a particular staff member. I did as I was told, signed a contract, and was hired as a Visiting Design Critic. My job was to show up two evenings a week for a design studio class. I accepted this first teaching job not for the mercenary reasons described earlier but out of sheer curiosity. Being a design critic was something I hadn't done before, so I was curious what it would be like. Plus, because of its stellar faculty, the AA had an elite ring to it, or so it seemed to me at the time. It no longer does.

At the beginning of the semester I was the students' favorite critic, or so they told me. I recall one of them telling me that I made the most sense. This honeymoon, however, didn't last long. Once the students started preparing presentation drawings, I became quite unpopular. Why? Because I insisted on certain conventions, such as that all drawings be the same size; that all plans, sections, and elevations be drawn in the same scale; and that all drawings be drawn in the same medium and not one in ink, another in pencil, and yet another in pastel. The students objected that I was cramping their creativity and started referring to me as a Nazi. An assistant dean had to be called in to mediate the dispute. He sided with me, which settled the matter but made me even less popular with the students. So much for my first teaching experience. The question of whether or not I'd be asked to teach the next semester never arose, because by the time the spring semester started, I was on a boat bound for America.

My second teaching experience took place between 1972 and 1974 at the School of Architecture at the University of Tennessee in Knoxville. Those were the years when I was developing my design consulting practice and when my major client was in Knoxville. Consequently, in those years, I was spending ninety to a hundred days per year in that city. Never more than three to four days at a time, but many trips nevertheless. Flying was easier in those days, when you could show up at the airport just twenty minutes before departure and when there was no such thing as a nonrefundable ticket.

Knoxville is a lively, small, university town, so meeting people was easy. It didn't take long before I met Don Hanson, the newly appointed dean of the School of Architecture. Don was a flamboyant fellow from Chicago who was in the process of assembling his faculty. The idea of hiring a visiting professor from New York who was also consulting for a leading local firm appealed to him. He offered me a job on the spot, without seeing any of my designs. My title was Visiting Associate Professor of Design. I was to teach a fifth-year design studio.

Like in London, I didn't have the nerve to refuse what was offered to me without my asking for it, but unlike in London, this time I accepted purely for mercenary reasons, or to put it more charitably, for reasons of convenience. It was just too good to have one more reason to commute to Tennessee, while the School of Architecture and my client split the cost of my plane tickets. I started teaching in the fall of 1972.

The School of Architecture had a rather showy method of assigning students to design studios. I didn't know whether it was instituted by Dean Hanson or if it was an established tradition, but here is how it worked. At the beginning of each semester, all the students gathered in a large assembly hall. Posted on the wall were the names of the professors who were going to teach design studios. Each professor in turn then jumped on the table in the middle of the room and described the project the students would be designing in his or her studio. Once the professors were done with their presentations, each student wrote on a piece of paper his or her first, second, third, and fourth choice of studio and threw that paper into a large cauldron. A secretary then took the pieces of paper and transcribed the student choices into columns of names under each studio. The dean then distributed the students to the studios according to their choices and his judgment.

Beginning with the first semester I taught, my studio classes were always oversubscribed. I think there were three reasons for that. First, I was the only member of the design faculty who was also practicing; all the others were teaching full time. Second, I was from New York, which in Tennessee commanded respect. Finally, the projects in my studio were those I had worked on for my client. Typically, they were proposals for housing or commercial developments in and around Knoxville for sites with which the students were familiar. That provided a dose of reality, which the students liked.

Whatever the reasons, the fact that semester after semester most of the students wrote Holub Studio as their first choice didn't make me popular with my colleagues. However, because there was precious little I could do about it, I didn't let it worry me. After all, I was an outsider; I didn't belong to the faculty community. My teaching assignment in Tennessee came to an end with my departure for Tehran in January 1975.

My third and last teaching job was in New York some eight years later at the School of Architecture of the New York Institute of Technology. Once again, the job came to me unsolicited. Out of the blue, the dean called me and asked if I'd be interested in teaching a fifth-year design studio. It turned out that I had been recommended by Julius Varosy, an architect acquaintance of mine who taught there and was leaving. And once again, when I met the dean and he offered me the position, I didn't have the nerve to say no, even though I didn't like the feel of the place. This time my title was Adjunct Professor of Design, and my teaching load amounted to two evenings per week.

My initial feeling proved to be correct: it was a terrible school. A preponderance of students were spoiled, rich kids from South America. I've been told that the school has since improved, but the following incident will illustrate its caliber at the time. It is only because of this incident that I remember the thesis project. It was a design for a community center that included a library, a restaurant, a dance studio, meeting rooms, and a multifunctional performance space—a complex project that was appropriate for a thesis project. One of the students had attended the first two sessions, during which he did not ask any questions, and then did not show up again until three weeks before the deadline, at a time when other students' designs had long been developed and they were then busy preparing their presentations. At that class, the fellow in question brought me three or four rudimentary sketches, the kind one brings to the first session to discuss a concept. Preparing those drawings couldn't have taken him more than a couple of hours. Despite his atrocious English, he proceeded to volubly explain how wonderful his design would be.

I interrupted him, saying, "Mr. Iglesias (I no longer remember his real name), architects express themselves by drawing, not by talking. I cannot comment on your drawings, because they don't tell me where the entrances are to the dance studio, to the library, or to the restaurant, where the bathrooms are, where the loading dock for the deliveries is, where people park, how many parking spaces you allowed for, and many other essential things. Once you show me drawings that contain the required information, I'd be happy to give you my comments. However, even if you work twelve hours a day every day from now on, I seriously doubt that it's humanly possible for you to complete this project before the deadline." The fellow looked at me angrily and said, "Professor Holub, do you know how much money my parents have been spending over the last four years to keep me in this school? And you are now telling me that you are not going to help me?"

The next thing I knew, the student complained about me to the dean, who called and asked me to come to his office for a meeting with the student. I had the presence of mind to tell the dean to ask the student to bring along the drawings he had shown me. Once he saw those drawings, the dean agreed with my assessment, but I could see that it was painful for him. He then told me that I could leave; the student stayed behind, and I have no idea what went on behind that closed door. It wouldn't have surprised me if the dean cut some deal with the student allowing him to graduate. I resolved to no longer teach at that school, but I was spared the task of announcing my resignation to the dean. When I saw the list of the design faculty for the next semester, my name wasn't on it. And that was the unceremonious end of my teaching career.

My Mother's Mink Coat

My mother was many things in her life: a lawyer (who never practiced), a housewife, a student of art history, a political prisoner, a professor of art history, a dissident, and a writer. However, when this story took place, it's fair to say that she was a spoiled rich kid, nineteen years old and in the first year of law school at Charles University in Prague. The reason she was in law school was that her father believed that—no pun intended—lawyers had the best balls. (His strategy worked because she met my father at one of those balls.)

That first winter in Prague my mother used her allowance to buy herself a mink coat. When she returned home for Christmas and her father saw the coat, he hit the ceiling. He told her, "In our family, we don't show off! The purpose of a fur coat is to keep you warm, which is why the fur belongs on the inside. When you return to Prague, go to Rosenbaum (at the time the best couturier) and have the coat refashioned so that the mink is on the inside as a lining." My mother got the point, didn't argue, and did as she was told. The coat with the mink lining served her well many years since.

My mother told me this story when I was a grown man and she was sharing with me the errant ways of her youth. Let's fast-forward some fifty years to the time when my mother was long dead, the story of her mink coat was long forgotten, and I was a recent widower spending my weekends in the country reading my grandfather's diaries. My grandparents had a particularly unhappy marriage, and keeping the diaries evidently provided my grandfather an escape from his sad personal life. There were many hardcover notebooks neatly written in my grandfather's elegant longhand.

In the notebook dated December 1932, I found the following entry:

> Another example of the wrong values my wife instills in our children: today my daughter returned from Prague in a flashy new mink coat that she bought from the allowance we gave her for her studies. Where did she get the notion that wearing a fur coat with the fur on the outside is the right and proper thing to do? It could only have come from my wife. All along, I have tried to teach my children to not show off our wealth and I thought they understood, until this. However, I was pleased to see that Miluška quickly saw the error of her ways and agreed to correct it.

Design Philosophy

I've already mentioned that I attended a total of six schools from primary school to high school because of my family history, which was rendered turbulent by the communist putsch. Now, from first grade through twelfth grade, teacher after teacher told me, in so many words, the same thing: "Holub, you are very smart, but you are lazy." Hearing the same thing repeated by so many different teachers over so many years, I came to believe it. When I was approaching adulthood, I gave the matter some thought and concluded that being lazy was a great handicap and, if I wanted to make it through the rest of my life honorably, I'd have to make some adjustments. I came to believe that a lazy man takes more time to perform any task than does an industrious man, and, consequently, I'd have to find ways to save time.

To do so I decided to simplify everything that could be simplified and to pare down everything that was not essential. This attitude saved me later from smoking, because always worrying about having enough cigarettes on me, plus the lighters or matches, was clearly nonessential and could be eliminated. So no smoking for me. Next, I decided that when I had to wear a tie, it would be a bow tie, so that I wouldn't have to worry about any other ties. Further down the road, to save the time it took to shave, I grew a beard, which I have to this day and which I have to trim only every two to three weeks. Imagine the time saved not shaving for more than fifty years!

All these adjustments were, of course, trivial, but I do believe that this attitude, consciously or subconsciously, came to influence the way I design. I have always tried to achieve the simplest possible expression with nothing superfluous. Every element has to have a reason—no fluff. Before I introduce any feature in my design, such as a jog in the wall or a change of material or a step in the floor, I ask myself, "Is it really essential? Would the design work without it?" Unless I am absolutely convinced that it has to be there, I don't include it.

Come to think of it, I am writing these scribbles in much the same way. I am trying to convey what I want to say in as few words as possible. I subject each word, each sentence, to the same scrutiny as I do my designs. You be the judge of whether I've succeeded.

My father as a law student at Charles University in 1920.

My Father

My father was born in 1900, so I always easily knew how old he was. I write about him reluctantly and do so only because this collection of memories would not be complete without him. Why reluctantly? Because in comparison with those of my mother, my memories of him will seem far less warm and fond, yet through no fault of his own.

But first, a word about my parents' disastrous marriage. It came about only because, when they met at one of the lawyers' balls, my mother's family was in turmoil after her father's unsuccessful suicide and the presumed bankruptcy of his business. At that time—in sharp contrast to her family—solid and steady Dr. Holub, who was thirteen years her senior, appeared to my mother as the rock of Gibraltar, which she found appealing. But after the dust had settled, she came to realize that she and my father were two completely different chips off the block. In some cases, a marriage of opposites may work; in their case, it didn't.

My mother's family members were entrepreneurs, used to taking risks, working hard, and playing hard. My father's father was a civil servant, and his mother was a housewife. My father himself was a civil servant, although he had a private law practice on the side. When he married, he expected his wife to be a housewife just as his mother had been. That was not going to happen, however. At the time my mother married, she was a doctor of jurisprudence. Although she had no desire to practice law, she didn't want to be a housewife either. You can see conflict in the making.

My mother suggested a divorce some four years after they got married. My father said fine, so long as he got to keep me. My mother wouldn't accept that, and they carried on for another three years until, when I was six years old, he finally agreed that my mother could have custody of me. They were divorced in the blink of an eye, because my mother made no demands for alimony or for any support whatsoever, since money from her family was still plentiful.

I recall absolutely no trauma or distress in connection with my parents' divorce. A child has no reference points, so whatever is presented to him or her, if done gently and lovingly, appears as normal. I still remember how my mother broke the news to

On a canoeing trip down Vltava River in 1930.

My father at the Adriatic Sea in 1935, two years before he married my mother.

me that my father was no longer going to live with us. It was at the end of my summer vacation between first and second grade, and I had just returned from my first Cub Scout camp. After I regaled my mother with some stories from camp, she said that she had something to tell me as well.

She began by saying that sometimes things develop between parents in such a way that they would be happier living apart, and that had happened between my father and her. That was why Daddy had moved out and was now living in another part of town, though it was easily accessible by a tram. He would be stopping by every Wednesday after work, and I would be spending every weekend with him. Plus, I could stop by his office after school anytime I wanted to see him and call him anytime I wanted to speak to him. It so happened that my father's office was very close to my school. Given that I had only known my parents treating each other in considerate ways, had never heard an argument or a raised voice, and had never doubted their love for me, I found the new arrangement perfectly reasonable and was looking forward to my first weekend with my father, just the two of us guys, as a new adventure.

So began perhaps ten years during which I had a weekend father. In those days, weekends started on Saturday afternoon. Until I became a young adult and had other things to do on the weekends, each Saturday after lunch with my mother, I'd take a tram to Podolí, a quarter full of suburban villas and small apartment buildings in one of which lived my father. Until he remarried some three years later, it was just the two of us, and I have pleasant memories of those times. We did manly things, such as throwing toy hand grenades or building fires. Before the communist revolution, my father was the Commissioner of Health for the city of Prague, and he later married an employee of the Health Department who'd now be called a psychiatric social worker. She was a family friend while my parents were still married, was a frequent visitor to our home, and was very fond of me. I'd called her Aunt Marie, so when my father married her, it seemed perfectly natural.

Except for Sunday morning breakfasts, my father and I mostly ate out. Once Aunt Marie moved in, the weekends took on a more domestic character. She was a great cook, so we had fine Saturday night dinners and Sunday lunches at home. Sunday mornings my father and I would typically take a walk in a nearby park, and after lunch we'd go to the movies. Then we'd stop in an ice cream parlor, after which I'd take the tram home for dinner with my mother. This routine wasn't interrupted even when my mother was in prison. The only difference was that instead of setting off for my father's place from our nearby apartment, on Saturday afternoons I'd take a bus from Poděbrady, a town some fifty kilometers from Prague, where I was in boarding school. In time, I learned to pocket the money my father gave me for bus fare and, instead, would hitchhike both ways. When my mother was released from prison, the weekend routine continued. The only thing that changed was the location of our apartment.

Apart from the weekends, my father was involved in my life when I attended Boy Scouts and later YMCA summer camps: it was he who came to see me on parent visiting days. Another tradition that lasted through my young adulthood involved my birthdays, which were always celebrated at my father's house. Because my mother could not make the kind of cake Aunt Marie could, on each of my birthdays until perhaps my late teens, my mother and I would go to my father's place where Aunt Marie would serve a fine dinner, culminating with a splendid birthday cake. To my knowledge, this was the one time a year my parents saw each other. As I write this, a memory comes to my mind, so I'll allow myself a little diversion.

Although I don't remember my tenth or twentieth birthdays, I have a clear memory of my sixteenth. That year, dinner at my father's house ended around 10 o'clock; when my mother and I were leaving, I told her that I was planning to meet my buddies in Alfa Bar on Wenceslas Square. At the time, I was already going to dance classes, an important rite of passage to adulthood that included bar hopping after the classes. My mother knew that was the reason, on the night of the classes that ended at 9:00 p.m., I didn't come home until after midnight; so on my birthday she didn't object to my going to a bar. At Alfa Bar four or five of my classmates were waiting for me with a bottle of Scotch already on the table. In those days, the communist authorities worried about young people's ideological purity, not about underage drinking. In fact, there was no such thing as a minimum drinking age, and whether a youth was served a drink in a bar was up to the discretion of the bartender. Even with my baby face, I don't recall ever having been refused a drink.

Once we killed the bottle of Scotch, we felt the night was still young, so we went to another drinking establishment along Wenceslas Square, where there was also dancing. I remember that it was the first time I encountered young women of a different gene pool from the girls in my high school. Dancing was then still a new adventure for me and, I guess, for all of us, so we danced until the wee hours. When I crawled onto my mattress in our miniscule apartment where my mother and I slept inches from each other, I was convinced that she was fast asleep. Much later, I learned otherwise. I fell asleep that night satisfied that I'd celebrated my sixteenth birthday in style.

But back to my father. Our weekend rituals started petering out perhaps right after my sixteenth birthday. Whenever I called him and said that I wouldn't be able to come, usually because of a Saturday night ball or a Sunday afternoon tea dance, or most likely both, he was always understanding. Then during my university years, I stopped spending weekends at my father's house. I recall, from time to time in those years, my mother asking me, "When did you last call your father?"

My father was of the generation in which classically educated men, of which he was one, showed their wit by spicing their conversation with aptly selected Latin proverbs. He was fluent in German and French and quite embarrassed that his command of English was less than perfect. At his time, he was considered by others and considered himself a well-traveled man on the strength of having been twice in Paris and once each in Berlin and Venice. Yet he never flew in an airplane or learned to drive.

Although he couldn't carry a tune, his first love was music. Up until the communist take-over of 1948 he was an accomplished pianist and, until a few years before he died, when he could no longer go out at night because of his advanced glaucoma, he was an avid concertgoer. His knowledge of classical music was encyclopedic. After hearing just a few bars of music on the radio, he'd say with great self-satisfaction, "This is andante sostenuto, the second movement of Brahms's Symphony No. 1." And of course, he was never wrong. It used to bother me that he didn't do anything with this vast database of knowledge; he never put it to any use. He would have been a great music critic, but that idea never crossed his mind.

My father was truly crushed by communism. At the time of the revolution he was forty-eight years old, at the height of his career, and highly respected both as a public servant and as a lawyer. Then, overnight, he found himself labeled an "enemy of the people," he was dismissed from his job, and his law practice was closed. The government instituted a currency reform, whereby a modest amount of the old currency could be exchanged for the equivalent amount in the new currency. However, whatever money exceeded that modest amount (I now forget the threshold) could only be exchanged in the ratio of fifty to one. Consequently, in one stroke, everyone had more or less the same amount of money. This meant that my father had to get a job, and the only work available to enemies of the people was manual labor. His first job after the revolution was digging ditches at the construction site of a new dam about thirty kilometers south of Prague. It was too far to commute there, so five days a week my father had to stay in the on-site dorms, coming home Saturday afternoons and leaving gruesomely early on Monday mornings. Sometimes he was so tired that he sent me word via my mother not to come for my weekend visit because he needed to rest.

His life after the communist revolution was horrible, but my father was hardly alone in that predicament. There were many enemies of the people, and the new government was doing a good job of rounding them up and sending them to dig ditches. After all, the liquidation of the bourgeois class was the first task in building socialism. As he later recalled, there were more doctors, lawyers, entrepreneurs, and industrialists at the dorm he stayed in than there were genuine laborers. By his own admission, many of his fellow members of the bourgeois class took their fate with more panache and humor than he was able to. At the time, no one of that class thought that the communist regime would last for more than forty years. Communism was considered a temporary aberration, bordering on madness, that would blow away; sound reason would prevail, and things would return to where they were before the revolution.

Hard as it was, the ditch-digging phase of my father's new life lasted only a little over a year. Its most visible casualty was his piano playing. He claimed the sensitivity of his hands was permanently destroyed by the manual labor, and because he was no longer able to play piano the way he used to, he'd rather not play at all. He did not touch the piano again for the rest of his life.

After the year of ditch digging, my father managed to be transferred to a concrete testing lab, where he transported concrete cubes. He was pleased with this change because the new job was indoors. After another year or two in the concrete testing lab, my father finagled yet another transfer. Using his lifelong hobby of photography, he obtained a job in a photo lab, which was a major improvement. First of all, the lab was in Prague, which meant no more commuting. And second, he was no longer doing manual labor. Instead, he was developing pictures. We all rejoiced over this happy development.

The photo lab job lasted perhaps five years, after which my father secured the best position of his postrevolutionary career: he became a librarian at the Czechoslovak Institute of Architects. Happily for me, his working there coincided with my time in the School of Architecture. When Western architectural magazines arrived at the library, I was perhaps the first person in Prague who got a chance to peruse them. It was in this job that my father coasted to retirement: he retired at the first stroke of sixty, the earliest he could. As I write about the succession of my father's postrevolution jobs, I realize that they mirrored the political climate of the country, which was getting gradually milder, culminating in the Prague Spring.

It so happened that my father and Aunt Marie retired at about the same time, after which they divided their time between their apartment in Prague and a house in the country. Typically, they would stay in the country from mid-May to mid-October. I was then riding a motor scooter, so each summer I'd pay them a visit over a weekend. They loved being in the country and complained about the winters in Prague. For my father, the redeeming feature of the city was the music.

My father's country house sounded grander than it actually was. It was an old German farmhouse in the border area formerly called Sudetenland, which had been settled for centuries by ethnic Germans. In fact, they were the first instance of "guest workers" being invited to move from their homes to work in another country. At the beginning of the fifteenth century, the Bohemian kingdom was experiencing a labor shortage, and King Václav IV invited German artisans and farmers to come to Bohemia to work. Many came and settled on the Bohemian side of the border between Germany and Bohemia, where they stayed until World War II. Many of them also became Nazi sympathizers, and since, at the end of the war, it was practically impossible to determine who was and who was not, then Czechoslovak president Edvard Beneš decided to expel all Sudeten Germans back to Germany. Because some of them were simple farmers who had done nothing wrong, the expulsion was a very controversial decision. Still, it was done, and as a result, there were many empty German farmhouses available for purchase for a pittance from the government.

I don't know how it started, but artists and musicians began buying houses in the small village of Říčky in the mountains of northeast Bohemia. Because my father was a great admirer of both artists and musicians, in the late 1940s he bought a house in Říčky as well. It was a charming but simple affair with a great view, but no indoor plumbing or electricity; those improvements came about ten years later. My father and Aunt Marie spent all their vacations, and substantially more time after they retired, in that house. I don't think they ever traveled anywhere else. My father sold the house several years after Aunt Marie died.

This was the state of affairs when I left the country in 1967. Of course, we all thought that I would be back in a year. Instead, it was another seventeen years before I saw my father again.

During my seventeen years apart from my father, just as I had with my mother, we were in contact through letters, but while with my mother I exchanged more than fifty letters a year, with my father there were perhaps only six per year. Although I felt a filial bond, I just didn't have much to say to him. He wrote me about which of his friends had died and how many funerals he attended, and I wrote him about where I was skiing or some such nonsense.

Perhaps the following story captures my father best. At the time when I was flying two to three times a year between New York and Tehran, stopping on the way either in London or in Paris, my

My father in 1975 at his country place, wearing a shirt I sent him.

mother, perhaps feeling guilty that she got to see me while my father did not, came up with an idea. She wrote me to suggest the following: "Instead of Paris or London, why don't you just once stop in Vienna? It's only a few hours on the train from Prague, your father would certainly get an exit permit, and he could join you there for a few days." I thought it was an excellent idea, so I wrote as much to my father, adding that I would, of course, cover all his expenses in connection with this trip. He wrote back thanking me profusely for my invitation. However, after seriously discussing my proposal with Aunt Marie, they concluded that it would be harmful for his health. Seeing me after such a long time and only for so short a period before parting again would just be too emotionally taxing for him, which is why, with great regret, he had to decline.

When my father was a law student in the early 1920s, he was part of a group of friends who frequently got together to carouse. After they graduated, the young lawyers kept on meeting at various times and places until, to facilitate the scheduling, they established a rule that they would get together for dinner in the restaurant U Schnellů the first Monday of each month. That tradition lasted without interruption for more than fifty years, until they started dying off. When, out of some six or seven friends, my father was the last one left standing, he wrote me—without any sense of humor or irony—that he'd discontinued his dinners at U Schnellů, because dining alone was no fun.

My father was no hero. Unlike my mother, he did not sign Charter 77. However, when he was forced by circumstances to make a moral decision, he always made the right one. My mother shared with me one example of this trait. During the German occupation, as a high official in the city government, my father had a German supervisor. It so happened that this particular German was a cultivated man who discovered in my father someone he could talk to about art and literature, and he wanted to befriend him. To that end, he invited my father to accompany him to the National Theater to see an opera. My father wanted so much to attend, but to have been seen in the theater with a German officer would have labeled him a collaborator, which to my father was unacceptable. And so at great risk to himself, he declined the invitation. Fortunately, there were no consequences, because the German seemed to have been not only cultured but also a decent fellow who understood why my father had to decline.

My mother also shared another story about my father's moral sense. My father was a lifelong member of the Social Democratic Party. Shortly after the communist take-over, to boost the number of party members, the new government declared that the Social Democratic Party would merge with the Communist Party. Those social democrats who did not object to the merger didn't have to do anything and were simply handed Communist Party cards. However, those who did not want to join the Communist Party had to state so publicly. Becoming a member of the Communist Party would have been highly beneficial to my father, who was at the time digging ditches, whereas stating that he did not wish to become a communist put a blotch on his ideological dossier. Still, my father chose not to join the Communist Party.

Although they divorced in 1945, my parents were always in touch because of me. For example, when he had not heard from me for longer than usual, my father would call my mother and ask her if I was all right. My mother would then write me to write to my father. She was not the most practical person, but compared to my father, she was a paragon of practicality. After Aunt Marie died, my father was totally helpless. He was not embarrassed to call my mother to ask her where to buy coffee. My mother took pity on him and provided him with basic practical advice. She told him where to buy an electric heater when the heating in his apartment conked out, how to get his laundry washed, and so on. As my father got older, traveling to his country house by a combination of train and bus was becoming more and more onerous for him, and so my mother offered to drive him to Říčky for the summer. My father wrote me how exceedingly helpful that was and how grateful he was to her. I was very glad that my parents were so civil with each other.

Then came December 1983, the time of my first visit back to Prague. Even before I arrived, my mother wrote me that the question had arisen with whom I would spend Christmas Eve. I knew that I would be staying with my mother and visiting my father, but did not care whether those visits would include Christmas Eve. However, several days before I left for Prague, I received a letter from my father, in which he wrote, "During my phone conversation with your mother, I found out what she thinks of me and, because of my health, I have resolved not to see or speak to her again for the rest of my life." Wow! Because I was leaving for Prague in a few days, I did nothing.

When in Prague, I told my mother about the letter I had received from my father and asked her what had happened. Uncharacteristically contrite, my mother replied, "It was not my proudest moment. While trying to convince me that, as you'd be staying with me, the least I could do would be to let you spend Christmas Eve with him, your father said, 'Why, I really don't care, but what would my friends think if, after so many years, my son did not even spend Christmas Eve with me?' Perhaps because it was so typically your father, it somehow opened the floodgates of long-buried memories and I just let him know how I felt about what his friends would think. As I said, it was not my proudest moment."

I was amazed. At the time, my parents had been divorced for thirty-eight years, both of them had remarried, and one was divorced and the other a widower; still, the passions of long ago were dormant somewhere down there in the subbasement of consciousness, ready to be ignited by a most benign spark. My father stood by his words and never spoke to or saw my mother again.

Aunt Marie died of colon cancer in 1979, and my father turned eighty as a widower. It was a hard blow for him, as theirs was an excellent marriage, if only because she was totally devoted to him. However, it didn't take long before another woman appeared in his life. I have no idea how they met. He wrote me about her almost sheepishly, as if embarrassed. The reason for that was she had been a hat maker, before she retired, which was beneath Dr. Holub's station. As he explained to me in a

My father at his apartment in Prague in 1979, the year his second wife died.

My father in 1984, a year before he died.

letter, "You know, it's hard to find the right woman when you are over eighty."

Her name was Zdenička, a diminutive of Zdena. I met her during my first visit back to Prague in Christmas 1983. She was a lovely woman, perhaps fifteen years younger than my father. She could not believe that someone of his stature would be interested in a simple woman like herself. The second time I saw her was two years later at my father's funeral. It was from her that I learned how he'd died. They were having lunch at a restaurant near her apartment and everything seemed fine, until my father leaned toward her, saying, "Zdenička, I don't feel well." Then he leaned over some more: "As a matter of fact, I don't feel well at all." Whereupon he keeled over, fell to the floor, and that was the end of him. When the ambulance arrived, he was pronounced dead. He was one month shy of eighty-five.

Perhaps ten years later, sometime in the mid-1990s, while I was visiting my mother in Prague, it suddenly occurred to me that I didn't know where my father was buried (i.e., where the urn with his ashes was). I asked my mother if she knew, but she did not. So I called Líba Lerl. When Aunt Marie had worked at the Department of Health of the City of Prague, a much younger Líba was among the staff Aunt Marie supervised and became her mentee. I suspect that she was a substitute for the daughter Aunt Marie never had. In any case, the two women became lifelong friends. Once Líba married Zdeněk Lerl, they became the young friends of both my father and Aunt Marie. They used to spend all their vacations at my father's country house, and after Aunt Marie died, they were very helpful to my father. And after my father died, they made all the funeral arrangements, which was why, when I wanted to find out where my father was buried, I called Líba.

When I asked her where my father's urn was, she replied, "Nowhere. It was your father's express wish to have no plaque or sign indicating where his ashes were; he wanted to disappear without a trace. So we strew his ashes in the meadow in Strašnice Cemetery. Next to the meadow is a wall full of plaques with names and dates, but there is none for your father."

I was familiar with that meadow from the funerals I attended at Strašnice Cemetery in my youth; I saw no point in going there.

Kazimir Jones

While working at Kahn & Jacobs Architects, I became friendly with a Chinese interior designer named Eunice Chan. We had the same take on a number of our colleagues, as well as a similar sense of humor, so we lunched together often. Eunice was a one-woman interior design department of that august firm. After its demise, she bounced from job to job until she settled in the Facilities Department of the New York office of Prudential Insurance Company where, over the next ten years or so she rose to the rank of vice president of facilities. Meanwhile, I had started my design consulting practice, first spending ninety to a hundred days per year in Tennessee where my major client was and then leaving for four years in Tehran. Throughout those years, Eunice and I had stayed in touch.

When I returned from Tehran, Eunice and I continued our friendship, lunching together frequently, as well as having occasional dinners. While she was with Prudential, in addition to hiring architects, Eunice was the liaison between the architects designing its office spaces and the contractors building them. Her frequent theme during our get-togethers was complaining about incompetent architects who produced terrible drawings on which the dimensions didn't add up, sheets were not properly cross-referenced, and important details were missing—all of which created a lot of headaches during construction. I remember it was during one of our conversations, when Eunice was once again ranting about incompetent architects she was dealing with on a particular job, that I could not help myself and blurted out, "Eunice, why don't you ever hire me? You know my design work, you know what kind of construction drawings I prepare, so why not hire me?"

Her response still rings in my ears: "Martin, even if you were the world's most talented and competent architect, there is no way under the sun that the Prudential Insurance Company would ever hire a sole practitioner. Martin, you have to project an image of a firm." Well, OK, I got that. At the time, I was indeed a one-man firm, working out of an office in one of the two rooms of my apartment. At the time there was a magazine, *Progressive Architecture*, that carried a column chauvinistically called "Firms and Men," or some such title. This column published news about promotions of top personnel in large offices, moves of top people from one firm to another, office mergers, establishments of new offices, firm relocations, and so on.

Immediately after I hung up with Eunice, I tried to think of a most ludicrous and unlikely name for an associate and came up with Kazimir Jones. Then, on a lark and as a private joke between Eunice and me, I picked up the phone and called the offices of *Progressive Architecture*. I asked for the editor of "Firms and Men," and when she came on the phone, I dictated the following announcement for the column: "The office of Martin Holub Architects & Planners is pleased to announce that Kazimir Jones was promoted to the position of Senior Associate." I also printed new stationery to reflect the change of the name of my firm from Martin Holub Architect to Martin Holub Architects & Planners.

Progressive Architecture was a monthly, and it happened to be near the end of the publication cycle, so that the next issue came out the following week, with my announcement in it. I called Eunice and asked her to look at the "Firms and Men" column. She did and could not stop laughing. When she finally did, she said, "I'll see if Prudential will hire this august firm where Kazimir Jones is a Senior Associate." I was, however, never to find out whether Kazimir Jones made any difference to my chances of being hired by Prudential Insurance Company because, shortly thereafter, in some corporate reshuffle, Eunice was transferred to another position within Prudential in which she no longer hired architects.

However, the Law of Unintended Consequences kicked in in a way neither of us had foreseen. It appeared that there were marketers who followed those announcements in "Firms and Men"; shortly after the announcement, Kazimir Jones started receiving mail and phone calls. It was the usual junk mail all architects receive: offers of insurance, samples of wood veneers, catalogs of shower doors, and so on. What was meant as a private joke between Eunice and me cast a shadow over the next thirty-plus years and counting, because while Eunice has been long retired and living happily in California, Kazimir Jones is still receiving junk mail and calls to this day.

Naturally, everyone who has ever worked at my office has wondered just who this guy who received all that mail and all those calls without ever setting foot in the office was. Eventually, Kazimir became an office phantom, a kind of in-joke for the initiated. There was a steady flow of banter: "I have to check with Kazimir, what would Kazimir think about it, I don't think Kazimir would like that," and so on. Not long ago I ran into Richard Perry who used to work in my office until perhaps ten years ago, when he set out on his own. His first question was, "And how is Kazimir?"

My Troubles with English

After my parents' divorce, it was agreed that my father would pay for my piano and English lessons. I started going to the English-for-Children classes at the Language Institute in precommunist Czechoslovakia when I was in second grade. We sang "Old MacDonald Had a Farm / E-I-E-I-O" and similar songs but did not learn much else. Seeing my lack of progress after a year or so of attending the Language Institute, my mother engaged the services of her colleague from the Art History Department of Charles University, Olga Šilková, who had spent the war in England and was now teaching English to children. With Olga, I learned about Humpty Dumpty, but I don't remember much else. My third English tutor was Mrs. Weiner, whom I've mentioned in an earlier story. It was around this time, when I was nine or ten years old, when the following incident happened. For years to come, it became family lore concerning my pursuit of English.

During my summer vacation, perhaps between fifth and sixth grade, I was spending time at my father's place in the country. One day my father remarked that he had not seen me open my English textbook even once since I'd arrived. So I went to fetch the book and brought it to the dining table where we were sitting. I opened it to a page on top of which was written "FIRST LESSON." I looked at it and then, innocently and un-self-consciously, asked my father, "Dad, what is the meaning of 'first'?"

Without saying a word, my father rose from the table, walked over to the telephone, dialed the operator, and asked to be connected with my mother's number in Prague. (There was no direct dialing of long-distance calls at the time.) When my mother picked up, my father asked her in his low, measured voice, "How long has Martin been taking English lessons?" They agreed that I had been taking them for more than four years. My father then said that he might as well have been throwing his money out of the window, because, after four years of studying, her son didn't know the meaning of the word "first."

The problem was that I had not been studying English for four years; instead, I had been attending classes or taking lessons in English—which was a big difference. I am sure that after I returned to Prague, my mother read me the riot act, but there was just nothing that would make me open a book and study in those years. Shortly thereafter, my mother went to prison, I went to the boarding school, and both my English and piano lessons were discontinued. While my piano lessons were never resumed (well, they were, but not for long; see "Piano Lessons"), soon after my mother returned from prison and I from the boarding school, she enlisted Mrs. Bassová to continue the thankless task of my English tuition (see "Early Sex Stories," about my lessons with Mrs. Bassová).

Several years later, when I was already attending dance classes and was a regular fixture at the Prague balls, there appeared on the scene an exotic beauty, the daughter of an Argentinian ambassador to communist Czechoslovakia. I still remember her name, Arabella Adriens. We were all mesmerized by her grace and beauty. Rumor had it that she spoke English. Although I was far from being able to converse fluently, the years of English lessons had left some residue in my brain, so that I was able to put a few sentences together and ask simple questions. At one of the balls, I plucked up the courage and asked Arabella to dance. We danced well together, so much so that people stopped to look. The conversation, however, was halting. I was flummoxed by the fact that, whenever I said something that had nothing to do with seeing, she'd comment, "I see." I could not fathom what it was that she was seeing, because at the time I only knew the literal meaning of the verb "to see." All the other meanings came later, much later.

After high school, I put learning English on the back burner. At the university, we had to choose one of the Western languages (English, German, or French) to study, and I picked French. A few years after graduation, I was offered a job in Munich and started to feverishly study German. I was amazed how quickly one progresses when one actually studies. Of course, my application for an exit visa was returned with a note saying, "Your trip is not in the interest of the Czechoslovak Socialist Republic." Nevertheless, the German I learned stood me in good stead a few years later during my first trip to the West. And it was only then, after my return from that first-time-out trip, when the possibility of being allowed out again became more realistic, that I started studying English again. And this time around, I was really studying in earnest, not just attending classes. Building on the foundation of whatever I remembered from the previous years of lessons, I progressed quickly. Also, it helped that it was no longer my father who paid for my tuition, but me footing the bill.

I took lessons from two native English speakers—Mrs. Black, an Englishwoman, and Mrs. Wheeler, an American—both of whom were living in Prague. Both ladies liked my zeal and tried to help the best they could. I saw each of them twice a week, and soon we were conversing only in English. In addition to those lessons, I studied on my own seven days a week. Each day I would read some English text, looking up words I didn't know not in an English-Czech dictionary, but in an English-English dictionary, which would lead me to look up more words. In a few months, I started reading English novels. Mrs. Black recommended *The Time Machine* by H. G. Wells, which was the first novel I read in English. The next one was *The Heart of the Matter* by Graham Greene. In the process of reading those novels, I looked up each and every word I didn't know. Mrs. Wheeler and Mrs. Black were both delighted with my progress and told me that my diction was fine and easily understood. Because I had no trouble understanding either of them, I thought I'd be OK.

By this time, I'd already gotten a visa for a year's stay in England. Regarding my English-language skills, I am embarrassed to admit that I was almost cocky. I was naïvely convinced that just as I could easily converse with Mrs. Black and Mrs. Wheeler, I would be able to do so with the rest of the population of the British Isles. The first shock came in the Customs Hall of the port in Dover, but let me first explain how I got there.

I was traveling with my friend and colleague Jasan Burin. We both worked in the architectural office of the contracting firm Konstruktiva, which designed the new Czechoslovak Embassy in London. Jasan was part of the design team, and in that capacity, he had been posted in London a year earlier to work with an English architectural firm that was preparing the construction drawings. After a year in London, he returned to Prague for vacation and was heading back for his second year. It so happened that his return to London coincided with my departure, so he offered to give me a ride in his car. We took five days to get to London, stopping on the way in Frankfurt, Düsseldorf, Amsterdam, and Brussels.

Having taken a ferry across the Channel, we found ourselves in the Customs Hall of the port in Dover, waiting for the customs officer. When he came by, he said something at length, of which I didn't understand a single word. It was my first encounter with a native English speaker in his native land, and my confidence was shattered. I asked Jasan if he understood what the officer had said and he shook his head. However, he seemed to be less perturbed than me by this fact. Neither of us had the presence of mind to tell the officer that we didn't understand him, so when he left we just stood there, waiting to see if he would return. Well, he did not return, so after a while we picked up our suitcases and returned to the boat, retrieved Jasan's car, and drove to London. I was to report for work the following morning.

At the office, all my colleagues were complimenting me on how well I spoke English. That may have been true, but what they didn't know was how poorly I understood the conversations around me. Hoping to improve my understanding, I enrolled in a class called English-for-Foreigners. It turned out to be one of the smarter things I did. I am not sure if it improved my understanding, but it improved my command of English immensely. A knowledge of grammar and basic vocabulary was assumed, and the class was all about usage. It was taught by an excellent teacher who wrote the textbook we were using. I still remember her name, Ona Low, and I still have that book.

We learned colloquial English that came naturally to a native speaker, but that a foreigner had to learn, such as saying "do me a favor, make no mistake," rather than "make me a favor, do no mistake," even though the latter phrases are grammatically correct and perfectly understandable. At the end of the year, I passed an exam called the Lower Cambridge Certificate in English Language (there was no such thing as a Higher Cambridge Certificate), and I thus became a certified speaker of English. What a joke! Fifty years later, I still don't consider myself a flawless speaker of English.

Colloquial expressions follow no rules and simply have to be learned. The Department of Architecture of the Greater London Council (GLC), my first employer in London, employed many foreign architects, so that the native-born employees were familiar with foreigners' struggles with English. Going out to lunch one day, I ran into an English colleague who asked me, "Where are you off?" Seeing my puzzled look, he realized that I didn't understand the expression and quickly spelled it out for me: "Oh, ef, ef, meaning where are you going?" When I asked my team leader a few questions, he responded, "Put it all down, Martin; we'll talk about it at the meeting this afternoon." I had to ask my colleague, "What does he want me to put down and where am I to put it?" My colleague was amused and explained to me that the leader meant for me to write it down. I recall many moments like these over the years.

And then there are the words one encounters in books that are hardly ever actually spoken. While still in Prague, when reading some English text, I looked up the meaning of the word "firmament." I liked that word, so I kept on using it. It wasn't until my third year in London, when I said something about the cloudy firmament, that my friend Mark Ransom just couldn't take it anymore: "Martin, for God's sake, just say sky. Firmament sounds pretentious and downright silly." I was surprised that no one had told me that earlier. Such are the pitfalls of a neophyte English speaker.

Late in 1969, before I left London for New York, I watched the film *Easy Rider*. There is a scene, which takes place shortly after the character played by Jack Nicholson is killed, when Peter Fonda and Dennis Hopper are sitting by the roadside, smoking and repeating to each other, "Oh, we blew it, we blew it." Once again, I was puzzled; what did they blow? That sense of "blowing it" was not used in British English. It wasn't perhaps until a year later that I learned the meaning of "to blow something."

At Frost Associates, my first employer in New York, a colleague was regaling the office with a story about his dinner the night before with a fellow who used to sit at the same desk I was using. When he told him that a Czech was now sitting at his desk, the fellow asked, "Oh, does he bounce?" The whole office cracked up with laughter, while I had no idea what was so funny: in England checks don't bounce; they are returned. It took another half year or so before I got the joke.

Sometimes my poor command of English even jeopardized my romantic life. During my early years in New York, I found myself at a party in downtown Manhattan, where I noticed an attractive young woman, who was just my type. The trouble was that she was with a young man. After a while, when her escort was speaking to someone else, I found an opportunity to talk to her. We talked at great length, and she seemed to enjoy our conversation. I grew fond of her and eventually plucked up the courage to ask about her relationship to the man she came with. She responded, "Ah, it's all very tenuous."

By then, including my stay in London, I had been in an English-speaking environment for more than four years, yet I didn't know the meaning of "tenuous." In my ignorance, I thought that it meant that the relationship was full of tension, which I further interpreted to mean that it was hot. So with great regret, I did not pursue her anymore that evening. When I got home I grabbed the dictionary and looked up "tenuous." I could have kicked myself! The word meant the exact opposite of what I thought it meant. And I hadn't even asked for her telephone number. Her name was Gabriela…

When I started working as a design consultant and before I set up an office in my apartment, I was renting a desk in an office of my first client, David Specter. It was in an old office building on Broadway and 70th Street, which at the time still had an elevator operated by a uniformed operator. One day, I found the operator standing in the lobby next to the elevator. When he saw me, he announced, "The elevator is down." It seemed to me a perfectly reasonable statement, as there was a basement where some tenants kept storage spaces, so I waited for the elevator to come up. It seemed to be taking a long time. While waiting, I noticed that the operator was eyeing me with a quizzical expression on his face. Eventually, he said, "I did tell you that the elevator was down, didn't I?" I replied that I had heard him and that I was waiting for it to come up.

Now the guy lost his patience and said, "It ain't comin' up; it's down, it's down!" Only then did it hit me, but trying to get back at him, I said, "You meant to say that it's broken down, except you left out the broken part, yes?" The operator got furious that I was teaching him English, but he didn't know what else to say, except for repeating "It's down, it's down!" After I climbed seven flights of stairs, the whole office had a good chuckle when I related my conversation with the elevator operator.

I could go on with similar stories, but you get the idea. I have never stopped learning English. English has three times as many words as French, German, Spanish, or Czech, so there's no end to learning the language. For the last ten years or so I have subscribed to the Word-of-the-Day emails from Merriam-Webster. The word for today was "minatory," as in "the minatory mutterings of the Delphic Oracle." That word's bound to come in handy one day.

Building Together

Architects who do residential work often find themselves in the role of a therapist. Building something together—whether it is a new house, an addition, or just a kitchen remodel—often releases strong emotions in couples. The notion of building something permanent seems to stir up all kinds of issues. Why this is so I am not qualified to say. However, I can say that my own experience confirms that this is indeed the case. It is because of this experience that, when one-half of a couple asks me if they should get married or even move in together, I always advise, "Before you do it, first build something together. Remodel your bathroom, install a new skylight in your bedroom, build a gazebo in your garden, whatever." Many have thanked me for this piece of advice.

During the course of my many residential projects, I have witnessed spousal quarrels that I'd rather not have seen. Those were moments when I felt like crawling under the table or disappearing altogether. One example that comes to mind involved a young couple, John and Rita. John sold commercial real estate; Rita was an aspiring opera singer. They bought a five-story brownstone on the Upper West Side and were planning to live on the lower three floors and rent out the top two floors. My job was to connect their three floors and create one triplex residence. The project progressed as well as it could. Both spouses were present at all my presentations. Rita was an accomplished cook, and her focus was the new kitchen. She had reviewed the layout of all the appliances at my schematic design presentation and then again at the end of design development. At the end of the construction documents phase, I called for one more meeting to review the drawings before sending them out for bids.

The drawing showing the kitchen was the same one Rita had already seen several times during the design development presentations, except now it had dimensions and notes as well. Looking at an elevation showing the two built-in ovens, she turned to her husband (interestingly, not to her architect) and said, "What, one oven above the other? Not next to each other? Do you want me to break my back by bending over each time I open the lower oven?" Looking dumbfounded, John replied, "But honey, you've seen these drawings many times before. You can see that there is not enough space for the ovens to be next to each other." Rita countered, "Well, if there is not enough space, you might start looking for another wife, because I am not cooking in that kitchen." And with that, she stormed out of the room.

Half embarrassed and half apologetic, John asked me to do nothing and wait until he called me. It took more than two weeks before he told me that I could send the drawings out for bids. During the ten months of the subsequent construction, John and Rita lived in one of the upstairs apartments; however, on my supervisory visits I only saw John; Rita was not in evidence. The matter of the ovens was not brought up again.

When the project was completed and John and Rita were settled in their new triplex, I got invited for dinner. It was the first time I saw Rita in well over a year. She was charming, as if nothing untoward had ever happened. I am happy to report that, twenty-five years later, John and Rita are still married and appear to be happily living in their triplex. I say "appear to be," because I have no way of knowing just how happily they live together as our contact has been limited to the exchange of Christmas cards.

This next story, although far less typical, is an extreme example of the same phenomenon—how building something together can trigger marital discord. It starts with Anthony Kettaneh, a Lebanese American businessman whom I met in Tehran. Anthony was the scion of a family that owned a refrigeration plant in Cairo, olive orchards in Brazil, a cement factory in Bombay, and the largest Ford dealership in prerevolution Iran—and those businesses are only what I can readily remember. After the Iranian Revolution, he moved to New York and bought a house with a large garden in the Riverdale area of the Bronx. Perhaps four years later, he commissioned me to design a gazebo overlooking the Hudson River. Anthony was divorced, but maintained cordial relations with his ex-wife Lalleh and her significant other Hans, who lived together in Winchester, Massachusetts. When Lalleh and Hans decided to build a house addition, Anthony recommended me as an architect. I flew to Winchester to meet them, and we hit it off immediately.

They were two very smart people. Lalleh was a professor of mathematics at MIT, and Hans taught computer science at Boston University. They'd been together for more than five years. A year earlier, they had bought a large house in Winchester. Like most traditional houses, it was a warren of dark rooms. They yearned for a bright, light, and airy contemporary space in which to live and entertain. Although they were both equally enthusiastic about my design, it was clearly Hans who spearheaded the project. He was about five years older than me, and we found we had similar life trajectories. He too had a bad early marriage from which he ran away, and he also spent three years in London before immigrating to America. His first stop was Stanford University, where he did postdoctoral work for three years before moving to Los Angeles to take up a job with a computer company. After five years in Los Angeles, he went to Tucson to work for another computer company. Then he met Lalleh at a symposium in Chicago, and over the next two years, they had a long-distance relationship before he found the teaching job at Boston University and moved in with her in Cambridge. Two years later, they bought the house in Winchester.

After one of our meetings, when Lalleh left and Hans and I were having a beer in the garden, he told me, "See Martin, after bumming around for years more or less aimlessly, I think I have, at fifty-five, finally found myself. I have found a woman I want to keep, and I have found this place where I want to stay. I would not mind if I never go anywhere else and stay sitting right here drinking my beer under this oak tree." Meanwhile, the project progressed very satisfactorily. Having enthusiastically approved the concept, Lalleh and Hans then signed off on the design development drawings, and I was beginning to work on the construction documents. Throughout the process, they had generously lavished praise on me: "Martin, you've hit the nail on the head! This is precisely what we wanted."

Then, one day out of the blue, Hans called me, "Martin, we have to put the project on hold for a short while. Lalleh and I need to sort out something; it won't take long. I'll call you soon." I was stunned. Up until now it had been full speed ahead, and suddenly they needed to sort out something? I had other projects to work on, so I wasn't just sitting around and waiting, but still, after I had not heard from Hans in three weeks, I called him. When he answered, I told him I was calling because, for work-scheduling purposes, it would be helpful to know when we'd be able to resume the project. Hans sounded quite cheerful. I still remember that he told me, "Oh, we'll be back on track soon enough." I never heard from him again.

About a month or so later, Anthony Kettaneh called: "Martin, Lalleh asked me to call you. Hans is dead. Suicide. She also wants to know if you are owed any money. Are you free for a drink tonight after work?" We met at the bar on the roof of the Peninsula Hotel. Once we found a small table to sit at and Anthony had ordered an expensive bottle of Bordeaux, he began to talk. During the course of the design of the addition, Hans was getting more and more settled in his conviction that this was what he wanted to do—to stay put at that place and drink beer under that oak tree for the rest of his life. But the opposite was happening for Lalleh.

Although she liked the design, observing Hans's growing enthusiasm for it and for what it meant for the two of them, Lalleh realized that she was far less certain than Hans that staying together for the rest of her life was what she wanted. Eventually, she became convinced that it was decidedly not what she wanted. When she shared her feelings with Hans, he just fell apart. His universe collapsed. Over time he became hateful and vindictive. He hanged himself in the stairwell, so that when Lalleh came home and started climbing the stairs, her head would hit his feet.

Anthony clearly felt for his ex-wife. What was there to say, other than I was extremely sorry to have heard all that I had. This is an extreme example, to be sure, but I've also witnessed countless far less drastic ones. Perhaps it is the permanence that the construction signifies—building something that is meant to last—that throws relationships that feel less than permanent into a tailspin.

My Grandmother's Ashes

Despite the fact that she lived 150 miles away from Prague, I was very close to my maternal grand-mother Maryan. She lived in Skrchov, a small village in Moravia, because that's where the family paint factory founded by my grandfather was located. When my grandparents divorced, my grandfather retired and moved to Prague before I was born. After that, my mother's older brother, my uncle Milek, ran the factory, with my grandmother helping out with the business end of things. During the first ten years of my life, my mother and I spent a lot of time with my grandmother and my uncle in Skrchov: two to three months each summer, plus two to three weeks each over Christmas, New Year's, Easter, and All Saints Day. That made for a lot of face time together. I loved those visits, which all came to an abrupt end with the communist putsch of February 1948.

My grandmother and my Uncle Milek escaped from communist Czechoslovakia shortly after the putsch. They settled in Gargas, a little town in southern France where my uncle found employment running a paint factory—the same thing he was doing back home, except there it was his factory, whereas in France it was his employer's. My grandmother unexpectedly died in the fall of 1950, a great shock both to my mother and my uncle, because they were all very close. Some years later my uncle found a better situation in Bourges, a larger city in central France. He didn't marry until he was in his early fifties, whereupon in rapid succession he sired three children, my French cousins, before he died from pancreatic cancer at the age of fifty-nine.

The first time the communist authorities gave my mother an exit visa for a visit to see her brother in France was in 1965; the siblings had not seen each other for seventeen years. After she returned home and was describing the visit, among other things my mother told me was that she had asked Uncle Milek where their mother, my grandmother, was buried. He told her that the urn with my grandmother's ashes was at the Pere Lachaise cemetery in Paris, in the *deuxieme souterraine* of the columbarium. And then he added, "I don't advise you to go there; it makes no sense."

In her memoir *Necestou Cestou* (although never translated into English, the title could be understood as *Off the Road, on the Road*), my mother describes her visit to Pere Lachaise cemetery during her next trip to Paris. Here is an excerpt from her prose, very inadequately translated by me:

Unforgettably and very precisely, I remember going down the steps and down some more, the words "deuxieme souterraine" ringing in my head and apart from those words "deux-ieme souterraine," what came to my mind were my brother's words—"I don't advise you to go there; it makes no sense." Finally, there, at the bottom of penumbrous catacombs. All the walls full of niches or, rather, plaques covering the niches, plaques with names, next to each other, on top of each other, below each other. One thing is certain—all foreign names. Mostly, of course, French—Florence, Constance, Marcel, Rene, Jacques, Charles—and the surnames that go with them—Duval, Riviere, Corbullier—plus all manner of French narrative, naturally also foreign, totally foreign, completely foreign when, all at once, dangerously close, right in front of my face, I stare with consternation at a cri de coeur—"Mami!"

In Czech, in our way. A plaque with a Czech name, so absolutely unique name of our mother—with the precisely correct diacritical marks, hooks, strokes, all as it should be—and under the name, chiseled into the stone, that one word with an exclamation mark—"Mami!"

Nothing more. Absolutely nothing more. No dates, when was she born, when she died, nor how she got here. That much I understood; no one in this far-flung foreign land would care to know those details. But that my brother just could not contain his grief and had that one more word with an exclamation mark chiseled into that stone, that made me almost faint…

The next thing I remember—I was again outside in the daylight, sitting on a bench surrounded by lush verdure and weeping with loud sobs that I could not suppress. I don't think I had ever in my adult life wept that hard. Streams of tears were pouring out of me, flowing down my cheeks, dripping into my lap, on my knees, on the ground, like a spring flood.

My mother died in 2001 and Karen in 2010, so it was perhaps around 2005 when Karen and I were visiting Paris, that I thought of my grandmother and wanted to see that plaque in the *deuxieme souterraine* at Pere Lachaise. Karen knew the story and was intrigued, so off we went to Pere Lachaise. We found the columbarium easily enough and descended to the *deuxieme souterraine*: I could see why my mother described it as catacombs. It is a cavernous, gloomy space. Having grasped the enormity of the task of looking for one plaque amid thousands, we decided to proceed systematically. We started in one corner, with Karen going one way and I the other, looking for the plaque that would say:

Maryan Jeřábková

Mami!

It took us more than an hour to meet in the corner diagonally across the one from where we started. Those simple two lines should have been easy to spot, but neither of us found the plaque. By the time that we met at the opposite corner, Karen was on the verge of a claustrophobic fit, so we had to get out of there. I wished I could have told my mother that we tried to find it but were unsuccessful, but she was no longer available.

My grandmother died in 1950, when I was eleven years old. I guess it was because she died young (she was sixty-three) and suddenly that my mother assumed that she had died of a heart attack. My mother died fifty years later, in 2001. When I was liquidating her apartment in Prague, I came across my uncle Milek's diary, in which he was describing his first years of exile in France. My uncle's widow Christa must have sent the diary to my mother because it was in Czech, which neither she, nor any of her children, could read.

When reading my uncle's diary, the first surprise was that, from his description of my grandmother's last days, it did not seem as if she had died from a heart attack. The medical care available in rural southern France in the 1950s appeared to have left a lot to be desired. The nearest hospital to Gargas was two hours away in Avignon. When my grandmother developed abdominal pains, my uncle picked one of the two local doctors available in Gargas, who cared for her until she died a week later. We'll never know what killed her.

The second and bigger surprise was Uncle Milek's description of my grandmother's funeral in the Gargas cemetery. What? So there had been a funeral, and she had not been cremated. But what about her urn in the *deuxieme souterraine* at Pere Lachaise? I was positive that my mother had not made up the story she told me, just as I was certain that my uncle was writing the truth in his diary. There was no one I could ask to solve the mystery.

Fast-forward eight years to 2009. On what turned out to be our last trip abroad, Karen and I were touring around Provence. While staying in a little auberge outside Avignon, I was studying a map and spotted Gargas. It was a two-hour drive from where we were staying. Having looked for my grand-mother's plaque at Pere Lachaise four years earlier, I asked Karen if she'd be game to look for her grave in Gargas cemetery. She said, "Let's go."

Gargas is decidedly not a tourist destination. There's nothing to see there, which perhaps was why an elderly waitress in the restaurant where we were eating lunch asked us what brought us to Gargas. I told her that my grandmother died in the town in 1950, and we had come to look for her grave at the local cemetery. That piqued her curiosity and she asked, "*Quel était son nom?*" I told her what I imagined to be a French pronunciation of Maryan Jeřábková and then spelled it for her in French. The waitress shook her head. "*Non, je ne la connaissais pas.*" I told her that her son, my uncle, had run the local paint factory. Her face lit up, "*Ah, un monsieur tchèque? Très charmant et élégant? Je l'ai connu, car quand j'étais jeune je travaillais dans l'usine. Et maintenant, je me souviens de sa mère aussi, mais je n'ai jamais su son nom.*" ("Ah, a Czech gentleman? Very charming and elegant? I knew him, because when I was young, I worked at that factory. And I remember his mother as well, but I never knew her name.")

Amazing! But in a small town perhaps not so amazing—I am sure that in the Gargas of 1950 my grandmother and my uncle must have stood out. We asked the waitress for directions to the ceme-tery and, having paid, promptly went there. Unlike the catacombs of the *deuxieme souterraine* at Pere Lachaise, Karen and I found the Gargas cemetery to be a lovely and inviting place. It was located outside the town on a beautiful meadow; it was a rectangular area surrounded by a low stone wall, with no church or parish house around; inside the enclosure, there were rows of graves. It was an early autumn day, sunny but not hot—perfect weather for the task at hand. Just as we had done at the *deuxieme souterraine*, we split up, with Karen starting at one end of the rectangle and I at the other, and then, walking through row by row, we proceeded toward each other until we met in the middle. It took us all of half an hour. Once again, we did not find Maryan's grave. I was puzzled, not knowing what to think.

Of my three French cousins, over the last forty years, I've been in touch only with Constance, the youngest one. When Karen and I returned from France and I was responding to an email from Con-stance, I mentioned to her the unsuccessful search for our grandmother's grave in Gargas. In her response, she wrote, "I recall, long ago, my mother telling me how my father had such bad mem-ories of Gargas, having been mistreated by his employers and then his mother dying there, that upon his move to Bourges, where his circumstances had improved substantially, he had his mother exhumed, cremated, and the urn with her ashes placed in the columbarium at Pere Lachaise." Well, that answered the question of why we did not find Maryan's grave in Gargas cemetery, but not why we did not find her plaque in the *deuxieme souterraine* at Pere Lachaise. I mentioned as much to Constance in my next email.

Constance wrote back that she did not have an answer for me, but that she'd ask her mother. She said that her family would be spending Christmas with my Aunt Christa in Bourges and that she'd ask her then. That was the Christmas that Karen spent in the hospital, and then in February 2010 she died, so I had other things to worry about than my grandmother's ashes and let the matter slip from my mind. It wasn't until about March or April when I received an email from Constance. She wrote that she had asked her mother about our grandmother's ashes and that Christa confessed that, in her distress after her husband died, she neglected to pay the fee for the niche at the columbarium; after several reminders, Pere Lachaise disposed of our grandmother's urn and rented the niche to the next party on the waiting list.

The mystery solved, my grandmother thus joined my father and my grandfather Bohumír, her ex-husband, as my ancestors without graves.

Asia Society

For perhaps ten years, from about the mid-1980s to the mid-1990s, I was the court architect of the Asia Society, all because of my acquaintance with Jan Arnet. Jan was its vice president and treasurer. Because the president seemed to be doing full-time fundraising, for all practical purposes Jan ran the Society. The Asia Society occupied then (and still does) its own building on Park Avenue and 71st Street, designed in the late 1970s by the well-known and well-respected architect Edward Larrabee Barnes. Either Mr. Barnes was having a bad day when he designed it, or he was given insufficient instructions by his client, because the building didn't function properly and was hated by the folks who worked in it.

The building's shortcomings were many. There was no service elevator between the workshops in the basement and the galleries. Consequently, the sculptures or paintings that were prepared in the basement had to be transported to the galleries on upper floors in one of the two passenger elevators, which caused obvious problems. In addition, even though the building was chronically short of space for all its functions, there was a huge, completely equipped, state-of-the-art commercial kitchen in the basement that was never used. Somehow no one had informed Mr. Barnes that caterers do not prepare food on the premises. They bring it with them, and all that's needed on site is a small serving area.

Then there was the issue of the toilets. To save space, Mr. Barnes designed the employee bathrooms so that men's rooms were on the odd floors while the women's rooms were on the even floors (or maybe it was the other way around). Eighty-five percent of Asia Society employees were women, so if a woman was working on a floor without a women's bathroom, each time she needed the facilities, she had to travel one floor up or down, while the men's room on her floor remained unused. The employees hated that.

Further, it appeared that no one had told Mr. Barnes that most of the Asian sculptures were of sandstone before he designed a grandiose outdoor sculpture garden on the second floor. The sandstone sculptures couldn't tolerate the freeze-thaw cycles of our climate, so that sculpture garden was never used and the artworks were languishing in basement storage.

What bothered Jan Arnet the most, however, was the appearance of the entrance lobby. It was a gloomy space with no character and without a clear orientation to the location of the galleries, the restaurant, the bookstore, the shop, or the offices. On entering, one wasn't sure if one was in an office building or a bookstore.

And the Society was also in dire need of more space. This certainly was not Mr. Barnes's fault. Whoever put together the initial program didn't properly foresee the space needs of the growing organization.

Although Jan Arnet's background was in finance, he was a closet architect who loved to think about how to improve the functioning of a space. He was determined to make the Asia Society building work, if not perfectly, then at least better than it did. His first step was to hire Martin Holub Architects and ask us to prepare a feasibility study showing how the said shortcomings could be remedied. Over the next ten years, Jan commissioned a total of four studies, each successive proposal being more ambitious than the previous one. Each showed different ways of improving the circulation and orientation in the lobby, enclosing the sculpture garden, adding a service elevator, using the space taken up by the never-used kitchen, and solving the bathroom situation. For example, we found a way of installing a smaller ladies' room on each floor with the men's room staying on every other floor. The last of the four studies also showed how to increase the floor space by adding a bay to the building.

The only one of our proposed improvements that was actually implemented was the addition of the women's bathrooms. The trustees didn't approve money for anything else. Then, some two years later, an unexpected budget surplus enabled Jan to ask for yet another study. As the years passed, the space needs of the Society had grown more pressing, so the emphasis of this fifth study was on increasing office space. It was the most ambitious design proposal of them all. Still, given the responses to the previous ones, I really did not expect that anything would come of it. However, this time I was wrong.

A few months after the submission of our last proposal, a jubilant Jan Arnet called. He told me that on its basis, the president of the Society had raised $20 million from a Hong Kong financier and that the project was bound to go ahead, because that money was earmarked for the building's renovation and could not be used for anything else. I was jubilant too! But it soon became apparent that both Jan Arnet and I were very naïve. We truly believed that because the money was raised on the basis of my design, it followed that I would be the architect who'd be commissioned to develop it.

Ha! It turned out that every trustee had his or her favorite architect. A list was drawn up of architects who were to receive the RFP (Request for Proposal). It included the stars from the New York architectural firmament, such as Richard Meier, James Stewart Polshek, Rafael Viñoly, Hugh Hardy, and Charles Gwathmey—all heading firms with more than one hundred employees—plus a few less well-known names. Jan Arnet had to intervene—pointing out that if it weren't for me, there would be no project—to get me on the list. My inclusion was, of course, a joke, since at the time I had two employees. I didn't stand a chance, yet having received the RFP, I felt obliged to submit a proposal. As with all proposals, we did our best. Predictably, in due course, we received a form letter informing us that we were not selected.

Eventually, the winner was announced. I was genuinely pleased that it wasn't one of the stars, but instead a medium-size firm headed by Bartholomew Voorsanger, with whom I was acquainted. We were not friends, but we knew each other. Jan Arnet told me that Bart Voorsanger was given my drawings. To let him know that I did not harbor a grudge, I called him to congratulate him. His secretary put me through to his voice mail, and I left a lengthy message congratulating him and telling him that I was happy that he, rather than some of the big guns, was selected. He never called me back. Many years later, whenever we run into one another at the Century Club, we are forcibly cordial.

Teenage Obstreperousness

Ever since I started taking dancing lessons at fifteen, a standard rite of passage to adulthood in the Czech lands to this day, I was obsessed with dancing. I happened to be a good dancer, so girls liked to dance with me, and I loved this way of communicating with the opposite sex.

At the time, there were many balls in Prague. Naturally, every high school had its prom, which we called a graduation ball. In addition, every school of Charles University and of Czech Technical University, as well as all art schools, had their yearly balls. So there was a Medical Ball, a Lawyers' Ball, a Philosophers' Ball, an Engineers' Ball, an Architects' Ball, and so on. There was also a National Gallery Ball, a National Museum Ball, an Academy of Sciences Ball, and balls of many other institutions. Considering that the liquidation of the bourgeois class was the reigning ideology of the communist regime, I find it fascinating that this culture of the balls was allowed to go on, because there can be nothing more bourgeois than a ball.

I loved going to the balls, but my mother believed that there should be some relationship between the time I spent dancing and the grades I brought home from school. That was an idea that, at the time, I just could not abide. So when my grades were not very good and my mother forbade my going to balls that week, I developed a subterfuge.

Each apartment in our building had a storage compartment in the basement used primarily to store coal for heating. My mother had also installed there an armoire for our overflow clothes, which was where I moved my tuxedo. After dinner on the night of a ball, I'd say to my mother, "I am going to Hans Bílek's (my classmate), and we are going to study French (or math, or history)." Then, instead of going to Hans's house, I would go down to the basement where I changed into my tuxedo and then hastened to the ball.

In those years, we were too poor to have a telephone, so there was no way for my mother to verify if I was indeed at the Bíleks. Moreover, even if we'd had a telephone, I don't think my mother would suspect that I could sink so low as to lie to her. Long after midnight when I returned home, I went first to the basement where I'd shed the tuxedo and put on my regular clothes. Then I'd go up to the apartment, open the door quietly, undress in the foyer, and creep into my bed, thinking that my mother was sleeping soundly. As I learned much later, that was not always the case. So much for the first example of my terrible teens.

Another involved my next passion after dancing: skiing. Not surprisingly, just as with dancing, my mother was convinced that the time I spent skiing should correspond with the grades I was getting at school: this notion was also unacceptable to me at the time. One winter when I was in tenth or eleventh grade, I was planning to go on a ski trip with my buddies during the midyear break. My mother forbade me to go but told me that if I improved my grades, I could go skiing over the Easter break. To prove that she meant what she said, she locked my skis in our basement cubicle and kept the key.

She didn't know that, because of my shenanigans with the tuxedo, I had made a duplicate key. On the day of my planned departure, when my mother was at work, despite her expressly forbidding me to go, I took the skis from the basement and, filled with righteous indignation, left for a week of skiing.

When I returned, I told my mother that she had no right to forbid me to go skiing. I had paid for everything myself from my summer jobs earnings: I had bought my skis and boots and paid for the whole trip. It was my right to go. My mother responded, "Yes, you did pay for your ski trip yourself. But tell me, who paid for the shirt and pants and shoes you are wearing? And who pays for the food you are eating? And who pays the rent? Once you're financially independent, you may do as you please, but doesn't it make sense that, while you accept your keep from me, I have some say in the way you live?"

I immediately saw the error of my ways and was embarrassed by my own obtuseness. My mother saw that I was genuinely sorry and we embraced. I remember realizing in that moment, for the first time, that I was already taller than she was. I don't remember any more collisions with my mother. I guess I grew up.

Divorce

I've described the circumstances of my first wedding, as well as those of my first honeymoon, so I think I ought to say a few words about my first and, so far, only divorce. I decided to leave Eva at the end of 1968. To explain why is not for these pages. Because I was the one doing the leaving, I planned to move out of our London abode. However, once Eva understood that I meant what I said, she wanted to be the one to move out, and eventually, she did. It was the simplest parting conceivable. There were no children, we had no money to speak of, and we had no furniture since we lived in a furnished room. The only things left to divide were some kitchen utensils, pots and pans, cutlery, and china. Presto.

Throughout my last year in London, we maintained friendly contact and saw no reason to file for divorce. The same applied to my first five years in New York. We both thought that until one of us found someone whom we wanted to marry, there was simply no reason to go through the trouble of the divorce process. However, my mother felt otherwise. First in her letters and then when she arrived for her first visit in 1974, she vehemently argued that I should get a divorce. She was convinced that living apart for so long without getting a divorce sent the wrong signal to the women I might be interested in; people might think that I harbored some morbid attachment to my wife that prevented me from seeking a divorce. In short, she thought that I was being foolish not to get a divorce. She also told me that she had spoken with Eva's mother, who was equally bothered by our still not being divorced.

I soon saw the wisdom in my mother's words, so I sat down and wrote Eva a letter. I told her that, just as we had not seen any reason to get a divorce, I also didn't see any reason not to get divorced, and because divorcing would please our mothers, why not do it. A few weeks later, instead of getting a response from Eva, I received a letter from a London solicitor informing me that my wife had filed for a divorce.

It must have been one of the easiest, simplest divorces ever. There were no children, no claims, no money or property to divide; there was mutual consent; and the parties had been separated for more than five years and even lived on different continents. Still, there was one unresolved issue: who was going to pay the expenses of getting a divorce? Eva wrote me, "I've filed for the divorce; I am going to pay for it." I replied, "It was my suggestion; therefore, I am going to pay." Eventually, we agreed to split the cost. It was ridiculously inexpensive. Once the British pounds were converted to dollars, the total came to something like $144. And our mothers were delighted.

C of O

Karen and I bought the parcel of land on which we were going to build a house because of the views it offered. When I climbed the trees near the house site, it became obvious that with each foot I got higher, the view got dramatically better. That is why, before I even started designing, we resolved to build a vertical house as high as the zoning would permit. A vertical house means a lot of steps, and since I didn't want an interior full of long flights of stairs, I decided to break the three-story house into seven levels, with never more than three or four risers (with one exception) between the levels.

Thus there was an entry level, below which were two levels with one guest bedroom each; the next one up from the entry level was a living-room level, and then there was a kitchen/dining/terrace level. Another four risers up was the study/office level. The longest flight of stairs had seven risers (the one exception) from the study level to the master bedroom level. The living room, kitchen/dining, study/office, and master bedroom were to be one open space, programmatically articulated by the levels.

When I was done with the conceptual design, my structural engineer pointed out to me that the New York State (NYS) Building Code doesn't permit wood-frame construction in structures higher than two stories. The simplest solution would have been to frame the house with metal studs and joists, which in theory should be less expensive than the wood framing. In practice, however, because carpenters are typically not skilled in assembling metal frames, builders tend to charge extra for metal framing. Because we were working within a budget and I didn't want to spend money where it wouldn't be seen, I was not keen on using a metal frame.

Then Larry, my longest-time employee, came up with a brilliant idea: "Martin, why don't we call the third floor a mezzanine?" I looked up the definition of mezzanine in the NYS Building Code and learned that it is a space open to the floor immediately below, with and area less than one-third that of the floor immediately below. The first requirement posed no problem, because the third floor containing the master bedroom was basically a loft open to the living, dining, and study spaces immediately below. Interpreting the second requirement, however, was not so simple, because in the given design, the meaning of "the floor immediately below" was not entirely clear.

Since immediately below the putative mezzanine was an open space consisting of three indoor levels and one outdoor terrace, could we count all of them as the floor immediately below? If yes, then the area of the third floor would be less than one-third of the area of the floor immediately below, and we could then call it a mezzanine. After all, the code did not say "enclosed area on the floor immediately below." If, however, we interpreted the code literally, then the area immediately below would include only the area of the living room level, in which case the master bedroom level wouldn't fit the definition of a mezzanine.

Not wanting any surprises down the road, I decided to seek preliminary approval from the building inspector of the Town of Stanford. I still remember that his name was Mr. Davis. I FedExed him the plans and followed up with a phone call a few days later. Poor Mr. Davis appeared totally flummoxed by all those levels, never having seen anything like that before. I told him that the levels were of no concern, since the code put no limitation on their number. My main concern was the determination that the area of the mezzanine was less than one-third of the area of the floor immediately below. I further explained that, according to my interpretation of the code, the floor immediately below included all levels, as well as the terrace below the mezzanine, and I asked Mr. Davis if he agreed with that interpretation. He said he would have to get back to me on that.

When I hadn't heard from Mr. Davis for more than a week, I called him. Because he just couldn't decide how to interpret the phrase "immediately below" in a multilevel house, Mr. Davis had sent my plans to the code enforcement officer in Albany. He said that, if I wanted to, I could call him, and he gave me the officer's name and phone number. I waited a few days and then called Albany.

To my great surprise, I lucked upon a smart and thoughtful government official, a rare occurrence indeed. The code officer told me that the code was written for conventional buildings, while my design was anything but. He further said that in such cases, it would be wrong to go by the letter of the code, but one must try to interpret its spirit. And according to the officer's interpretation of the code, the top floor of the house I designed conformed to the code's definition of a mezzanine. He would call inspector Davis to tell him that. I was elated, convinced that this hurdle was behind us.

In those years my office was busy, so that I could work on the house only on weekends and in the evenings, which is why it took another two years before the working drawings were ready for construction. After six months, during which there were several rounds of bidding, we found a contractor; Mr. Davis then issued a building permit, and the construction started. The house was completed fifteen months later. Consequently, it was a little more than four years since the mezzanine issue had been resolved when I called the Stanford Building Department to ask for a Certificate of Occupancy (C of O). I expected to speak to Mr. Davis, but was told that he had retired. The new inspector told me that before issuing the C of O, he needed to conduct an inspection. That is standard procedure, so I expected it.

I no longer remember the new inspector's name, so let's call him New Inspector. The first thing he said as he walked around the house was, "This is a three-story house, and the code doesn't permit three-story, wood-framed houses." I pointed out that the top floor was a mezzanine. New Inspector said, "I see." However, when we walked inside the house and reached the second multilevel floor, New Inspector looked up at the open top floor and said, "Come on, Mr. Architect, this ain't no mezzanine; you must know that. I don't need to measure it to see that its area is way over one-third of the floor below."

I didn't want to start arguing about the methods of calculating the area, so instead I pointed out that the plans of the house were approved by the Building Department, a building permit had been issued, and the house was built according to the approved plans. New Inspector countered, "Well, all that means is that my predecessor made a mistake. It doesn't mean that I am going to make a mistake."

Only then did I remember the code enforcement officer, so I said that the plans had also been approved in Albany. That revelation seemed to take New Inspector's breath away. He dropped his chin and repeated, "In Albany?" I explained that his predecessor had sent my plans to be reviewed by the code enforcement officer, who had then approved them. "What was his name?" I had to admit I didn't know. "Well, if Albany calls me and tells me that they had approved your plans, I'll give you the C of O." With that, New Inspector got in his car and drove away.

I was worried because not only did I not know the code enforcement officer's name, but I also didn't have any record of my conversation with him from four years ago. I thought that perhaps Mr. Davis might know the officer's name, but when I called the Town of Stanford Building Department and inquired about his whereabouts, all the secretary could tell me was that he had moved to Florida. When I explained the situation to Karen, she was on the verge of a nervous breakdown, fearing that we'd have to remove the top floor of our house. She calmed down when I explained to her that the worst-case scenario would be that we wouldn't get the Certificate of Occupancy; that might be a problem when we'd be selling the house, but other than that, nobody cared whether or not we had a C of O.

I found the Albany phone number I had called four years prior in my appointment calendar of that year. My hopes for a satisfactory result of that phone call were not high. I told the man who answered my call that I was looking for the code enforcement officer with whom I'd spoken four years ago about a code issue and whose name I didn't know. While I was explaining that, it struck me how preposterous my inquiry was. The man on the other end of the line asked me, "Do you remember what code issue you discussed?" I said that it concerned an interpretation of the definition of a mezzanine, which applied to an unconventional design of a multilevel house.

To my inexpressible delight, the man responded, "I remember that issue. I was the officer you spoke to. I remember the design of the house with all the levels. So how can I help you?" I could not believe my luck! I told the officer that the inspector he dealt with had retired and that the new inspector was interpreting the code literally; he found the house at variance with the code and wouldn't issue the C of O unless a code enforcement officer from the state office in Albany called him and told him that the house was code compliant. The officer replied, "Don't worry; I'll call the inspector. It is the Town of Stanford, yes?" I confirmed that it was indeed the Town of Stanford; he said, "OK, good-bye," and hung up. I didn't even have a chance to thank him. Incredibly, I also didn't have the presence of mind to ask the officer's name, so that to this day I still don't know the name of my savior.

From that point on, things proceeded predictably. A few days later, I had a voice mail from New Inspector, telling me that I could pick up the C of O at the Stanford Building Department. Once we had it in our hands, Karen and I celebrated with a fine dinner at L'Absinthe. This was the second time I had gotten into trouble in connection with a Certificate of Occupancy and a retiring building inspector.

The first time took place some five years earlier, when an almost identical scenario occurred, except that time I was not so lucky. It was in connection with my design of the Roosevelt Island Cultural Center, my firm's first public project with a New York State agency as the client. The center included three distinct components: an eighty-five-seat theater, a dance studio, and a synagogue. Because all three were places of public assembly, meeting the egress requirements of NYS Building Code was of paramount importance.

New York State projects in New York City are not administered by the New York City Building Department, but fall under the jurisdiction of the Urban Development Corporation (UDC), a state agency with its own building department. Once my schematic design was approved by all three user groups as well as by the client agency, I then requested a plan review by the UDC. Knowing that the building code is often subject to interpretation, I just wanted to make sure that the examiner who would be approving the plans and issuing the building permit interpreted the code the same way I did. I still remember that the examiner's name was Mr. Schwartz, an affable man in his sixties. He reviewed the plans and found them code compliant. I didn't think much of it, because I expected that he would do so.

From the time of that meeting, it took us another year to complete the design development phase and the construction drawings phase and then to prepare the bid documents. Then followed some six months of bidding before we selected the contractor. The construction then took one and a half years, so by the time we were seeking the Certificate of Occupancy, it was close to three years since my first meeting with Mr. Schwartz and two years since he issued the building permit.

The first thing I learned when I called the UDC was that Mr. Schwartz had retired. I was then connected to his successor, Mr. Kaplan, and we made a date for his final inspection before issuance of the C of O. I had no reason to be worried about its issuance, yet when I first saw Mr. Kaplan, I sensed trouble. He was a young man in his early thirties, new on the job, and determined to make a mark. He was clearly looking for some instance of noncompliance: he measured the heights of railings and grab bars, checked the width of the doors to the toilet rooms that had a handicapped stall, and tested the smoke detectors, the fire alarm, and the emergency lighting. Everything checked out, and Mr. Kaplan looked disappointed. Then he found something, or so he thought.

The synagogue was accessible through a large foyer that was to function as a gathering space for socializing before and after services. There was an exit door from that foyer leading directly outside. When Mr. Kaplan walked through the space of the future synagogue and saw only one exit leading outdoors, he asked where the second exit was. I pointed to the exit sign above the entry door leading to the foyer and explained that the foyer itself was a fire-rated area with an exit directly to the outside. In other words, the foyer functioned as a fire-rated corridor leading to the exit.

Mr. Kaplan found this unacceptable. According to him, all exits from a place of public assembly had to lead directly outside. I didn't want to contradict him, so I said that the plans were approved and the building permit had been issued by his predecessor Mr. Schwartz. In words almost identical to those I was going to hear five years later from New Inspector of the Town of Stanford, Mr. Kaplan declared, "Just because my predecessor made a mistake does not mean I am going to make one." He also said that before he would issue the C of O, he needed to see one more exit directly to the outside. This was serious, because, unlike with a single-family house where nobody cares whether or not it has a C of O, a state agency cannot operate spaces of public assembly without one.

From both the design and construction points of view, installing another exit door was simple. However, because this was a public project, securing approval for an extra expense requiring a change order was never simple. The contractor's quote for cutting through the concrete wall and installing another door was $20,000. Once I had that information I called Alyce Russo, the representative of the Roosevelt Island Operating Corporation (RIOC), my client. I briefed her on what happened relative to the C of O and told her that in my opinion Mr. Kaplan was flat wrong since nowhere in the code did it say that exits had to go directly to the outside. Then I told her that she had to decide whether to fight Mr. Kaplan or come up with the $20,000 for the extra exit door. She said she would get back to me.

The next thing I knew, I received a letter from the president of the RIOC. It was a terse missive, asking me to explain in writing what method I had used to assure code compliance. I swiftly responded that the method I had used was to have a consultation with the code enforcement officer who found my design code compliant, which was later confirmed by his issuance of the building permit. That his successor interpreted the code differently was something beyond my control, although I was convinced that his interpretation was wrong. I never heard back from the president, but a week or so later, Alyce Russo called to tell me that RIOC had decided to pay the extra $20,000 and that I was authorized to prepare whatever was necessary architecturally for the installation of the new exit door. I was astonished: one public agency would rather pay than challenge another public agency, even when that agency was patently wrong.

The door was installed and the C of O was issued in short order, but the project, once completed, fizzled. There was no opening ceremony, no ribbon cutting, nothing. I never heard from the RIOC again. It was as if the totally unnecessary door cast a pall over the whole undertaking. Mr. Kaplan certainly made his mark. I did, however, hear from the users of the three spaces, all of whom were quite ecstatic about their facilities. The Roosevelt Island Theater Company sent me free tickets to their plays for years afterward, and Karen and I enjoyed many a fine performance there.

Robbery in Catania

Sicily was the last leg of our trip through southern Italy, and Karen and I spent four days driving around the island. After seeing Cefalu, Monreale, Segesta, Agrigento, and Siracusa, we were driving north along the east coast of Sicily on our way to Taormina, our last stop on the island before flying back to Rome and then to New York. To get to Taormina we had to drive through Catania, the second largest city in Sicily after Palermo. Karen couldn't handle a stick shift, so I was driving. Rental cars in Italy at the time did not have air conditioning, and we were driving with the windows rolled down.

Anyone who has ever driven in Italy knows that kids weaving in and out of traffic on Vespa motor scooters are a common sight. Consequently, I wasn't at all perturbed when, all of a sudden, two boys on motor scooters appeared in front of our car. However, when we realized that they did not appear by accident but were slowing me down intentionally, it was all over. A series of perfectly coordinated actions took less than ten seconds.

Exactly at the moment when I had to stop or hit those boys, another motorcycle with two men on it pulled up by the open window on the passenger side of the car. A beefy man stepped off the back of the motorcycle and came to the open window; with his long arm he reached down to the floor by Karen's feet, grabbed what he thought was her handbag, and threw it to yet another man on another motorcycle who came by just at that exact time. The first man then got back on the motorcycle that sped away in one direction, while the motorcycle with the man who caught the bag sped off in another direction. When I looked in front of me, the boys were gone.

The whole operation was so perfectly choreographed and so flawlessly executed that it must have been rehearsed. It was almost a work of art. By the time we realized what was happening, it was over. I stepped out of the car to see if I could spot a policeman, but none was in evidence. Then it hit me that I was standing in the middle of a busy street with cars whizzing by, so I got back in the car and we drove off.

Karen then told me, "They took your bag." It was a black canvas bag with a wide shoulder strap, which I used to take on planes as a carry-on. We went over the things that were inside: maps of Italy we used along the way and would no longer need, my cheap camera, sunscreen lotion, and the paperback book I'd finished reading the day before. On the whole, we didn't lose anything precious. The photos we had taken along the way, which were still in the camera, were the biggest loss.

While checking in to our Taormina hotel, we told the receptionist what had happened to us in Catania. Totally unimpassioned, he told us that, yes, that sort of thing happens in Catania and that "they don't need money. They are after passports." He then regaled us with a story he'd heard about a woman who was stopped in Catania much in the same way we were, except that instead of a handbag, they took her whole suitcase and sped off on a motorcycle with it. I felt almost sorry for the robbers that after such an immaculate performance, all they got from us was a cheap camera, sunscreen lotion, a worn-out paperback, and some maps.

Boarding School

In 1950 while in boarding school.

I was eleven when my mother was taken to prison in mid-June 1950, and I had only two more weeks of school left before the two-months summer vacation would begin. I spent the first month of the vacation with my father and his wife at their house in the country and the second month with various relatives and family friends, who each took me for a week at a time. For the following school year, my father enrolled me in the boarding school George of Poděbrad in the town of Poděbrady, about fifty kilometers east of Prague, on the River Labe (Elbe). George of Poděbrad was a Bohemian king in the sixteenth century who was quite popular and well liked. The boarding school bearing his name was based in his castle.

It was a boarding school that reflected its time. A number of kids were there because one or both of their parents were in prison. An equally large group consisted of children of communist apparatchiks who had been sent to the West either as part of the diplomatic service or as business representatives. And so it happened that one of my roommates was Václav Havel, whose father was in prison, and another one was Jiří Kaiser, whose father was the communist ambassador to Mexico. Because the communists didn't even trust one of their own, Jiří was not allowed to go with his parents to Mexico, but had to stay behind to assure that his folks would return. This was the case, even though Jiří was a grandson of Antonín Zápotocký, at the time the prime minister and, three years later, the president of Czechoslovakia.

My roommate Václav Havel was two years older than me, which when one is eleven years old makes a huge difference; so we were not close friends. However, as I found out forty years later, he had remembered me. The year was 1990, and Václav Havel arrived in New York for his first official visit as the president of Czechoslovakia. There was a reception for him at the Guggenheim Museum, which Karen and I attended. After the speeches, Havel stood at the head of a long receiving line, filled with all the people who wanted to shake the hand of the new president of the newly free Czechoslovakia. I was one of those people. While we were in boarding school, Havel's nickname was Bumblebee because he was a chubby kid. So when my turn came, I addressed him in Czech, "*Jak se máš, Chrobáku?*" (How are you doing, Bumblebee?).

Karen was standing nearby, watching this encounter, and later told me that Havel seemed at first a little startled; he then stepped back, looked me over, flashed a smile, and said this phrase to me in Czech: "*Pokoj sto čtyřicet tři*" (Room 143). I remember thinking, "So this is why you are the president, because if my life depended on it, I would not have recalled the number of our room in boarding school."

In 1950 while in boarding school.

We then exchanged perhaps twenty sentences during which we established that he knew my mother from the days of Charter 77 and from her he knew that she had a son who was an architect living in New York. Then I sensed that my time was up and I had to move on to allow the people standing in a long line behind me to greet him as well. During his next visits to New York, I had more occasions to talk with Havel. Each time he knew immediately who I was. The last time we met was in the Bohemian Hall on East 73rd Street. He knew that I was the architect of its renovation and complimented me on it.

But back to the boarding school. It was a tough place where brawn ruled. The school comprised grades six through thirteen. I was then in seventh grade, so the vast majority of my schoolmates were bigger and stronger than me. Most of the dorm rooms were at the top floor of the castle. One day, just for the hell of it and because they could, two of my roommates who were four or five years older, held me by my ankles and suspended me from the window. I remember hanging there, head down, some eight stories above the ground. I was not frightened, because I had full faith that they would not drop me. Still, I didn't like the fact that I had no choice in the matter.

The boarding school encouraged toughness: it was considered cool to be strong, hardy, and tough. One example of how it celebrated toughness was the annual St. George Swim. Given that the school was named for George of Poděbrad, St. George was, if not exactly its patron saint, as close to it as you could get under the communist regime. I'll never forget that St. George's feast day is on April 24. The St. George Swim consisted of swimming across the River Labe and back. It was not about breaking any speed records, but about braving the cold water, and there was a competition between the rooms to see how many boys from each would manage to swim across and back. Rumor had it that a few years earlier, boys had to swim among ice floes.

In April 1951, there were no ice floes, but the water seemed diabolically cold. There was a lot of peer pressure to tough it out and get it over with. Yet some boys jumped in, made five or six strokes, turned around, and swam back to the shore: they simply could not face staying in that freezing water for the time it would take to swim to the other shore and back. I remember jumping in and swimming the crawl stroke as fast as I could, kicking furiously, not allowing myself to think about how cold the water was. Once I reached the other shore, however, I was so out of breath that to get back I could only swim

In 1950 while in boarding school.

the breaststroke, which took much longer. And it was on the way back that the frigid water got to me. It seemed an eternity before I got back. Some older boys helped me out of the water and proceeded to rub me with Turkish towels while I sipped the hot chocolate that was handed to me. I realized later that I became a minor hero because not many other boys my age ever completed the swim. I'll remember that experience for as long as I live.

On weekends, I returned to Prague to be with my father. At the time, weekends did not begin until Saturday afternoon because there was school on Saturday mornings: two-day weekends came some ten years later. My father gave me money for the hour-long bus ride back and forth between Prague and Poděbrady. However, I learned from my schoolmates to hitchhike, so I pocketed the bus money my father gave me and hitchhiked instead. Going back on Sunday in late afternoon, I'd take a tram to the end of the line, where the road out of Prague started, and then hitchhike my way to Poděbrady. Soon, hitchhiking became the norm.

To promote manual dexterity the boarding school operated several workshops, and each student had to enroll in one. There was a woodworking shop, a book binding shop, a metal shop, and an electrical shop in which boys learned how to build crystal radios. However, only boys from ninth grade and up could enroll in the electrical shop. I was too young, so I chose woodworking instead. I remember building a tray for Aunt Marie, my father's wife, to carry dishes from the kitchen to the dining table. She lovingly kept and used this crude artifact long into my adult years. The compulsory attendance at those workshops, the 6 a.m. reveille followed by a rigorous workout, and the daily roll call before dinner at 7 p.m. were the only three attempts I can think of to instill some discipline in the students. Otherwise, after school, we were pretty much left alone to do as we pleased.

To call the George of Poděbrad establishment a boarding school is a bit of a misnomer, because there was no school in the castle; in Czech, it was in fact called an *Internát*. We only lived, took our meals, and had our workshops, study rooms, and gym in the castle: for our classes we went to a regular public school in the town. As in all high schools, there were five-minute breaks between classes and one twenty-minute snack break at 10:00 a.m. During the snack break, the school provided a glass of milk, and the students who lived at home took out the rolls or buns or cakes their mothers had packed for them and proceeded to snack. The *Internát* of George of Poděbrad did not provide snacks, so those of us who lived there had to do with milk alone.

Shortly after the beginning of my first school year in the Poděbrady public school, a girl—one of my seventh-grade classmates—came up to me during the snack break and asked me if I'd like a buttered bun. I said yes, and she handed me a neatly wrapped package containing a generously buttered fresh bun. From that day on, throughout the rest of the school year, that girl whose name I no longer remember brought me a buttered roll or bun at each snack break. It didn't occur to me to write a thank-you note to her mother nor to share my good fortune with the other two boys from the *Internát* who were in the same class. I can only surmise how this girl came to bring me a roll or bun each day. Probably she mentioned to her mother that the boys from the *Internát* didn't have any snacks, and the mother took pity on us; she then told her daughter to pick a boy she liked and ask him if he'd like a bun. I'll never know if that is really what happened. Even worse, I'll never be able to thank that good soul.

After sixteen months in pretrial custody, my mother was released from prison in the late summer of 1951. I stayed in the boarding school through the first four months of my eighth grade, and at Christmas I moved back to Prague to live with my mother in our new proletarian apartment. In retrospect, those one and a half years of boarding school were both good and bad for me. One result was that, having lived practically on my own for that long, when I came back, I considered myself a completely independent person with no need for any adult to tell me what to do or not to do. From my perspective of today, that was a little too early for so much independence.

At the same time, being without moral guidance for that long at that impressionable age severed certain inchoate moral fibers, which then took a long time to mend and prevented other such fibers from forming for some time.

For example, perhaps three or so years later, when I was in high school, I fell in with a bunch of bad boys, the kind who might today be called juvenile delinquents. I recall one evening walking with them along a row of parked cars as one of them kept trying all the car doors until he came to one that was not locked. He opened the door and noticed on the seat a pair of fine leather gloves. He tried them on, and they fit, so he pocketed them, saying, "At long last, a good find." Though I knew what he did was wrong and would never have done something like that myself, I was not so morally outraged by his actions as to break away from that crowd. Instead, I continued to hang out with them. That's what I meant when I said that certain barely formed moral fibers got severed during my one and a half years in the boarding school. They were later mended, but it took time.

Thick Skin

While still living in Prague, I was distantly acquainted with a young couple my age, Peter and Charlotta Kotík. Peter was a flutist and an avant-garde composer, and Charlotta was an art historian. They had a distinguished lineage: Charlotta was a great-granddaughter of Thomas Masaryk, and Peter was a son of Jan Kotík, a well-known abstract painter. In addition, my mother and Charlotta's mother were both art historians and friends. After the Soviet invasion of Czechoslovakia in 1968, the couple emigrated to the United States, and through the grapevine, I learned that they had settled in Buffalo, New York, where Charlotta was working as a curator in the Albright Knox Gallery, while Peter was trying to make it as a musician.

During my mother's first visit to the United States in 1974, out of the blue I received in the mail an invitation to a concert given by Peter Kotík in Westbeth Auditorium on Manhattan's West Side. The invite announced a solo performance by a flutist and composer who'd be playing his own compositions. I had no idea how he found my address, because we were not in touch. My mother and I concluded that, because of my acquaintance with both Charlotta and Peter and her friendship with Charlotta's mother, we couldn't not go. And so on the given date, we arrived at the Westbeth Auditorium.

I remember that it was a Saturday afternoon. At five minutes before the announced starting time, there was only one man sitting in the second row of the three-hundred-seat auditorium. On the stage was a stand for music next to a set of drums. Doubting that we were at the right place, I asked the man if this was where Peter Kotík would be playing. He responded that it was what he came for, so my mother and I sat down in the same row but at the opposite side of the aisle from the man. Eventually, an elderly couple then came in and sat down in the first row. Soon after, two young men came and sat down next to the man who was there first. Counting my mother and me, there were now a total of seven spectators in that large auditorium.

A few minutes after the stated beginning, Peter walked onto the stage with sheets of music in one hand and a flute in the other. It was the first time I had seen him in more than ten years. He wore black pants with a black shirt buttoned up to the collar. His expression was stern. He put the music on the stand, surveyed the auditorium, bowed deeply, and proceeded to play. I was not sure if he recognized me. If he did, he made no sign of it.

There are two kinds of avant-garde composers: those whose music is listenable, such as Philip Glass or Steve Reich, and those whose music is not. It quickly became apparent that Peter Kotík's music was of the latter category. Given that it is hard to play flute and drums at the same time, his composition alternated solo flute whistling with robust percussion playing.

About five minutes into the performance, the elderly couple promptly fell asleep, with the man emitting occasional light snores. The next thing I noticed was that the man who was there first took out a notebook, jotted down a few notes, stood up, and left. I concluded that he was a critic. The next to leave were the two young men who, at about twenty minutes into the performance looked at each other, nodded, stood up, and departed. That left Peter playing to my mother and me, with the elderly couple sleeping soundly.

My mother and I looked at each other, hoping that in recognition of the absurdity of the situation, Peter would shorten his program. But no such luck: he kept on playing interminably. Then at one point, he hit the drums a little too strongly, which woke up the elderly couple. They sat up looking alarmed, not quite knowing what hit them. Once they realized where they were, they both looked at their watches, then at each other, after which they stood up and left.

Now my mother and I were the only spectators left in the auditorium. As we clearly could not leave, we were now sure that Peter would acknowledge the humor of the situation and stop playing. But we were wrong again: Peter continued to play. We soon started enjoying the theater of the absurd, in which we were the principal actors, but continued to wonder how long this could possibly go on. Peter kept on playing for at least another half an hour; he did not shorten his program by a single note.

When he finished, he bowed, and my mother and I clapped. He didn't flash a smile, still looking deadly serious. He gave no sign that he considered the whole scene even slightly a bit off. Initially, my mother and I had intended to take Peter out to an early dinner, but seeing his stern face, I instead decided to play along. I walked up to him, shook his hand, and congratulated him on a splendid performance. His face still serious, he thanked me, turned around, and walked backstage.

Going home, my mother and I wondered aloud, "So this is how thick your skin needs to be if you want to make it as an avant-garde musician!" It took a long time, but make it he eventually did. Forty years later, Peter Kotík got his own orchestra. In New York, there is an audience for anything, and that includes Peter Kotík's kind of avant-garde music.

My Time in the Czechoslovak Army

One peculiar irony of communist Czechoslovakia was that, in a regime dedicated to the eradication of the bourgeois class and hailed as a worker's paradise, and where everyone was to be equal, there was one instance in which the intellectuals, who typically tended to be suspected of disloyalty, were actually accorded preferential treatment, and that was in the case of military service. There was a two-year compulsory service for all able-bodied males over eighteen years old from which, however, university students were exempted. Well, not entirely exempted but had their time of service significantly reduced.

Here is how it worked in my case. During four of the six years of the architecture program at the Czech Technical University in Prague, male students had to attend military training one day a week. We were given uniforms and gas masks, which we kept at home, and once a week, typically on Thursdays, at an ungodly early hour of the morning, we had to report to an open space at the outskirts of Prague; there we marched, crawled, threw blind hand grenades, and practiced other military nonsense. In addition to those one-day-a-week exercises, during two out of five summer vacations, we had to spend four weeks in a military camp located in the countryside out of town. We uniformly hated all of it, but we took our military training in stride, first, because it was something we had to do if we wanted to graduate and, second, because we were grateful for not having to spend two years in the army. At graduation, we all received one stripe on our epaulets. I don't know the English term for that lowest of military ranks, but it was one tiny step above the regular grunt.

Then, after graduation, having received all that military training during our time at the university, we had to serve only six months instead of the standard two years. These days, six months goes by in the blink of an eye, but when I was twenty-four, it seemed like an eternity. I was drafted just after I was transferred from my banishment in the provinces to an architectural office in Prague, and I was eager to show the world and myself what I could do; I found this half-year delay very hard to take. I was posted to Marienbad, an unlikely location for a barracks. Before the war, it was an elegant spa town, but in the early 1960s it was as drab as any other provincial city during the communist era in Czechoslovakia.

My strongest memory of those barracks is the smell. I was assigned a bed in a room with perhaps twenty other guys. The water in the bathhouse was hot only once a week, so you can imagine the body odor. In addition, most guys smoked then. The mixture of body odor and cigarette smoke produced a miasma that made it impossible for me to sleep. So on the very first night, after the lights were turned out, I took my blanket, left the room, and started roaming around the barracks in search of another place to sleep. After a while, I spied an unlocked room, which turned out to be a storage closet for blankets: it was full of stacks of folded blankets. The tops of those stacks provided a flatter surface to sleep on than the bumpy mattress of the bed I had abandoned. There was even a window that could be opened to let in fresh air. That room became my lair for the rest of my days in those barracks. Sometimes I hid there even during the day to take a nap or to study French. That single stripe on my shoulders made it easier for me to hide, because it exempted me from participation in drills or morning exercises.

I no longer remember how—perhaps he'd seen a questionnaire I filled in—but the commanding officer of the barracks, a colonel, noticed that I could print in neat block letters (as all architects can). He summoned me to his office and asked me to hand-letter several announcements for the officers' bulletin board. The colonel liked my lettering and, perhaps, even my company, because from then on, he called me in at least a couple of times a week. Eventually, I got to design posters for special events, something I actually enjoyed doing. In addition to getting me this task, which allowed me to spend several hours a day doing something I liked, my association with the commanding officer served me well in another way. Whenever my lower-rank superiors couldn't find me, they assumed I was with the colonel—even though, more often than not, I was in my lair studying French.

I was so determined not to waste the time I had to spend in the army, to have something to show for those six months, that learning French became my obsession. I brought with me an excellent textbook, *Langue Francaise de A a Z*, which I carried on me all the time. It is amazing how fast you can learn a language if you study every day. When I returned home at the end of my service, I picked up Camus's *L'Etranger* and was thrilled to find that I could read it with ease. But I am getting ahead of myself, because I am not yet done describing my six months in the army.

One would think that, with the lettering of announcements and designing of posters for the colonel, studying French, and sleeping in the storage closet in fresh air, my life in the barracks would be bearable. From my perspective of today, it certainly would seem that way. However, from the impetuous perspective of a twenty-four-year-old, I found my existence in the barracks stultifying, and I devised a subterfuge to escape, albeit only temporarily.

It so happened that one of my skiing fractures had left a small fragment of bone that had grown into my left tibia bone about two inches above the inner ankle. The result was a tiny protrusion on my shin. It was not visible, but when one pressed a finger to the bone at that spot, one could feel a little bump. It also showed up on X-rays. At the time of the fracture some five years earlier, the attending orthopedist told me that removing that bump would be a simple little surgery, but suggested I wait and see if it caused me any discomfort. If it did not, then why bother with surgery? Because it caused me no discomfort whatsoever, whether walking, running, or skiing, I soon forgot about it. Once I was in the barracks, however, the bump came in handy.

Feigning a slight limp, I walked into the infirmary in the barracks and saw the army medic. I told him that I was experiencing an excruciating pain in my left leg whenever I wore my army boots. He felt my left leg, and as I expected, he found the bump. Very pleased with himself for discovering the cause of my suffering so quickly, he told me I needed an X-ray, wrote me a day's pass out of the barracks, and sent me to a Marienbad hospital. Having seen on the X-ray the lump of bone that had grown into my tibia, the civilian doctor in the Marienbad hospital pronounced that it had to be removed and wrote me a prescription for the surgery in the Army Hospital in Prague. That was precisely the outcome I'd hoped for!

The next day I was on the bus for Prague. I had dinner with Eva and my mother, spent a night at home, and the next morning reported to the Army Hospital for the surgery. In those days things in hospitals didn't move very quickly. All the pre-op tests and preparations took two whole days, so that the surgery, such as it was, didn't take place until the third day. Today, I'd be sent home the day of the surgery, but back then, I was not released until the wound was healed and the stitches taken out. All in all, it took two whole weeks before I was discharged. After another dinner and night at home, and a bus ride back to Marienbad, I was back in the barracks.

Although my leg felt perfectly fine and I could run a marathon if I had to, according to military procedures, and to my inexpressible delight, I was pronounced a convalescent and ordered to the infirmary "to complete my recovery." I was the only occupant of the infirmary, so I had peace and quiet for my study of French. After a week of this nirvana, the medic certified me as recovered, and I was released into my platoon. The net outcome of this totally unnecessary operation was that it removed me from the barracks for three whole weeks. At the time, it struck me as a very good bargain. And on top of that, removing that piece of bone from my shin could only have been beneficial. Who knows if in later years it might have bothered me?

The week after I was released from the infirmary, I was working in the colonel's office on a poster for an officers' dinner when I noticed on the bulletin board an announcement for the Annual Army Ski Championship, with training sessions starting the following week. I asked the colonel if it was open to all soldiers or just the officers. He replied, "To any soldier who can ski." I told the colonel that I could ski and asked him if I could go to the training sessions. He said he could not see why not and suggested that I speak to my immediate superior, a captain whose name I've long forgotten. The captain was a little flummoxed over how someone whose leg was just operated on could want to participate in ski races, but because he knew that the colonel had sent me, he approved my participation in the training.

And so the next day I was once again sitting on a bus to Prague, this time to pick up my skis and head to Špindlerův Mlýn, my favorite ski resort in northern Bohemia and the site of the Army Championship. The races didn't start until the following week; the first week we were to practice, and practice we did.

I couldn't believe my luck. A month earlier I had to have my leg cut open to get away from the barracks for three weeks and now, without having to do anything except knowing how to ski, I got away for two weeks of skiing. Well, I did have to do something: I had to race. After a week of unsupervised practicing (i.e., skiing), the races began. The first was the slalom, the next day the giant slalom, and on the third day was downhill racing. There were around fifty racers in each category, and although I did not win any medals, I placed among the first twenty or so which was better than I expected. Much as I love skiing, I have never enjoyed racing. Having to ski through the gates seemed somehow contrary to the free spirit of skiing. Nevertheless, since in those days racing typically provided a free week of skiing, I always went for it.

In conclusion, here is the sum total of my military service: with my leg surgery and the ski races, I only ended up staying in the barracks twenty-one of the required twenty-six weeks. Considering that my time in the barracks was divided between hand-lettering announcements, designing posters, and studying French, from my perspective of today, no one should have felt sorry for me. Yet that was not how I saw it at the time. Instead of enjoying the ride, this uncalled-for interruption of my work made me furious. When thinking now of my impetuous attitude of those days, a benign smile spreads across my lips.

Leaving London

From time to time, I am asked why I left London for New York. The answer is that I didn't think one could be a citizen of the world, something I aspired to be, without experiencing life in America. In London, I had a satisfying job, a good enough apartment, and all the papers, such as a labor permit and permanent residence, required to live and work in the United Kingdom indefinitely. There was simply no reason for me to leave London, except for this itch to experience America. But that itch was not without some reservations.

Although none of my English acquaintances ever said anything openly anti-American to me, the prevalent view in England at the time was that America was a cultural desert where everyone

Late 1969 in London, before leaving for New York.

was just chasing money and where no sensitive person could possibly survive. I recall an acquaintance, Rosy Hardy, whose father was in the House of Lords and who was fond of traveling, especially to Canada and Mexico. When she was once again about to leave for one of those two countries, I asked her if she had ever visited the United States. Her brisk response: "Never! That country simply doesn't interest me whatsoever!"

I did not realize until later how much of this attitude I had absorbed, as if by osmosis, during my two and a half years in London. To be sure, American tourists were doing a good job reinforcing this perspective. It was the Beatles era, the time of shaggy hair and bell-bottom pants, and there walked these apparitions down Oxford Street with their crew cuts and high-water pants, loud and confident, but looking as if they came from another planet. Those were American tourists. Naturally, I assumed that they represented typical Americans.

Still, when I opened an American architectural magazine, I liked what I saw in it more than most of what I saw around me in England. This is no longer true, but it was in the 1960s. So despite all my reservations, I was determined to go to the United States. Although I had no fixed schedule in mind, I was convinced that it was going to be a temporary adventure and that, after some three or four years of working in America, I'd return to civilization—which in my case meant London. I was so certain that I'd eventually return that I left in my friend Tony Medwin's basement a trunk packed with stuff I didn't think I'd need in America.

When the news circulated among my coterie of friends and acquaintances that I was indeed going to America, the reactions were mixed. Some were genuinely puzzled because they just could not fathom why anyone would do such a thing. Since, at the time, salaries in the United States were uniformly higher than those in England, they assumed that I must be going there for the money. Then there were those who were truly disappointed. They didn't say so aloud, but they seemed to think,

"So we were not good enough for you?" That reaction was harder to take because throughout my stay in England, I always felt warmly welcomed.

People also started giving me advice. The father of a friend counseled me, "Martin, buy yourself some clothes of natural fibers like cotton or wool, because all there is in America is polyester." That was pure nonsense, as I soon found out, but not knowing that, I went to Simpson's at Piccadilly and bought myself a bunch of flannel and corduroy slacks. The only guy in the office I worked in who had actually visited the United States told me, "Martin, Americans don't read, but they like pictures. Everybody has a slide projector, so why don't you take with you some pictures of Prague that you could show after dinner? You'll be very popular." I followed that advice as well, and it actually stood me in good stead during my first year in New York.

During my first five years in New York, I didn't give a single thought to the question of whether I'd ever be returning to London. It wasn't until my mother's first visit in 1974, when she asked me where was my cast iron pot that I had bought in London, that the question occurred to me. I then remembered that it was in the trunk I left behind in Tony Medwin's basement. It didn't take us long after that to realize that I was not going back to London. I wrote to Tony, explained that I would not be returning anytime soon, sent him some money, and asked if he could ship the trunk to New York. By that time, Tony was married to an American wife and understood completely.

That my impressions of my English friends' reactions to my going to America were not far off the mark was confirmed during my first visit back to London, on a stopover en route to Tehran in late January 1975. I invited a bunch of friends for lunch at Bricklayer's Arms, an old architects' hangout. They all came, curious to see me after the five years, but their former warmth seemed palpably tempered.

A Stunningly Beautiful Woman

My office in Tehran was in a suite that included a large foyer/waiting room, three offices, one conference room, a kitchenette, and a bathroom with a shower; it was on the second floor of a six-story office building owned by my client, on Shahreza Avenue. My client kept the largest of the three offices for himself, I used the second one, and a Swedish salesman of a variety of earth-moving equipment rented the third office.

The suite came with two servants, Hamze and Oyad. They were from a village in the countryside, where they kept their wives and children. While they were in Tehran, they lived in that suite of offices. They kept their futon-type roll of bedding in a closet; in the evening, they would unroll it in the foyer, where they would sleep. Their job was to clean the offices, prepare tea or coffee, and run errands. They were clearly not overworked. Most of the time they sat in the kitchen and drank tea.

My client's hours were highly irregular. If he showed up at all, it was sometime before lunch, which was delivered to his office by one of his house servants. After lunch, he typically slept for an hour, and soon after he left. The Swedish salesman spent most of his time on the road. Tehran was his base, but his territory also included Saudi Arabia and the Emirates. I saw him at most once or twice a month. As a result, most of the time, other than the servants, my draftsmen and I were the only people in the entire suite.

Hamze and Oyad were barely literate and were very proud that they could sign their names. In dealing with them, I made the mistake that many Westerners commit when dealing with servants: I treated them as equals. When I asked them for something, I said the Farsi equivalent of "would you please," and once they did what I had asked them to do, I thanked them. For generations, they were used to being treated by their masters like dogs, so when I treated them as my colleagues, they interpreted it as some kind of weird weakness on my part and lost all respect for me; I became a sort of laughingstock for them. But they still liked me because, weird as I was, I was one of them. They liked it when I practiced my Farsi on them and were eager to teach me new words. Despite my many attempts to have them call me Martin, they kept calling me Mr. Martin. My last name was just too hard for them to pronounce.

In those years, I worked until dinner time, which in Tehran was around 9 p.m. However, I had convinced myself that I needed to have a glass of Scotch every day at about 6 p.m. I kept a bottle of Black Label in my file cabinet, so when the time came, I rang the bell, Oyad or Hamze would come to my office, and I'd say, "*Lotfan yek livan ba yach*," which was Farsi for "One glass with ice, please." They knew very well why I wanted that glass. As good Muslims, they disapproved of drinking alcohol, and to show their disapproval, when one of them brought me the glass, he handed it to me with his arm outstretched and his face turned away.

One day when I was at the office alone, both Oyad and Hamze came in and, out of the blue, asked, "*Aghaye Martin, kchanum mikchaid?*" which meant "Mr. Martin, do you want a woman?" In my broken

Farsi I responded, "Oh, absolutely, I do want a woman!" Although at that time it was a statement of fact, I meant it as a joke and promptly forgot all about it.

Now, I must digress for a moment to explain something about Iranian culture at that time. For a young Iranian woman from the emerging new middle class, snatching an American husband was a coveted prize, tantamount to winning a lottery. This was not true for the high rollers of my clients' cohort, who had degrees from US universities, made weekend shopping trips to Paris, and vacationed in Bali. But for those women one level lower on the social strata, from the first generation with college degrees, an American husband was a trophy.

About a month later, Oyad and Hamze came once again to my office, strangely gloating, and announced, "Mr. Martin, the woman is here. She's waiting for you in the conference room." I had no idea what they were talking about, so I stammered in Farsi, "What woman?" They responded, "Well, you did say you wanted a woman, so we brought you a woman. She is waiting for you in the conference room; come and take a look." Suddenly I remembered what I had asked for and started sweating.

Hamze led the way to the conference room, opened the door, and ushered me in. When I walked in, my jaw dropped. On a chair pulled away from the conference table sat a stunningly beautiful young woman, with a fashion magazine type of beauty. Indeed, she could have just walked in from a fashion shoot for *Vogue*, with her tailored dress, perfect makeup, impeccable nails, flawless eyebrows, the hair done just so and sitting with crossed legs to show off her shapely gams. To complete the image, she was smoking a cigarette in a cigarette holder. She didn't show the slightest sign of nervousness; on the contrary, she looked composed, calm, and confident. I was mystified. How did these two half-literate villagers come up with this beauty?

I asked her if she spoke English. She responded in Farsi, "Not one word." So I switched to Farsi and asked her what her name was. I have not seen her since, but I still remember that her name was Shahla. I sat down across the table from her and attempted to start a conversation. I asked her where she lived and what she did. She gave me the most succinct answers possible. I felt something was odd, and then it hit me: Shahla never flashed a smile. She sat there with a stern, composed look, totally unengaged.

Out of desperation, I asked her if she'd like to have dinner with me sometime. For the first time, she became somewhat animated and responded, "First, you have to come and speak to my father." When I asked her if she needed permission from her father to have dinner with me, she repeated, "You have to come and speak to my father." That sentence became her refrain. Whatever I said, she replied, "You have to speak to my father." Feeling like an actor in the theater of the absurd, I started enjoying the bizarreness of the scene and asked her if her father spoke English. A quick answer came: "No."

There was a notepad on the table. Shahla took it, tore out one sheet, scribbled a phone number on it, said something in Farsi that I didn't understand, said, "*Kchoda hafez*," and headed for the door. I walked her to the front door, said "*Kchoda hafez*" as well, and that was the last I saw of her. I shared this incident with a number of my Iranian acquaintances, and most of them were as baffled by it as I was. One woman was convinced that Shahla came expecting that she would receive a marriage proposal.

Subterfuge

When I returned from Tehran in January 1979, I continued to work at the office that I had in my New York apartment, which I had kept during my four years in Iran. Of the two interconnected rooms, my drawing board, file cabinets, and flat-file drawers were in the smaller one. I had earlier built a loft bed directly above the flat-file drawers and some shelving. The living room was in the larger of the two spaces. There was a writing desk there, but other than that, it was a typical living room with one fancy leather sofa that converted into a bed, two armchairs, and a low coffee table. There was a dining alcove between the living room and the kitchen. During the annual St. Martin's parties, the combined spaces could accommodate more than fifty people. I thought that for a single man this was an entirely satisfactory living/working arrangement.

Eventually, as I needed drafting help, I designed another drawing board that I had built into the bay window in the living room. I made it an integral part of the window so that it did not take up much space. I also needed more flat-file drawers so I turned the coffee table into a flat-file cabinet that also still functioned as a table. And when I needed to buy a copier, the only place I could put it was on the low bench in front of the nonfunctioning fireplace that I was using for wine storage. It was a nice-looking, shiny black box, but still, it was a copy machine in the middle of the living room.

And so it went, until one day in the mid-1980s when, during a visit, my mother remarked, "I don't think you realize, my dear son, that you no longer live in an apartment. You live in an office." It didn't take me long to see that she was absolutely right. On some subconscious level, I knew all along that what I was doing was postponing the inevitable, which was either to turn my apartment into an office and find another place to live or to move the office someplace else.

Without any idea whether I wanted a space to work in or a space to live in, I started looking, hoping that the space I'd find would be more suitable for one or the other use, and that would help me decide accordingly. And that was exactly what happened. After a year of looking and seeing more than a dozen spaces, I found one that was perfect for my office. It was on the top floor of an old residential hotel on the south side of West 72nd Street. The two tiny rooms totaling four hundred square feet in the middle of the hustle and bustle of 72nd Street were quiet because they faced south and west, and as such they were also full of light.

The location was perfect as well, less than fifteen minutes' walk from my apartment on West 89th Street and a stone's throw from Lincoln Center.

The residential hotel was the kind of establishment Henry James wrote about: a place where young ladies and gentlemen from good families from outside the city could come into town and stay, enjoying all the conveniences of a regular hotel—maid service, a change of linens, a restaurant on the ground floor to take meals if they wanted to—but where they could also cook at home if they preferred that. To that end each unit was equipped with what at the time was called a Pullman kitchen. It amounted to a stainless-steel counter with a sink, a two-burner gas stove, and an undercounter refrigerator. And, of course, there was a bathroom with an extralarge tub, as was customary at the time.

After World War II, residential hotels fell out of favor, and the building was converted into regular apartments, chiefly by installing kitchens with larger counters and full-size refrigerators. The landlord had the nerve to call those tiny two-room units, in which the back room was accessible only through the front room, one-bedroom apartments. In the early 1980s, the building was converted into a co-op, and it was one of those co-op apartments that I bought. Or, strictly speaking, I bought shares in the cooperative and obtained a proprietary lease for that specific apartment.

In the arcana of New York City co-op laws, there is a phenomenon called "unsold shares." It so happened that the shares belonging to the apartment I bought were unsold shares. Those are co-op shares pertaining to the not-yet-sold apartments that are still held by the co-op sponsor, typically the former owner of the building. There are two advantages (if that's the proper word) that accrue to those who buy unsold shares: first, the buyer doesn't have to be approved by the co-op board, and, second, if the buyer wishes, he or she can be appointed to the co-op board. I wanted to avail myself of both. However, before buying those shares, I wanted to be doubly sure that I could have an office in the apartment I bought.

The first person I asked was the sponsor from whom I was buying the apartment, who assured me that, absolutely, I could have an office there. He pointed out that many people had offices in the building. Looking at the list of names on the intercom, I saw that, indeed, there were several CPAs in the building, as well as several lawyers and therapists.

The next thing I did was to look at the New York City zoning book, where I found "Home Occupation" as an allowable use at the given address. The definition of "Home Occupation" was tailor-made for a small architectural office: it allowed for two employees. The only restrictions were that there could be no beauty parlors and nothing could be sold on the premises. To make sure that I was not missing anything, I asked my lawyer friend David Soeiro, who was assisting me with this real estate transaction, to confirm that I could have an office there. David did so. And on the basis of this triple assurance, I went ahead and bought the apartment.

Having bought the apartment, I set out to design its gut renovation. Other than changing the bathroom from the one with a large tub to a much smaller one with a shower stall and installing a smaller kitchen counter in the passage between the two rooms instead of in the front room, the rest of the renovation consisted of installing built-in desks, cabinets, and shelving. The idea was to create four workstations plus a conference table by using every last square inch of the four hundred square feet of space. I even managed to include a flip-down bed for occasional overnight stays. In between working on client jobs and after hours, it took me four months to prepare the construction drawings. During that time, as a new board member, I attended the monthly co-op board meetings. Once the job was approved by the Building Department, I put it up for bids. I selected a contractor, paid him a deposit, and, the next day, flew to Geneva to meet my mother at her cousin Jean's in Fernay-Voltaire. I felt mighty pleased with how things were coming along and could not wait to move into my new office.

When I returned from Europe, my first full-time employee Louise Dunford told me that the managing agent of the co-op had left several messages and wanted to speak with me. I called the agent, only to be told that the board didn't want any more offices in the building and that it had ordered a halt to the construction. I then called the contractor, who told me that just when they had completed the demolition part of the renovation, the managing agent and two men who identified themselves as the president and vice president of the co-op board came by and asked him and the workers to leave the premises. I called the managing agent back and asked for the phone number of the president of the board. When I called the president, he confirmed what the agent had told me—namely, that the board wanted to keep the building residential and, to that end, did not want any new offices. I knew that the following week there was going to be a board meeting, so I didn't bother to explain my position over the phone, but kept my arguments for the meeting. I was naïve enough to believe that my position was so strong that I was bound to prevail.

At the meeting, I argued that the board could not possibly prevent me from setting up an office in the space I had bought, given the following:

1. The co-op sponsor had assured me that I could operate a small architectural office out of the unit I bought from him.
2. The New York City zoning law permitted the "Home Occupation" use at that location. I passed around copies of the page from the zoning book with the definition of "Home Occupation" highlighted.
3. The Building Department approved the office use at this location. I produced a set of plans stamped APPROVED by the building department.
4. There already were a number of offices in the building. How could those be allowed and not mine?

In conclusion, I pointed out that by allowing more offices, they'd be adding value to the building since office space costs more than apartment space. I was quite pleased with the calm and even-handed delivery of my arguments. In an equally even-handed manner, the president responded, "Well, Martin, it's all very nice, except that we don't give a damn about what the sponsor told you. We don't care about the zoning law or the Building Department. And as to the offices already in the building, they are grandfathered in because they were here before we established the no-more-offices policy. Consequently, you cannot have an office in this building. You need to sell your unit."

I was stunned. From the assured and relaxed way in which the president talked, I could see that he was quite confident in the power of the board to prevent me from having an office there. Although I was still a board member and could have stayed on and participated in the rest of the deliberations, I told them that I would think about my options and let them know what I planned to do at the next meeting. Then I made my farewells and left.

My head was reeling. How did I find myself in this pickle? The option of selling this unit and looking for another space horrified me. It was not just that I would surely lose money—the real estate market was softening, and I would certainly not be able to sell the unit for anywhere near what I paid for it, plus I would never get back the money I paid the builder. Even worse, I would lose all the time that it took me to find that space and to design and draw the construction drawings for its renovation. That was totally unacceptable to me. But what were my options?

The next morning, I called David Soeiro and told him what transpired. His reaction? "Well, Martin, there you have a prime example of the arbitrary power of New York co-op boards. They operate as autocratic fiefdoms. I am surprised they even gave you a reason, because they didn't have to. Do you remember how Richard Nixon or Madonna could not find a co-op that would accept them? No reason was given." I asked David if he could think of a way around the board, but he could not. This situation was an unintended consequence of the fact that, as a buyer of unsold shares, I didn't have to be approved by the co-op board. If I had sought approval, it would have come up immediately that I could not have an office there, I wouldn't have bought the unit, and all I would have lost would have been the time it took me to find the place. That was still a loss, but it was peanuts compared with what I was about to lose.

Communist totalitarian regimes are full of idiotic, nonsensical rules and regulations, and those of us who have lived under those regimes have developed a fine art of circumventing them. Indeed, my art of rule circumvention was particularly finely honed. It was perhaps the combination of my righteous indignation with my art of circumvention that helped me come up with a subterfuge that would trick the board and enable me to have an office in the space I had bought.

I would tell the board that, since they didn't want me to have an office in the building, I was going to sell the unit I'd bought and get out. However, to be able to sell it, they had to let me complete the renovation. As it was, I had a demolished wreck on my hands, which I couldn't even put on the market. But then, once the renovation was completed, instead of selling the unit, I would quietly move in and proceed to operate my office. What could the board do then?

I ran this scenario by David Soeiro. He thought that it was a brilliant idea and that, indeed, once the renovation was completed and I had moved in, the co-op board, if they tried to evict me, would not have a leg to stand on; as long as I was paying my maintenance payments, there would be nothing they could do to get me out. "But," said David, "too much is riding on this, so let me run it by a friend whose specialty is New York co-op law." The next day David called and said that the co-op lawyer confirmed that, once I was in, the law would be on my side, and as long as I operated the office according to the Home Occupation rules, there would be nothing the board could do to prevent me from doing so.

Nervous as a cat, looking at all of them and none of them, I presented my proposal at the next board meeting. It was a seven-member board of which I was one, so there were six other members present, but only three addressed me: the president, the vice president, and the female treasurer. The other three members never said a word, and I had the feeling that some of them might have even been sympathetic to my plight. Having listened to me, they all nodded, and then the three leaders of the meeting conferred, whereupon the president said that they understood my proposal but wanted me to put it in writing.

Oy, it is one thing to say that you will do something that you have no intention of doing, but quite another to put it in writing. Still, I swallowed hard and wrote, "Per your request, I am pleased to confirm that, after its renovation is completed, I intend to put my apartment on the market to sell it." I faxed the letter to David Soeiro for his opinion. He thought that, from a legal standpoint, it was a completely meaningless and unenforceable document. His advice: "Go ahead and send it. If they accept it, you'll be fine." I then faxed the letter to the managing agent. He called me back in a few days and said that the board had decided to let me complete the renovation. I breathed a deep sigh of relief, fully aware, though, that the matter was far from over. I dreaded the inevitable confrontation that was bound to come once the board realized that I had tricked them.

It took another six months to finish the renovation, so it wasn't until April 1988 when I moved in to my completed office. The moment the construction was finished, I called the real estate agent who'd found me the space, explained to her my situation, and asked her to put the apartment on the market at the price I paid for it. It had been more than a year since I'd bought it, the residential market was way down, and the agent agreed that there wasn't the slightest chance that someone would pay that price at this time. Meanwhile, throughout the renovations, I had attended the monthly board meetings. On a few occasions, when the board faced construction issues, I had even managed to make myself useful.

The move to the finished office was quite discreet. Because all the furniture was built in, all I brought were a couple of chairs and a bunch of file folders, catalogs, and rolled-up drawings from the flat files at my old office. Chairs for the conference table were delivered a few weeks later. The new office worked out beautifully; it was a small but efficient space with all the conveniences I needed: four phone lines, a separate fax line, a large-format copier, a fax machine, a printer, and a coffee machine. I was very happy there, and my two employees claimed to like working there as well.

After I started operating the office, each time I attended a board meeting, I feared that one of the members would ask me, "So Martin, how is your apartment doing on the market? Any offers yet?" If someone had asked me, I was prepared to answer that my apartment was on the market, but so far, I'd had no offers. It was for the purpose of answering that question alone that I had put the unit on the market. But three months later, even six months later, no one had asked me that question. The dreaded confrontation never happened. My relationship with the board members was becoming more and more cordial.

So it happened that one of the most potentially unpleasant situations in my life just fizzled: there was no denouement. I wonder to this day what made the board drop the issue. Was it that they had seen through my subterfuge, realized that once I was in, there was nothing they could do to get me out, and so just let it be? I'll never know. To this day, thirty years later, the subject of my office has never been brought up by any board member. About ten years into my occupancy, we even held a board meeting in my office, and everyone remarked, "What a nice office!" I was appointed to the board because I bought unsold shares, but after that, each year I had to be reelected at the annual meeting of shareholders. Unlike some board members, I was reelected each year. After twenty-five years, I decided to no longer run for reelection and stepped down.

Jasan

These scribbles wouldn't be complete without one about Jasan. Unwittingly and without trying, he managed to play a significant role in my life, so much so that I can say that without him, my life wouldn't have been the same. I met Jasan after I was released from my banishment to the border region of Bohemia and was transferred to the architectural office of the national enterprise Konstruktiva in Prague. Jasan Burin was the most senior architect of the group I was assigned to. He was exactly ten years older than me and was extremely popular, for good reason: he was funny, he worked hard, and he played hard. We soon discovered that we had a similarly skewed sense of humor and that we both liked to drink and party, so we became fast friends.

I looked up to Jasan and was thrilled that I could count him among my friends. At that time when drafting was done manually, an architect's graphic skills were highly valued, and those that Jasan possessed were formidable. He was not only an excellent draftsman but also a fine renderer with a great flair for freehand sketching. I learned a lot from him, and my presentation skills improved considerably. Jasan and I also shared a desire to get out of Czechoslovakia and work in the West. His turn came first.

As a part of the team that designed the Czechoslovak Embassy in London, in 1966 Jasan was posted to London for what was to be a two-year stay; he was assigned to work with the English firm of architects that was preparing the construction drawings for the embassy. At the end of his first year in London, Jasan returned to Prague for a vacation. As mentioned, it so happened that his return to London coincided with my departure for London, so Jasan offered me a lift in his car.

I was delighted to accept, because that way we'd get to see a bit of Europe. We took five days to get to London, stopping along the way in Frankfurt, Düsseldorf, Amsterdam, and Brussels. In all those places, we stayed with acquaintances I had made during my previous trip to West Germany or with friends of those acquaintances. That way, while Jasan was providing the transportation, I was providing the lodging.

In London Jasan proved to be of great help to me. He invited me to stay with him in his small apartment until I found my own place. In fact, I am not sure how I'd have managed without Jasan, since before my first paycheck arrived, I had a miniscule amount of money. However, it was also in London that I experienced my first disillusionment with my hero.

It had to do with the way Jasan spoke English. Given that he had already spent one whole year in London working with English architects, I expected that by the time I got there, his English would be perfect. Instead, Jasan spoke haltingly, with many mistakes and with so heavy an accent that my English friends who met him had to really concentrate hard on what Jasan was saying to understand him. Worst of all, his wit and humor somehow didn't carry over from Czech to English. When he tried to be funny in English, it fell flat. It was painful for me to see the difference between Jasan speaking

Czech and Jasan speaking English. I felt sorry for him, yet when I suggested that he take an English class, he brushed the idea away with a wave of his hand.

During the year that we were both in London, although Jasan was moving in his circle and I in mine, we still found time to see each other at least once a month. However, I felt guilty when we saw each other, because even though Jasan introduced me to his friends, some of whom I am in touch with to this day, I was embarrassed to introduce him to my acquaintances, with a few exceptions. When my first and Jasan's second year in London came to an end—almost to the day on which the Russians invaded Czechoslovakia—it soon became obvious to both of us that we wouldn't be returning home anytime soon. At the end of 1968, Jasan found himself a job in Indianapolis and left for America. I spent first another year and then yet another year in London, before I followed him.

While we were apart those two years, we stayed in epistolary contact: Jasan was an excellent letter writer. His letters, most of which he illustrated, were hilarious, and his good humor remained intact in Czech. In Indianapolis, Jasan was invited to join a new firm of housing developers to become its architect in residence. When the firm got a contract to develop a large tract of land in Knoxville, Tennessee, it moved its headquarters there, and Jasan followed.

By the time I arrived in New York, Jasan was already living in Knoxville. The first time we saw each other in over three years was late 1970 or early 1971, when Jasan paid me his first of many visits to New York. I remember I was still working at Kahn & Jacobs. We spent days in the museums and nights bar hopping on the Upper West Side—these were good times like in the old days in Prague or London. I threw a little party for Jasan, and my friends were charmed by him. His English had improved somewhat over those three years, although not by much, but Americans have a much higher tolerance and acceptance of garbled English than the Brits had at the time.

Perhaps six months later, I lost my job at Kahn & Jacobs and started looking for another one. But I didn't want just any job; I wanted a design job. After two weeks and a number of interviews, I still had no offers, and I already envisioned myself in a gutter on the Bowery. So I panicked and called Jasan. He said, "Come on down; there's plenty of work here." I took my portfolio, hopped on an airplane, and flew to Knoxville. I made the phone calls, lined up the interviews and, while Jasan was working, he let me use his car to drive to my appointments. The third firm I interviewed with, Barber McMurry Architects, offered me a job as a lead designer of the office and for more money than I was making at Kahn & Jacobs. I returned to New York relieved that I wouldn't end up on the Bowery, but also apprehensive because I didn't want to move to Knoxville. I liked New York. So I continued interviewing.

Someone suggested that I see David Specter, who had a small office of four to six architects and might need a designer. David and I hit it off immediately, but after he reviewed my portfolio, he said, "Look, I have one housing project that would be right up your alley, but I cannot well offer you a full-time job on the basis of this one project alone. However, if you'd like to do it on a freelance basis, you can start tomorrow." I accepted his offer enthusiastically. When I prorated the hourly rate that David offered on a per annum basis, it came to more than what Barber McMurry offered me.

The next day I called Ben McMurry, told him what happened, and then added that if they had a project for me, I'd love to design it for them on a freelance basis. Ben said he would talk to his partners and get back to me. He called back the same day and said that, yes, they would be happy to have me design for them on a per-project, freelance basis—and he wanted to know how quickly I could come down. Thus started my three-year collaboration with Barber McMurry Architects, the most visible product of which is Rokeby Condominium Tower in Nashville, a fourteen-story, high-rise apartment building. And it was during the first year of my commuting to Knoxville that I met the dean of the School of Architecture at the University of Tennessee, where Jasan was already teaching, and got appointed a Visiting Associate Professor of Design.

It was during my frequent trips to Knoxville that I really got to know Jasan. None of the trips were more than three or four days long, but I made many of them, so that in those three years I ended up spending ninety to a hundred days each year in Tennessee. During the first year or so I always stayed with Jasan. He would either pick me up at the airport or I'd take a cab directly to the office of Barber McMurry, where he would fetch me in the evening.

Jasan had a large apartment, and I think that he actually liked having me stay with him. Eventually, however, I rented a studio apartment in faculty housing. In my second year I also bought a car—a 1966 Ford Galaxie—for $100, so I no longer needed to be dependent on Jasan for my mobility in and around Knoxville. The Galaxie was as big as a church, and instead of shifting gears with a lever, you had to press buttons. The moment I drove it out of the used car lot, the gas tank fell out. For another $100 I got a new gas tank, and from then on, the car served me well for two years. When not in town, I kept it in the parking lot at the airport.

Even when I was no longer staying with Jasan while I was in town, we spent all our after-work time together; most of the time we spent it with his friends and, later, with my friends as well. It was during those many dinners, parties, and excursions to the Smoky Mountains and to university functions that I became aware of Jasan's extraordinary sexual appetite.

I had known for some time that he was catnip for women; I just wasn't aware of the large numbers of them or of his capacity and willingness to accommodate them all. Jasan also liked to share his sexual escapades with me—not to brag, but just because he needed to talk about his sex life. And he shared everything, down to the minutest anatomical details. He was my only male friend with whom I ever had those sorts of discussions, although "discussion" was not the right word since he was the talker and I the listener. I also suspect that I was his only confidant and that, with other people, he was perfectly discreet.

I recall one of Jasan's birthday parties, thrown by his lady friend of the moment, where there were more than a dozen women in attendance: some were single, and some were with their husbands or significant others. At one point when Jasan and I were standing alone, he whispered to me, "I slept with all of them." Again, not in a bragging way, but simply to state a fact. I was positive that none of those women had the slightest suspicion of that fact.

One woman, who stayed with Jasan longer than any other I was aware of, was a certain Caroline. She was married to a real estate developer and owned an art gallery in downtown Knoxville. As Jasan was not only a good architect but also an accomplished artist, Caroline gave him many solo exhibitions showing his watercolors of landscapes, flowers, or cityscapes. I attended many an opening at

Caroline's gallery. She and Jasan appeared to be genuinely fond of each other, and, as with his other women, Jasan described their sexual acrobatics to me in graphic detail. Once or twice, when Jasan was out of town, Caroline and I went out for dinner together.

I noted a peculiar change in his appearance while Jasan was living in Tennessee. In Prague and in London he had always worn crisp white shirts and ties, and his hair was cut short, but in Knoxville he went "country." He wore boots and cowboy belts with big buckles and let his hair grow over his ears and collar and down his forehead, where it formed bizarre bangs that hung right down to his eyebrows. I was always slightly embarrassed when he came to pick me up at the office of Barber McMurry.

One day when I arrived in Knoxville on one of my many trips, a crestfallen Jasan told me that Caroline had divorced the real estate developer, married a Baptist preacher, and moved to Atlanta. Exactly how dejected Jasan was I only found out perhaps six months later, when Caroline was visiting Knoxville and sought me out. Over lunch she told me that after she had moved to Atlanta, Jasan tracked down her address, and ever since, each morning she found on her porch a fresh bouquet of cut flowers with a note from him. She felt sorry for Jasan and asked me to tell him that those flowers would not change anything and that he needed to please stop that insanity. I asked how long Jasan had been doing it; she wasn't exactly sure but thought it was at least two months or maybe three. I asked if she found fresh flowers every day. Caroline replied, "Seven days a week, without fail."

I was astounded by that revelation. To drive from Knoxville to Atlanta took at least three hours. To deposit those flowers by 7 a.m., Jasan had to leave Knoxville before 4 a.m. and then would not get back until 10 a.m. at the earliest. Doing this day after day for months seemed to me an obsession bordering on lunacy.

When Jasan and I had dinner that evening, I told him that I had lunch with Caroline and asked him if it was true that he drove down to Atlanta every morning to leave a bouquet of flowers on her porch. He said that it was true. I then told him, "Jasan, this is sheer insanity. Why are you tormenting yourself?" He looked at me dejectedly and said that it was simply something he just had to do. By this time Jasan and I had known each other for more than ten years, and I had never seen him so downhearted. He was always the life of the party. It was painful for me to see him in that state, but there was precious little I could do to help him.

Architecture in the United States is a regulated profession, meaning that to be able to practice, an architect, like a lawyer or doctor, needs a license. The licensure process is administered by the states. To obtain a license, an architect has to pass a license exam. And to be eligible to take the exam requires a degree from an accredited school of architecture, plus three years of practice under the supervision of a licensed architect. Architects can now take the license exams online, one subject at a time; in the early 1970s, however, there were seven exams stretched over three days, which was quite an ordeal. The most unnerving part was that one was allowed to fail no more than two subjects. If that occurred, one could then retake the one or two failed subjects later. If, however, one failed more than two subjects, none of the passed subjects counted, and one had to retake all seven exams. I took the exams in December 1970 and managed to pass all but one part, that on Construction Administration. I retook it the following June, so that by the summer of 1971 I was a licensed architect.

To serve as the in-house architect for the housing developers who brought him from Indiana to Tennessee, Jasan had to be licensed, so he took the exams after moving to Knoxville. He passed only one out of the seven exams, the Design part, and failed all the rest. He got so discouraged that he did not take them again. He had, however, an advocate. A Knoxville architect who was sitting on the Board of Architecture of the Office of Professions in Nashville was so impressed by Jasan's design talent and his presentation artistry that he convinced his fellow board members to invite Jasan in for an interview. Once the board members saw Jasan's drawings, they decided to bend the rules for him. They told him that all he had to do to get a license was to pass the Administration exam. Something like that would never be possible in the North, but this was 1970 in Tennessee where things were more relaxed.

Jasan took the Administration exam, but unfortunately failed it. Six months later he took it again and failed again. He decided not to try again, which meant that he would never be able to practice on his own and would always have to work for other architects. The housing developers had to hire a licensed architect, who became Jasan's boss.

On my next trip to Knoxville, some three weeks after my lunch with Caroline, as was our routine, I called Jasan late in the afternoon from Barber McMurry's office to find out what the plan was for the evening. In an uncharacteristically stiff voice, Jasan told me that he was otherwise occupied. He knew that I'd be around for another three nights before returning to New York, but he said nothing more. I felt as if someone had poured a bucket of cold water on my head.

I no longer remember what I did that night. It was the first evening in more than two years of my commuting to Tennessee that Jasan and I didn't spend together. The following afternoon I was teaching a studio class at the School of Architecture, and while there, I ran into Jasan in the hall. I asked him if we were going to see each other while I was in Knoxville or if he was otherwise occupied every night. He said he was otherwise occupied. There were students all around us so that was clearly neither the time nor the place for a discussion. We went our separate ways. Ten years passed before we saw each other again.

Perhaps two weeks after my return to New York, I received a letter from Jasan. I still have it. Without looking at the letter, I still remember one pivotal sentence from it: "I came to hate you with such intensity that whenever I see you, I feel like demolishing kitchen cabinetry with dinnerware inside it."

There was no explanation as to what caused that hatred. It was the fall of 1974, I was leaving for Tehran in January, and I had probably no more than two trips to Knoxville left before my work for Barber McMurry and the semester would be done. So I had plenty of things to worry about other than Jasan. Still, his letter was a shock: I had absolutely no idea what had come over him.

Our first contact after that hiatus was perhaps two or three years after my return from Tehran when, out of the blue, I received another letter from Jasan. The tone of the letter was casual and witty, as if nothing untoward had ever happened between us. Jasan told me that he had moved to Columbia, South Carolina, where he had been offered a better job; plus, after fifteen years, he'd had enough of Knoxville. He then spent a few lines describing his work, before he wrote: "Oh yes, I do owe you an apology. My weird behavior was all attributable to my infatuation with Caroline. I was just insanely jealous of you because I thought that you had hanky-panky with her and that drove me crazy. I now know that it wasn't true, but at the time my judgment was clouded."

And that was all. We resumed our epistolary relationship, and occasionally Jasan phoned.

In the summer of 1984 Jasan called to tell me that he and his Iranian girlfriend (about whom he had written) were driving from South Carolina to Maine, and he asked if they could stay one weekend night with me in New York. I told him that I was spending my summer weekends in Westhampton on Long Island, in a beach house that I was sharing with a bunch of friends, but if they wanted to, they would be welcome to sleep on a convertible sofa in the living room.

And so it happened that late one Saturday afternoon, Jasan and his lady friend pulled up in a station wagon loaded with camping equipment. It was the first time we had seen each other in ten years, but Jasan acted as if we had last been together just a month ago, as if we were the same bosom buddies we had been before. I went along with that, although I knew that our friendship could never be the same. I found myself unable to erase from my memory what had happened. I was also worried that what had happened once might happen again, which made me feel, as far as Jasan was concerned, like I was walking on eggshells.

Jasan was then in his midfifties, and his Persian lady looked as if she could be his daughter. She had the fashion-model type of beauty, was very docile, and seemed totally devoted to Jasan. At the time, my Farsi was still quite serviceable, and I enjoyed practicing it on her. As before, Jasan shared with me the intimate details of their sexual congress. After he checked out the convertible sofa, Jasan asked if they could pitch a tent on the beach side of the house while whispering to me with a wink, "For privacy purposes." Clearly, his libido showed no signs of weakening.

My housemates found Jasan's English amusing, and Jasan himself intrigued them. After dinner at the house, we all went dancing at a country music place on Montauk Highway. Jasan acquitted himself well on the dance floor, and I made a fool of myself by singing along with the orchestra, so once again, we were wild and crazy guys like in the good old days. On Sunday morning after breakfast Jasan and his lady folded the tent, packed up the car, and continued on their way to Maine.

The next time I saw Jasan was four years later, in 1988. Karen was already firmly in my life, and I had just moved my office out of my apartment to 72nd Street near Columbus Avenue. During those previous four years, we had been in touch via perhaps two letters and one phone call a year. Mostly Jasan called to tell me the details of his latest sexual adventures. When he called in the fall of 1988, he told me that he was coming up to New York to pick up a nurse whom he was importing from Slovakia and whom he intended to marry. He knew about my office and asked if he and his bride-to-be could stay one night there. As usual, he traveled with an inflatable mattress and a sleeping bag for two. Although by then I was pretty much inured to any surprises in connection with Jasan's women, this news astounded me. The man to whom women flocked like flies to honey needed to import a mail-order bride?

When Jasan came to my office with his nurse, I saw trouble ahead. All the other women I had seen with him over the years were visibly enamored of him, but this one very clearly was not. I saw a cold, calculating woman. This was not Jasan's perception, so I said nothing. Karen also met Jasan for the first time. She understood our long history—by then he and I had known each other for twenty-five years—but other than that, she had little use for him.

The four of us had dinner in a restaurant near my office, and it was a disastrous evening. It turned out that the nurse's English was practically nonexistent, and Jasan's English was still problematic. I was used to listening to his English, but I realized that people who were exposed to it for the first time had to concentrate hard to understand what he was saying. As a sensitive person, Jasan realized the awkwardness of the situation, and, to amuse Karen, he started clowning, making faces, and saying limericks, all of which amused the waiter, but not Karen.

My premonition regarding the nurse turned out to be spot on. She used Jasan to get her into the United States, and after less than six months in South Carolina, she left him and married a wealthy local dentist. Unlike years earlier with Caroline, this time Jasan recovered rather quickly, and then he pulled off something remarkable, something you read about in racy novels but never expect to actually encounter: a real-life a real-life *ménage à trois.*

He told me about this threesome in his letters and our occasional phone conversations. Jasan was in his early sixties when he met a female lawyer at an office party; she was a counsel for the firm for which Jasan worked. As usual, in short order, they became lovers. Not long after, he met a librarian at the Columbia public library, and they too quickly became lovers. What Jasan didn't know was that those two women, the lawyer and the librarian, were lifelong friends and confidantes. They exchanged notes about Jasan and agreed that they were both fond of him and that they both wanted to continue seeing him. So for a while, Jasan would alternate, sleeping one night with the lawyer and the next night with the librarian. Then one evening, after the three of them had dinner together, they all ended up in Jasan's house and, eventually, in his bed. They liked this better than the previous arrangement. So from then on, several times a week, the three of them converged for the night in Jasan's house.

Soon, however, Jasan's quarters felt too cramped for this new form of cohabitation. Because none of the three lived in apartments that were large enough, they pooled their resources and bought a house in which they all lived happily for more than two years. After the first year, things were working so famously that they decided to make it official, even if only among themselves. The librarian researched which African countries permitted men to have more than one wife. Of the many countries that allow for multiple wives, they picked one; I think it was Ghana or Gabon, but I am no longer sure. I still remember, however, Jasan's elated phone call when, after their return from Africa, he called me and announced, "Martin, I am finally a married man."

This idyll lasted another year before it fell apart. I never got out of Jasan any details of how it came undone, except that it was amicable. All that Jasan ever told me on the subject was that, after more than two years, they'd all had enough and wanted something else.

In Jasan's case, that something else was a woman in Prague. But before I get to that story, I want to say that, throughout all his escapades, Jasan continued to work hard and produce an impressive body of work. Sadly, he was not recognized for it, because he wasn't a licensed architect and could not work under his own name. That is why, instead of satisfied clients, he left behind a number of satisfied employers who were all very happy with his work. I knew that was the case in Knoxville, where I knew some of them. They were all uniformly in awe of Jasan's design talent and drawing prowess, and I have no reason to doubt that it wasn't the same in Columbia.

Back to the woman; the time was some eight years after the fall of the Iron Curtain and the Velvet Revolution, and travel to Prague was easy. After thirty years in America, Jasan decided to move back to Prague. I felt sorry for him when he told me that he was moving back, because it meant that, despite all those years and all those women, he had not been able to put down roots anywhere the way I had in New York. The next thing I knew, about six months later, I received in the mail an invitation from Jasan to his wedding in Prague.

Jasan was then in his early seventies and was about to enter his first legally binding marriage. So the move back to Prague did work out for him after all! The date of the wedding was only about a month away, and there was no chance that I could take time off to travel to Prague, so I called Jasan. I still remember that conversation. I found out the following information about his bride-to-be: she was an art historian working in the Museum of Applied Art in Prague, in her early fifties, divorced, with no children. I noted that it was the first time Jasan talked to me about a new woman of his without giving me the details of their sexual doings. I took this to be a good omen, meaning that this one was different from all the others. She sounded like a perfect match for Jasan, and he seemed very happy. So I sincerely congratulated him, gave him my best wishes, and started thinking about an appropriate wedding present.

About a month later, a few days before the date of the wedding, another piece of mail arrived addressed in Jasan's recognizable hand. Inside the envelope was a slip of paper with a photocopied announcement: "Jasan Burin wishes to announce that his wedding to [so and so] has been canceled."

Just to make certain that I didn't have to worry about sending a wedding present, I called again. I never got out of Jasan the full account of that debacle, and because I had not met his intended, I had no opinion of my own. The best I could surmise was that, based on her behavior regarding Jasan's purchase of an apartment in which they were to live, Jasan got the impression that she was marrying him for his money. In my later conversations with him, it appeared that there was also a disagreement over money Jasan had loaned her. So instead of the wedding, there was, eventually, a lawsuit.

That was one way Jasan was spending his time in Prague: waging lawsuits. In addition to the one against his formerly intended bride, he filed another one against the Czech government. Regarding the former suit, I simply didn't know enough to have any opinion; however, regarding the latter, I was 100 percent on Jasan's side. The lawsuit concerned his 1904 Daimler Benz motor car, which the communist government had confiscated after Jasan failed to return from his posting in England and which he was now trying to get back from the democratic Czech Republic.

During the past thirty years, the historic automobile had been exhibited in the Technical Museum of Brno, a state institution that didn't want to give it up. The museum's position was that it was in the public interest for this unique historical automobile to remain on exhibit. Jasan's position was that, even though the exhibit might be in the public interest, it was his property, which was illegally confiscated and should be restituted to its owner. He even offered to will it to the museum after his death.

Surprisingly, the court sided with the museum. Jasan kept on appealing; the courts kept on denying him. This was sure evidence that, even after more than ten years since the Velvet Revolution, the Czech Republic had not yet completely shed its communist past.

After my mother's death in 2001, my visits to Prague grew less frequent, but each time I was in town, I continued to get together with Jasan. He was then in his midseventies, and I was amazed to see that his libido had not flagged. Each time I saw him, the first item on his agenda was talking about his latest woman and giving me a detailed description of their copulation. Once she was a well-known actress; the next time she was the wife of a former communist apparatchik. When he was sleeping with the wife of the communist, Jasan convinced himself that it was his revenge for the forty years of communism Czechoslovakia was forced to endure.

Then disaster struck. Around the time Jasan turned eighty, his eyesight started rapidly deteriorating, and eventually, he was diagnosed with an irreversible case of macular degeneration. At the time, he was at work on a book about his architectural designs. Soon, he could no longer work by himself on his book, although with help, he did manage to publish it. It is an impressive book about a little-known architect.

A few years later, he was no longer able to read my emails, even when I typed them in large block letters, so our communication was reduced to occasional phone calls.

The last time I saw Jasan was when I visited Prague with my third wife Sandra, who knew him from Knoxville. In fact, without Jasan, Sandra and I would never have gotten together. After Karen died, it was Jasan who suggested to Sandra, with whom I hadn't been in contact for thirty-five years, that she write me a condolence letter. So to his help in London and then in Knoxville, Jasan added one more thing I owe him for.

When Sandra and I saw Jasan in Prague, he was walking somewhat unsteadily with a white cane that blind people use. He was then in his mideighties and had aged considerably since the last time I had seen him, perhaps four years earlier. His old vim and vigor were gone. He even had to be helped down the steps of the tram he had taken. Knowing that he wasn't poor, I asked him why he didn't take a taxi. He responded that sometimes he did, but most of the time it wasn't necessary. I recognized Jasan's old frugality, which, however, wasn't uniformly applied. When it came to buying cars, it had to be the top-of-the-line Porsche or some such expensive model. When he was drinking in a bar, frugality went out the window, and he kept on ordering round after round. When, however, it came to paying rent, after his leases expired, he would rather move than pay the increased rent. During the course of his fifteen years in Knoxville, he moved nine times; I couldn't fit all his addresses in my address book and had to add a page.

It is always with great sorrow that I think of Jasan these days. To think that after the multitudes of women in his life, he lives alone, half blind, in Prague fills me with inexpressible sadness.

Childlessness

Ah, what a subject! I could go on forever, but I'll try to be brief. Whether you look at it from a religious or a biological point of view, it appears self-evident that procreation is an integral part of human existence. Consequently, those of us who have not had children cannot be fully human. We are misfits, going through life without experiencing it fully. I find it impossible not to ask, "What's wrong with me? How come I haven't experienced the urge to have children, something that to the vast majority of people comes naturally?"

Because of Sandra's grandchildren, over the last five years I've had many opportunities to observe up close what it takes to care for a child. My head is still reeling! To have gone through that effort, or not to have gone through it makes for such vastly different life experiences that I am amazed that those of us who have gone through it and those who have not can even talk to each other.

Of course, I am talking about people in my lifetime, when most parents raise their children themselves. Until World War II, members of the upper-middle and upper classes outsourced childcare to highly qualified, certified nannies and governesses, a class of professional help that no longer exists. Consider my own mother: first of all, during my preschool years, she was a housewife; second, we had a live-in maid; third, as if that weren't enough, my mother hired a nanny who came six days a week to take care of me.

One could divide humankind into three groups. In the first would be people like my mother, my third wife Sandra, and many other women (and some men) who've told me that, ever since they came of reason, they knew they wanted children. When they married, it was specifically to have children. In the second group would be the tiny minority who've told me that, ever since they came of reason, they knew they did not want to have children. Those were mostly self-centered, egoistic types who considered their work so important that they simply could not do it while having children.

I belong to the third group: those of us who neither wanted nor didn't want to have children. I just never gave the subject much thought, with one exception: in the early 1980s, when I was infatuated with a woman from Minnesota, I found myself fantasizing about having a child with her. I don't think it was a sudden awakening of my dormant urge to have children; rather, I was infatuated and wanted to have a child with that particular woman. That was the only time I consciously thought about siring a child. While I was married to Eva, I think we both considered ourselves too young, and our marriage too wobbly, for the subject of having children to ever come up. And when Karen and I got together, she had already had her hysterectomy, so that the subject of having children was moot.

The older I get, the more aware I become of what a sensible life arrangement it is to have children, to have someone to pass on to not only one's wisdom, such as it is, but also the material stuff one has accumulated. Both my apartment and my house are full of valuable objects, most of which were passed on to me by my mother, with a few from my father. A baroque chest of drawers from eighteenth-century Bohemia, a Persian carpet my grandmother bought in Egypt before World War I, a Ming dynasty Chinese plate my father bought at auction, and many more—all of which are dear to me and all of which I'd love to pass on to my children if I had any.

However, here comes the rub: I was able to live the life I lived, choose the work I wanted to do, and live and work in four different countries only because I just had myself to support. If I had to support children, my choices would have been severely limited. During my employment days, I wouldn't have had the luxury of taking only design jobs; I'd have had to take jobs that paid more money. I don't think I could've left for Tehran if I had a family. If Eva and I had children, chances are we'd never have left Czechoslovakia, and, boy, am I glad I did! So herein lies the contradiction. On the one hand, I miss having children. On the other, when I imagine what my life would have been like if I had kids, I am glad I led the life I did. Selfish? Sure, but life is like that.

Guilt

While attending university, like most students, I wanted to make some money during summer vacations. To that end, each summer I took a job for one of the two months of vacation. The first summer I worked for a month in the coal mines. I was genuinely interested in experiencing what it would be like to be so deep underground. There was also the macho element of coal mining that, at the time, appealed to me. The money was good, and last but not least, doing manual labor greatly improved my ideological dossier. The following summer I worked for a month as a truck driver's assistant. I helped load and unload the goods we were delivering around the country, but most of the time I was paid for sitting in the cabin of the truck. The third summer a bunch of us sprayed hops in western Bohemia with pesticide.

By far, my favorite summer job was surveying undocumented baroque churches scattered all over Bohemia and Moravia. The head of the Department of History of Architecture was compiling a book about forgotten churches, and she secured money to survey them from the Ministry of Culture. After completing the third year of the six-year program, students of architecture were deemed competent to survey the complex geometries of baroque plans, which is what I applied to do. Crews of two students each were deployed to villages for approximately two weeks to measure the undocumented churches, and then they had another two weeks or so to prepare the plans of the churches they had surveyed.

Those were wonderful adventures. In the summer of 1960, my crew mate Miloš Mytiska and I headed to Český Rudolec, a small town of around nine hundred people in southeastern Bohemia, to survey the baroque Church of Jan Křtitel (John the Baptist). We checked into the only hotel in town, across the little square from the church, and the next morning we set to work. Next to the church we noticed a little parish house, and although we were not instructed to do so we thought that it would be a good idea to introduce ourselves to the priest and tell him what we'd be doing.

Although the official ideology was that religion was the opium of the masses, the communists did not have the nerve to abolish the church in Czechoslovakia outright. (The Czech lands at the time were and, I believe still are, 95 percent Catholic, so when I say "the church," I mean Roman Catholicism.) However, the communist government did something diabolically clever: they nationalized all the church's properties, and then to control the priests, they put the clergy on the state payroll. The parish priest turned out to be a pleasant chap. Happy to have someone to talk to, he invited us in for a cup of coffee. Interestingly, even under communism, the government paid for a housekeeper. The coffee was prepared and served by an elderly local peasant woman.

It didn't take long for the priest and us to reach a tacit understanding that our views of the communist regime were identical.

At that time, before the advent of television, there was a marked difference between life in the city and life in the country. Miloš and I stood out in Český Rudolec just as a person from Český Rudolec would have stood out in Prague. During our two weeks there, we became local curiosities. As we ate dinner in the local pub, often some daring local person would come up and politely ask if he or she could sit down and talk to us. Naturally, we always said we'd be delighted, and we actually were. These conversations provided us with a peek into a slice of life to which we were not exposed. Most of the townspeople worked in the local agricultural cooperative, and their stories were fascinating. They also made us appreciate the fact that we did not have to live year-round in Český Rudolec.

During our breaks from surveying, I'd often climb up to the church loft and play the organ. The only difference between playing organ and piano is that on an organ, you have to manage pedals and registers, which was something I taught myself very quickly. One day, when he heard me playing the organ, the parish priest came by and asked me if I could play a few hymns during Sunday mass. I had to confess that I was playing like a gypsy, by heart, because I never had learned to read music. The priest then asked, "Does that mean that you can play by heart whatever melody you hear?" I told him I could do that. The priest continued, "What if I sing you a hymn; would you then be able to play it?" I said that, unless it was a very complicated melody, I would very likely be able to play it. The priest replied that it wasn't a complicated hymn and proceeded to sing it. Next, we sang it together, after which I was able to play it with the priest singing along. I remember he had a lovely voice and clearly enjoyed singing (and hearing himself sing). He then taught me another hymn so that, after some practice, on Sunday I could accompany the congregation's singing of two hymns. That afternoon Miloš Mytiska remarked, "I never thought the day would come when I would hear Martin Holub, in communist Czechoslovakia, playing Roman Catholic hymns in the church." But life under communism was full of surreal paradoxes.

Although it took longer than we expected, the day arrived when we were done surveying the Church of St. John the Baptist in Český Rudolec and were headed back to Prague. Before going to the train station, we stopped at the parish house to say good-bye to the priest. He was interested in how long it would take us to plot the plan of the church from our sketches containing all the measurements and to prepare a scaled drawing. We told him it would take about two to three weeks. The priest then asked if he could buy a copy of that drawing for the parish. I was about to tell him that all he'd have to pay for was the cost of reproducing the drawing, when he offered, "How about two thousand crowns; would that be enough?" Before I could say anything, Miloš responded, "Oh yes, Father, that would be more than enough." The priest then opened a drawer in his desk, took out two 1,000-crown notes and handed them to Miloš. We thanked him, and then he thanked me for playing the organ. We shook hands and left for the train station.

I was dazed. Walking to the station, Miloš handed me one of the 1,000-crown notes and said, "Your share." When I told him that we shouldn't have taken the money, this was his response: "Why not? We didn't ask for it; he gave it to us. Plus, I am sure it wasn't out of his own pocket." I was troubled but kept the money. Back in Prague, Miloš and I worked quickly to complete the drawing of the plan so that we could turn it in before the start of the fall semester and get paid for it. Coincidently, as if the priest had divined it, our contract with the History Department was also for two thousand crowns. Today two thousand crowns would be around $80, but in 1960, for a student, it was a fortune. To put it in perspective, the monthly salary at my first job after graduating from the School of Architecture was 1,200 crowns. Surveying the Church of St. John the Baptist earned me more money than working in the mines.

As we walked out of school after we'd turned in the drawing of the church plan, Miloš and I both suddenly remembered, "Oh, my god, we forgot to have a print made for the priest!" We would have to go back, borrow the drawing from the History Department (which would involve completing some paperwork), take it to a printing bureau downtown, then wrap it up, and take it to the post office to mail to the priest. In hindsight, it is obvious to me that we should have stopped in our tracks right there and gone back to do what needed to be done. But of course, it was just not convenient to turn back right then. We both had places to go to, so we decided we'd do it the following week. But the next week the fall semester started, and we were busier than ever. And so it went. I am embarrassed to admit that during the next two years at the School of Architecture, we never found the time to get that drawing printed and to send it to the priest.

After graduation, I kept running into Miloš at parties and balls and in pubs. Each time we met, I'd tell him, "Miloš, we've just got to find time to get that drawing printed and send it to Český Rudolec. We cannot go on like this forever." Miloš appeared far less perturbed by the situation, and finally, one day he said, "Come on, Martin. Let's just forget about it. The statute of limitation has long expired on it." Interestingly, at the time it never occurred to me to print and send it myself.

That is, until 1967, fully seven years after we surveyed the church and took the priest's money. I just could no longer live with myself without rectifying this wrong. Not yet knowing that it was the last year I would be in Czechoslovakia for a long, long time, I took time off work and rode on my scooter to the School of Architecture. It was the first time I was back since I'd graduated. The Department of the History of Architecture was still in the same place, but I was surprised to find that the professor who commissioned the survey of John the Baptist Church in Český Rudolec was no longer the department head. I was received by a young (meaning younger than me) assistant professor, who told me that he had heard of the program of surveying the forgotten baroque churches, but unfortunately, he had no idea where those drawings might be. He called a colleague of his who came to the office but said the same thing: he had heard of the program, but had no idea where those drawings might be. They promised to ask the new department head and to let me know what they learned. I jotted down the name and phone number of the first assistant professor, thanked them, and left. That happened probably in March or April.

As things developed, I was to leave to take up a job in London that August. Before I left, I called the assistant professor at the History Department at least twice. The first time he told me that the new department head also didn't know where those drawings might be. I no longer remember what he told me the second time, except that he had no answer for me. That was the end of the line, or so I thought. The next time I was in Prague was seventeen years later, at Christmas of 1983. Because of the political situation related to my first visit home (described in "First Visit Home"), I didn't have the time to look for the drawing of the plan of the John the Baptist Church. But it did cross my mind. All those years, it was somewhere in the subcellar of my consciousness.

After the Velvet Revolution, in the 1990s while my mother was still alive, I visited Prague at least once a year. During each of those visits, there would be a party or a dinner at which I'd run into Miloš

Mytiska, and each time I'd bring up the matter of the money we took and the drawing we didn't deliver. I asked him if he could find out if that survey of forgotten baroque churches in Bohemia and Moravia was ever published or if he could track down the old department head and ask her if she knew where those drawings might be. Each time Miloš looked at me almost solicitously, as if he were worried about my sanity. Given that it was then well over thirty years since we had surveyed the church, his feelings were probably justified.

About twenty years later, I took my third wife Sandra for her first visit to the Czech lands. After some five days in Prague, we drove to Moravia because I wanted her to see the village of Skrchov, where my grandfather founded the paint factory, my mother was born, and I spent all my summer and winter vacations during the first ten years of my life, before the factory was nationalized. The plan was then to drive from Skrchov to Munich to visit our German friends, parents of my godson, before flying back to New York. Because the drive from Skrchov to Munich would take longer than I like to drive in one day, we planned to break up the trip by staying one night in Třeboň, a charming little town in southern Bohemia dating from the Renaissance era. When I was plotting on the road map our route from Skrchov to Třeboň, I saw that we would be passing close by Český Rudolec, the town where, fifty-four years earlier, Miloš Mytiska and I had surveyed the church of St. John the Baptist. I immediately decided that we would be stopping there.

What a difference half a century can make! The first surprise was how shabby and rundown the church looked: its walls were dirty, patches of stucco were peeling off, and where there once was a lawn with flower beds, now there was dirt and debris. The second surprise was that when we walked into its vestibule, we found the sanctuary locked. In the middle of the vestibule was a low table on which stood an urn with a slot on its top labeled DONATIONS. The third surprise was that the parish house's windows were boarded up, its door was padlocked, and there was a FOR SALE sign with the name and phone number of the real estate agent. The sign had a look of having been there for a long time.

I found all that shocking, but then it came to me: after the Velvet Revolution, all church properties nationalized by the communist government were restituted to the church, and the priests and other church employees were no longer on the state payroll. The church in the democratic Czech Republic had to take care of its people and its properties, and clearly it lacked the resources to do so. And so the paradoxical fact is that the small congregation of believers in Český Rudolec was better off under communism than in the free Czech Republic, a member of the European Union.

An elderly local woman noticed two obvious out-of-towners loitering around the church and came up to us to ask if we needed anything. I explained that I was revisiting the church I had measured a half century earlier. I added that I was surprised to find the church locked, because at the time of my first visit, it was never locked. With a measure of pride, the lady identified herself as a local native who had never left the town. She explained that shortly after the church and the parish house were restituted, the resident priest was transferred to a larger parish and the house put up for sale. That was more than twenty years ago, and the house was still empty because nobody wanted to live on the square so close to the church. Then she told us that a priest came from Jindřichův Hradec (the nearest larger town) to say a mass every Sunday, but that the church was then locked until the next service.

When the Pew Research Center conducted a poll asking a sample of one thousand people in the countries of the European Union a simple question, "Do you believe in God?" the country with the largest number of those who answered no was the Czech Republic. Perhaps this fact has something to do with the sorry state of the church in the Czech lands.

Before leaving the town, Sandra and I went back to the church vestibule, where I counted an equivalent of $200 in Czech crowns and stuffed it in the slot of the donations urn. Thus concluded the longest guilt trip of my life.

Piano Lessons

Czech kids of my generation invariably took either violin or piano lessons. There were two reasons, of the two possibilities, I started taking piano lessons: first, at the time we still lived in a large apartment in whose living room we had a Petrof grand piano, and second, my father was an accomplished amateur pianist. I remember I was in the third grade when I started taking lessons. My mother enlisted Professor Grunerová, whose day job was teaching students at the Conservatory how to play piano. She came to our apartment twice a week to give me lessons.

When my mother first announced that I would be taking piano lessons, I was not thrilled. Learning and practicing piano meant less time to play or make mischief. However, to everyone's surprise, I took to the piano like fish to water. My mother later told me that I practiced daily without being prompted. Once we were done with scales and fingering exercises, I started playing simple pieces, like Mozart's *Lullaby* or Beethoven's *Für Elise*. Professor Grunerová was delighted with my progress, so much so in fact, that about a year after I started the lessons, she asked my mother if she could take me to the conservatory to demonstrate to her students what, following her technique, a child could learn in a year.

My mother, of course, agreed, so one afternoon after school I reported to the Conservatory. I was taken to a large auditorium full of students who, being at least ten years older than me, looked to me like grown-ups. My performance was not a success—not because of my playing, but because of my deportment. As Professor Grunerová told my mother and my mother later told me, here is what happened: while other kids my age would be frozen by stage fright and, between playing the rehearsed pieces, would sit motionless, I appeared totally relaxed; between playing, while the professor was talking to her students, I looked visibly bored, kept on yawning, and had to be told several times not to twirl around on the piano stool. Clearly a disobedient child, I was not asked to come to the Conservatory again, but my lessons with Professor Grunerová continued.

Shortly after the communist putsch of February 1948, Professor Grunerová lost her job at the Conservatory, but our lessons continued for the next two years until June 1950, when my mother was imprisoned and I was shipped to the boarding school in Poděbrady. However, by then I had acquired enough proficiency in playing that, due to my good ear and with a simple left-hand accompaniment, I could play, without sheet music, pretty much any tune I heard. There was an upright piano in one of the halls of Poděbrady Castle, where the boarding school was located, and over the eighteen months I stayed there, I spent many hours playing it. I became a kind of gypsy, playing without music the classical pieces I remembered from my lessons, as well as folk songs and any pop tune that I had heard, mostly just for myself but sometimes for the amusement of my schoolmates. Eventually, I developed a way of playing all my own, on a scale that included mostly black keys, using both hands to play progressively more complex melodies, all by ear alone.

When my mother was released from prison and I returned home from the boarding school, she was furious with my father for not arranging for the continuation of my piano lessons in Poděbrady, and she immediately found me another piano teacher. I no longer remember why it was not Professor Grunerová, but this time it was Professor Weltzelová who taught me. She was an older lady (meaning she was probably in her fifties), and her sole occupation was to teach children how to play piano. She did not make house calls; children had to go for their lessons to her apartment. I did not like going there because of the smell; her apartment was infused with an ever-so-slight, but persistent and most unpleasant, sweet, fishy smell. It was many years later when I learned that it had to do with poor female hygiene.

I still remember my first lesson with Professor Weltzelová. When I sat down on the piano stool, she said that she understood that I had had three years of lessons before they were suspended for one and a half years. I told her that was correct. Then Professor Weltzelová asked whether I had learned some pieces by heart during those years of lessons. I responded that I had indeed. Next, she asked me if I could play something that I remembered, so that she could assess my level of proficiency. I don't remember what I played, except that it was some simple classical piece in a recognizable scale. Professor Weltzelová's face was expressionless. She asked if I could play something else. So I switched to my gypsy mode, using the black keys scale, and played by heart some fast and rhythmical current popular tune. I was quite proud of my complex left-hand accompaniment.

Professor Weltzelová then asked if during those one and a half years without lessons I had kept playing. I replied that I had. Then she said, "Dear Martin, I am sorry that I have to tell you this, but during the time you played without supervision, you managed to completely ruin your hands. If you want to bring your playing even just to a modicum of competence, you'll have to unlearn all the bad habits you picked up. To do that, you'll have to stop playing on your own, and we'll have to start from the beginning, meaning scales and fingering exercises. Go home now, think about it, and let me know if you want to do it. The lesson is over. There will be no charge for this lesson."

I was not thrilled with the prospect of practicing scales and doing fingering exercises all over again, but my mother convinced me that if I didn't do what Professor Weltzelová suggested, I'd be forever stuck at the level of playing I was at without any prospect of improvement. So I resumed the lessons, but they were not a success. For one thing, my music-reading prowess was not very good even when I was taking lessons. Before starting to learn a new piece, Professor Grunerová always played it first for me to hear how it should sound; the problem was that once I had heard it, I didn't have to look at the music anymore, because I could play it by heart. After the hiatus, during which I played only by heart, I lost altogether the skill of reading music and was very slow in relearning it.

Another problem was that I could not stop myself from playing by heart; consequently, my bad habits were not being unlearned, and Professor Weltzelová was not pleased. In addition, I just was not diligent enough in practicing the scales and doing the fingering exercises, which also did not please her. And so it went until, after perhaps six months of lessons, my mother told me that Professor Weltzelová wrote her (at the time we were so poor that we did not have a telephone) to say that she saw no point in my continuing them, because I was not making any progress. I guess that, at the time, my mother had too many other things to worry about—namely, making a living—so she let my piano lessons slide. She didn't even get mad at me for my dismal performance and the resulting waste of money.

Playing and singing at a ski lodge in 1961.

So that was the end of my piano lessons, but by no means the end of my piano playing. Although I never relearned to read music, I continued to enjoy playing by heart. When I'd come home from school and while my mother was still at work (if she had work), the first thing I'd do was to spend an hour or so at the piano, playing whatever came to my head. And contrary to my mother's prediction, the more I played, the better I got. At the time, my buddies and I followed passionately the latest American pop songs on Radio Luxembourg, so I began to sing while accompanying myself on the piano, imitating the songs of Bill Haley, Fats Domino, the Everly Brothers, Marty Robbins, and many others whose names I didn't even know. My English was poor at the time, so when I didn't understand the words, I just imitated their sound.

Around the same time, I started going to dance classes and hanging around Prague's bars and pubs.

And in a corner of many of those bars or pubs, there was an upright piano that no one played. Often, after a few drinks with my buddies, I'd sit at the piano and play while singing American pop songs. Hearing those songs in a Prague bar was highly unusual, plus they had an added attraction of being forbidden fruit, since the official ideology was that those were bourgeois songs coming from the morally corrupt, capitalist West. So it usually didn't take long for a crowd to collect around the piano, encouraging me to keep on singing. Other venues for my self-invited performances were ski lodges. They provided a more relaxed atmosphere because there was less of a danger that an eager communist would report to the authorities that an unruly youth was contaminating his contemporaries by singing songs from the decadent West.

One of the favorite student hangouts was a pub in the old town called Rybárna (meaning "fishmonger," although the place had nothing to do with fish). There was a piano there that I had already played a number of times. One night after I stopped playing and singing, I saw the manager of the place, whom I knew only by sight, come to the table where I was sitting with my buddies. I froze. Flashing through my mind was this thought: "This is it. He's coming to tell me that he's reporting me to the police, that uninvited, I was disseminating decadent Western culture in his establishment." At the time I was in the first year of the School of Architecture, and it ran through my head that the police would report my subversive activity to the school and that on the strength of that activity I'd be dismissed from the university.

Imagine my surprise when the manager asked me if I'd be willing to perform at the bar on a regular basis for as much beer as I'd want to drink! Uncharacteristically for me, I managed to collect my wits and told the manager that I'd be delighted to play once a week, but that I wasn't much of a beer drinker and could he make it wine instead. The manager responded, "Done deal!"

I no longer remember how our arrangement ended (except that it happened amicably), but while it lasted, I felt so very grown up performing every Monday night at Rybárna. It was outrageous that I even had the nerve to sing publicly, given that I knew perhaps only 60 percent of the song lyrics: the rest I just made up in English-sounding mumbo-jumbo. Amazingly, no one called my bluff; no one said, "Hey, young man, why don't you learn your lyrics first and then come back!"

Until I left for London about ten years later, I continued to play piano when no one else was at home, just for my own amusement. Once I started working, there was less gallivanting and, consequently, less playing in public. I believe it was during this time when my playing reached the level my mother had predicted years earlier—that is, it reached the point beyond which it wasn't getting any better. However, by continuing to play, I maintained the level of proficiency. Even more surprising, I managed to maintain that level for more than twenty years after leaving Prague, even though in that time, I never lived in an apartment with a piano and the chances I got to play elsewhere were few and far between. It wasn't until the late 1980s, when I started visiting Karen and later moved in with her, that I once again lived in an apartment with a piano.

Karen was a reasonably proficient piano player herself, but she was unable to produce a sound unless she was reading music. She was absolutely amazed and charmed by my ability to play by heart whatever melody I heard. She urged me to play each time I visited, and I gladly obliged, because I was delighted that my ability to play had not disappeared over the many years that I had not touched the piano. However, as time passed, I found myself playing less and less.

It's hard for me to pinpoint the cause, except perhaps that, as I got older, I became a little self-conscious about my gypsy-like playing. Once I was in my fifties, I thought that a man of my age should either play like a grown-up or not at all. Then again, it might have had something to do with the location of the piano. While the piano was in her living room, I passed by it each time I moved from the living to the dining room and played it each time I visited. When I moved in, as part of my redesign of the apartment, I moved the piano to the master bedroom and found myself playing less. Later, when we moved the piano to one of the guest bedrooms of our house in the Hudson Valley to make more space in our bedroom, I stopped playing altogether. Another period of perhaps twenty years passed without my touching the piano.

However, as my ability to play had survived the first hiatus of twenty-some years, I was confident that, should I ever want to play again, I could pick up where I left off. That proved not to be the case. Perhaps a year ago, on a weekend in the country while Sandra was shopping at Sam's in Kingston, something moved me to go down to the guest bedroom with the piano and start to play. But my playing was not coming along; I could not figure out the black keys scale I used to play in. When you cannot read music, memory is all you have, and when that fails, you are up the creek. I haven't touched the piano since, and it is likely that my piano playing days are truly over. Had it not been for that first interruption of my piano lessons while my mother was in prison, I might have been a concert pianist instead of an architect. Enough has been said, though, about the kinship of architecture and music.

Church Pistols

Around the mid-1980s my good friend Sally Kuhn asked me to redesign her apartment so that it would have an entry area, which it was lacking. I created a foyer by designing a number of custom cabinets: some open, some closed, some standing on the floor, and some suspended from the ceiling. Sally then hired Ed Krieger, a painter, who was making a living as a cabinetmaker in the employ of the Whitney Museum, to build and install those cabinets. I made Ed's acquaintance during my supervisory visits as he manufactured and then installed the cabinets. Ed complimented me on my drawings for the cabinetwork, saying he'd never worked from such comprehensive and well-detailed documents, which made his task a lot easier. Sally was thrilled with the result, which she enjoys to this day.

Perhaps two years later, I got a phone call from the Chase Manhattan Archives. The archivist said she was calling at the suggestion of Ed Krieger, who had just installed some shelving there. She explained that they were looking for someone to design a traveling display case for the Church pistols and that Ed had recommended me. She promised to explain about the Church pistols when I came down to the Archives, provided, of course, that I was interested in the job. I said I was keenly interested, and we made an appointment. At our meeting, the woman I spoke with on the phone introduced me to her colleagues, and they explained about the pistols.

John Church was a British Army colonel sympathetic to the American Revolution who became rich by providing arms to the Continental Army. Later he also provided the pistols used in the 1804 duel in which Aaron Burr killed Alexander Hamilton. The archivists were impressed that I knew everything about that duel (I had read *Burr* by Gore Vidal). Alexander Hamilton was a founder of Chase Manhattan Bank, which grew out of the Manhattan Water Company that Hamilton had transformed into a bank. That is why Chase Manhattan kept the Church pistols in its custody ever since the duel. At present, the custodians of the pistols were the Chase Archives.

To promote the long history of the bank, a vice president in charge of publicity had the brilliant idea to hire an Italian gunsmith to produce twelve faithful replicas of the Church pistols. He then envisaged building twelve display cases that would circulate throughout the more than five thousand branches of Chase Manhattan Bank in the United States. The missing piece was the design of the display case, which was the reason the archivist called me.

I designed a sleek case in the shape of an octagonal column, made of dark-blue anodized, polished aluminum and plexiglass. I had no idea where the managers of the individual branches would place the display case, which is why I chose the octagon shape; it would allow the case to be placed in a corner, by a wall, or in the middle of the room. It also didn't hurt that the Chase logo is in the shape of a dark-blue octagon. The archivists loved my design. However, the vice president, who was spearheading the whole project, was less enthusiastic. I never met the guy; he was just too high up the ladder to bother with things like meeting an architect. He communicated with the archivists and the archivists communicated with me. Apparently, he found my design too sleek and modern: he had in mind something more traditional. The archivists asked me if I'd like to take another stab at the design to see if I could come up with something more traditional. I said that I couldn't, that traditional was not in my design genes. They understood.

It seemed that the archivists were more crushed by this rejection of the design they liked than I was. As solace for my efforts having come to naught, they offered to introduce me to the staff of the Chase Facilities Department. And that's how I secured the most lucrative assignment of my career. It wasn't the most exciting assignment, but never before nor since have I made more money per unit of time. Two things had to occur for it to happen. First, a year earlier, I had designed a floor for handicapped residents in a residential hotel where the City of New York housed its homeless. Second, the ADA (Americans with Disabilities Act) was about to become the law of the land, and large corporations were all scrambling to make their facilities accessible.

When the architect who interviewed me at the Chase Facilities Department saw on my list of projects that my office had designed a handicapped-accessible floor at a hotel run by the city, he asked me if I'd be willing to make one of the Chase branches in Brooklyn compliant with the ADA. Hoping that I would thus get my foot in the door and that it might lead to something more interesting in the future, I said my office would be happy to do it.

Making the branch handicap accessible was strictly a technical affair involving the installation of a new elevator, a new ramp at the entry, a new sidewalk, a lot of new railings and grab bars, and a number of new, wider doors, as well as a redesign of the bathrooms and reconfiguration of private safe-deposit booths. A week after we submitted the completed construction drawings, I got a call from the architect who had interviewed me at the Facilities Department. He said that they were extremely pleased with the quality of our drawings and wanted to do the same ADA compliance work with another forty branches in Brooklyn. Forty branches! My chin dropped, as I knew I didn't have enough people to do forty branches, but what I said was, "Oh, thank you for your trust. We'd be delighted to do another forty branches."

Luckily, the whole construction industry was in the middle of a recession in the early 1990s, so there were many unemployed architects walking the streets, and it was relatively easy to staff up. The problem was that my office had space for only four people, as I never anticipated hiring more staff. I called David Specter, whose office was nearby, and asked if he had any empty desks I might rent from him. David's business was also very slow at the time, and he was happy to loan me not only two empty desks but also two underemployed draftsmen. So in short order, I had eight architects working on the project: four at my office and four at David's office. It took us six months to redesign all forty Brooklyn branches, after which we got another fifty-some branches in the Bronx and Queens, and then another thirty-plus branches in Westchester. Throughout the entire eighteen-month process, I had not drawn a single line: all I did was supervise, coordinate, and check.

There are more than five thousand Chase branches in the United States, so clearly many other archi-tects were doing the same ADA compliance work. Our clients at the Chase Facilities Department in New York told me that they were sending our drawings to Facilities Departments around the country to be given to other architects working on ADA compliance as a standard to be met. Despite that and other signs that they were very pleased with our work, we never got another job from Chase, which is something that puzzles me to this day.

What did I do wrong? Or what did I not do? God only knows. At Christmas, we sent the Facilities Department a basket of the finest, handmade chocolate truffles. Was that the wrong thing to do? Or was that gift not generous enough? The staff at the Facilities Department had our office brochure, which included many photos of our completed buildings, so they knew that we were capable of producing work other than installing elevators and designing ramps and railings. Only once, about a year after our ADA compliance work was completed, did we receive an RFP (Request for Proposal) for the design of a new Chase branch somewhere on Long Island. It was a project for which we were eminently qualified. We submitted a fine proposal but were not selected. Worse yet we were not even short-listed.

How Communism Warped People

At the time I lived in Tehran, more than a hundred thousand Americans and a proportional number of other Western nationals also lived there, making for a lively expatriate community. Still, compared with the total number of Tehran inhabitants, the number of Westerners was just a drop in the bucket, so that the people one saw on the sidewalks were nearly all Iranian. Because Westerners looked different and also walked differently from the local population, it was easy to spot one among the multitudes of the locals. One day walking to the office, I noticed a Westerner a distance away walking toward me. As he came nearer, he appeared somewhat familiar, and then the thought occurred to me that he could be Czech. And then when he got even closer, I realized I knew the man but could not place him. When we were about ten feet away from each other, the man spotted me and exclaimed, "Goodness gracious, Martin, what are you doing here? I thought you were in America! So good to see you," all the while shaking my hand.

I had, by now, realized that he was Karel Kofránek, an engineer from the national enterprise Konstruktiva, my former employer in Prague. Although we never worked together, Karel and I sat in the same office for more than four years. I remembered liking him then, and I was looking forward to getting together with him and hearing some gossip from my old office. However, it was not to be. As we were shaking hands, his expression suddenly clouded, a frown appeared on his face, and, not looking at me, he said, "Martin, please, I hope you'll understand and not hold it against me, but you can imagine what a stroke of luck it is for me to be posted abroad, and I just cannot afford to risk it all by talking to an emigrant. So please excuse me, but I just have to go." He dropped my hand, turned around, and walked away. I was left standing in the middle of the sidewalk and, with mouth open, watched his back as he walked away. I counted my lucky stars, grateful for the fact that I didn't have to live in the country that was turning good people into creatures like Karel.

One of the ironies of the Cold War era was that the Socialist Republic of Czechoslovakia was doing brisk business with the ultrarightist, capitalist, pro-Western regime of the Shah—and not only in the field of oil and sugar refineries but also in the arts. Specifically, they were working together on exhibition design projects, which was one of the few things in which communist Czechoslovakia excelled. The Shah was building a self-celebratory, memorial museum called Shahiad, whose interior was entirely designed and its artwork installed by artists from Czechoslovakia. Consequently, there was a large contingent of Czech architects, designers, and installers working in Tehran in the mid-1970s.

One of my projects in Tehran required acoustical consultants, and I retained a firm of British acousticians who had an office in Tehran. When they found out that I was Czech, they told me that they were working with Czech architects on the Shahiad Museum. One day when leaving the acousticians' office, I ran into Emil Sirotek, a classmate of mine during my first four years of grade school. We had not seen each other since we were ten years old; now we were in our late thirties and, amazingly, recognized each other instantly. Emil told me that he was posted in Tehran by the national enterprise

EXHIBIT, the firm that was installing the exhibits in the Shahiad Museum, and that he had come to pick up some acoustical devices from the British acousticians. We were both in a hurry but made plans to meet the same day after work at the Excelsior Bar, a popular ex-pat hangout.

At the Excelsior, I found out that Emil never went to university and that he was working for the EXHIBIT firm as one part driver, one part gofer, one part carpenter, and one part whatever-needs-to-be-done. He was very convivial, and once he learned that I was an architect, he asked me if I knew Radka Lomikarová. As it happened, I did know Radka well because she was my classmate in the School of Architecture. Emil told me that she was working with the EXHIBIT firm as an architect and that she had designed one whole floor in the Shahiad Museum. He suggested that the next time we got together for drinks, he'd bring Radka along. I said that would be wonderful. Recalling my encounter with Karel Kofránek, I was surprised how unconcerned and carefree Emil was in dealing with an emigrant like myself.

However, for our next meeting at the Excelsior, Emil showed up by himself. When I asked him where Radka was, he sheepishly shrugged his shoulders and said, "Well, she didn't want to come. She said she was not going to ruin her ideological dossier, and thus her chances for another posting abroad, by meeting with an emigrant." I asked Emil why he was not afraid of the same thing. He replied, "For one thing, the stakes are higher for an architect than for a chauffeur like me. For another, some people are just scared more than they need to be." Several years later, in 1977, when only a little more than two thousand people signed Charter 77, my mother repeated the same sentiment: people were scared more than they needed to be.

Fast-forward some twenty-five years, perhaps a decade after the Velvet Revolution, I was dining in Prague with two old friends; she was a physician and he an architect. We had known each other since high school days. They mentioned that the previous summer they had traveled to Malta with Radka Lomikarová and her husband Zdeněk. I asked if I had already told them how Radka refused to meet with me in Tehran. I detected a hint of oh-here-he-goes-again when they replied, "Oh yes, Martin, you told us that already. When are you going to forgive her? After all, she didn't really harm anyone."

Walking to my hotel after the dinner, I felt terrible. What was wrong with me that I could not forget something like that? Upon reflection, I concluded that even though I didn't think that people who behaved the way Karel or Radka had should be punished, I still believed that they should be ostracized from the company of decent people. But clearly, my Czech friends felt otherwise. Perhaps that's the reason why I live here and they live there.

The Mattress Principle

From time to time, usually when we were lying in bed on a Sunday morning, Karen would say, "Martin, we need to buy a new mattress." My usual response was something like "Ah, we don't need a new mattress; there is nothing wrong with the mattress we're sleeping on." Until one day, Karen insisted, "Martin, we need to buy a new mattress. I've been sleeping on this mattress for over thirty years!"

Only then did it hit me that I didn't have another thirty years, so if we were ever going to buy a new mattress, postponing the purchase made no sense. The next week we bought a new mattress. It was the last mattress we were ever going to buy.

We started calling this purchasing principle the "Mattress Principle." Once you reach a certain age, it becomes an extremely useful guide. When Karen and I noticed that the fabric on the cushions of the built-in seating in our living room was beginning to show its age, we asked ourselves how long it had been since those cushions were purchased. The answer was twenty-two years. We concluded that, in another twenty-two years, if we were lucky enough to still be around, we'd probably have other worries than reupholstering our cushions, so we decided to have it done straightaway. Once done, it was the last time we'd ever have our cushions reupholstered. By the same principle, last winter I bought my last pair of skies.

School in Nature

In Czechoslovakia, fifth grade is the last year of grade school, and to promote the appreciation of nature in inner-city kids, all public schools in Prague (there were no private schools) organized during fifth grade a program whose name could be literally translated as "School in Nature." It was a four-week excursion to a mountain or lake resort taken by the whole class, which typically had around thirty pupils. Bohemia is geographically defined by mountain ranges on all four sides, so there was no shortage of mountain lodges that, in the off-season, were happy to accommodate a class of kids. In addition to hotel rooms, all lodges had dorms, so one dorm was for boys and another for girls; one of the dining rooms was converted to a classroom, and school carried on. The teacher who taught in the city came along and taught in the country. Usually two mothers volunteered to help supervise the kids and accompanied the group as well.

By the time that I was in the fifth grade, I had already been to three Boy Scout summer camps and one YMCA camp, so being away for a month was not a big deal for me. However, for many of my classmates the School in Nature was the first time they were away from their families for that long a time. Our lodge was in the mountains of north Bohemia, in a beautiful meadow within walking distance of a small village. In the mornings we had classes; after lunch we played games, took walks, and played some sports. I remember a long-distance run on which I didn't do too well. Our teacher was Mrs. Válková, a humorless, authoritarian woman who, as such, was not well liked.

A classmate who was snooping around the lodge while the rest of us were playing outside reported that Mrs. Válková kept a chamber pot under her bed. A popular soft drink at the time came in powder form. You could buy packets with different flavors, empty the powder in a glass, fill it with water, and it would fizz dramatically into a bubbly drink with a foamy head. That gave me an idea for a prank. First, I purchased a packet of that foamy drink powder in the village store. Then after dinner one evening, while Mrs. Válková was still conversing with the two mothers, I slipped upstairs, entered her room, pulled out the chamber pot, emptied the powder from the packet into it, and returned downstairs. After the light was out in our dorm, I told the other boys not to go to sleep just yet because we might have some entertainment from our teacher.

The only public telephone in the lodge was at the foot of the stairs. As if on cue, we heard Mrs. Válková dashing out of her room, running down the stairs, and dialing a number. We pushed the door to our dorm ajar so that we could hear better, but we still couldn't hear much. However, we did manage to make out the words "urgency," "doctor," and "urinary." The next morning Mrs. Válková was not in evidence, and one of the mothers told us that she had gone into town to see a doctor. Instead of having class, we played games under the supervision of one of the mothers. Never in my wildest dreams would I have expected that my prank would succeed to that degree. Its effectiveness went to my head, and I boasted to my classmates that I was the reason why we were playing instead of sitting in the classroom. Since Mrs. Válková was uniformly disliked, I expected a measure of loyalty and the corollary code of silence.

I was wrong: someone squealed. Later that afternoon I was called into Mrs. Válková's office, which was a hotel room with a desk in it. She did not ask me to confess my misdeed; in fact, she didn't bring it up at all. With her usual stern face, she simply announced that, because of my insubordination, I'd be sent home. As the weekend of the parents' visits was coming up, she said she'd send me home with my mother. This was very bad news. Not only would I miss the remaining two weeks of the School in Nature, which was work I'd have to make up, but also my grade in conduct would most likely be less than "Immaculate." The next lower grade was "Satisfactory," and the kids who got "Unsatisfactory" in conduct were typically sent to the reformatory. The word in class was that "Holub will be sent home because of what he did to Mrs. Válková." What I had done was now an open secret.

When my mother arrived, I fessed up and told her everything. As she told me much later, she barely managed to hide her amusement and to keep a serious look on her face. She said she would talk to Mrs. Válková. Later that day I saw the two of them sitting on a bench in the backyard of the lodge, engaged in a long conversation. When it was over and Mrs. Válková was gone, my mother told me that I would be able to stay on. I was so relieved that I didn't even ask her how she managed to convince Mrs. Válková to let me stay. It wasn't until many years later, when I was a grown man and my mother and I were reminiscing about that incident, that she told me that she literally had bribed that woman.

In 1949 when I was in the fifth grade, nylon stockings were a coveted item in Czechoslovakia. My mother told Mrs. Válková that if she kept me in the School in Nature for the remaining two weeks, my mother would give her a pair of nylon stockings. That's all it took.

———————

Here is another memory I have about the same sojourn in the School in Nature. The lodge we stayed in was not a fancy place, particularly not in the off-season, when the school kids were the only occupants. The hot water was on only once a week, so we washed only once a week. The place of our ablutions was the hotel laundry room. Once a week we piled into the room, first the girls and then the boys. There were no showers, but there were a lot of wooden tubs used for washing bed sheets. At the time, there were no washing machines, and the laundry was done by hand.

Those wood tubs were just the right size for ten-year-old kids. After they were filled with hot water, we jumped in and washed under the supervision of the two attending mothers. I didn't mind stripping naked in front of those adult women, but what happened next was another matter.

After I soaped and scrubbed my entire body, one of the mothers washed my back and then, with a look of mysterious significance, handed me the soap and said, "Now wash yourself!" Having just washed myself quite thoroughly, I was puzzled. I didn't understand why I was being asked to wash myself again, but I started soaping and rinsing my body all over again. The woman touched my arm and with a stern look told me, "I said, wash yourself." Even more confused, I kept on soaping and rinsing, until the woman lost her patience, took the bar of soap from my hand, and started lathering up my private parts. I was mortified, but having finally understood what she meant, I took the soap from her and finished the job. It was a humiliating experience for me.

A New York Moment

I was standing on a crowded 79th Street cross-town bus when I noticed a gray-haired woman of my vintage, who was standing nearby, looking at me. When she realized that I had noticed her staring at me, she offered, "I was just admiring your coat." In reply, I said only these two words: "Issey Miyake." She responded, "I thought so. He's the best." End of conversation. At the next stop, we both got out and went our separate ways. Only in New York…

More than One Life

F. Scott Fitzgerald said, "You've written one book, pff, you've written one book. You've written two books, you are an author!" By that standard, my mother just barely achieved the status of an author, having written a total of two books: first, a novel that was translated into English as *More than One Life*, and then a memoir that exists only in Czech. If it ever got translated into English, it would be called "Off the Road, on the Road." How the novel got translated into English is the subject of this story, but to explain it, I have to digress.

My mother's second husband Miroslav Mikšovský was a scientist working at the Czechoslovak Academy of Science. In the early 1960s, he was part of a team that collaborated with the University of Michigan in Ann Arbor on a research project involving semiconductors. It was a long-term collaboration that included a year's stay of an American scientist at the academy in Prague, followed by a year's stay of a Czech scientist in Ann Arbor. Miroslav was chosen to be that Czech scientist. This exchange, however, did not include spouses, so Miroslav went alone. In fact, even if it had included spouses, my mother could not have gone along. She was teaching at the Academy of Applied Arts and was unable to take a year off.

At the time, to be able to spend a year in America was such a phenomenal stroke of luck that my mother was happy for Miroslav and harbored no grudge. It was an interesting feature of the communist era in Czechoslovakia that, while all civil structures were decimated, no open discourse was allowed, and all printed matter was censored, scientists were pretty much left alone. Of course, the president of the Czechoslovak Academy of Science had to be a party member, but other than that, the scientists were allowed to pursue their science undisturbed. Still, allowing any contact with the capitalist West was highly unusual during the dark ages of the Cold War. It was perhaps because this exchange was totally apolitical, concerning pure science, that the communist government permitted it. Even more unusual was that Miroslav, who was not a party member and, moreover, was married to an "enemy of the people," was allowed to go. But anomalies like this did happen from time to time.

While in Ann Arbor, Miroslav fell in love with a graduate student Lyn Coffin, decided not to return to Czechoslovakia, divorced my mother, and married Lyn (who later became a noted poet, writer, and translator). Miroslav's defection angered Professor Mason, the leader of the semiconductor research project at the University of Michigan, because he was worried that the Czechoslovak Academy of Science, seeing that the collaboration with the West had led to the defection of a prominent scientist, might terminate the project. That did not happen, but Professor Mason took enough umbrage at Miroslav that he did not write him the requisite letter of recommendation. Without that letter and without being able to give Professor Mason, his only American contact, as a reference, Miroslav was unable to find a job in which he could use his knowledge of semiconductors, either inside or outside of academia. In fact, as I later learned, he had trouble finding any job at all and, for a year or so was eking out a living pumping gas at a gas station.

When I arrived in New York in 1970, Miroslav and Lyn were living in Maplewood, New Jersey, and he was selling insurance. About two years later, Lyn left him for another man. It was another five years or so before he met and later married his third wife Marlee. My mother forgave Miroslav for leaving her, and during her visits to New York the two of them maintained friendly relations. Marlee adored my mother, and the two women became good friends. Sometime in the early 1980s Miroslav and Marlee moved from New Jersey to Old Lyme, Connecticut. Then in 1992 in early June, Miroslav committed suicide. I remember the time because Karen and I got married on May 16, 1992, and Miroslav and Marlee were at the wedding. When we returned from our honeymoon in Italy and Sicily in early June, I had to call Marlee for some reason. It turned out that I had called her on the very day that she had found Miroslav hanging from the rafters in the garage.

Only after he was dead did I learn from Marlee what a financial struggle Miroslav had endured ever since he left the University of Michigan. I guess he was too proud, as my ex-stepfather, to even drop a hint to me about how hard it was for him to make ends meet; I had no idea. Marlee told me that without her modest salary as a librarian, they couldn't have kept the house. She was convinced that he had killed himself because he didn't want to be a burden to her and his two sons. By pure coincidence, at the time of Miroslav's death my mother was a Bunting Fellow at Harvard and was living in Cambridge. When I called her to tell her about Miroslav's suicide, she took the news calmly and inquired about the funeral arrangements.

And so it happened that all three of Miroslav's wives were present at his funeral in Old Lyme. My mother took the train from Boston, Lyn came from I don't remember where, and I drove up from New York. The first time my mother met Lyn, the woman for whom Miroslav had left her thirty years earlier, was at the reception after the funeral. When Lyn learned that my mother had written a novel, she wanted to read it. She was able to read Czech and had translated some Czech works into English. In fact, on the basis of her translations, Jaroslav Seifert received the Nobel Prize in literature in 1984, which, I thought, was a pretty good recommendation for a translator.

My mother was, of course, delighted that someone wanted to read her book, so she asked me to send Lyn a copy of the book in Czech. The next thing we knew, Lyn called my mother and told her that her book was wonderful, that it simply had to be translated into English, and that she wanted to do the translation. She said she had plenty of contacts in the publishing world and that she was sure she could help get the book published. She asked my mother's permission to translate the book. Of course, my mother was thrilled and said yes. Lyn then recruited the help of her friend Zdenka Brodská, a Czech-born professor of English literature at Ann Arbor, and the two women together translated my mother's book.

After the book was translated and Lyn's publishing contacts proved unavailing, I was left with playing the role of my mother's literary agent, which was something of a bad joke. While I had no contacts in the world of publishing, I knew people who did, particularly my good friend Peter Kussi. Peter was the head of the Department of Czech Language and Literature at Columbia University, as well as a translator of a number of Kundera's novels into English. He was also a great admirer of my mother, read her novel in Czech, and liked it very much. Clearly, when Professor Kussi from the Czech Department at Columbia recommended a book, editors listened. Still, it took about two years before Peter found someone who was willing to publish the book. Susan Harris, an editor at Northwestern University Press, was interested, but only on one condition. She liked the novel, but thought its translation was somewhat wanting: she found it a little stilted and thought that it did not flow well. She said she'd publish it if we improve the translation. Peter reread the translation and found himself agreeing with Ms. Harris. He then recommended that I engage his former student Alex Zucker to improve the translation.

Alex is a Brooklyn-born American who graduated from Columbia with a degree in Czech Language and Literature. After graduation, he spent five years in Prague, during which time he became fluent in Czech. Alex read my mother's book in its original Czech, as well as its translation, which he thought he could improve. While today Alex is a well-known and respected translator of Czech literature into English, at the time he was just starting out. Given that he would not be translating from scratch but improving an existing translation, he agreed to do the job for $2,000, which I was happy to underwrite. Now there remained the delicate task of breaking the news of this latest development to Lyn Coffin and Zdenka Brodská. I called Lyn. She completely understood that, if we wanted to see the book published, we had no choice but to do what Northwestern University Press requested. She said she was curious to see how Alex would improve their translation. Because she and Zdenka had not gotten paid for their work, I didn't mention that I would be paying Alex.

When Alex was done with his retranslation, I sent it to Susan Harris at Northwestern. Comparing the two translations, Alex's definitely seemed more readable. Although it was less literal, I didn't think that it distorted or lost anything from the original. Susan Harris apparently agreed, because in short order, she called me and said that Northwestern was going to publish the book. Then she asked me how I wanted the translation credit to read.

I threw that ball back in her court by saying that, of all people, she was best acquainted with the relative merits of the three translators and knew the standards of the industry; therefore, I would defer to her judgment. She agreed to write the credit. As it turned out later, leaving this to her was a mistake.

All my contacts, including Peter Kussi, who knew about the ways of the publishing industry told me that publishers typically pay for translations. So I called Susan Harris and asked her if Northwestern would reimburse me for what I had paid Alex Zucker. I was prepared for an argument, but there was none. Susan simply asked how much I had paid Alex and when I told her $2,000, she said, "OK, send me an invoice and we'll reimburse you." That was all it took. I thought that the publishing industry was a field of gentlemen, but clearly that's not the case. If I didn't ask, the reimbursement would not have been offered…

About six months later, in July 1999, seven years after Lyn Coffin and my mother met at their ex-husband's funeral, *More than One Life* at long last came out. The translation credit read, "Translated by Alex Zucker with Lyn Coffin and Zdenka Brodská." It seemed fine to me. At the end of that year, Susan Harris called me and said that the book was selling better than they expected and that, more than likely, there would be a second printing. She was ecstatic. Everything looked rosy.

Everything seemed rosy—that is, until Lyn and Zdenka became unhappy. About six months or so after the book was published, they came to the conclusion that the translation credit didn't do them justice. After all, it was they who translated the book; Alex Zucker had just polished their translation,

Jacket of *More than One Life*.

but he was getting the major credit. Zdenka Brodská called me and inquired who wrote the credit line. Even though I told her that Susan Harris had written the line, she was very unhappy with me, as if it were my fault.

A month or so later, Susan Harris called me. Until then, she had been so overly friendly and sweet that she sounded almost on the cusp of smarmy. Now, in a completely changed voice, she told me that Lyn and Zdenka had hired a lawyer and had a meeting with her boss and a Northwestern lawyer expressing their concerns about the translation credit. She said that Northwestern wanted to avoid a lawsuit at all cost, and, consequently, they agreed that for the second printing, they would change the cover, as well as the title page, and that the new credit would read, "Translated by Zdenka Brodská, Lyn Coffin, and Alex Zucker." It was to be an alphabetical listing, indicating equality of the three translators. Susan Harris concluded by stating, in a very cold tone, that she was very disappointed, never having expected this development. Again, I was being blamed for this state of affairs.

I too would never have expected this development; I would never have imagined that Lyn and Zdenka could be capable of such small-mindedness. Yet it was hard for me to get mad at them, because without them my mother's book would not have been translated in the first place. Furthermore, they labored without pay, translating it out of sheer enthusiasm for the book alone, without any thought of economic gain.

Their settlement with Northwestern Press, however, could not be a better example of a Pyrrhic victory. Having agreed that in the second printing they would change the translation credits, Northwestern University Press made sure that there would never be a second printing. They simply pulled the book out of all listings of books available from the press. Ever since Susan Harris decided to publish the book, every month I received a list of books available from Northwestern University Press. First, *More than One Life* was listed in the "Soon to be Published" column and then in the "Books Available" column. After the settlement, it disappeared, so that no one could ever order it. I will never know if they did not reprint it for economic reasons, because of the cost of changing the cover and the title page, or just out of spite. From the tone of Susan Harris's voice in her last phone call to me, I suspect the latter.

I have not heard from Lyn or Zdenka since, so I am not even sure if they realized that they killed the book they created. However, they didn't kill it completely. There are still a few copies of *More than One Life* left from the first printing, and they are available at large stores like Barnes & Noble or on Amazon.

A Foolhardy Flight

During the years of my commuting to Tennessee, my closest male friend was Gerry Jonas. Gerry was an architect working on a freelance basis for David Specter's office; we met when I was renting a desk there. He turned out to be one of the most talented people I ever knew. While architects need to know a little something about specialized disciplines such as structural calculations, heating and cooling, electrical, plumbing, acoustics, elevators, lighting, and so on, we cannot be experts in all those fields, and so we hire those specialists as our consultants. Well, Gerry was an expert in all those fields. He could calculate the cooling loads and determine the size of the air conditioning ducts, he could size the steel beams and design the armature in concrete slabs, he could size plumbing pipes and design electrical circuits. And if that weren't enough, he had a flair for freehand sketching and was in high demand as a renderer. In addition, he was also a well-read person who could quote Shakespeare and had a passable command of Latin and Greek. However, what's relevant to this story is that Gerry also became a pilot.

When we first met, Gerry was taking flying lessons at Teterboro Airport in New Jersey. I knew he was very dedicated to those lessons and wouldn't let anything interfere with them. The next I heard about his flying was about a year into our acquaintance, when I was in Tennessee. Gerry knew I was in Knoxville and, without telling me, overjoyed upon obtaining the pilot's license, on the spur of the moment, decided to rent a plane and to fly to Knoxville to bring me back. Late one afternoon the phone rang in the office of Barber McMurry, and it was Gerry telling me, "Martin, cash your return plane ticket. I came to get you. I am at Island Home Airport, so come and pick me up. We'll fly back tomorrow; you were returning tomorrow, right?" He continued, "I just got my pilot license and I felt I simply had to fly someplace."

Gerry was correct in that I was indeed scheduled to return the following day, but on United Airlines. That was a small detail, since in those days plane tickets were readily refundable. I told Gerry that I'd be at Island Home in short order. It was an airport for private planes on the east side of Knoxville. Because I was leaving the office earlier than usual, when I saw Ben McMurry, I told him about my conversation with Gerry. Having heard me out, he then said, "Martin, help me understand: you'll be flying the seven hundred miles to New York City on a rented two-seater, single-engine propeller plane, piloted by someone who has just obtained his pilot license. Did I get that right?" I told Ben that, yes, he got it right. He thought I was crazy. Crazy or not, I couldn't well tell Gerry that I wasn't flying with him. I trusted his judgment implicitly.

Gerry knew my Knoxville friend Jasan from Jasan's previous visits to New York, so the three of us had a fine dinner in the Orangerie, the only French restaurant in Knoxville. The next morning Jasan drove us to Island Home Airport because he wanted to see us take off. We threw our bags behind the two seats of the tiny plane, climbed in, and closed the cockpit bubble. Gerry then spoke to the traffic controller and got permission to taxi to the runway; he started the engine, the propeller started to turn, and we began to move to the runway. Then after another communication with the traffic controller, permission to take off was granted, and off we flew. It all appeared very easy.

Once in the air, I soon relaxed. Gerry inspired confidence, as he seemed to be in complete control of the machine. It was a new experience of flying for me: we flew slower and at a lower elevation than I was used to on commercial airliners. We were lucky and had clear skies; the weather and the forecast were good for the rest of the day. However, after the initial excitement of taking off and the first half hour of experiencing the flight, I found sitting in that noisy small plane more than a little boring. Fortunately, in about two hours, there came a break.

The small plane could not make the seven-hundred-mile trip on one tank of gas, so we had to refill midway, which necessitated an intermediate landing. Gerry located a small airport somewhere in northern Virginia and we landed. The airport was operated by one employee and consisted of one runway, one shack with bathrooms, and one gas pump. The chief duty of the employee was to operate the gas pump. We filled the gas tank, went to the bathroom, and took off. Then came another two hours of a more or less boring flight before we came to the vicinity of New York.

As we were approaching Teterboro Airport and saw the Hudson River with the whole of Manhattan beyond it, a spectacular sight, I asked Gerry, "Do you think we could fly over Manhattan?" Gerry liked the idea, got in touch with the Teterboro traffic controller, and was told that we could fly over Manhattan. The only restriction was we had to stay at a certain elevation; I think it was five thousand feet.

So we spent more than an hour flying all over Manhattan. An altitude of five thousand feet is a very intimate height: you can see people walking in the streets. First, we crossed the Hudson, flying over the George Washington Bridge and then above Broadway down to West 89th Street; we then flew east above 89th Street so we could see the brownstone I lived in and then went farther east across Central Park. Next, we flew south to the East Village and saw the building where Gerry lived on Tompkins Square, and so on. If someone had told me that he had flown for more than an hour all over Manhattan in a rented, tiny airplane piloted by someone who had just received his pilot license, I would not have believed him, yet there we were, doing just that.

We were watching the gas gauge and before we ran out of fuel, we turned toward Teterboro Airport, where we soon landed. We took a taxi to the city, and that was the end of this adventure. At the time, I didn't think much about it; it was just one of those things that happens in life. In hindsight, however, I marvel how all that was possible and legal.

Gerry Jonas died fifteen years later, at the age of fifty-one, in Arizona while trying to take off in a one-person aircraft of his own design. Just as he could calculate the steel beams and size the ducts, he'd convinced himself that he could also design an airplane, which turned out to be his undoing. Much as I loved Gerry, I thought he died of hubris.

Patriotism

It's hard to write clearly about something that is not clear in one's mind, yet that is exactly what I am attempting to do. The subject is patriotism or my feelings about it, or, more accurately, my lack of feelings about it. It most probably would have been a nonissue for me had it not been for my mother. She gave me the opportunity to observe up close a pure, genuine, unvarnished patriot. She was someone to whom the fate of the Czech nation truly mattered, so much so that, when she saw an opportunity to do something to better it, she did it even at great peril to herself.

I recently reread the twenty-five-page letter she wrote me on August 21, 1968, the day of the Soviet invasion of Czechoslovakia. It is such an emotional document, written as if the Soviets were violating her personally. After the invasion, even though it took a few months for the Soviets to seal the border during which time my mother could have left if she wanted to, she decided to remain in Czechoslovakia. It was, in fact, the second time she decided to stay in her country. The first time was twenty years earlier in 1948 when, after the communist take-over, both her mother and brother left for France; yet my mother decided to stay.

Another example of her patriotism was her signing of Charter 77. As she told me later, she did not see it as an act of bravery but, on the contrary, as motivated by cowardice. She was afraid that she could not look at herself in the mirror for the rest of her life if she did not sign it, and so she signed. After the Soviet invasion, she was torn: her mother's heart was glad that I was safely in the free world and didn't have to live in the "normalized" Czechoslovakia, but her patriot's heart was sorry to see people like me leaving. However, her mother's heart was a lot bigger than her patriot's heart, and so even though I could have returned, she never put any pressure on me to do so. Soon the communist government sentenced me in absentia to four years of hard labor for my crime of not returning, which made coming back a moot point.

Is it any wonder that, with a mother like that, I feel a measure of compunction for not having her intensity of patriotic feelings? Or, rather, not sharing her feelings of patriotism raises an unanswered question for me, similar to my wondering why I have not experienced the urge to have children. And that unanswered question keeps on nagging me as I observe world events. For example, two million Vietnamese fled communist Vietnam after 1975. Many of them left as children and later became successful professionals or businesspeople. Since Vietnam launched a capitalist version of communism similar to that in China, many of those Vietnamese Americans have been gripped by the desire to return to their motherland.

Whether to seek profit in the nascent developing economy of Vietnam or for purely altruistic reasons to help their home country, many Vietnamese Americans have returned to their native country. There have been so many returnees that the locals made up a word for them: they are called *Vietkey*. Naturally, when I read about the *Vietkeys*, it caused me to question why I had not experienced the desire to return, when it became possible after the fall of the Iron Curtain, to the free Czech Republic, a member of the EU.

To be sure, there were Czech emigrants who, having lived in the United States for more than twenty years, picked up and returned home the moment their return became possible. I must confess though that I took a dim view of the folks who returned so quickly, wondering how it was possible to have lived somewhere for twenty-plus years without putting down any roots, without being integrated into their community or workplace. The communist regime in Czechoslovakia (as elsewhere) collapsed so unexpectedly that no one could have prepared for it. In 1990, which was the first year that return was possible, even if I had wanted to go back (which never crossed my mind), it would have taken me years to disentangle myself from all my obligations, to finish all the projects that were in progress, to close my office, to sell the real estate I owned, and so on.

Curiously, patriotic feelings can jump a generation. A number of children of my compatriots living in the United States, who were born in this country, are now living in the Czech lands. They first went there after college, just for an extended trip, and they liked it so much that they ended up living there permanently. I know three such young people who now live in Prague while their parents continue to live in the United States. And this phenomenon is not just restricted to children of Czech émigrés. My godson Mark Roth, son of David and Marja, was born in New York, studied at Harvard and later in France, then married a Finnish girl, and has been living in Helsinki ever since, while his mother, who was born in Finland, continues to live in New York.

How do I feel when I visit Prague? Just like a tourist. It is a weird feeling to be in the town I was born in and where I spent the first twenty-eight years of my life and to feel like a tourist, yet that is how it is. I've forgotten the names of the streets and the routes of the trams and trolleys, so I often have to ask for directions. I speak the language, but I don't often know the latest expressions. I am not familiar with the restaurants. I am, clearly, a tourist. Does that bother me? No, but I am intrigued by the feeling that I no longer belong to where I came from.

Could it be that this patriotism thing is something that pertains only to people in small nations? Graham Greene spent half of his life living in France, yet I feel certain that he didn't worry about not being patriotic enough. On my travels, I met a number of Americans who spent their lives living abroad, in Paris, Tehran, London, or Rome, and I am sure the thought that they were not patriotic enough did not cross their minds. Yet we from small nations, we have this complex. But perhaps not every small nation is burdened by it; I am not certain, but I suspect that the Danes, Norwegians, Dutch, and Finns do not suffer the same affliction. Could it be a specifically Czech impulse to question the patriotism of, say, Josef Škvorecký, a writer and publisher who continued to live in Toronto after the Velvet revolution, or Milan Kundera, who continues to live in Paris and writes now in French?

Does homesickness equal patriotism? I don't think so. In December 1968, when I was living in London with my first wife, Eva, we were visited by Honza and Zdena Líman, whom we knew in Prague. Honza was one year ahead of me in the School of Architecture, and Zdena, a physician, was my high school classmate, so they were acquaintances of long standing. The Límans were returning from an eighteen-month stay in Halifax, Nova Scotia, where Honza had worked for an architectural firm; on their way back home, they made a stopover in London. It was four months after the Soviet occupation of Czechoslovakia; by then, the Soviet-installed regime was in complete control, and the process of "normalization" was being implemented with the full force of a police state.

Eva and I were shocked that the Límans were voluntarily returning to that situation; perplexed by their decision, we asked them if they realized that what they were doing amounted to a one-way ticket home. Zdena admitted that she would have preferred to wait and see how things at home would develop before returning, but Honza wanted to go home no matter what. He told us that, after being away so long, he just needed to spend some time at home, whatever the political situation was there—even if it meant that he might not be able to get out again for a long time. It was the strongest expression of homesickness I was ever exposed to, and I am convinced that it had nothing to do with patriotism. When it came, eight years later, to deciding whether or not to sign Charter 77, neither of the Límans signed.

This recollection raises another important question for me, that of homesickness, something that seems to afflict a lot of people. There is an entire body of literature dealing with this feeling. The Human Resources Administration (HRA) in New York City has an array of social services that help uprooted, transplanted people cope with homesickness and adjust to their new environment. So another of my unanswered questions is, "Why is it that I have never experienced homesickness? Am I so shallow? Or does it mean that my roots in my homeland were not deep enough?" Again, I just don't know the answers.

Yes, my heart beats faster when I visit Skrchov, the village in Moravia where my grandfather founded the paint factory more than one hundred years ago, where my mother was born, and where I spent all my summers, Christmases, Easters, and Halloweens during the first ten years of my life. However, I don't think that's homesickness, because I quite happily leave Skrchov and don't think about it again until my next visit, which may be five years down the road. And I feel the same way about Prague. I love visiting it, but I also love leaving it and coming home to New York City.

So what conclusion can I reach? Simply saying different strokes for different folks seems too facile, so I'll just leave those questions hanging…

Mr. Heckert

After my parents divorced in 1945 and my father moved out of our apartment, my mother stayed on with our live-in maid and me. It was a large apartment with three bedrooms, two bathrooms, and a maid's room, so in the three years between the end of the war and the communist take-over of 1948, my mother would rent out the spare bedroom to foreign journalists. She did this not to economize but to practice her foreign-language skills.

Our first lodger was a French lady named Madame Beaume. I later learned that she was working for the recently founded *Le Monde*, but at the time my mother simply told me that Madame Beaume would be staying with us and that, even though I liked to roam about the apartment, her room would be off-limits to me. Most of the time Mme. Beaume dined out with her colleagues, but once or twice a week she would have dinner with my mother and me. While they were yakking in French, I was royally bored and excused myself from the table as soon as I could. Mme. Beaume stayed with us a little over a year before she returned to Paris. My mother continued to exchange Christmas cards with her over the next forty-plus years.

Our second lodger was an English lady, Miss Ashford. I no longer remember what newspaper or agency she worked for. She stayed with us for about six months, and it was much the same as with Mme. Beaume. Whenever she dined with us, she and my mother spoke in English, which was then incomprehensible to me, and I couldn't wait to get away from the table.

Our third and last lodger was Mr. Robert Heckert, an American journalist from Philadelphia, who worked for the UPI agency. By that time, I was in third grade and was attending English classes, at the Prague language school. Mr. Heckert was of my parents' generation, and he differed from the two previous lodgers in that he took a fatherly interest in me. I was fascinated by him. He was thin and tall with sharply chiseled features, sort of a Clint Eastwood type. He exuded dignity and commanded respect, yet he still was interested in a little brat like me. Unlike the other lodgers, Mr. Heckert dined with us almost every night. Although I didn't understand the conversation between my mother and him, I wasn't bored and I didn't rush to get away from the table. Instead, I watched him, listened to the mellifluous sound of his English, and admired his bearing, his gestures, everything about him.

One clear memory that has stayed with me is of a Sunday when Mr. Heckert took me to an air show at Ruzyně Airport near Prague. I remember watching in amazement as the planes flew in tight formations and did all manner of acrobatic tricks. Mr. Heckert and I couldn't communicate verbally, because despite my taking English classes, my English was practically non-existent and he didn't speak a word of Czech. All the same, we managed to communicate nonverbally. I always knew what he wanted me to do and was eager to please. And, strangely, it appeared that Mr. Heckert seemed to enjoy my company. As my mother told me much later, she didn't ask him to take me to that air show; it was his idea. Clearly, of all our lodgers, Mr. Heckert was my favorite: I just loved having him around.

To say that he was my surrogate father would be an overstatement because my own father was very much in evidence, but he came close to it.

Then, all of a sudden, this idyll came to an abrupt end with the communist take-over of the government in February 1948 when, among other changes, all foreign journalists were summarily expelled. Mr. Heckert announced that he had been asked to leave, and it was a sad parting. However, as a nine-year-old kid, I soon forgot about Mr. Heckert and got absorbed in other aspects of growing up. So much for my childhood memories of Mr. Heckert.

It wasn't until I was in my late teens that my mother told me the whole story. It so happened that Mr. Heckert fell head over heels in love with my mother early on during his stay with us. My mother, though she liked and even admired him, did not love him, which he came to understand and respect. Perhaps the reason why he was so nice to me was that he understood that one way to my mother's heart was to be kind to her son,

Robert Heckert in 1947, before he was expelled from Czechoslovakia.

but I'll never know. However, ever the gentleman, just before the Iron Curtain came down, Mr. Heckert offered to marry my mother, just on paper, to make it possible for her to leave the country. My mother, not yet knowing that in two years she'd be in communist prison, declined.

Over the next twenty-two years we stayed in touch with Mr. Heckert, if only by yearly Christmas cards, so that his phone number was one of the few contacts I had when I arrived in New York in January 1970. One weekend soon after I settled in my apartment, I called Mr. Heckert. I recognized his booming voice as he said, "Oh, Martin, your mother wrote me that you were in New York, so I was expecting your call. You must come to visit me in Philadelphia." We decided that I'd pay him a visit on a weekend two or three weeks later. When I arrived at the 30th Street Station in Philadelphia on a Friday night, I immediately spotted Mr. Heckert waiting for me on the platform.

The last time we had seen each other I was nine and he was in his early forties. Now I was thirty-one, and he was in his late sixties. His shock of hair was still parted in the middle as I remembered it, except it was now completely white. As always, he was wearing a suit. When I came up to him, he claimed to have recognized me straightaway, and we formally shook hands. Mr. Heckert suggested that I must be hungry and, because it was dinnertime, that we stop in a restaurant and have something to eat, which was what we did.

During dinner, all we talked about was my mother. Mr. Heckert, even though he knew the bare facts, wanted to hear from me how long my mother had been in prison, where I was staying while she was incarcerated, how we lived after she was released, when she became a professor of art history at the Academy of Applied Arts, when she got married, and when she divorced. When the check arrived and even though I wanted to pay, I still remember the peremptory manner in which Mr. Heckert grabbed hold of the check and paid it. After dinner and a short bus ride we reached Mr. Heckert's apartment building, and I was in for my first shock.

It turned out that this distinguished gentleman lived in a one-room apartment. There was also no entry space; you opened the door from the hallway, and you were in the apartment. (At the time, I didn't yet know that this was not unusual in America, even in large apartments.) Behind a curtain along one of the walls was a counter with a tiny bar sink, a small undercounter refrigerator, and a coffeemaker on top of it. Mr. Heckert noticed that I was taking in the layout of the room and said that he ate all his meals out. "Cooking is not my thing," he said.

Three of the four walls of the room were lined with books from floor to ceiling, with a stepladder nearby to reach books on the upper shelves. In the fourth wall was a large window with a writing desk under it and a sofa next to the desk. There was a small coffee table in front of the sofa. The only chair in the room was the one at the desk. There was a worn, but still very nice, large Persian rug on the floor. When Mr. Heckert noticed that I was looking at it, he said, "It's not mine; it came with the room." Then he asked me if I'd like some Courvoisier before we tucked in. Of course, I said that I'd love some, but what was really on my mind was how and where we were going to tuck in. Once again Mr. Heckert read my thoughts, saying, "You are going to sleep on a cot, which is in the closet and which we are going to assemble, and I am sleeping on this sofa, which converts into a bed." And that is what we did.

After a snifter of cognac and talking some more about my mother, Mr. Heckert took out of the closet a cardboard box from which he produced a number of tubes and a piece of heavy canvas fabric. The tubes fitted into one another and then into the loops in the fabric, and soon there was a perfectly adequate cot. I was familiar with it since I had brought a similar one with me from London. Mr. Heckert then provided sheets and a blanket, and I was ready to tuck in.

When I put the empty cardboard box back in the closet, the only one in the apartment, I had an opportunity to survey Mr. Heckert's wardrobe. I saw two jackets and two pairs of pants hanging there. It meant that in addition to the one he was wearing, Mr. Heckert owned a total of three suits. Also hanging were three white shirts and a winter coat. I didn't count the number of underpants and socks on the shelves, but there weren't many. There were two pairs of shoes on the floor of the closet. That was the entire extent of Mr. Heckert's wardrobe.

When I returned from the bathroom, Mr. Heckert was already tucked in.

We wished each other good night, but I could not fall asleep: my head was reeling. When he lived with us in Prague with his dignified deportment, perfectly tailored suits, and crisp white shirts, Mr. Heckert always exuded an air of a man of substance and consequence—and now he was living in a room without a kitchen! I couldn't wait to write about it to my mother. Eventually, I fell asleep. What woke me up in the morning was Mr. Heckert, fully dressed, talking in fluent French on the phone. He apologized for waking me up, explaining that he had to call the French ambassador. Then he said that he needed to take about a half hour to write a few letters before we could go out for breakfast. When I was done with my ablutions, Mr. Heckert was still bashing away on his typewriter. His typing speed was formidable. And now, I was in for a second shock.

While waiting for Mr. Heckert to finish his typing, I started looking at the books on the shelves. I still remember that the first one that jumped into my view was *Memoirs of the Second World War* by Winston Churchill. I pulled it off the shelf, opened it, and on the title page inside I saw a handwritten inscription: "To my dear friend Robert, fondly—Winston." I could not help interrupting Mr. Heckert's typing to ask, stupidly, "Mr. Heckert, you knew Winston Churchill?" He replied, "Oh yes, when I was reporting from London during the war, we became quite good friends. We lunched together often."

The next book that caught my attention was *Les Grands Discourse de Guerre* by Charles de Gaulle. Once again, when I opened the book I saw an inscription on the title page: "*A mon cher ami Robert, affectueusement—Charles.*" Once again, I interrupted Mr. Heckert by asking him how he got to know Charles de Gaulle personally. He responded, "Oh yes, after I was kicked out of Prague, I spent five years reporting from Paris, during which time I interviewed Charles numerous times, and we became quite well acquainted."

Next, I pulled out *The World as I See It* by Albert Einstein. You can imagine what I found when I looked inside. Mr. Heckert's response when I asked him how he met Albert Einstein was, "Oh, we met before the war, when I lived in Princeton while I was studying for my PhD. We used to play chess together and took long walks, as we were both fond of walking." Double wow! Neither my mother nor I had any idea that Mr. Heckert had a PhD. Coming from a culture where people address each other by their academic titles, this was an astounding revelation. I asked Mr. Heckert in what field he had earned his PhD. He replied, "Ah, English literature; perfectly useless."

When Mr. Heckert was done typing, we went to a coffee shop across the street to have breakfast. The rest of the day we spent taking in Philadelphia's sights: we went to Independence Hall and saw the Liberty Bell before lunch and the Philadelphia Museum of Art afterward. On Sunday, we visited the Museum of the Academy of Fine Arts, Society Hill, and the Rodin Museum before I took a train back to New York.

One event from those two days stands out in my memory more than any art I saw that weekend. Mr. Heckert and I were walking down Market Street, the Philadelphia equivalent of Fifth Avenue, when out of nowhere appeared a well-dressed, rather thin, middle-aged woman who came up to us and started hitting Mr. Heckert on the head with a small, closed umbrella. The spectacle was all the more absurd because it would have been hard to imagine an elderly gentleman who exuded more dignity than Mr. Heckert. I didn't know what was more startling to me: the act itself or Mr. Heckert's reaction to it.

All he did, while he kept on walking, was to raise his right arm to deflect the blows. Then, as the woman continued to strike him and he continued to walk at the same pace, he deftly grabbed the umbrella and handed it back to her. With a look of surprise, she disappeared into the crowd. Throughout, Mr. Heckert remained totally unperturbed, his face showing no emotion. When it was all over, I asked Mr. Heckert what that was all about. He responded, "Oh, nothing. She was a crazed woman, that's all." Not satisfied with that answer, I asked whether he knew the woman. He said he had never seen her before. Case closed. Neither of us ever mentioned it again.

During our many talks that weekend, Mr. Heckert mentioned that he very much liked visiting New York City, because as a young reporter in the 1920s he had lived there for more than five years.

Consequently, before I boarded the train at 30th Street Station, I told Mr. Heckert that I had brought with me from London a knock-down cot similar to the one I slept on in his place, and if he'd be comfortable sleeping on it, he'd be welcome to stay with me in New York City as often as he'd like. At the time, I had no idea how enthusiastically Mr. Heckert would accept my offer.

Over the next four years, he came up to stay with me at least twice a year. Compared to his quarters, my apartment, which had two rooms, a kitchen, and a dining area, must have felt like a palace to him, but Mr. Heckert never made any comment about it. He was a model houseguest, scrupulously neat and clean. Typically, he arrived on Friday night and left on Sunday afternoon. He always insisted on one meal out, whether it was Friday night dinner, Saturday lunch, or brunch on Sunday, for which he paid. He knew his way around the city, so the rest of the time he was on his own. Still, over his many visits, we became quite well acquainted. Interestingly, he never asked me to call him Robert, so until the end of his days, he remained for me Mr. Heckert, while he continued to call me Martin. Because of our great age difference and because he knew me as a child, that was fine with me.

Then came 1974, which was the year when my mother was allowed to leave Czechoslovakia for her first visit to the United States. Once she wrote me that she had an exit visa stamp in her passport, I told Mr. Heckert about her visit. He got very excited and asked me when I thought it would be appropriate for him to pay my mother a visit. I told him that she'd call him herself to let him know. And so some two weeks after her arrival, my mother called Mr. Heckert. I was at home then, and I remember being struck by her calling him Robert. They made a date for him to come up for a visit perhaps two weeks later. When they last saw each other, my mother was thirty-five and Mr. Heckert in his late forties; now she was sixty-one and he in his early seventies. It was the first time he stayed in a hotel, because when my mother was staying with me, there was no room for him in my apartment. I was not home when he arrived, and when I returned home, Mr. Heckert was about to take his leave. They had spent the whole afternoon talking and both seemed exhausted. After he left, I asked my mother how she found him. She said, "Ever a gentleman, such as they no longer make, but surprisingly we didn't have a whole lot to talk about. Still, we made a plan for another visit in about a month."

It was during Mr. Heckert's second visit to my mother when, out of the blue, he told me, "Oh, by the way, Martin, I recently met an interesting chap who is an architect. We started playing chess together. He told me he had an office in Philadelphia. I told him about you and he was impressed with your design consulting practice. He'd like to meet you, so why don't you give him a call? He gave me his phone number." I asked the architect's name. When Mr. Heckert responded, "Louis Kahn," I almost fell off the chair. Mr. Heckert certainly had an uncanny knack for attracting exceptional people. After Churchill, de Gaulle, and Einstein (and who knows who else, because I only discovered those three accidentally, pulling books out of Mr. Heckert's library), now came Louis Kahn, one of the most significant American architects of the twentieth century.

I asked Mr. Heckert how they had met. He answered, "Oh, in downtown Philadelphia, in a coffee shop. We sat next to each other at the counter and he struck up a conversation. We found out we both liked playing chess and we've already played twice since." Louis Kahn—who was at the time building the State Capitol of Bangladesh, teaching at the University of Pennsylvania and, as we found out later, maintaining three separate families, of which only one was with his legal spouse—found time to play chess with Mr. Heckert! I did call Louis Kahn and told him I was calling at Mr. Heckert's suggestion. "Ah yes," Kahn said. "Robert told me about you. If you'd like to come down to Philadelphia, I'd love to see your designs." He then passed me to his secretary, and we made a date about a month later for me to go and meet Mr. Kahn. But that's another story; this one is about Mr. Heckert.

My mother returned to Prague in October 1974, and in January 1975 I left for Tehran. Over the following four years of my flying between New York and Tehran with stopovers in London and Paris, I did not see Mr. Heckert at all. When my Iranian adventure came to an end in 1979 and I returned from Tehran for good, I was too busy chasing work and women to think much about him. So it wasn't until sometime in 1980 or perhaps even 1981 when Mr. Heckert called and asked if he could come for a visit during one of the upcoming weekends. Naturally, I said, "Of course," and we set a date.

During the six or seven years in which we had not seen each other, Mr. Heckert had aged appreciably, but in his eighties he still cut an impressive figure. He no longer had to sleep on the cot, because I had since acquired a fine convertible sofa that folded out into a comfortable queen-size bed. As usual, Mr. Heckert arrived Friday night, and we went out to dinner at a nearby restaurant. I remember I was impressed with how well informed he was about the circumstances of the Iranian Revolution. What was, however, not usual was how my telephone was ringing off the hook while Mr. Heckert was in town. All the callers were women asking for him. When I told them that he was not in, they all wanted to leave a message. When Mr. Heckert came back on Saturday evening, I handed him a page from my note pad full of names and phone numbers and asked him who all those women were. He responded, "Ah, Martin, here is something that might be of interest to you. They are all Single Booklovers."

It turned out that, just like me, Mr. Heckert was looking for a woman. Single Booklovers was the equivalent of a dating website in that preinternet age, disguised as a club of people interested in discussing the books they had read. It was a club one couldn't just join; one had to be introduced by a member, and Mr. Heckert offered to provide me with that introduction. Other than being single, the only other requirement for membership was having earned an advanced degree. I was grateful to Mr. Heckert for the introduction to this club, because over the next five years or so until my first date with Karen in 1986, it provided me with yet another avenue in my search for the right woman. Although I did not find my woman through Single Booklovers, I did meet under its auspices a number of fine, interesting women, and some are in my orbit of friends to this day. Unfortunately, most of them were not interested in remaining friends. They were looking for a husband, and once I didn't pounce, they moved on. But back to Mr. Heckert.

After his visit during which he introduced me to Single Booklovers, I did not see Mr. Heckert for a number of years, although we spoke on the phone at least once a year. Each time he assured me that he was fine. Then sometime around the mid-1980s Mr. Heckert called and, once again, asked if he could come up for a visit. When he arrived, I was shocked to see how much he had aged. He was visibly senile now, with a permanent tremor in his chin, and everything I said he repeated twice in a whisper to himself. He was also much shorter: he used to be taller than me, but now I was looking down at him. His shirt, however, was still crisp white, and his suit appeared freshly pressed. I never knew his exact age, but he must have been in his late eighties by then. It was dinnertime on Friday night so as usual, I asked Mr. Heckert if he'd like to go out or if he'd prefer to stay in. I said I could fix some salad and pasta. I heard him whispering to himself, "I could fix some salad and pasta," and then, for the first time ever, he said that pasta and salad would be fine.

When we sat down to dinner, Mr. Heckert revealed the true purpose of his visit. He said that he had found himself in a financial pickle and that he needed $250 toward his next rent check. He didn't want to ask me on the phone, so he came up to see if I would loan him that money. Then he said that the good news was that he would soon be receiving a large sum of money, and he'd be able to pay me back in short order. When I asked where that large sum of money was coming from, he answered, "Oh, I won the first prize in some sweepstakes." Upon further questioning, it became obvious to me that Mr. Heckert had fallen for the most basic of scams, whereby you are notified that you have won some big sum, say, half a million dollars, but that to get that money, you have to pay a small processing fee of only a few hundred dollars. It turned out that Mr. Heckert had already paid that processing fee, though he never let on how much it was. Nor did he tell me how much money he was going to win.

It was heartbreaking. I tried to prepare Mr. Heckert for the possibility that the large sum he was counting on might never materialize, that there were bad people out there, but he dismissively brushed me off as if I didn't know what I was talking about: "Martin, it's a fait accompli; trust me." The next morning after breakfast, to my great surprise, Mr. Heckert announced that he was going back to Philadelphia. He looked so frail that I didn't want to let him take the subway and carry his satchel to Penn Station by himself, so I made up a story, telling him that I had some business to take care of on 34th Street and that I'd go with him. When I handed him the check for the $250, I told Mr. Heckert that I didn't need that money back anytime soon. He replied, "Oh, Martin, you'll have it back soon enough." On Central Park West I saw a taxi, so I hailed it and we got in. Mr. Heckert didn't object. When we were saying good-bye at Penn Station, my instinct was to hug him, but I just couldn't bring myself to do that; it was not what one did with Mr. Heckert. So we formally shook hands as always and walked away. It was the last time I saw him, but not the last time we spoke.

When, perhaps, a half year had passed and I had not heard from Mr. Heckert, I didn't have the heart to call and ask him if he had received the large sum of money he was expecting. Plus, I was positive that if he had received it, he'd have paid me back the $250 I loaned him. My hunch was proven correct about a year later, when Mr. Heckert called again and, using almost the same language ("I find myself in a financial pickle"), asked for another loan. This time it was for only $150, and he didn't say he'd pay it back in short order. About six months after I sent him that second check, I called Mr. Heckert to inquire how he was doing. When I dialed the number, I heard, "The number you have called is no longer in service. No further information is available." It occurred to me that his phone might have been cut off because Mr. Heckert hadn't paid his phone bill, so I sent him a letter marked PLEASE FORWARD. It came back stamped, "No forwarding address available." Mr. Heckert had disappeared without a trace. I knew that he never married, I had never heard him mention any relative, and his last friend of whom I knew of was Louis Kahn, who died in 1974. I knew no one whom I might have called and inquired about him.

Third Marriage

The death of Karen has been the biggest disaster of my life, bar none. Consequently, after I lost her, the idea of looking for another companion was something that simply didn't enter my mind. Also, somewhere in the basement of my consciousness was the awareness that it had taken me seventeen years to find Karen, making the possibility of my ever finding another woman extremely remote. Then, out of the blue, about a month after Karen died, I received a condolence letter from Knoxville, Tennessee, which read,

Dear Martin—

You may not remember me. We used to know each other over thirty-five years ago in Knoxville. At the time, my name was Sandra Chittick. I learned from our mutual friend Jasan about your wife's passing. Having gone through a similar experience myself, I am writing to extend my condolence.

Warm regards,

Sandra Sanders

As it happened, I did remember Sandra very well. We had met in the early 1970s, when I was spending a lot of time in Tennessee. I have described earlier the circumstances of my frequent stays in Knoxville in those years.

Among the many people I met then through Jasan was a young couple, Sandra and James. They were not yet married but were clearly heading that way. Ours was a rather superficial relationship, and I never saw them without Jasan being present. From time to time, the four of us went out to dinner, and I remember we had several dinners at Sandra's apartment. She was a graduate student of French history at the University of Tennessee; James had graduated a year earlier with a master's degree in English literature and was then dabbling in real estate. Both my consulting work and teaching in Tennessee concluded by the end of 1974, and in January 1975 I was leaving for Tehran. I had not heard from or of Sandra for the next thirty-five years, which was why she wasn't sure whether I'd remember her when she wrote me that condolence letter.

I thanked Sandra for her condolence with a postcard that had my email address on it. We then started emailing. I learned that she had, indeed, married James and had two daughters with him. When the daughters were grown, she divorced him and married an Englishman, Norman Sanders, who was a professor of Shakespeare at the University of Tennessee. Norman was sixteen years older than Sandra and had died in 2007. When Sandra wrote me that condolence letter, she had been a widow for three years. Knowing from her that her marriage to Norman was an excellent one, I was keenly interested in how she dealt with her loss and about the stages of mourning she was going through. I asked many questions, and soon we were emailing daily. The more we exchanged messages, the closer I felt to

The first time I visited Sandra in Tennessee.

Sandra. We discovered there was this symmetry between us: both of our first marriages went sour and we had both left our first spouses, and both of our second marriages were wonderful, but then both of our second spouses had died…

When Václav Havel married a floozy actress some two months after his first wife Olga died of lung cancer, Karen and I were appalled. A long time before she was diagnosed with lung cancer, Karen and I had made a pact, whereby if one of us dropped dead, the surviving spouse would wait at least a year before remarrying. Knowing that it had taken me seventeen years to find Karen, after which it took us another six years to tie the knot, the notion that one of us would want to remarry within a year of our spouse dying seemed totally absurd and preposterous; still, that was the pact we made. During the time that I was exchanging emails with Sandra, the possibility of developing a relationship with another woman didn't enter my mind: I was still very much a grieving widower. Strangely though, the pact Karen and I had made was on my mind.

The longer we kept up our epistolary relationship, the more we got to know about each other and, although we exchanged photos, the more curious I was to take a look at Sandra in person. So after a year of emailing, I invited myself for a weekend in Tennessee. Sandra graciously accepted, so for the first time in thirty-six years, I once again landed in Knoxville. She met me at the airport and we spent a very pleasant time together. Perhaps two months later, Sandra paid me her first visit to New York City. We spent time in the city, as well as in my house in the Hudson Valley.

We exchanged a few more visits before, in the summer of 2011, Sandra was appointed a district director of the Department of Labor in Tennessee. In that position, she had to be based in Nashville, so while keeping her house in Knoxville, she found a small apartment on the east side of Nashville. To help her settle, I brought down a bunch of prints of contemporary Czech artists I had from my mother, had them framed in Nashville, and hung them on the walls of Sandra's apartment. Over the next two years, we kept visiting each other in ever shorter intervals until we came to believe that we simply could not be apart for more than two weeks at a time. Because my time was more flexible, I traveled more often. Naturally, with each visit, we grew even closer.

Sandra at her house in Knoxville.

In the summer of 2013, after thirty-nine years with the Department of Labor, Sandra retired. We first rented a U-Haul van and carted the contents of Sandra's apartment to the basement of her house in Knoxville. Then we rented a large SUV, loaded it with the framed paintings and Sandra's clothes, and took three days to drive to my house on a hilltop in the Hudson Valley. Since then Sandra has lived with me in New York, and we've been visiting her house in Knoxville. When Sandra and I started living together, it felt almost spooky how seamlessly she filled Karen's space both in the apartment and in the country house. She sits in the same chair at the dining table and sleeps on the same side of the bed. At the beginning of our cohabitation, I felt as if someone had told me, "So your wife died? No problem, here is another one." Although it was more than four years since Karen had died, it seemed too early to start living with another woman. But I didn't want to wait any longer.

Sandra and I both believe in the institution of marriage, and a year later, in the summer of 2014, we felt that it was time to get married. It was the third wedding for both of us, and consequently, it was a low-key affair. We got married in Tennessee by an Episcopal priest on the terrace I designed as an addition to Sandra's house in Knoxville. It was a beautiful summer day. The toast I proposed was almost identical to the one that I had proposed twenty-two years earlier at my wedding to Karen. It went something like this:

Sandra visiting me in New York.

> Most people get married for a reason. The most common reason is starting a family, as it makes a lot of sense to be married when you are having children. Some people get married for health insurance reasons, to be added to the policy of an employed spouse. I know of people who got married for real estate reasons, in order to hold on to a rent-controlled apartment. None of those reasons applies to us, so why are we getting married? For romantic reasons alone. As an expression to each other and to the world that we mean this, that we are truly committed to one another. That's all—no other reason. Only for love, which is what this toast is about.

Later, Sandra, quite correctly, pointed out to me that there actually were practical reasons for our getting married. When Norman fell sick before they were married and Sandra came to see him in the hospital, she had no standing. When he was unconscious, she couldn't tell the doctors what to do or what not to do. They asked her, "Who are you?"

The similar toast I proposed at my weddings to both Karen and Sandra was a symbol of a number of uncanny similarities between the two women, some serious, some frivolous. To start with, they were of nearly identical age: Sandra is two days younger than Karen. They were both high-powered executives, Karen in the private sector, Sandra in the public one. They were both "one-firm people," meaning they both spent their entire careers working for one employer. They were both chemistry majors, and both regretted not having become doctors. They both had difficult, self-centered mothers, and amazingly, both of their mothers were teachers. They both had failed to finish their graduate degrees: though Sandra earned her master's degree in French History, she didn't finish her PhD studies, and Karen did not finish her MBA degree program. They were both self-made individuals, meaning they both got very little guidance from their parents. Unlike me, whatever they made of themselves, they made on their own.

At the Century Club in 2017.

On the frivolous side, they both had long legs and both looked much younger than their age (well, Sandra still does); they both had convinced themselves that they couldn't ice skate because they had weak ankles (orthopedists tell me there is no such thing as weak ankles). Although they both could swim, Karen wasn't and Sandra still isn't comfortable in the water, and neither of them would ever swim in the ocean, no matter how calm it was. Karen had, and Sandra still has, an atrocious sense of orientation. Karen, a born New Yorker, once managed to get lost in Central Park. Whenever we leave any building, Sandra always starts walking in the wrong direction. Isn't all this bizarre?

Without planning it, I went from one extreme to another in my search for a partner. While it took me seventeen years to find Karen, Sandra fell into my lap without my lifting a finger. I feel extraordinarily fortunate to have found her. And the thought that it was Jasan who made it happen makes it almost surreal.

Louis Kahn

In my story about Mr. Heckert, I wrote about how it happened that Louis Kahn expressed an interest in meeting me, how I called his office and spoke to him, and how his secretary then made an appointment for me to come down to Philadelphia and meet with Mr. Kahn about a month later. Naturally, I was very excited about meeting him. Although still a little astonished that someone who was considered by many to be the greatest living American architect would make time to meet with someone like me, I started preparing a portfolio just for Mr. Kahn. I put together six building designs that I considered to be my best, and I also included photographs of the only two buildings that actually had gotten built by that time. I could not wait to show it to him.

About two or three days before the appointment, my phone rang. It was Rosemary, Mr. Kahn's secretary, who called to tell me that Mr. Kahn was very sorry but that something had come up and he had asked her to reschedule our appointment. We rescheduled for three weeks later. Over the next six months, this scenario was repeated three or perhaps four times. Each time Rosemary called in a timely manner, two or three days before the scheduled appointment, and we rescheduled.

I was then a visiting professor of design at the School of Architecture at the University of Tennessee in Knoxville. At the end of the fall semester the dean of the school traditionally invited a noted architect to make the rounds of the studios and comment on the students' work. In February 1974 Dean Hanson invited Louis Kahn, who accepted.

When Mr. Kahn entered my studio was the first time I laid eyes on him, and I was surprised by what I saw. He was not an attractive man. He was short, had a scarred face, and a bad case of dandruff. The shoulders of his jacket were covered with it. However, as I soon found out, all that disappeared when he started speaking and his face became animated. When I introduced myself to him, to my surprise, he knew who I was. He said, "Ah, you are a friend of Robert Heckert, yes? And we have an appointment. In a few weeks, you are coming down to Philadelphia to see me, yes?" I responded yes and yes, and that I was very much looking forward to it. Mr. Kahn then walked around the studio, made a few, mostly complimentary comments on my students' work, and in ten minutes was gone.

On the evening of the same day, Louis Kahn was to deliver a lecture in the school's largest auditorium. The lecture was advertised in the local press and was open to the public. The auditorium was packed. It was an amazing spectacle, although not in the visual sense of the word: it was the only time that I ever saw an architect give a talk without showing pictures of his or her work. But then, Mr. Kahn was not talking about his work. He sat on a chair in the middle of the stage, his shoulders covered with dandruff, and, without any notes, talked about architecture in general. It was the first time I heard the now well-known Kahnian phrases, such as "I asked the brick what she wanted to be and she said she wanted to be an arch." Or "The sun never knew how great it was until it hit the side of a brick wall." And so on. In this manner, this little man held the audience spellbound for more than an hour.

It turned out that that was Louis Kahn's last public appearance. Less than a month later, in March 1974, after returning from Bangladesh, he was found dead in the men's room at Penn Station in New York City. He was seventy-three years old. After his death, it was revealed that he was $400,000 in debt. I marvel to this day over the fact that at the time that he was completing the National Assembly Building of Bangladesh, when he had a number of projects in the United States on the boards, and when he was that much in debt, Louis Kahn still found the time to play chess with Mr. Heckert, to schmooze with students, and to deliver a talk at the University of Tennessee—and had he not died, he would have made time to meet with Martin Holub. I find all that beyond amazing. And, even more amazing—although not known at that time—was that Mr. Kahn had maintained three households, only one of which was with his legal spouse.

More Childhood Memories, This Time Not Sexual

The end product of Teluria, the family enterprise started by my grandfather in Moravia, was a finely ground powdered pigment that, when mixed with water in the given proportion, produced an exterior paint. At the time, that powder was distributed around the world in extrastrength paper bags. Those bags were made of several layers of very sturdy paper, but still, if you took a sharp nail to them, they could be punctured. After my grandfather's retirement, Uncle Milek ran the factory, and my grandmother remained in charge of accounting and administration. On our many visits, I was allowed to roam around the factory area. I was instructed not to touch any moving machinery, but other than that, no space was off-limits, and I was free to observe what was going on. The workers got used to the sight of me and paid me no mind.

The incident I remember must have taken place in the summer of 1945 or 1946, so I was six or seven years old. One day on my wanderings through the factory compound, I picked up a sharp, long nail. Then, in a shed next to the loading dock, I spied a row of filled paper bags ready to be shipped out. The temptation to take that nail to one of those bags was irresistible. I had to push hard, but eventually the nail went in. When I pulled it out, a stream of bright yellow powder started trickling out and would not stop. I licked my forefinger, put the wet tip to the hole from which the yellow powder was pouring out, and that stopped it.

Now, an irrepressible curiosity got hold of me. Did all the bags contain the same yellow powder? Without thinking of the consequences, I punctured the next bag, and whoa, a red powder started trickling out. The next bag produced green powder, and the one after that blue powder. What fun! I managed to stop the trickles with my wet finger, but it proved to be only a temporary measure, because once the saliva dried, the powder started trickling afresh. And so it happened that by the time I had stopped the last trickle, the first one started pouring out again. Unable to do anything about it, I fled.

At the dining table in the evening, while the cook was serving supper, my grandmother announced, "Someone punctured six bags of paint that were in the shed prepared for the shipment to India, so that they had to be rebagged. By any chance, do you know anything about it, Martin?" I stammered, "Oh no, I don't know anything about it." My grandmother continued, "Well, just think about who might have done it, and if you get any ideas, let me know." I said I would.

Later, when my mother and I were alone, she told me how very stupid I was not to fess up to something that only I could have done. Then she gave me the following piece of advice: "The best thing is never to lie. Life is much easier that way. However, if a situation develops when you must lie, then you'd better make sure that the lie you plan to tell is airtight before you say it." As an example of a lie that was not airtight, my mother repeated the one I had just told my grandmother. "Just think, who else but a stupid child would do something like puncturing those bags. Certainly, not any of the workers, because their livelihood depends on that paint being sold. The factory is secured, so no stranger could have come in. That leaves Uncle Milek, you, and me. I'll let you ponder who of the three of us is most likely to have punctured those bags."

Lastly, my mother suggested that it would be a good idea if I apologized to my grandmother for lying to her. It was a bitter pill to swallow, but I found everything my mother told me compelling, and an apology was the only logical conclusion. So the next morning before breakfast, I went to my grandmother and mumbled my apology. She was predictably gracious, praised me for acknowledging the error of my ways, and then said, "It's all right to make mistakes, Martin, as long as we recognize them, correct them, and don't repeat them." I remember that to this day.

———————————

Unlike present-day parents, my mother felt comfortable leaving me home alone in the evening from the time I was seven or eight years old. True, I wasn't completely alone, because we had a live-in maid Amálka. However, after Amálka served me supper, she retired to her room behind the kitchen, and I had the whole apartment to myself to make mischief in. And mischief I made.

Of the two bathrooms in our apartment, one had a toilet, a sink, and a bidet; the other had a tub and a sink. During a kids' party at the Schauers—family friends who had four children—Jirka, the eldest of the four, who was a year older than me, showed me something in their bathroom, which also had a bidet: when you turn on both cold and hot water faucets at the same time and at full throttle, the water from the bidet's spigot shoots up all the way to the ceiling. Naturally, when I was home alone, I tried to do the same thing to the bidet in our bathroom, and—lo and behold—it worked just the same. Ever since, whenever I was home alone, I couldn't resist the temptation to splash the bathroom ceiling with the water from the spigot of the bidet. What fun! Of course, even when I turned the faucets off, after the water hit the ceiling, it would splash all over the bathroom, making the towels and the bathmat wet.

My mother was not amused. She was even less amused when the paint of the ceiling started peeling and the bathroom had to be repainted. Then she read me the riot act and issued an ultimatum that, if she ever found me repeating this misdeed, there would be corporal punishment. At the time, corporal punishment consisted of lashes with a leather belt on my bare buttocks. The number of lashes was subject to negotiation. Sometimes I succeeded in convincing my mother that the number of lashes she proposed to administer exceeded the severity of my misbehavior, and then she'd agreed to reduce it; mostly, however, my argument did not succeed.

———————————

Another temptation I found hard to resist during my times alone in the apartment was supplied by the rococo armchair in our living room. Yes, this was the very same armchair that some seven years later found its way inside the bathtub of our two-room, cold-water flat on the ground floor of a proletarian tenement in Žižkov. However, at the time of this particular temptation, we were still living in our large, bourgeois apartment. The legs of the armchair in question were hidden by tassels suspended from the bottom of the body of the upholstered armchair, and it was the dull uniformity of those tassels that cried for some intervention. I could not resist taking a pair of scissors to those suspended threads and making them less uniform by cutting bunches of them at uneven heights. One or two notches at a time, and soon the whole row of tassels at the back of the armchair were a work of art. Fortunately, I had the presence of mind to do this on the back of the armchair, which was close to the wall and, consequently, not in plain view.

The irony was that my mother did not notice this barbaric piece of vandalism until after her release from prison, when the armchair was being moved in and out of the bathtub during our ablutions. At that time, I was thirteen and beyond suspicion of being capable of doing something so stupid, so my mother attributed it to the malice of the communist movers. When I confessed that it was I who cut those tassels when I was six and was home alone, she probably had second thoughts about the wisdom of having left me unsupervised at that age.

Another way I discovered of amusing myself when left home alone was climbing in and out through the window of one of the bedrooms that was facing the street. It was a large double window with a post in the middle, separating two casement windows. When they were open, I would sit on the sill inside and stick my legs out on either side of the post. Then, while holding onto the post with my arms, I would start slowly rotating around it until my legs were inside and my body was outside the window. Continuing to swivel around with my arms wrapped around the post, I'd eventually end up in my starting position, sitting again on the sill with my legs out on either side of the post. That was great fun for me.

Although I had absolutely no fear of heights, there was a measure of thrill in doing this on the third floor. Some evenings I'd do three or four turns around the post. Then one night, having completed the circumnavigation of the post, I looked down to the street and saw a crowd of people looking up at me. It was dark, and the light in the bedroom made me backlit and clearly visible from the street. So I turned out the light and went to bed.

A few days later my mother told me that a neighbor, whom we vaguely knew because she had a son my age with whom I used to play in the playground, stopped her in the street and asked her if she knew about the antics her son was performing in the window of our apartment. My mother asked me if I could tell her what that neighbor was talking about. I said that she was probably talking about my turns around the post between the two windows, and I explained what I had been doing. I still remember my mother's response, because it impressed me.

She said, "While I know that you are a very competent and careful tree climber and rock climber and that you use the same caution when turning around the window post, other people don't know it. If they thought that you were doing it with my permission, it would make me look like a bad mother, which is why I am asking that you don't do this trick anymore." I fully comprehended what my mother was saying and felt satisfied that she talked to me like I was an adult. That I had the power to make my mother look bad was a new idea for me. I certainly didn't want to do that, so I respected her wish and never again did that trick.

Metaphysical? Supernatural?

The year was 1989, and it was the first time my office was considered for work in the public sector. The project in question was a community center for Roosevelt Island; the client was the Roosevelt Island Operating Corporation (RIOC), a New York State agency.

The architect selection process started with the publication of the project in the *Contract Reporter*, a newsletter publishing all public projects in New York State. We responded, expressing our interest in being considered for the design of the community center and enclosing our office brochure.

About a month later, we received a letter from the RIOC informing us that we were among the firms asked to submit a proposal; the letter also asked the qualifications and experience of those who'd be working on the project. Another month later, there was a request for more photographs of our completed projects. We were thrilled, because we thought all those requests were proof that we were being seriously considered.

Next came a request for letters of recommendation from our former clients, and finally, we were informed that we were short-listed and that, as the principal of my firm, I would be called in for a personal interview.

The community center was to have three components: a black-box theater, a dance studio, and a synagogue whose sanctuary would also be used as a community auditorium. Consequently, there were three user groups, and we were told that two representatives of each group would be present at the interview. Together with four folks from the state agency, it meant that I would be interviewed by a committee of ten people. Because the user group representatives all had day jobs, the interview was set for 7 p.m. at the offices of the RIOC on Main Street on Roosevelt Island.

The date set for the interview was more than six months after our response to the advertisement of the project in the *Contract Reporter* and, given all it took to even get to the interview, I was nervous as a cat. Never before had I been this close to getting a public project.

Under normal circumstances, getting from my office at Columbus Avenue and 72nd Street to Roosevelt Island takes about half an hour: I would take the B train to Rockefeller Center and, from there, the Q train to Roosevelt Island. To be safe, I allowed one and a half hours for the trip, but as we'll see, it was not enough. It's clear to me now that I must have been so strung out that my judgment was severely clouded, because I made one blunder after another.

The first mistake occurred as I was leaving my office at 5:30 p.m. It suddenly struck me that the case in which I carried my portfolios was unnecessarily big and that I had a smaller case that would look much better. With my assistant's help, transferring the portfolios to the smaller case took five minutes. On leaving the building, I saw a cab. Because my reserve of extra time had been reduced by those five minutes, instead of walking to the subway, I jumped into the cab and asked to be taken to the subway station at Rockefeller Center. That was the second blunder.

As soon as the cab turned south on Columbus Avenue, we got stuck in a massive traffic jam. The driver informed me that President Bush (senior) was in town and that the whole of midtown was grid-locked. My third blunder was not getting out of the cab right then and there and walking to the subway stop at Central Park West. Had I done that, I would have been fine. Instead, I stayed in the taxi, stewing and biting my nails. By the time we got to Columbus Circle, it was ten minutes past six. I could have walked there faster than that.

The traffic seemed to be moving along 59th Street, so instead of going down Broadway to Rockefeller Center, I asked the driver to take me to the subway stop at Lexington and 63rd Street, where I'd pick up the Q train. My fourth blunder was not asking him to take me all the way to Roosevelt Island. It seems incomprehensible to me now that I did not think of that.

It was half past six when the driver dropped me at Lexington and 63rd Street. The station is very deep underground with long escalators, so that by the time I got to the platform, it was 6:35 p.m. If the Q train had arrived within five minutes, I would still have been on time. However, five minutes passed, then another five minutes, and there was no Q train in sight. In sheer panic, I ran back up to the street in search of a taxi.

It was now clear that I would be late; the only question was by how much. I foresaw the biggest embarrassment of my life. It took me six months to get to that point, and now I was going to blow it by being late for a meeting where ten people were waiting for me. There were no taxis on Lexington Avenue, so I started walking along 61st Street to Third Avenue. I was walking in the street along the parked cars in order not to miss any taxis, but there weren't any to miss.

Suddenly, I heard "honk-honk." I looked and saw an old, beat-up white Toyota, somewhat dirty, pulling up alongside me. Its driver was rolling down the window. He was a slightly greasy-looking black man wearing a rumpled suit, a not very clean white shirt, and a tie. With an engaging smile, he asked, "What's your problem, buddy?" I was so unnerved by the situation I was in that I didn't even question what made him stop and ask what my problem was. Instead, I blurted out, "I desperately need to get to Roosevelt Island and I cannot find any cabs." In a mild, reassuring way, the fellow responded, "Well, get in; I'll take you there."

Without much reflection, I got in, and we were on our way. Church music was playing on the car radio, a rosary was dangling from the rearview mirror, and a statuette of Jesus was on the dashboard. (I remember that it made me think of the jingle, "I don't care if it rains or freezes long as I have my plastic Jesus.") I asked the guy if he knew how to get to Roosevelt Island. He could tell how nervous I was, and again in his mild, reassuring way, he said, "Don't worry, buddy; I know how to get there."

It was 7:00 p.m. when we were crossing the 59th Street Bridge and 7:10 p.m. when we arrived at the given address on Main Street on Roosevelt Island. I asked the fellow how much I owed him. He responded, "Oh, don't worry about it." I insisted, "Come on; you have to take something," and I handed him three twenties (which was all the cash I had after paying the exorbitant fare of the first taxi). With his engaging smile he responded, "Well, if you insist," and he took one of those three twenties. I thanked him profusely, he wished me luck, and he drove away.

So I ended up being a little over ten minutes late to the interview. This was inexcusable in my book, but the committee was gracious (acknowledging that the Q train was known for running very irregularly), and the interview went well.

It wasn't until a few weeks after we were told that we were awarded the commission that I first reflected on this incident. I found it more than a little odd and have wondered ever since just who it was who sent that chubby black cherub who saved me from potentially the biggest embarrassment of my life.

Park East Synagogue

John Hill is a contractor who built a few of my firm's commercial projects in the 1980s and who kept recommending me to potential clients because he liked working from our drawings. Of course, he also knew that if we got a commission because of his recommendation, we were bound to recommend him as the builder. One day he called and said that I should call Rabbi Schneier of Park East Synagogue. John was finishing a minor renovation project in the synagogue and found out that they were looking for an architect to design a new chapel inside the synagogue building. He also issued a warning: "Martin, if they hire you, make sure to front-load your billing, because you will not get paid your last invoice."

Park East Synagogue, with an entrance on East 67th Street, is a nineteenth-century building in Moorish Revival style whose sanctuary seats more than five hundred people. In the 1960s, a contemporary building housing a Jewish Cultural Center and synagogue offices was added directly to the north of the main synagogue, with an entrance on East 68th Street; the two buildings are connected. In addition to the large sanctuary space, the congregation needed a smaller, more intimate worship space for daily prayers and weekly services. That was the reason for the new chapel, which was to be located on the second floor of the Cultural Center.

During my interview with Rabbi Schneier (at the end of which I was hired), he mentioned to me the major players behind the new chapel. The chief one was Leona Helmsley, a member of the congregation who had agreed to underwrite the cost of the chapel. (Those of you who have never heard of Leona Helmsley, just google her.) The second one was Yacov Agam, a well-known Israeli painter and sculptor, who had agreed to donate his design of the tabernacle. Rabbi Schneier was a great admirer of Yacov Agam, and it soon became apparent to me that my role was to design a space in which Yacov Agam would deign to design his masterpiece. The chapel was to be known as the Agam Chapel.

Rabbi Schneier also retained a liturgical design consultant, who advised me that, according to Jewish Orthodox tradition, men and women had to sit separately, divided by a low wall or a screen. The first humorous incident occurred during one of my presentations of the chapel design—including its seating layout—to the synagogue's chapel committee. A member of the committee asked Rabbi Schneier, "Arthur, can you picture Leona sitting behind this screen?" The rabbi quickly grasped the situation and said, "Oh no, that won't do! We have to come up with something." After a long discussion, it was decided that, because Mrs. Helmsley didn't attend services very frequently, on those days when she did come the screen would be removed. I was directed to design a screen that would be easily removable.

After my design got the OK from the liturgical design consultant and the chapel committee, it had to be approved by Maestro Agam, who divided his time between New York and Israel. When he was next in New York, Rabbi Schneier and I were summoned to his apartment on East 58th Street one day early in the morning. I was relieved to find that for Mr. Agam, early in the morning meant 10 a.m. On the appointed day, I showed up at the given address, the doorman announced me, and I was sent up in the elevator. I remember it was above the thirtieth floor. In the spirit of I-am-a-great-artist-and-regular-conventions-don't-apply-to-me, Mr. Agam welcomed me in his pajamas. Not pajamas as an artist's outfit, but crumpled ones in which he obviously had slept. This was the first time we met. He clearly knew who I was, so no introductory niceties were required. In a loud, peremptory manner, he commanded me to wait in the living room. He instructed me, "While waiting, you can look at all the books written about me. They are on the shelves. The latest one is on the counter."

Happily, I didn't have to wait long, as Rabbi Schneier was announced shortly thereafter. At the time of this meeting I was in my late forties, the rabbi looked to be in his early sixties, and Mr. Agam was perhaps in his late seventies. Having greeted the rabbi perfunctorily, Yacov Agam asked him very loudly, "Have you seen the latest book about me?" The rabbi stammered, "No, Yacov, I haven't had a chance yet." This time Agam almost shrieked, "What, you haven't? Then go see it now; it's right over there on the counter." Obediently, Rabbi Schneier walked to the counter and started turning pages in the book.

What followed then was a priceless piece of theater that could have been called "a meeting of two peacocks." The counter was in front of a wall that was faced with a mirror. The rabbi in a dark suit, white shirt, and a tie stood facing the mirror; Yacov Agam in his pajamas, sipping coffee, sat on the sofa with his back to the rabbi; and completing the triangle, I sat in an armchair looking at the two men in profile. I saw that Rabbi Schneier, while turning the pages, was not looking at the book at all. Instead, he was looking in the mirror. Turning the pages while watching himself in the mirror, he was exclaiming, "Oh, Yacov, this is just great! Fabulous! Simply splendid! Oh, just wonderful! What a great book, Yacov!" All that, without casting his eyes at the book even once.

Satisfied with the rabbi's effusive praise, Yacov Agam now turned to me and said, "OK, let's see the plans." I brought along a rendered plan and elevations of the proposed chapel, which I now took out from the folder and propped against the mirror on the counter. The space for Agam's tabernacle was clearly marked. Mr. Agam stood up from the sofa, walked to the counter, took one look and, in less than fifteen seconds, said, "Fine, I can work with that." It was the first time he saw the design. It would have been quite impossible, even for the most brilliant architect, to grasp its intricacies—such as varying ceiling heights, floor and wall finishes, the lighting—in one perfunctory look. Be that as it may, with the purpose of the meeting accomplished, the rabbi and I were dismissed with "You can leave now." We rode the elevator down in silence. Knowing how much the rabbi worshipped Agam, I just didn't know what to say. Once we were on the street, the rabbi said, "Now, full speed into the construction drawings." We shook hands and parted.

While developing the working drawings, my office followed with increasing concern the legal troubles of Leona Helmsley. After she went to jail for tax evasion and lying to the jury, the inevitable call from Rabbi Schneier came: "Martin, stop the work. We just have to put this project on hold until Leona is back from jail. I'll be in touch." I never heard from the rabbi again, nor do I know if Yacov Agam ever created any design for the proposed tabernacle. And, true to John Hill's warning, I did not get paid for our last invoice.

What Kind of Dogs?

After the communist putsch of February 1948, it took more than a year before the Iron Curtain clamped down tight. Until then, it was relatively easy to walk through the forest and cross the border either to Austria or to West Germany. A number of my relatives, including my grandmother and my uncle, did so. However, by the early 1950s the new regime managed to make the border nearly impassable. Many people died trying to cross it. From the accounts of the few who did manage to get through, we slowly learned how the border was guarded.

The trees were cleared all along the border, creating about a forty-foot-wide strip of clear ground. At the far end of that strip were two parallel barbed wire fences about ten feet apart. The border guards with guard dogs walked in the corridor between the two fences. Whoever managed to cross the border had to cut holes in those two fences and crawl through them to freedom.

When in 1967 I arrived in London, one of my contacts was Karla Smutná and her husband Jan. Karla was my mother's colleague from the School of Art History at Charles University, who after the communist take-over stopped her studies and, with her husband and two-year old daughter, walked through the forest across the border to West Germany. Eventually they settled in England. By the time I arrived they had already lived in London for close to twenty years. They were empty nesters as their daughter was then studying in the United States, and I became their frequent Sunday lunch guest. They were interested in hearing from me a fresh perspective on the doings in their old country, and I was grateful for their pointers concerning London. It was from Karla and Jan that I heard the following story.

There was in Prague an old family called the Bednars. They had two grown sons, Ivan and Michal. At the time of the communist take-over Michal was twenty-eight and Ivan was twenty-five. Their father, the senior Mr. Bednar, was the largest distributor of pharmaceuticals in Czechoslovakia. We were not acquainted but knew of them. My father used to point out to me the Bednar's villa in the most expensive part of town: it was a grand edifice. Thus Mr. Bednar was clearly a prime example of "an enemy of the people." He saw the writing on the wall and, while it was still possible, decided to emigrate with the whole family. At the last moment, Ivan, in love with a young woman who would not leave with him, decided to stay behind, defying his parents' pleas to join them. Eventually, Mr. and Mrs. Bednar left with Michal alone.

Observing the communist atrocities and his love affair having gone sour, Ivan soon saw that he had made a big mistake and started planning an escape to join his family in London. By then, however, it was the early 1950s, and the border was closed shut. In addition to what I described earlier, the authorities had instituted along the border a half-mile-wide no-entry zone, a patrolled area that no civilian was allowed to enter. Ivan was aware of this and planned accordingly.

He was an old Boy Scout, camper, and backwoodsman, experienced in orienting in the woods at night and spending time by himself in the forest. He did his research as to the best place and best time to attempt his escape. Having packed enough food for three days, a compact sleeping bag, and the sharpest wire-cutting shears he could find, he then enlisted the help of a trusted friend who drove him to the chosen area, a place from which he could immediately disappear into the forest of the forbidden border zone.

Ivan crawled the entire night through that half-mile strip of border-zone forest until, early in the morning, he spied the clearing with the barbed wire fences some forty feet away. He burrowed into a bush and spent the whole day observing and monitoring the movements of the border patrols inside the corridor between the two fences. He found that the patrols walked by at fairly regular intervals, but there were variations in who patrolled. Some patrolmen walked by themselves, sometimes there were two of them walking together, some had dogs on a leash, and some walked without a dog.

The biggest surprise and biggest danger for Ivan were the dogs running by themselves with no guard in sight. That was an unexpected and unpredictable wild card. Ivan decided to wait and see if the unaccompanied dogs were running at night. He also determined that the window of time in between the patrols was not long enough to cut through both fences. He'd have to first cut a hole in the near fence, withdraw to the bush, and let the next patrol pass; he would then crawl through the first hole, cut another one in the far fence, crawl through that one, and run for his life to freedom.

When night fell, Ivan was on the lookout for the dogs running by themselves. When by midnight he hadn't seen any, he concluded that unaccompanied dogs were a daytime occurrence, and he decided to go for it. Up until then, everything had gone more or less according to plan, but now Ivan hit a snag. When he crawled to the near fence and started cutting, he found that it was much harder to do and went much slower than he had expected. The communists scrimped on everything, but not on the barbed wire: it was industrial-strength wire, extremely difficult to cut.

Ivan quickly determined that what he hoped to accomplish in two steps would take four: first, he'd cut only half of the wires required for the first hole, crawl back to the bushes, wait for the patrol to pass, crawl back to the fence and finish the hole, then back to the bushes, and so on until the last wire of the second hole was cut. This, of course, added considerable time to the operation, thereby increasing the possibility of being caught should there be any irregularity in the movements of the guards, but there was no other way to get through.

By daybreak, exhausted, Ivan pulled himself through the hole in the second fence and ran. In short order, he was then reunited with his family in London. His head was still reeling, however, from what he had gone through. Many people were killed while trying to cross the border, but he had done it! He kept reliving those thirty-six hours he was lying in the bushes or crawling back and forth between the fences and the bushes. He was elated and eager to share his good fortune with people other than his family. Then one night his parents took him along to a cocktail party. They told their friends what their son had just been through, so soon, a group of curious people surrounded him. Ivan was delighted that, at last, he had an audience.

He started by explaining what the Iron Curtain he had just crossed consisted of—the cleared strip of ground, the two barbed wire fences, the no-entry border zone. He then minutely described his own harrowing progress through it: the night of crawling through the border zone, the day of lying in the bushes. Throughout, however, he felt that he was somehow not connecting with his audience. There were no questions, no exclamations of surprise. People stared with blank faces, sipping their sherries. Ivan proceeded to explain the difficulty of cutting through the barbed wire and, still, no reaction, no connection. It wasn't until he mentioned the guards with dogs when one woman excitedly interrupted, "And what kind of dogs were they?"